A Collective Sharing: the Spiritual Community Speaks

Endorsements for *Journey Through Ten Thousand Veils*

"Alhamdulillah! The excellency of this transmission of the spiritual journey is apparent inasmuch as Sheikha Maryam is swimming consistently in a realm of ever-increasing light, constantly breathing and inhaling its luminescence. This is a voyage inspired by Allah *subhana wa ta'ala*. Her swimming is in an ocean rarely travelled."

—Sheikh Harun Al Faqir
Sheikh of the Mustafawiyya Tariqah
Originating in Senegal, West Africa

"*Journey Through Ten Thousand Veils* is not simply 'another book': it is a testimony that allows you to highlight your experience in the Way of God, your experience of Divine Love. It is the realization in all humility of our need to assume the responsibility to share with others these experiences as a potential catalyst for their awakening and spiritual transformation."

"This book is a witnessing and bringing to completion of the teachings discovered on the journey to God. May the Lord bestow this Grace upon all beings!"

T0306851

—Sheikh Aly N'Daw
International Sufi School
of Sheikh Ahmadou Bamba,
Pout, Senegal

"The book you hold in your hands is more than a memoir of one soul's inspiring journey toward Ultimate Reality. It is a roadmap for any soul that yearns for sojourn to the Divine, a trustworthy travel companion for all who answer the inner call to discover their highest self, and a proof that genuine spiritually awakened Guides still exist. Sheikha Maryam masterfully shares her most intimate, perilous, and profound moments as she is guided to the company of some of the greatest Muslim Spiritual Masters of the modern age. Her story is both unique and universal, for after reading about her Journey Through Ten Thousand Veils, we realize that we in fact have been journeying with her all along. It is the same journey of hope, healing, and homecoming embarked upon by different bodies, expressing a single Spirit, desiring one transcendent Goal."

—Shaykh Adeyinka Muhammad Mendes
Founding Director of
Sacred Service for Human Liberation

"Journey Through Ten Thousand Veils contains Maryam Kabeer's autobiographical account of her lifelong search to become closer to God, ultimately via Sufism, in Islam, and what a journey it is! The memoir is all the more impressive, because the author is a historical person in her own right. This book will be highly valuable to any seekers of God, as she examines all of the multiple dimensions of a quest. It is also a treasure as a record of a precious and significant part of American Muslim History."

—Dr. Khalid Yahya Blankinship
Head of Graduate Studies, Department of Religion,
Temple University, Philadelphia, PA

"Who is a Sufi? What does Sufi mean? Do you know one? If one of the definitions is a Seeker, then Sister Maryam is an embodiment of the term. Since we met in the early nineties, I was drawn to her tireless efforts to be travelling on the Path. Her home and heart are open to all. With a smile and kind hospitality she listens, shares, and teaches by example. Her life is a great journey that reflects the beauty of Faith. It is a blessing for seekers yearning for guidance that she is generous to share her story and make it available to those who want to learn, reflect and be inspired to be seekers on the Path."

—Dr. Manar Darwish
Professor of Religion, Bryn Mawr College

"This book is a magnificent beacon of love and light that kindles an awakening of the Divine journey in our lives. In a time when "extremist" messages are transmitted through peoples' hopelessness, disconnection and despair, Sheikha Maryam spreads the message of hope and connection by describing how Allah, *subhana wa ta'ala*, through His deep subtle

Love and Compassion, is always gently and gracefully guiding each and every one of us towards our own awakening to the Divine—the Divine Light of Love and Connectivity. We can see many parallels in her life that reflect our own individual and collective journeys. Sheikha Maryam describes each new step as an unfolding Divine beauty being bestowed upon her, revealing her realization that all lives are interconnected and that the journey of enlightenment is one in which we naturally find many others on the same path on which we all form a collective, a coalition of souls, united in love and peace."

—Moaz Choudhury
Social Worker,
Toronto, Canada

""Maryam Kabeer is one of those rare seekers after knowledge, a qaland-ar in Sufi terminology, a traveler to many lands in search of wisdom from the teachers of the era. It is an adventurous and loving journey, and her descriptions and prose are heartfelt. I thoroughly enjoyed the journey. And she is still at it, ever seeking knowledge of God. Her life is an example for all who love and struggle in His Name."

—Irving Karchmar
Author of *Master of the Jinn*

"Maryam's journey with her son to Medina and Mecca, and their visit to the Ka'aba, is probably the most exaltedly symphonic and overwhelming of her pivotal experiences in the book, as she journeys in her relentless search for transformative liberation and the Truth of Certainty."

—Daniel Abdal-Hayy Moore
Inspired Poet of The Ecstatic Exchange

"Maryam Kabeer lifts the veils, to expose the spiritual bond between God, humans, and all lives. She shows her readers that life can be lived and should be lived, by seeking nearness to God."

—Dr. Aisha Michelle Byng
Department of Sociology,
Temple University, Philadelphia, PA

"The story of Sheikha Maryam's compelling narrative of wisdom and inspiration is particularly meaningful to me as it is offered by an inspiring spiritual sister. Sheikha Maryam's absorbing life journey fluently guides the reader through life's tender moments, intense challenges, and keen spiritual insights. For anyone seeking a path of spiritual renewal, read this book! It is an enchanting inspiring journey of transformation which allows the reader to exit from a narrow definition of religion and enter into an enigmatic self-journey leading to Divine Discovery. You will find yourself inspired by the sheer dedication of the author whose self-sacrifice and service to humanity is deeply moving."

—Daisy Khan
Founder of Women's Islamic
Initiative in Spirituality and Equality

"This book will, no doubt, be an inspiration to many readers. It will lead many to join hereon the blessed pilgrimage."

—Dr. Mahmoud Ayoub
Professor Emeritus,
Temple University, Philadelphia, PA

"It is said that there are thousands of veils that separate the human heart from Reality, and it is rare that we can accompany a traveler on the subtle journey from the self and the world to the Divine Presence of God. Yet in her iconic memoir, Sheikha Maryam Kabeer invites us to do just that by allowing us to join her on a sacred quest from the materialistic life of a modern citizen to some of the most remote and hidden parts of the planet, ultimately culminating in a glorious celebration of divine light and spiritual awakening as a result of the persistent pursuit of the call to the Eternal Presence of the Divine. *Journey Through Ten Thousand Veils* is a living testament to the purity and beauty of the spiritual path of the sincere seeker and is an incredible account of what is possible when a human being has the courage to follow his or her heart on the path to the Truth."

—Emil Ihsan-Alexander Torabi
www.spiritualexcellence.com

"Sheikha Maryam has given birth to a purely profound memoir. This beautiful interwoven narrative does not feel like that of the mundane but that of the sublime. It would seem that Sheikha Maryam is a vessel that the Divine uses to inspire others to go on a spiritual and transformative journey."

—Issa Kabeer

"Sheikha Maryam is a great living witness to the beauty, simplicity, and spiritual power of traditional Islam, a living tradition that is increasingly marginalized and threatened by the reactionary forces of political Islam in our times. Her luminous presence at our spiritual retreats has been a true blessing for us, allowing us to experience firsthand the fruits of a life of a sincere seeker seeking the Face of God.

This book, Sheikha Maryam's autobiographical account of her spiritual quest, is especially relevant for our times because of its ability to awaken within all of us a sense of nostalgia and longing for the company of God and His Beloved Messenger (saw). The stories Sheikha Maryam shares in this volume are not only motivational but also profoundly humbling, as we discover that the journey to God is a life-long endeavor and not a matter of instant gratification. The reader gets to accompany Sheikha Maryam as, fearlessly and consistently, she reaches new stations only to hop right back on the train of self-discovery, heading towards the next horizon of awareness.

In short, Sheikha Maryam unveils for us the timeless components of a life well-lived: the need to realize that we belong to our Creator, to find our purpose, to experience transcendence, and to share with the world how that can be done. Her memoir gives renewed hope in the human spirit and its ability to transcend the veils and reach inner peace.

For these reasons, this work is a spiritual classic for all seekers and a beacon pointing the way to the people of God and their powerful legacy of love and healing for all times. Sheikha Maryam is nothing less than a pioneer of Islam in North America and we are honored to have her history recorded so beautifully in this book so that we can all come to know our roots and divinely determined goals."

—Shaykh Hamdi Ben Aissa & Anse Shehnaz Karim
Sanad Collective,
Ottawa and Montreal, Canada

A JOURNEY THROUGH TEN THOUSAND VEILS

THE ALCHEMY OF TRANSFORMATION ON THE SUFI PATH

Maryam Kabeer

New Jersey

Published by Tughra Books
335 Clifton Ave,
Clifton, NJ 07011
www.tughrabooks.com

ISBN: 978-1-59784-947-0

In the Name of Allah,
the Merciful, the Compassionate
All Praise be to Allah
Lord of all the Worlds
The Merciful, the Compassionate,
Master of the Day of Judgment
You, Alone, do we worship
And You, Alone, do we seek for Help
Lead us on the Straight Path
The Path of those upon whom
Your Grace has fallen,
Not (the path) of those upon whom
Your displeasure has fallen
Or those who have gone astray. Amen
—Surat'ul Fatihah, The Holy Quran 1:1-7

Allah! There is no god but He!
The Living, The Self-subsisting, Eternal.
No slumber can seize Him nor sleep.
His are all things in the heavens and on earth.
Who is there can intercede In His presence except as He permits?
He knows what appears to His creatures before and behind them.
Nor shall they comprehend anything of His knowledge except as
He wills. His throne extends over the heavens and earth, and He
feels no fatigue in guarding and preserving them, for He is the
Most High. The Supreme (in glory).
　　　　　　　　　　　　　—Ayat'ul Kursi, The Holy Quran 3:18

Allah is the Light of the heavens and the earth. His Light is com-
parable to a niche, wherein is a wick, the wick is in a crystal, the
crystal is brilliant like a star. It (the wick) is kindled from a blessed
tree, an olive tree, which is neither of the east nor of the west, and
whose oil would almost glow forth of itself, though fire touches it
not, light upon light.
　　　　　　　　　　　　　　　　　—The Holy Qur'an 24:35

Allah's is the Sovereignty of the heavens and the earth, and all that
is between, and unto Him is the journeying.
　　　　　　　　　　　　　　　　　—The Holy Qur'an 5:18

CONTENTS

Foreword xv

Chapter 1   *Impressions Which Formed Me* 25
            Southern California, 1946-62

Chapter 2   *UC Berkeley - Flying into the Open Sky* 41
            Berkeley, California, 1962-69

Chapter 3   *Setting out on the Path* 59
            Orient Express and Afghanistan, 1969

Chapter 4   *Entrance to India* 65

Chapter 5   *In Search of Maharaj-Ji* 71
            Crisscrossing India and Nepal, 1970

Chapter 6   *An Oasis in the Desert: Meeting With A Mystical Sheikh* 85
            Discovering Islam in the Holy Cities of Tabriz and Ma
            shad, Iran, 1970

Chapter 7   *Saved by Grace - Iran, Turkey and Bulgaria, 1971* 95

Chapter 8   *Who Am I? In the City Flowing with Light* 101
            Amsterdam, 1971

Chapter 9   *Life in the Monasteries* 111
            Chevetogne, Belgium and the French Alps, 1972

Chapter 10   *Culture Shock, Longing to Return to Sanctified Land* 121
            California, Colorado and New Mexico, 1973

Chapter 11   *Embracing Islam in El Khalil, The Place of
            Abraham (as)* 129
            Jerusalem and Hebron, 1974

Chapter 12   *Praying in the Dome of the Rock* Jerusalem, 1974..........139

Chapter 13   *Building the Adobe Mosque* 149
                Watering the Seeds of Islam Planted in the Holy Land |
                Lama Foundation, Taos, New Mexico, 1975

Chapter 14   *Arrival in the Presence of the Awakened One* 157
                Philadel phia, 1979-1986

Chapter 15   *The Resonance of Allah, the Ever-Deepening*
                Experience of Prayer Colombo 173
                Sri Lanka & Philadelphia, 1980-2000

Chapter 16   *The Vale of Kashmir, Deeply Blessed and*
                Deeply Stressed..195
                Srinagar, Kashmir, 1992

Chapter 17   *Mecca, Medina and the Mountain of Light*......................205
                Saudi Arabia, 1996

Chapter 18   *Return to the Continent of Origin* Allahu Wahidun!........225
                Senegal, West Africa and the US, 1999–2001

Chapter 19   *Walking in the Footsteps of the Friends of God* 245
                Dakar, Gabon, Lambarene
                and Mayumba, 2000

Chapter 20   *The Therapy of Liberation, a Journey of Consecration* 259
                Senegal, Mauritania,
                Morocco and Mauritius, 2003

Chapter 21   *Traveling on a Mission of Healing and Peace*.................275
                India, Nepal, Bangladesh,
                Pakistan and Kashmir, 2003-2004

Chapter 22   *In the Time Allotted Before We Must Go* | 297
                Out of the Context of Time and Space
Chapter 23   *Surely, with Difficulty Comes Ease*................................ 317

Chapter 24   *A Prophetic Legacy is Revealed*...................................... 329

Chapter 25 *The Way of Muhammad as Manifested in the Life and Teaching of Sheikh Harun Faye al-Faqir* 338

Chapter 26 *Guidance on the Inner Journey* 355
Sacred Words and Teachings Come to Life

Chapter 27 *Transmission of Grace Through the Coalescing Network* 365

Chapter 28 *Uniting in the Light* 375

Chapter 29 *The Unending Circle of Praise* 387

Chapter 30 *The Alchemy of Journeying with the Sheikh* 399

Chapter 31 *As We Become Sanctuaries of Peace and the Spiral Ascends* 409

Chapter 32 *Through Doorways of Life and Death, For All Humanity, A Call to Prayer, A Call to Awakening* 429

Chapter 33 *Lailat'ul Isra Wal Mı''raj The Exalted Night Journey of The Holy Prophet (saw) And Its Significance for Humanity* 441

Chapter 34 *The Endless End: Eternal Prayer* 457

Foreword

Ages unfold on the pages. Light is moving in synergy and synchronicity with Divine Sound. The dot of light is a materialization of the Divine Order moving through the pages of the book of destiny. Beholding this wonder, one feels inspired to travel on this journey of light. As the veils are lifted, you see that you are a journeying dot of light, at first marveling at the universe, and, at the end you have become integrated into its hidden fabric of light, as you are traveling forever in this majestic journey of pilgrimage.

The journey takes you through the Book of destiny, the Book of unity, the Book of light, finally arriving at the Book of all things! As Sheikha Maryam journeys across the earth, and her realization of the deeper patterns of light becomes more and more profound, she realizes that this unfolding message is not haphazard. She comes to understand her duty and to realize her place in the Book of light. As she travels through the Book of light, pages by pages are flowing, as the completion of one circle leads to the next which then leads into an even greater track.

She gazes into one vast circle after the next, spiraling through higher realms, and then suddenly, she finds herself — back in her booth — selling Treasures from the Silk Road.

As she is journeying through the book of her life, she understands that only when she gives up, she will rise up. She must not linger, asking questions or she may miss the light caravan as it travels through higher tracks of light. As she travels from one station to the next, from the smaller to the bigger and bigger circles, through India, Europe, Jerusalem, Africa, the Americas... she delves into deeper and deeper meanings and receives heavier and heavier instructions related to the completion of her pilgrimage.

The silk road woman asks no questions, but gazes into the deeper and deeper meanings and receives the instructions without losing focus. As she beholds it, the dot of light starts to write on the page in synergy with the Divine Order.

Travelling with Sheikha Maryam, one must journey through the pages and simultaneously through the expanding tracks of light, through the higher realms, and be guided on the path of one's own unfolding journey of light.

—Sheikh Tamer Degheidy Qaderi
Spiritual Guide, MD Fethiye, Turkey

On the road that leads to the Beloved
Every stone is made of gold.
Every step we take brings knowledge to us.
Even what appears to be a mistake, or an error,
Can bring us closer to purity and truth.

Every good intention, thought and action
Guides the soul toward the Goal.

Every true word that is heard,
Every understanding received,
Every challenge met,
Every station, by God's Grace, attained
Leads the traveler
Through the labyrinth of steps and tests surely, to the One,
Who has left, at every turn in the Road,
Signs of His Existence,
Clear signs showing the Way
That leads to Him.

Not only do our successes show us the way,
But even more deeply, our apparent failures—
Those moments in our journey
When we are most deeply humbled
And realize our limitations,
Realizing that every step we take
Is not due to our own power or will
But occurs by the Grace of God.
The journey that leads to the Beloved is guided by His Love.
The traveler is like a leaf
Blown in the wind of the Divine Will.
I was blown from one place to the next
Then, carried to another place, and on and on.

Thus, was I guided, without doubt, and witnessed on every
mountain path and in every valley, in every city, on every street,

the signs that He unveiled before my eyes,
Signs of His Love, His Power, and His Truth,
The signposts clearly delineating His path,
That the Beloved enabled me to see.

I was guided in my journey to see and love deeply
lands and people of great beauty
That, no longer exist in this world,
lands and people that can never be found again
In this world
But are alive in my heart.
They are alive within me.
And it is my loving duty
To bear witness to their life and legacy.

By the Grace of God, the Most Merciful,
I was guided through the countries to appreciate all the details of
the life there that I could see, before the devastating floods covered
the land.
In this very lifetime we have witnessed the vast transformations
of the earth, the nations, the peoples, powerful natural disasters,
as well as wars and oppressions,
all of which elicit
the deepest prayer, supplication, and compassion.

I met, on the journey, the Ancient ones.
and received the gifts that they placed in my hands before they left
this world and went on their way.
What remains of all the places and the people we have met along
the way
after the form of the flower has wilted and disappeared, back into
the earth,
is the essence of the fragrance,
the essence of the truth that they imparted to us
in the precious time allotted before they left this world,
leaving us here to carry on the work and the journey.

And the underlying truth revealed
through all that we are witnessing and learning is,
as the Holy Qur'an tells us,
(as difficult as it is for us, ultimately, to grasp)
"And everything perishes but the face of your Lord, full of majesty
and bounty" (55:26-27).

I pose the question to myself:
How can a creature that will perish
Comprehend this truth?
In every land through which I traveled in my search,
I found the pieces of a puzzle,
Pieces of beautiful, colored glass.
Piece by piece, every piece found its place
In the stained glass window — my life —
Until, the picture began to be complete.

And then, suddenly the Divine Light,
Nur Muhammadiyyah,
Came shining through,
Illuminating the total picture,
Causing my soul to proclaim,
"What a wonder!
So that is what it was all about!"

I followed the map only God gave me,
and was led from one situation
and station to the next,
from one Teacher to the next,
everywhere, in every land and in every state,
in every holy place and gathering,
collecting clues and messages,
following the guidance
as it was given.

Thus, step-by-step

through the stages of awakening,
the stages of acceptance, understanding,
healing and transformation.
I followed the light of guidance
in search of its Source and End.

I came to see that, behind every veil,
is the One, Who sees all,
and behind every occurrence
is the Hand that moves all,
and not a leaf falls,
but He knows it And He wills it.
What makes every detail
of this story sacred and significant,
is that He willed it.

These are the messages, the gifts
that the Creator, Most Kind, gave to me as He drew me
through the veils of karmic bondage
into the light, the liberation,
of submission and divine peace.

I came to see that it is not my business to
judge the people that I happened to meet along the way.
They are all instruments of my awakening,
Just as I am an instrument of theirs.
We see, as we continue to travel in the way of God, that there are
no accidents or mistakes.
Every stone that we walk on,
every piece of ground that we cover is
is a part of the Way, itself.
And every stage, every new level of awareness
is a preparation for the one which will follow it.

To reach each new step,
we must let go of the one that went before it.
The past is gone.

We must let it go.
The person that we thought we were
is like water in the river that has passed by.
What is awaiting us, at every stage of the journey,
is an unlimited new dimension of awareness,
that we cannot attain, except by letting go
of at least some of the false concepts and patterns that we had
been dragging along with us
and are now ready to release.

Sometimes the veils are washed away
in the rain of Divine Mercy,
and sometimes, they are burned away in the fire of
Divine Love.
Moment by moment, stage by stage,
the divine alchemy,
if we are willing and able to go through
the complete process,
is powerful and intense.

Sometimes we wish we could get out of that fire
and just go for a pleasant walk in the park.
but we are like fetuses in the Divine womb
and we cannot come out of the fire
until, we are gold.

Just as the baby becomes perfectly formed
in the womb
and then, exactly at the right moment, emerges
what an amazing divine process!
Like this, does our soul — the purified life
emerge from the crucible
radiant with the light of God, its own true nature.
Such is the nature of the profound process
Of transformation, and once we have begun,
we must go all the way through that deep tunnel.
Like the baby in the birth canal

We cannot turn back.
As difficult as it seems to be to carry on, from time to time, what
an amazing journey it is -
The journey of unveiling,
the journey of the opening of our inner eye!

What I saw, in the beginning,
through a glass, darkly,
is becoming,
through the process of unveiling, brilliantly clear.
In truth, what I saw was always perfectly clear.
It was I who was obscured
and could see it only through the densities of veils.

But the truth within me
was magnetically drawn to the truth in whatever form
it was hidden and then revealed.

Everywhere I traveled, I searched for the treasures -
The Divine Attributes and Messages -
And found them in every land, manifesting in different people
and places more, or less clearly.
Wherever I saw them,
sometimes, even, hidden in the dust,
I recognized their great value
and collected them into my heart, saying, "This is what I was
looking for!"

And, thus, through traveling for the sake of God, has the heart of
the seeker for truth
been restructured in the form of truth.
For as we gather the treasures of Divine Knowledge into our
heart,
in truth, we become united with
that, for which we have been seeking.

I sought my Beloved everywhere that He led me,

and there was not a moment in the journey
of my seeking Him
that He was not with me.
No doubt, I felt it,
and my heart was warmed and inflamed by His nearness,
and yet, I had to continue to travel, for years and years,
penetrating the veils.

As close as He was,
I could not find Him and know Him, until, I came to know
myself.
But, what is this knowing? Knowing myself in Him
is to be the drop that disappears in the Ocean.

CHAPTER ONE

IMPRESSIONS WHICH FORMED ME

Southern California, 1946-62

Each second we live is a new and unique moment of the universe, a moment that never was before and will never be again. And what do we teach our children in school? We teach them that two and two make four, and that Paris is the capital of France. When will we also teach them what they are? You should say to each of them: Do you know what you are? You are unique. In all the world, there is no other child exactly like you. In the millions of years that have passed there has never been a child like you. And look at your body — what a wonder it is! Your legs, your arms, your cunning fingers, the way you move! You may be a Shakespeare, a Michelangelo, a Beethoven. You have the capacity for anything. Yes, you are a marvel.

—Pablo Casals, *Joys and Sorrows*

I was born as a mystery within a mystery, descending to this earth and manifesting here for a reason known only to the One who created me and sent me here. The mystery of where I came from and why, exactly, I came here is a divine mystery. This is a mystery that all created beings share.

We, as souls, emanating from the light of our Creator, have the capacity for anything only because He has the capacity to do everything. And He created us for a reason. As much as Shakespeare and Michelangelo and Beethoven had a reason and purpose, a mission to fulfill, a unique song to sing, so do each of us. We came to this limited world, from the unlimited realm of souls where we existed within the Divine Presence, with precise tasks to fulfill, tests to pass through, and lessons to learn.

From the vast sphere, that unlimited world, my soul was sent to incarnate in Hollywood, California, in 1946. And, although I happened to land there for a reason, yet was my soul deeply connected to many other parts of the world I would have to discover. My mission in coming here has been an endless process of discovery.

As, step-by-step, I learned to walk and, word-by-word, I learned to talk, and, sight-by-sight, I learned to see, I was amazed by the marvels unfolding around me. And the greatest wonder I came to discover was the knowledge that was within me, the secrets I brought with me when I was sent to incarnate on this earth.

Everything that unfolded was a dance, an interaction between the inner world and the outer world. Where did the reality truly exist? This book is the legend of the journey of the soul in quest of the realization of its true nature and return to its Divine Source. But the soul is implanted in a body which walks and talks, sees and feels. While the body and personality were growing up as a young girl in Hollywood, California, the Light of the powerful soul was hidden, within that child, unseen by the people around her but guiding and inspiring her steps.

I grew up in a liberal Jewish family. Throughout my childhood, I spent a lot of time in Jewish community centers and camps that were held in eucalyptus groves and other natural settings. The image I remember most was the assembling of the "circle," the joining of hands, the sense of invocation and belonging.

Even when I was a baby in the crib, my mother noted that she often found me in a state of great contentment, a kind of ecstasy. She did not understand the source of the joy that enveloped me. When I consider the way in which my life has unfolded, I believe that even then I was aware that I was surrounded by the light of the Divine and the souls of the illuminated ones, some of whom I would later meet on the spiritual journey.

In contrast to the joy and peace that surrounded me in the crib was the stress in my parents' relationship. I never really understood what was going on, but it seemed that there was ongoing conflict between them. When I was seven years old, they divorced. As they went their own ways, in a certain way, the stress was relieved. As this occurred, I began to understand each of my parents better and what principle each represented, what part each played in the saga of my life.

I have come to understand that in the continuously woven tapestry of our life's journey, not one thread is without its purpose. Every part of the vast picture is delineated through contrasts. As in stained glass, without the dark leaded lines defining the light portions, there would be no picture, no story revealed. Every aspect of my relationship with my parents was like this. I see now, there were no mistakes and that every part of the unfolding, whether apparently positive or negative, had to take place to create the conditions necessary to catapult the seeker within me into the quest.

Every liability is also an asset. Reflecting upon our childhood, my brothers and I recollect that we were left to our own devices a lot. Especially after my mother married my stepfather, she became so absorbed in her relationship with him that she did not have the time or energy to be really involved with my development.

But very early on she said to me, "I have found what is true for me. You must find what is true for you." This was a principle that she maintained strongly to the end of her life. Rather than forcing her ideas or way of thinking upon me, she wanted me to understand this one single idea— that I must discover the truth for myself.

Both my parents insisted upon this. Sincerely, they gave me the gift of freedom, which allowed me to journey very far, unfettered by their demands or expectations. While we may have often not understood each other, and, often, I felt like a stranger in a strange land, I am indebted to them for this one great gift — the unconditional freedom to discover the truth for myself. That was a gift more valuable in the long run than understanding, acceptance, or any kind of appreciation or praise.

When my parents were still together, we lived on Valley Heart Drive in a donut-shaped, redwood house with large glass windows. In the center of the house was a large grassy garden where we ran freely, along with our pet rabbit. But then, the heart split in two. Soon after, my mother remarried, and my brothers and I moved with her to a street called Lemona Avenue.

We lived a block away from school. I still remember my first day at Kester Avenue Elementary. I was sitting on the black asphalt, children running, shouting, laughing, and balls flying all around me. Sitting as though invisible in the midst of this swirl of activity, not knowing anyone and not known by anyone, I entered into a kind of mystical experience of being selfless, independent, and free.

It was a foretaste of states to come, though certainly I had never heard the word "mystical" and did not know, in that mysterious moment, where "I" had gone. After a short while, I made many friends and became integrated with the life there. But the most vivid memory I have of all of my experiences at school was that first one.

One block away from that school, I lived in the house of my mother and stepfather. It was their exclusive palace, in which I felt I did not really belong. I had a small room near the front door. My mother painted it pink, which was her favorite color but which I found somewhat suffocating. In this small, oppressive pink room, I, who loved turquoise, felt compelled to continuously create art. That was the first crucible in which I began to realize the vision and purpose of my life.

Love came to me in the form of a huge, grey, fluffy cat I called Tiny Lou, who was always with me, and in the form of Papa, my mother's father, with whom I was deeply connected. I sat at his feet for hours as he played the mandolin. We were bonded like this in silence, music and gentle peace. Eventually, Papa was afflicted by a serious stroke, was partially paralyzed, and could barely speak.

Still a young girl, I spent hours reading to him and drawing, playing games designed to help him learn to speak again. He never really did regain his speech, and I felt his sadness and frustration. Nevertheless, the love we shared was a language beyond words. In this way, I learned in my earliest years about love which transcends sadness, illness, and disability. That was the realm in which Papa and I truly existed and were united.

At the same time, I had to adapt to the world created by my mother and stepfather. My mother and her husband lived as Queen and King in the palace belonging exclusively to them. I was a marginal figure in their realm, wondering what I was really doing there. They expanded their bedroom with glass doors overlooking the garden. I, very tentatively, observed their world, how they played their parts with a sense of glory and mutual adulation, knowing that I had really no role to perform in their play. I had simply been dropped there as a visitor or observer for a period of time.

While I lived in the house as an exile, on the other side of the sliding glass doors was the backyard, the garden of my liberation. We had a large swimming pool, almost the shape of the state of California, surrounded by trees bearing fruits of all kinds — apricots, peaches, guavas, and avocados. I found my true self in the garden, radiantly free and contented, eating the delicious fruit provided so abundantly by the generous Source. Very often, I would invite a friend as a guest for the night. We would swim in the illuminated pool, eat from platters of fruit and other food, and sleep in chaise lounges in the garden, in peace and with great joy. It was a vision and experience of freedom, purity and sharing, a foretaste of communion with companions in paradise:

And give glad tidings, unto those who believe and do good works, that theirs are gardens under which rivers flow. As often as they are regaled with food of the fruit thereof, they say, this is what was given us aforetime, and it is given to them in resemblance. Thereof, there are pure companions. There, forever, they abide.

The Holy Qur'an 2:25

For the rest of my life, I have dreamt again and again of bodies of illuminated water and gardens. In waking life, too, I am always drawn to such places. All of this, we know, is for a reason. It is a metaphor, a sign, an invitation to return to a place we have been before and can, by the grace of God, return to again.

There was one picture I painted again and again at that time. It was of a child with arms raised up into the sky. In the sky was a huge eye from which tears or drops of rain were falling. This water was falling into the child's hands and around her, causing flowers and plants to rise up all around her. Although no one around me was acknowledging the existence, the reality, of God, the Divine Source, the signs of His Presence and the descent of His Mercy were revealing themselves within me.

While our family was not at all religious, understandings and moral values were nevertheless shared that were important to me. Almost every weekend, my brothers and I went traveling with my father. Usually, we went to Palm Springs where my father's parents had a hotel. I loved those desert journeys. I felt that I could relax completely and would be carried along, through no effort of my own, to our lovely destination.

My father, Lennie, sang all the way through the desert. Many of the songs were filled with messages relevant to the essence of my life as it unfolded. Those songs were so important to me that I have remembered them all my life. It was in this way that my belief system about the family of man evolved during my formative years, reinforcing the knowledge that I brought with me when I came into this world. Again and again, as we traveled, he sang songs like this:

If we could consider each other
A neighbor, a friend, or a brother
It could be a wonderful world,
O yes! It could be a wonderful world!

If each little kid could have fresh milk each day
If each working man had enough time to play,
If each homeless soul had a good place to stay,
It could be a wonderful world,
O yes! It could be a wonderful world.

If there were no poor and the rich were content,
If strangers were welcome wherever they went,
If each of us knew what true brotherhood meant,
It could be a wonderful world,
O yes! It could be a wonderful world!

I still remember the deep sense of peace and security I felt as I cuddled up in the backseat with my blanket, being carried gently through the night, desert winds blowing in the window, and these beautiful songs of brotherhood blowing through my consciousness, forming attitudes and understanding even as I slept. These trips also engendered in me the life-long love of travel.

Then, my father married Sophie, and we all traveled together. We often went to Family Camp in the mountains, where Lennie and Sophie were in charge of arts and crafts. That was a heavenly combination for me — art, nature, and family altogether. When I became the editor of one of the camp papers, I developed my love and capacity for creative writing. This was an activity I enjoyed very much and one that I would continue to enjoy and greatly benefit from.

For the first years of her life with my father, Sophie was continuously creating mosaics, and, for the next half, she was constantly engaged in the creation of stained-glass windows. Wherever she lived, the house became an ever-unfolding work of art. She would begin the mosaic at one end of a room and continue until the whole room was a mosaic. At eighty-seven, her house of many windows was a museum of stained-glass windows, which, for the next several years of her life, she did not cease to create.

The atmosphere of creativity that filled the house allowed me to be the budding artist that I was, not hidden away in my bedroom but right in the middle of the living room. I remember, for example, greatly enjoying sculpting a bust of Albert Einstein there. This was exactly the kind of thing you would expect to be happening in Lennie and Sophie's living room.

Lennie and Sophie moved freely from place to place. Wherever they were, their house was always filled with people from different countries, different walks of life. The guests would drop in, visit for a while, and often stay for unlimited periods of time. This atmosphere, this style of living, was very invigorating and liberating for me. I came to understand that our family included everyone.

Anyone who came to the door from any corner of the world could come in and immediately be a part of our family. Since then, I have traveled around the world more times than I can count and found, in every journey, my family everywhere. From the time I came to own a house, it has always been an open house, a refuge for wayfarers on the path, like all the blessed oases around the world where I was so graciously received. As the spark of the creative spirit was ignited within me and beginning to blaze, impelled to express it, I was drawn to the medium of theatre. I began acting at five and continued to be involved in theatre until the age of twenty-three, when I went to India and became an *actor* on the journey, on the world stage.

When I was twelve, I heard that a theatre company called the Alley Theatre in the San Fernando Valley was auditioning for actors. I went to audition. I held the scripts in my hands like sacred hieroglyphs. I read them like a blind person reading braille who then could begin to see. This I understood: I will follow the script and it will show me how to open my heart and be free.

Thus, I came from my mother's home, where I felt like I had no part to play, to the stage, where I could play any part I liked. I played a weaver in *The Emperor's New Clothes*, the Gypsy Shoemaker in *The Red Shoes*, the White Rabbit in *Alice in Wonderland*, and the Wicked Witch of the West in *The Wizard of Oz*. The script for me was a sacred key which opened the door of intimate communion. All at once, I was able to communicate with everyone. Although I did not know their names, I found the capacity within myself to touch the people in the audience, to share intimately with them. This was one important step in the journey of self-discovery. It was the understanding and experience of sharing generously from the wealth that my heart had inwardly received.

To confirm that this was a sacred moment in my development, I received a gift from the assistant director of the theatre company that was of great significance to me. It was a pastel drawing he had made of an ancient man walking in the mountains, holding a staff and lantern, with his long beard blowing in the wind. Written upon it was: *"Seek, and the truth shall make you free."*

In truth, I was living, within myself, in an entirely different realm than the world of the late-Fifties San Fernando Valley. This was a world that I was temporarily visiting. When I saw the image of the ancient seeker, I knew that it was *me*, and I began to follow that deep instinct like a magnet.

Throughout my childhood, I was aware of the existence of subtle realms, realities, and beings other than those of the apparent world in which I was living. I saw in one of many dreams that I was standing in the middle of a circle of seven ancient men who were blowing upon me, blessing and initiating me. This dream revealed the truth that I would meet such beings of light, who would initiate and lead me with the light of guidance.

Even at this time, *the spirit of guidance* was manifesting in the outer world, just as it was within, and various people appeared as beacons in my life, exemplifying the message my father was singing about, the message of universal love, justice, unity, and peace, which was already, truly, singing in my heart.

One of these people was Sophie's father, Abe Wieselman. Abe was an extraordinary being who had a great influence on my formative years. He was inspired to go from country to country, especially to those countries where conflict and suffering prevailed. He was somehow able to meet with heads of state, such as Ben Gurion, introducing himself as an *Ambassador of Peace*. He was an ambassador not sent by any governmental agency but by *peace itself*. And wherever he went, with buoyant spirits, he delivered messages such as the following great poem. For me, no poem written by a human being expresses more simply and more purely the true purpose and high noble goals we were created as human beings to fulfill.

I want to be the one.

I want to be the Proclaimer

That the world has finally
Concluded a true and noble peace.

I want to see ample food for everyone
    On earth who is hungry.

I want to be the healer for everyone
    On earth who is ill and ailing.

I want to be the smile on the face
    Of everyone on earth.

I want to be the eyes for all the blind on earth.

I want to be a friend to all the homeless
    On earth.

I want to be joy in the heart
    Of everyone on earth.

I want to be a home for every wanderer
    On the face of the earth.

I want to be a song in the heart of everyone
    To sing.

I want to extend my utmost gratitude to Mother Earth
For providing us with food and sustenance of life.

I want to be the lantern beacon that brings
Light and enlightenment to every human on earth.

I want to be free like a bird to fly without fear
    Throughout the heavens and earth.

And it is my fervent hope
That all peoples and all nations on earth
Shall live as one nation, one people
In eternal peace.

Toward the end of his life, Abe made a practice of visiting retirement homes in hopes of inspiring his fellow elders to live their lives to the fullest. He was reading the poem and had just uttered the line, *"I want to be a smile on the face of everyone on earth,"* when he died. For evermore, when I think of him, I know that he is smiling within me, smiling with joy, understanding, and compassion for all lives. It was a great blessing for me that, early in my life, I heard words such as his, which significantly contributed to the development of my character and vision quest.

Another wonderful example of the noble human spirit, who was shining through his words and deeds for us at this time, was Dr. Martin Luther King Jr. I was blessed to meet him and hear him speak in person at a local school gym. I felt the courageous truthfulness and purposeful clarity of his being and his mission and was always deeply affected by what he said and what he did.

Throughout my teens, I was passionately dedicated to the cause of racial equality and actively involved in CORE, the Congress of Racial Equality. Brought up as I was, from the time when I first began to think, to believe vigorously in equality and justice for all members of the family of man, when I came to realize the conditions prevailing for African Americans, particularly in the South, my heart was inflamed by longing for these grave injustices to be rectified and for the equality inherently due to all beings to be established in this world.

The ever-expanding Civil Rights Movement — in which people of all races and walks of life joined hands and hearts in the courageous, loving call for justice and equality for all — was manifesting what I most deeply felt.

I was greatly inspired and encouraged by the power of the human spirit that was expressing itself during this era. The impassioned, eloquent speeches of Dr. King that moved so many people to join together and walk for freedom and peace as well as the song rising up in the hearts of so many great singers and social commentators of the time — such as

Pete Seeger, Joan Baez, and Bob Dylan — all passionately affirmed the rights of human beings to live in equality and peace. It was a period when the heart of the people was singing strongly, even in the face of the unfathomable darkness of bigotry and oppression, and it was not weakened but strengthened by the encounter.

Almost fifty years later, in 2008, while I was visiting Sophie, she played for me a documentary of the wonderful folk singer and activist, Pete Seeger. Suddenly, I remembered secret dimensions of my life and how my heart was originally opened, here in this world.

In the midst of the unfolding social movements of the late Fifties and Sixties, I had finally understood what I was doing on earth and felt that I actually belonged in this world (albeit just for a time). I felt unified with kindred spirits (such as the great folk singers and all the people marching with Dr. King) and that we were all inherently dedicated to common high ideals.

In the documentary Sophie shared with me are scenes of countless thousands of people assembling in our nation's capital, not obstructing justice or threatening violence, but singing with unbounded love.

What strength for the country, I thought, that so many of its citizens were inspired to unite, surrounding the White House, somehow embracing that heart of our country and our people with the very spirit of liberty and justice for all. When I saw in the film all the countless beings joining hands to surround the capital, I remembered the impact of those moments upon my evolving life; they were indeed one of the great signs in my youth that God was alive and ruling His universe with His Grace and Love.

These were the values that were nurtured and respected by my family. And, they were also the very qualities that I later came to realize were most perfectly manifested in the Prophets and Messengers, peace be upon them, sent to this earth by a Lord Most Merciful who specifically requested and commanded that human beings treat each other with such love, justice, and respect. When I saw people gathering together to affirm these human values, I knew that inherently they were not so much *protesting* injustice, as *affirming* noble divine qualities and God-given rights.

By the Grace of the One Who is the Giver of all goodness, on November 4, 2008, a few weeks before this book's first publication, the news came that the dream of Dr. King — the song of all of us who have been singing for justice and equality, with hands and hearts joined, surrounding the heart of our nation and world — seemed to have manifested in reality. I do not speak about the political implications or consequences of this profound occurrence in our history, but about the fulfillment of the dream that all human beings have equal rights to attain the highest goals. This was a victory not for one person, but for humanity.

Watching the response to the election results on television, it appeared that the whole world was celebrating. What were so many people sincerely celebrating? Hope for the end of the racial divide, the opportunity for all to advance together. In the context of centuries of horrendous racism and apartheid, this was a victorious step for humanity on the journey towards justice and truth. May the One Most Merciful, Most Wise and Just, lead us on the path to the realization of true unity and equality.

So the victory was of love, mutual concern, mutual respect, and solidarity for the people of this country and the family of man. The fact that a person of color could be elected President of the United States was to be deeply celebrated and was a door opener and meaningful game changer in our political and cultural history.

The knowledge that all human beings were created equal and that equal rights for all were truly worth fighting for was not an understanding that I shared with most of my school mates. Their social interests seemed more superficial, like dating and going to parties. Still, I wanted to speak up, without speaking, for what I believed. Every day, I wore a big button on my coat that said, "Freedom Now! CORE." This became the name by which most people knew and addressed me, the message that defined me in high school, the words that people would call out to me when they saw me. Even if they chanted it as a taunt, it did not bother me because these words and all that they represented expressed what I truly believed in and who I truly was.

It was difficult to find many people of different races and cultures to link arms with, in the San Fernando Valley of the late Fifties, but the longing for union with Africa and with people of all cultures, countries, and colors was already resonating in my heart. Already, my hands and my heart were linked with theirs.

Being somehow deeply aware of this big picture, I could not easily fit into the somewhat limited life of the student body at Van Nuys High School. Certainly, my heart was beating to the beat of a different drummer.

Lennie and Sophie had now moved to Greenwich Village in New York City. That seemed to me to be an appropriate place for me, to continue to expand my horizons. So, when the summer came, I went to live with them. They had an apartment in Washington Square. It was filled as ever with people.

In the tiny kitchen, where the light would not disturb anyone, on many nights I used to read all night long. I remember specifically reading *Portrait of the Artist as a Young Man* by James Joyce, which nourished, inspired, and empowered the artist as a young woman within me. Books like this were sustenance for the visionary, the thinker, growing up within me, just like the water poured into budding plants which makes them rise up and bloom.

Those were nights of light and days of discovery. I fondly remember roaming through Greenwich Village and resonating with like-minded souls. When we are on the path of self-discovery, everyone we meet is a mirror and every word we read is a ray of guidance. That summer in Greenwich Village was full of signs and reflections.

I joined a theatre company in New York called the Fifty-Fourth Street Repertory Company and continued to explore the inner and outer dimensions of self-discovery and the loving art of sharing with others. I wanted to remain there and go to school at one of New York's performing arts high schools, but it was not possible to work out all the details. So, I had to go back and "do more time" (but not too much!) in the San Fernando Valley.

I returned to high school in California but knew that I could not last there for very long. I wasn't really able to fit into the "box" of the world, as we knew it then, a culture of pink mini-skirts and American Bandstand. Having skipped the sixth grade, I also skipped the twelfth grade. I missed the prom and all related rites of passage and went to the University of California in Berkeley at the age of sixteen.

CHAPTER TWO

UC BERKELEY — FLYING INTO THE OPEN SKY

Berkeley, California, 1962-69

Onward and upward into the morning,
Free flash, O Soul, to the realms of Light
Move thou in Order
Move thou in Harmony
Freely shalt thou move with the children of Light.
　　　　　　　　　　—*Emerald Tablets of Thoth*

I was a bird released from its cage, flying into the open sky. Berkeley, in the early sixties, was a marketplace of spiritual teachings, an open-air market where the representatives of many spiritual lines brought their fruit and laid it on the table. I was delighted by this feast, very much energized by the currents of light and knowledge that came flowing into my consciousness.

But not without paying a price, did our generation pass through the door of awakening. I remember vividly standing in the Berkeley Student Union when the news of the assassination of President Kennedy was announced on the loudspeaker. This news pierced all our hearts at once. Everyone was paralyzed by its impact. It was a rite of passage that united us all. We lost our innocence and gained knowledge — knowledge of the vulnerability and mortality of all living beings, our President, ourselves.

From that moment on, death was always a part of the picture, as I perceived it — death as the end of a dream, and death as the beginning of the spiritual journey. I saw then how things were inextricably connected, the inevitability of death and the need to gain spiritual knowledge, the need for the liberation that transcends death. The door of the *dharma* was open. I read books such as the autobiography of Carl Jung, the life story of Milarepa, and *The Tibetan Book of the Dead*. I will never forget the power and truth of the introductory passage.

> *O procrastinating one who thinks not of the coming of death, devoting oneself to the useless doings of this life, improvident is one in dissipating one's opportunity. Mistaken indeed would one's purpose be now if one returns empty handed. Since dharma is one's need, would one not devote oneself to the dharma even now?*

At this time of the beginning of my awakening, in my sixteenth year and not apparently approaching death, as I was reading the book of my life,

I saw that every paragraph was introduced by this passage. Although young, with my whole life yet to unfold, I grasped with an inner intensity the awareness that life on earth was not permanent. It was but a preparation for an ultimate transformation leading from the impermanent to an eternal life. I wanted to learn and to practice, that *dharma*, the virtuous way of the higher truth, which would not leave me empty-handed and dissipated, unprepared, at the moment of the coming of death.

Through reading the stories of those who sought the truth, I knew within the depth of my soul the need to find the Master and become a disciple on the Path. But where was the true Master I was searching for, and by what means could I find him? All of the teachers were bringing their fruits and selling them. I tasted them, found sweetness and nourishment in the teachings, but I knew that none of these teachers were the Master I needed to find.

I gravitated to the Integral Yoga Institute in San Francisco, which was dedicated to the teachings of Sri Aurobindo. There, I made friends with the director, Dr. Haridas Chaudhuri, and entered the world of the teaching of Sri Aurobindo — a great Indian activist for social justice, teacher, and sage. Reading the writings of Sri Aurobindo about his experiences in prison, where he was interred for a year as a result of civil disobedience, had an effect upon my evolving consciousness.

What impressed me so deeply that I consider it a landmark awakening in my own journey was the description by Sri Aurobindo of the transformation of his consciousness while he remained in the prison cell. The experience of this teaching was in itself a meeting with the Master. It was not the person who was the guide I was seeking but the authenticity of his transformative experience that came through his words, simply ignited my soul and made me yearn yet more deeply for the Teacher and the Path.

He described his experience, at first, deprived of freedom, of contact with the books, situations and people he loved. Undergoing the anguish many prisoners face, especially those in solitary confinement, he found it impossible almost to meditate at all. On the contrary, it was necessary for him to experience for himself the despair and hopelessness of so many people who languish and even have mental breakdowns under the duress, the inhuman strain, of prison life.

This is the catalyst for awakening, as the Buddha also experienced it, the deep, empathic comprehension of human suffering. As he continued his journey within the cell, Sri Aurobindo came to understand what he had come there to learn. Although he was locked in the very same cell where he had suffered so much, he came to the state in which he felt completely embraced by the Divine and filled with love and wonder in his awareness of the nearness of that Divine Presence enveloping him, within and without. He began to perceive the Divine Presence in everything — in the bars of the prison cell, the prison guard, the bird flying outside his window. Thus, this experience in the prison cell became for Sri Aurobindo a profound spiritual awakening.

This story touched me deeply. In the transformation of one state of mind to the other, I saw the power of the spiritual path, and knew that I must make that journey myself. To further come to the state in which, although apparently imprisoned, one perceives God in everything was all the more amazing and marvelous. This was greatly inspirational to my yearning soul. This was a concept of absolute transformation, which, from the moment I read about it, I have constantly yearned to attain: to embrace all lives as my own, and to perceive the Divine Presence in everything. This is truly where my heart and soul were; this was the state of realization that I truly yearned to attain.

But my life was manifesting on other planes at the same time. So, in speaking about my first year at the University in Berkeley, I do not want to convey the sense that everything was so profoundly serious. In fact, life was also delightfully enjoyable. I was free, out of my mother's house, and in my own element. I was going to a university where I did not need to wear shoes to class, studying Theatre, Folklore, Italian, and walking into the mysteries of my unfolding life.

I was walking barefoot along a stone ledge, one day, when a man with very long, golden hair and beard and an angelic face began to follow me. He said he would like to play music for me. I went with him to the Pauley Ballroom on campus. It was empty except for a large grand piano. He improvised galactic music for hours. I lay beneath the piano and then danced across the huge empty ballroom.

Charles and I began to live together in a small cottage on Blake Street and then moved to a house on Parker Street and joined together with artists of all kinds to celebrate the golden age of the sixties in Berkeley. Our life became a continuous series of artistic happenings.

My brother Michael, three and a half years older than I, was an inspired artist in whatever medium he engaged. At this time, his principal art form was creating events, sometimes lasting for as long as twenty-four hours. My brother took the time and care to think about what each person in our circle would most enjoy. He sought to know the inner life of that person and then manifest for him or her, an intricate series of experiences that would reveal to the person most poignantly his or her inner vision. That was truly a beautiful form of art and a deeply caring expression of friendship.

I also have another brother named Steve. He was at the University of Arizona while all this was taking place. I spent time with him, off and on, a little later in life. His love, support and kindness have been continuous throughout my life. His fundamental characteristic of loving kindness has expressed itself, throughout his life, in a love for animals and all creatures.

From the time that I came into this world, I was balanced by the two aspects that my brothers embodied, both brothers having both qualities. One was a kind of brilliant creativity and the other, compassionate kindness. I have a photograph of myself as a young girl standing with my brothers on a hillside overlooking a large lake. I am standing with these two aspects of my being, my brothers, surrounding and protecting me, all of us at ease, overlooking the lake of existence.

Another very pivotal member of our Berkeley circle in the Sixties was Charles's best friend, a poet named Daniel Moore (who would, upon embracing Islam, become the Sufi poet, Abdal-Hayy Moore). It was a spiritual experience even to visit his home. He lived in an apartment in San Francisco's Divisadero district. Daniel was a gifted Blake-like artist as well as a very inspired poet. The walls of his apartment were covered with illuminated manuscripts. I felt that these were like the walls of his heart and I was reading his poetry, perceiving his vision from within his heart.

For example, the poems that I read were like this one he would compose and publish much later in life:

"All My Poems Assembled Together"

I wonder if I put the entire machine of all my
poems together, like so many moving parts
what kind of thing or creature would
result, a Taj Mahal of translucent
ivory glowing pinkly in the rising or
setting sun, or a hairy monster out of
control, capable of searching out every sensitive
reader to devour them at one screaming
gulp, or a sea creature, vaguely prehistoric, of sweet
benignity, all puffy and docile, and smiling,
like a giant animate marshmallow

or would the resulting assemblage be more like a
a virgin forest, tall mysterious trees made of
various substances, coral, turquoise,
teak, cardboard,
rubies, coal, laced everywhere, with the densest
vegetation, birdsong, warbling and cooing.
rustling, at the sides, as you
walk, rustling of hopefully
benign creatures in their turn, exotic looking
lemur or tapir types. You sometimes catch
the phosphorescent glint of their eye-whites,
or a vast dusty plain, with one old
house standing on it, wood worn almost to
paper by the constantly howling winds, shutters and
doors banging, and inside an
old man in a wicker chair fallen asleep in
a heap of out-of-date magazines

I mean, put them all together, assembled, after all
into one whole totality, would all these
hundreds of poems be a
floodlit or shadowy
path to Paradise, as I hope.

                    Daniel Abdal-Hayy Moore,
                    I IMAGINE A LION

Now, approximately fifty years later, after Daniel Abdal-Hayy Moore (ra) has returned with such deep dedication and sincerity to the Beloved Source, we have come to behold the absolutely amazing assembly of his deeply inspired works which, we pray, have led him and all those inspired by the Divine Light and Love transmitted through him to the paths of paradise leading to the Divine Presence, the Lord of Infinite Mercy and Grace.

Daniel was the very essence and manifestation of the passionate poetic soul I had known was blazing secretly within me. He was my mystic counterpart whom I recognized and bonded with immediately. The passion was not personal but collective. We had work to do together, creating a vehicle for the ritual transformation of our extended tribe.

This was Berkeley in the Sixties. So many people were searching, but we did not know what we were truly searching for. At the very least, we knew that we wanted to transcend the isolation of the limited nuclear family system that prevailed in America in the Fifties and create a truly extended encompassing sense of community. And for the kind of tribe that we were forming, we needed rituals of collective transformation.

So, to channel the energy of so many people who were searching for a meaningful way of joining together not previously found in their experience of American culture, something they could not have found in the gathering of traders on the stock market or at a football game or wrestling match, we created a theatre company called the *Floating Lotus Magic Opera Company.*

Every weekend, we would perform in an amphitheater in the hills of Berkeley in John Hinkel Park. We had a large regular audience that came every week for this rite. We began and ended by sitting in a large circle meditating and chanting. In between these two periods of meditation, we would go through the steps and stages of invocation and transformation and then finally serve food to all.

In one play, I had the part of the goddess Kali. In the first half of the play, she unleashes a cyclone of dark forces. Then, she dies, is placed in a coffin, and is carried on a *bardo* journey around the stage. She is then reborn as the pure regenerated mother earth.

There was a very deep sense in which I had to experience this death and rebirth every week. By compelling confrontation with the force of darkness itself, this became a period of initiation. Sometimes, in the course of the process, I was unable to move for two or three days, in a week, and I would lie still, wait, and pray until the "spirit" rose up again, freed of some more impurities. Then, I would carry on cooking, working with the company and preparing collectively for the weekend ritual.

Now, as I write about this, so many years later, I have come to see how profound is the darkness of this time that we are living through. As the signs of destruction are manifesting, one after the next, I believe with absolute certainty that we are alive in a time such as this to transmute, by God's Grace, the darkness into light.

So, it is more important than ever for the earth and its inhabitants to travel with certitude and focus, under the guidance of a true Master, the guidance of true mastery on the path, which comes from God and leads back to God. We were searching and yearning for this even then in our amazing theater experiences in the Berkeley hills, but it is yet more amazing to consider how we ultimately found it.

Once or twice a week, I taught yoga classes in a very large, light-filled loft that belonged to John Argue, a very fine actor in the Berkeley Theatre Department and a member of our extended theatre family. It was a class for members of the Floating Lotus and for others. Many people came. I had studied with a yogi in San Francisco and was now passing on what I had learned.

At this point in our life, and collective journey, we were given the gift of timelessness. We were not bound and constrained by the sense of urgency beating at the door. The class did not seem to take place in a certain defined period, after which we had to get up and go. We entered into the eternity of the breath and allowed it to breathe through us. Our bodies, stretched across the room, were floating in the breath. We would assume one of the yoga postures for a while and then return to the formless peace. As the apparent facilitator of this process, I discovered that I could be a vehicle for peace.

When the theatre company, this assembling of our tribe, began, I was still living with the cosmic pianist named Charles. We had a small house on Parker Street. In the back was a garage that I lined with wood in a rustic style. This became my painting studio. It opened into a very small but very beautiful and magical garden, surrounded by a weathered lattice fence, heavy with fuchsia and bougainvillea flowers.

A lama from Mongolia used to come to our garden regularly to visit. He had many hundreds of disciples in Mongolia. In Berkeley very few people even knew that he existed. I accepted his appearance in our garden as the most natural thing and was delighted and blessed by his presence.

When he came to the amphitheater to see our performance, as I was flying across the stage, I looked out into the audience and saw no one but him. His illuminated face filled all of everything and that was all I could see. I believe that it was the purity of his practice, compassion and intention which generated the light that made him especially visible to me.

We were also deeply blessed and amazingly graced to practice meditation in San Francisco, in the meditation hall of the great Zen master Shunryu Suzuki Roshi. The first time I entered the zendo, a Japanese television film crew was filming a documentary. Not really knowing how things were arranged in the zendo, I went in and sat down on the men's side. It was a very Zen like way of entering the path of no-mind and no-planning.

Suzuki Roshi was, it certainly seemed to us, an awakened being, joyously engaged in awakening others. He was shining like the full moon in a dark night sky, illuminating the world with bright wisdom.

Just as a Zen master would, he spoke words that automatically dispelled the constraints of the ordinary mind. For example, he said:

> *To live in the realm of Buddha nature is to die as a small being, moment after moment. When we lose our balance, we die, but at the same time, we also develop ourselves, we grow. Whatever we see is changing, losing its balance. Then we see that the reason everything looks beautiful is because it is out of balance, but its background is always perfect harmony.*
>
> Shunryu Suzuki Roshi,
> *Zen Mind, Beginner's Mind*

This perspective, which integrated — into one reality — the state of imbalance and the state of perfect harmony, was useful and enlightening at all times and in all situations. Certainly, everything that was happening and everything that could happen could easily find its place in the comprehensive understanding that was being transmitted to us by the bright and shining Roshi. He also taught extensively through the ongoing practice of meditation, called *zazen*. I remember, in the midst of sitting in meditation for several days, I was served a meal on a tiny, rectangular ceramic plate. It consisted of one slice of celery, one slice of carrot, one slice of bean curd, and a few other carefully selected items.

In the context of those many hours of sitting, this small break was truly wonderful, and the meal, I felt, was the most delicious that I had ever eaten. Such was the grace of the purity of that spiritual practice and the subtle teaching about the interaction of imbalance and harmony that was being transmitted. And, outside the zendo, I was noticing the teachings at work in life.

Living in the small house on Parker Street with Charles and me was a large golden cat we called Yellowness. Every night, Yellowness knocked over the statue of the Buddha on our shrine and sat in its place. In this too, it seemed, the living teaching was manifesting.

We also had other mysterious visitors. Once, a German painter named Blalah turned up and moved in. He was very talented and pleasant, but when tear gas filled the streets during the Free Speech Movement demonstrations, some deep trauma in his past was triggered. I had stretched out a large canvas that I was meditating on in order to bring forth a vision from the whiteness. While we were out, the traumatized Blalah slashed the canvas with a knife and disappeared, never to be seen again. The slashing of the canvas was more significant than anything I might have painted on it.

We never knew who would turn up. The house was open. At another point, the actor, Roberts Blossom appeared. He seemed to be a very lovely, kind, and luminous being. As an actor, he had appeared in many movies and television programs, such as *The Great Gatsby* and *Northern Exposure*, always playing the part of a wizened old man, a seer. Just as he appeared in those movies, so did he in ours.

Whatever happened we accepted as the "unfoldment." A clairvoyant and inspired but also mentally unstable woman named Jennifer appeared, moved in, and lived with us for some time. She spoke continuously and transmitted a lot of interesting teachings from the masters, but she was possessed by different forces at different times, which destabilized our life and household. Then, she too disappeared.

At a certain point, both the house and life there reached their limit for me. I knew that I needed purification, transformation, and elevation. I needed to take the next step. I asked Charles to drive me to Mendocino and leave me in the middle of the wilderness, which he did.

I took with me only *The Tibetan Book of the Dead*. I walked deeper and deeper into the wilderness and became hopelessly lost. Having no idea where I was or how to retrace my steps, I sat down in a grove of trees as the sun was setting. In some sense, having arrived at my destination, I felt that death was overcoming me. It was an overwhelming experience. Immediately, I became the prey of hordes of insects, each taking large bites out of me.

I opened *The Tibetan Book of the Dead* and read prayers that I felt were being said for me and were being said to protect me in the midst of my plight:

> *O you compassionate ones possessing the wisdom of under-standing, the love of compassion, the power of acting, and of protecting in incomprehensible measure, one is passing through this world and leaving it behind. No friends does she have, she is without defenders, without protectors and kinsmen.*

> *The light of this world has set. She goes from place to place, she enters darkness, she falls down a steep precipice, she enters a jungle of solitude, she is pursued by karmic forces, she goes into a vast silence, she is borne away on the great ocean, she is wafted on the wind of karma, she goes where there is no certainty, she is caught in the great conflict, she is obsessed by the great affecting spirit, she is awed and terrified by the messengers of death. Existing karma has put her into repeated existence and no strength does she have although the time has come to go alone.*

> *O you compassionate ones, defend her who is defenseless, protect her who is unprotected, be her kinsman, protect her from the suffering in the depression of the bardo, turn her from the storm wind of karma, turn her from the great awe and terror of the Lords of Death, liberate her from the long narrow way of the bardo.*

I read passages such as these. The book I was holding in my hands and reading was no longer a physical object made of paper; it was the vehicle through which knowledge was being transmitted. I began to comprehend the moment of death, the moment of transition from life in this world to the journey that leads beyond this life. I understood very clearly that in that moment of transition, a choice would have to be made between the terrifying manifestations of the illusions of the mind, and the brilliantly clear light of Reality, the state of enlightenment.

The insects consuming me seemed to be manifestations of the dark forces of illusion. I was being instructed not to be afraid of anything, not to be daunted or awed, but instead to stay focused in meditation upon the clear light of Reality, which was my true nature. This experience was a physical and psychological ordeal. But it was truly a glimpse into another dimension of reality, a spiritual opening. I had come to this forest to confront my own mortality and was brought through this test by an unseen Power, loving and willing me to continue on the journey of my life.

On the next day, when I knew that the experience was complete, I got up and slowly began to walk. Step by step, my feet were guided out of the wilderness onto the path that would lead back to civilization. When eventually I looked in a mirror, my whole face and body were so swollen from bites, I could barely recognize myself. I could see that I had been changed.

No matter what, I knew that my intention to find the spiritual path that leads beyond death had been infused with life. I had to make the journey, wherever it led me, to attain that goal. Just as I was guided out of the wilderness back to the path leading to the next step in my journey, I knew that I would continue to be guided. But I had to let go of everything that was distracting me from pursuing the real point of my life and journey.

When I finally somehow arrived at our home on Parker Street, I knew I could never live there again. I could not resume my former life, but was impelled to take the next step, deeper into the spiritual journey. I moved out immediately and then into the large wooden hall where Daniel lived and the Floating Lotus group gathered. We all lived, rehearsed, meditated, and ate together in the beautiful wooden lodge with immense windows overlooking the wonderful gardens and woods of Williams College on the north side of the Berkeley campus.

It was a beautiful place, a grand building surrounded by a beautiful garden, which inspired in us deep nostalgia, as if we had seen it in our dreams and had returned to it at last. But this beautiful building did not belong to us. It had been lent to us and was not our real home. One morning when we woke up, the dream was over, and we had to leave.

Next, we moved to a place we referred to as "the land," an abandoned lumber mill where everything had simply stopped functioning. There, we lived a very strange life in semi-habitable dwellings. Approximately fifty years later, I received a film that had been made then of our community by a visiting filmmaker. Seeing the film touched me deeply. The camera was focused mostly on the feet of the ancient travelers navigating through rocky mountainous paths symbolic of our actual journeys through life that were to unfold. Daniel was guiding this hippie caravan with words of wisdom and inspired poetic grace, revealing even then, as we walked on those rocky paths the inspired transmitter of the messages of Allah's Grace that he was and ever more deeply and sincerely would become.

On the land, we did our prayers, meditations, and performances, as we had done in Berkeley, but our time together was fading out, and each of us was entering into his or her solitary journey.

We had performed many times in Berkeley in a relatively pure atmosphere. Every time, the rite was completed, and the regenerated, pure earth rose up out of the coffin. Then, one day, we came in from *the land* and performed in San Francisco at the Family Dog, a famous gathering place for rock music and New Age happenings. Many people in the audience were on hard drugs. We were incapable of processing that. We could not resurrect. The pure earth could not rise up out of the coffin. The Floating Lotus Magic Opera Company dissolved, and each of the core members went into retreat in preparation for the spiritual journey. I moved into a glass room in my brother's house in Berkeley and went into deep retreat. In search of my true self, I entered into a period of fasting and silence for many months. The room had two levels. On the lower level, I had a long puja table for spiritual offerings, upon which stood the pictures of many teachers and saints. I saw practically no one but them. They were the friends with whom I conversed.

My bed was on a raised platform that was surrounded by glass. The room was like a glass lantern, my soul, in its unfolding process, the light within it. Surrounding the glass room were trees, blowing in the wind, and the light itself constantly moving. I was in a womb, a crucible of light, being guided and prepared for my journey. In reality, it was my life that was laid upon the altar. I offered it and surrendered in the deep longing to be guided, inspired. I had many dreams and visions. Understandings of the spiritual path and the need to follow it were flooding in. The ancient texts, teachings of a variety of religions, were alive. I saw them written in light, heard them resonating, and wrote them in my journal:

> *Ageless, subtler than the mind's innermost subtlety, Universal Sustainer, shining sun-like, self-luminous. I am the Knowledge, the brilliant Lamp dispelling all darkness. I am the End of the path, the Witness, the Lord, the Sustainer. I am the Place of abode, the Beginning, the Friend, and the Refuge. I am the Breaking-apart and the Storehouse of life's dissolution. I lie under what is seen in all creatures, the Seed that is changeless. I am the cosmos revealed and its essence that lies hidden. The man of inner wisdom, I see as My very Self, because he alone loves Me because I am Myself the last and only Goal, the inner Truth of his devoted heart.*
>
> Bhagavad-Gita

> *Allah is the Light of the heavens and the earth. His Light is comparable to a niche, wherein is a wick, the wick is in a crystal, the crystal is brilliant like a star. It (the wick) is kindled from a blessed tree, an olive tree, which is neither of the east nor of the west, and whose oil would almost glow forth of itself, though fire toucheth it not, light upon light.*
>
> The Holy Qur'an 24:35

I went into the room in hopes of finding myself, but what I found there was the light of God, the words of God. These were the secrets that I found, as I was being prepared to make the journey which would lead me to the Source of the beautiful words that were resonating through my being.

Another beautiful passage I wrote in my journal, was especially meaningful as it referred to the "book" not written on paper. This "Book of God's Remembrance" was the one I most wanted to read.

But not a word is lost, for in the Book of God's Remembrance, a registry is made of every thought and word and deed. Then, when the world is ready to receive, lo! God will send a Messenger to open up the Book and copy from its pages all the messages of purity and love. Then, every man of earth will read the words of Life in the language of his native land and men will see the light. And man will be at one with God.

Levi H. Dowling,
The Aquarian Gospel of Jesus the Christ

Such were the words I was reading, contemplating and recording in my journal as a reference to the sea of universal messages that were resonating within my heart and mind, truly inducing a state of awe, wonder, and yearning to make the journey that would lead me to the Source. I went out very rarely, but periodically the spiritual teacher Ram Dass came to town, and I knew for some reason I had to see him. Each time he spoke, I sat directly in front of him and was amazed to hear that he was reading to these large gatherings many of the exact passages I had been writing in my journal.

It appeared to me that we were getting messages from the same source and that I should make the journey to India to see his guru, Neem Karoli Baba, or Maharaj-ji, who seemed to be sending these messages

— of universal love, universal truth — to me as well as to Ram Dass and others.

I shared this feeling with Ram Dass, and he sent me two letters, confirming my instinct that I must go see Maharaj-ji.

There is nothing you can do but be very calm, very patient and persistent in your sadhana. You must even watch your own desire for enlightenment... We are very blessed to have tasted of the sphere within. Your letter is so full of shakti that it is fairly ablaze in my hands. You certainly need not worry. The seed of the spirit is planted within you and is emerging as fast as you are able to handle the light. Attachment will fall away. Each day is a further unfolding.

Here we are eternally, Shanti, Ram Dass

In another letter he wrote:

> *I hear in my heart every twist and turn of your journey...our journey. The veil of purification that makes ready the vehicle of ten thousand suns. We are so ancient... almost old enough to be born. When birth is no birth...death is no death...longing and fulfillment are one. Bharat (India) is where we meet... Bharat is the consummation. You write our journey so good... such melodrama... the love affair with the Ancient One... Dissolving in the Ocean of Love. All the black magicians bow to the pure Spirit... the Devil knows not for whom he works. There is only One. What we seek, we are. When we arrive, we shall be.*
>
> *I love you, Shanti, Ram Dass*

These letters were inscribed as a seal upon the parchment of my unfolding quest. It was clear that India was the consummation of this stage of my journey, and I had no choice but to set out on the journey to that ancient land.

CHAPTER THREE

SETTING OUT ON THE PATH
Orient Express and Afghanistan, 1969

A man is said to be absorbed when the water has absolute control of him and he has no control of the water. The man absorbed and the swimmer are both in the water, but the former is carried along and borne by the water, whereas the swimmer carries his own strength and moves at his own free will. So every movement made by the man absorbed, and every act and word that issues from him, all that proceeds from the water, and not from him: he is present there as the pretext.

—*Discourses of Rumi*

Having chronicled the dreams, visions, and messages that made me know that I had to go forth on the spiritual journey and give myself entirely to it without looking back, I made a copy of this book of dreams and visions, gave one to every family member and close friend, and then left, as though I did not know if I would ever return.

From this time when I first set out, I never once followed a map or really knew where I was going, much less how to get there. But I discovered that I was perpetually guided and that there were certain people I had to meet who were, in fact, waiting for me.

First were the electronic composer Karlheinz Stockhausen and his companion, a wonderful person and artist in her own right, Mary Bauermeister, whom I had met in Berkeley. They lived in a house constructed, like his music and her art, of many floating rooms, many suspended planes and dimensions. It was an appropriate place to begin my journey into worlds beyond.

I had lived in London for a few months and was well into my next journal of paintings and writings of the dreams and visions that were coming in an ever-flowing stream. Mary seemed to understand what was happening. She showed me photographs of her journey to Sri Lanka, a place I was indeed destined to go. I left with her my dog-eared copy of the *Discourses of Rumi* and boarded the Orient Express bound east.

I once heard a very useful teaching relating to train travel. When you get on a train with your luggage, put your luggage down. You do not need to carry your luggage once you are on the train, because the train is carrying both you and your luggage to your destination. So, when I got on the Orient Express, I let everything go. I was like a *corpse in the hands of the washer*. I was being carried. I was traveling in the current, immersed in it, so much that I had no sense of who I was, other than the one that was being carried along on the journey.

Having abandoned the sense of self-direction, being absorbed in the current that was carrying me, I remember little of the externals of that trip except looking out the window and beholding an endless golden canyon filled with turquoise water reflecting the radiant sky. At that moment, the earth, the divine creation itself, opened up for me its splendor. And, as the train passed through this fantastic landscape, I beheld the unparalleled artistry of the One Who created it.

At last, the train arrived at its final destination in the east in order to return to the west. That is where I got out. I was in Afghanistan.

I began to travel by bus, but not the modern, streamlined buses we are used to seeing in all modern cities. The buses in Afghanistan were, with their plenitude of bells and tassels, hand-painted works of art. Brilliantly colorful and joyous, with no glass in the windows, and packed with equally colorful passengers, they were an expression of the culture, the innocent heart of the people.

I remember sensing an ancient stillness and light pervading the land, which was at that time still untouched and intact. In every city and every village, the people, dressed in beautiful robes, embroidered hats, and turbans, were sitting in circles, communicating, sharing, and drinking coffee or tea. I saw no violence, no festering fires of terrorism or the bleeding wounds of a country dispossessed or possessed, but a golden haze of stillness and peace. I sensed that life here was being lived as it had been for centuries. This was holy Afghanistan, where a boy like Jelaluddin Rumi could have been born and begun to grow up.

For me, this was a vision, something revealed to me that I needed to see. I do not know how accurately this vision presented the real state of the land and the people I saw. I am certain there were many things taking place there, within that complex culture, that I was not aware of. I saw only the dimension of ancient and eternal peace, and I did not want to leave it.

The memory of this holy time and place is poignantly precious to me now, since all things have been changed by the ravages of the times of destruction. The beautiful, golden, gentle, peaceful land of Afghanistan I saw then cannot be found again in this world, but it lives in the hearts of those who were blessed to perceive and internalize the beauty and grace of the Eternal One that was manifested in Afghanistan then.

What was that mystery which I was blessed to behold, to taste and to smell? Longing to return to that place, I have come to realize that it no longer exists in the physical world. Nothing in this world is permanent. I know so deeply that I had to move on and could never go back to that place and time.

When we realize that our true identity is as a seeker, a wayfarer on the path of God, we come to see more and more deeply that it is the path to which we are wed, the *path* to which we always return. And the path never lets us dwell in any oasis too long. However beautiful and enchanting any experience was along the way, I could never remain there but simply take the essence of each experience, the teaching, and continue to be carried along.

Now, I was continuing the journey on a bus with bells, beads, and tassels, rattling along as it bounced through the rocky terrain. The bus was wondrous, I discovered, in more than its appearance. I was amazed to see that suddenly, in the middle of the desert, the bus stopped, and all of the passengers got out and laid out their prayer mats in the desert to pray. This occurred on all the buses in Afghanistan at every time of prayer. The call to prayer would come lilting from a minaret somewhere in the desert, and all the people would get off the bus and lay out their prayer mats. I had never seen anything like this. It was a wonderful, amazing vision, outside of any political context, a vision of peace and piety, of people united in their love for the Creator. Wherever the people were going, whenever they had to get there, the priority and necessity for them was always to stop in the middle of the journey at the designated times, get off the bus and pray. This was the way in which I was introduced to the simple beauty and truth of prayer and of Islam.

This act of bowing down, of stopping in the middle of any journey to praise the Creator, was not something I learned about in a book — it was a reality that my soul witnessed. It was an awakening for the soul, an invitation to pray.

The way that such images are represented today in the media often suggests that when you see a group of people gathering together in the Islamic congregational prayer, you should be afraid, for when they rise up from their prayers these people may do something violent which will endanger you. But what I saw in the middle of the desert was the very opposite — it was absolutely peaceful, natural, and pure. It was for me a revelation of pure existence, in which human beings traveling upon the earth given to them to dwell upon by the Creator, bow down upon it in praise of Him, as He has decreed.

What has been decreed, by the Creator, I came to understand, in my discovery of the beauty of Islam, is mercy and kindness and peace, which come through submission and surrender to the Source of all things, the Most Merciful, Most Compassionate. The true believers bow down to praise the greatness and the glory of the One who created everyone. And the root of the word "Islam" is *salam* — peace.

This is what I learned about the nature of true Islam from the people of God I was destined to meet. Those who are in the state of true Islam do not bow down, beseeching God to destroy others, and then get up from prayer intent to kill. For, just as the Bible says, "Thou shalt not kill," so does the Holy Qur'an say, "If you kill one person... it is as if you killed all of humanity and if you save one life, it's as if you saved all of humanity."

This is the truth of submission to the Creator of all, Most Merciful, Most Compassionate, Most Clement, Most Kind. It is a truth, which is hidden in our world, today, behind a terrible veil of war, brutality, injustice, and strife. But what was revealed to me in that moment in the desert of Afghanistan was a vision of peace, not war, a vision and realization, which has constantly guided my journey toward the Source of eternal peace.

Signs are continuously being revealed to us to help us enter the stream of the Divine Attributes. For me, that eternal moment, that vision in the desert of Afghanistan was the opening of a doorway of perception that would lead me toward the Source of the stream. The simple, pure message was: *Stop in the middle of the journey and bow down to the One Who created you and enabled you to make this journey. Then, when you rise up and continue to travel, know that wherever you think you are going, the real journey is to Him.*

CHAPTER FOUR

ENTRANCE TO INDIA

The great thing in this world is not so much where we stand as in what direction we are going.

—Oliver Wendell Holmes

I found myself in a Pakistani town en route to India. I was in a hotel room with several other people, westerners on their way east. They were engaged in various kinds of activities and social games, which I observed as though I were a visitor from another planet.

What I remember is that I received a message there to cease to find provision for myself. I was not to buy any food or look for it, but only to accept what was offered to me. I said nothing, ate nothing, and was simply focused upon the path leading to the goal. I slept only in order to wake up. I slept very little, woke early, and left the hotel.

Immediately, as I began to walk down the road, I came across an extremely elderly man in a horse-drawn cart who seemed to be saying to me that he was waiting there to take me to my destination. Although he was much older, he had almost the same face as a teacher with whom I had studied tantric art and philosophy in the Berkeley Hills, Harish Jahori. Seeing my old teacher appear again leading me on the way, I understood the humor, the secret truth, and I surrendered to his guidance, sensing that he was the one designated to take me to the next stage of the journey. So, I got into the horse-drawn cart and off we went.

I remember the warmth and sweetness of the day, the fragrance of fires and incense burning, the pervading golden light, the peace, and the pace of the horse gently carrying me towards an unknown destiny. We traveled for some distance. Because this mode of traveling was so much slower than I was used to, and closer to the earth, it is recorded in my memory in an extended timeless dimension to which I long to return.

Finally, we arrived at the destination he had in mind, and he put me on a bus, gave respects to the light within me, and disappeared. The bus quickly started filling up with warm, friendly people. They all seemed to recognize and know me and treated me like a long-lost member of their family. They were going to a great wedding feast to which they enthusiastically invited me, as though I was an awaited participant.

I imagined, as the bus passed through the lush, rolling terrain, that I was being guided to this wedding feast, where I would certainly find the food that God would provide for me, the food He had told me to wait for, and maybe also find there my husband. I got right into the celebratory atmosphere that filled the bus, not knowing what wondrous events were about to unfold. After a period of camaraderie, the bus stopped, and absolutely everyone but me got out. They all got off the bus without looking back, without saying a word to me.

Then, the bus took off again, at an incredible speed, with just the driver and me. It seemed to me that we were flying through another dimension of existence. The marriage feast was a dream, an illusion that never took place, and this was like a dream, too, a dream of passage from one plane to another. I was flying across that river of light, deeply alone, but with the bus driver as my ferryman to the opposite shore. The bus seemed to be flying over the ground and moving at the speed of light. This timeless flight ended at the border of India, where he let me out.

I walked over to the border itself and sat down with the guards. There was a full moon in the sky. *Full moon in the valley of death,* I said to myself. So far, all the stages of my journey had corresponded to the stages in the mystic book *Conference of the Birds* by Farid ad-Din Attar. Now I had come to the seventh valley, the valley of death. Dispassionately I observed the signs and knew that in entering the mystic dimension that was India I would have to undergo some kind of death.

As I was sitting with the guards waiting for the border to open, looking up at the full moon, a young man came and sat down next to me and began to speak with me. He was Danish and very friendly and talkative. He indicated that he would like to travel with me, not in an intimate relationship, but as fellow travelers on the path. I knew that my journey was inherently solitary but accepted his offered friendship as part of the unfolding story.

He said he was going to be staying in the Green Hotel in Amritsar. I knew by then about the mystic aspect of the color green, and I took that as a sign that that was where I was to go next.

We arrived at the Green Hotel in the middle of the night. I looked up and saw the full moon. A small Indian man appeared and fell at my feet and kissed them. He got up and exclaimed, *"Devi, Devi!* How can we serve you?" I sensed that he believed that I was some kind of incarnation of the Divine Mother.

Whatever he may have thought, he certainly was offering me food, the first food offered since I had received the directive to eat only what was offered to me, and I knew that I had to eat that meal. Very ceremoni-ously, full of devotion, he laid out before me a beautiful meal composed of many dishes. I began to eat.

From the first bite, I knew that this meal was going to kill me in some way. It was a meal that I would never forget. I felt that it was a kind of initiation and I had to finish it. When I look back at this moment, I can think reasonably that it is not wise to eat whatever you may be given in a foreign country. In that moment of the journey, however, it was the initiation I had to go through.

He took us to a room, and as soon as we entered it, it was as though a fiery dragon took hold of my body. I was entirely overcome by fever, paroxysms, and vomiting. This continued for days. How many exactly, I do not know.

After a day or two, the young man excused himself, saying he was not really ready for this kind of spiritual journey and simply wanted to travel around the world and enjoy himself. I was left alone in that room for an unknown period of time.

Thus, did I enter India with the *full moon in the valley of death* and passed through the doorway of purification, so when I emerged from that room and was able even barely to take the next step, it was as one chastened and changed. I felt like a newborn colt walking on entirely new legs, as I emerged from the hotel into the bright sunlight. Now that I had the strength to *travel*, even tentatively, the journey must contin-ue. Since I was in Amritsar, the next stop was the Golden Temple. After seeing nothing but the dark room and the fires of purification for some unknown period of time, I beheld the Golden Temple like a resplendent vision I had seen in my dreams. The temple of gold, floating on luminous water, was filled continuously with songs of God's praise.

Was this the *Bharat*, Ancient India, about which Ram Dass had written, the place where we would meet? I found my seat in a place over-looking the shining water and breathed in, drank in, the divine music, as I awaited guidance, waited to be found. Incense filled the air, the sweet-ness of praise.

After some time, a tall, elderly man with a long beard, turban and Indian robes appeared. He was a Sikh elder. He told me that he had been waiting for me all his life and would like to take me to his home nearby, where he had been keeping a bed for me. I went with him to his room and saw the bed, which, he said, had been reserved for me. Then, he offered me food from a large pot covered with a towel. He lifted the towel, and under it was white rice with large black ants crawling in it. I knew that it could not have been *me* for whom he had been waiting all those years. As politely as I could, I refused and said that I could not really stop there but must continue my journey in search of my Master.

Chapter Five

IN SEARCH OF MAHARAJ-JI
Crisscrossing India and Nepal, 1970

A man sits wakeful through the dark night resolved to travel toward the day. Another man is traveling by caravan, upon a dark night and in a storm of rain. He does not know where he is passing or what distance he has covered; but when that day comes, he will see the result of that traveling. Whoso labors for the Glory of God, though he closes both his eyes, his labor is not lost.

—*Discourses of Rumi*

In search of the Master, my feet were next guided to the *kumbha mela*, a gathering of worshippers on the banks of the Ganges. In Indian tradition, the *kumbha melas* are sacred gatherings where gurus and disciples assemble for a time and live with many others on the shores of holy rivers for the exclusive purpose of worshipping God. It was being held this time at the confluence of three holy rivers in Allahabad. So that was where I went next in my search for the guru.

Upon arriving on the banks of the Ganges, I found many gurus. As far as I could see, there were campfires surrounded by gurus and their disciples, many of them naked, covered only in ash, most of them sitting in meditation. Somehow all of this was not surprising or shocking to me. I felt like I had seen it all before. It was buried in my subconscious mind, an ancient vision that was now manifesting before my eyes.

Still, I did not feel that I should walk from campfire to campfire, looking for my guru since, in many of these circles of naked ash-covered men, no one spoke English, nor, I thought, had they ever seen a western woman. The best thing, I felt, would be to leave them undisturbed and simply sit in meditation and allow the guru to find me.

After some time, the chief disciple in charge of Maharaj-ji's activities in Allahabad, having heard that I was sitting there, came to meet me. He had been told that I had come in search of Maharaj-ji. He was a very refined and soft-spoken gentleman named Dada (uncle). He took me to his home, which was exceedingly neat and clean. Everything was in perfect order, awaiting the guru's imminent appearance. The people were all patiently waiting, but they had absolutely no idea where he was or when he would turn up.

I stayed with these kind people for several days, but then, since there was no concrete sign that the guru was coming, I felt it would be best to return to the banks of the Ganges, where at least I could meditate with the *saddhus*, those who had renounced their households and consecrated their lives to God.

Shortly after I had returned to the *kumbha mela* and to the meditation, suddenly my yoga teacher from the Berkeley hills, Harish, himself, appeared. Very happy to see me in India, he invited me to come home with him. He lived on a piece of land owned by an herbal doctor named Vedgiy.

Knowing that nothing is an accident, I accepted his invitation. I had been searching for the campfire where I was supposed to sit, and I found it there. I was given a beautiful adobe-like outdoor house in which to live, pray, paint, and write. Next to the small adobe house was a fire pit, where every night into the night I met with Vedgiy and Harish under the starry Indian sky and discussed many interesting things, such as tantric art and understanding, and Ayurvedic medicine, both subtle, mysterious concepts and very practical teachings which are stored within the treasury of India's ancient wisdom.

For those eternal moments, I was happy on this blessed earth, beside the fire, under the Indian sky. It was peaceful and healing to my body, heart, and soul. I was at home in a way that I had never been in contemporary America. It is in moments like this that we find ourselves truly established in the state of being. There is a cumulative treasure of awareness gleaned from these moments of eternity that we take with us as we travel on. Yet, as contented as I was to be in that abode of peace, after a few days I thought, *I must not forget why I came to India. I must not be distracted by this natural beauty and peace but must continue to search for the Master.*

I had learned that Maharaj-ji had temples in many parts of the country. No one knew, at which one he might be at this time, so I would just have to go from one to the next until I found him.

From this point on, I traveled night and day on trains crisscrossing India in search of Maharaj-ji. I did not know that to get a seat on an Indian train you have to get a reservation even for second class. So, for many days, I traveled standing, gazing out at the amazing landscape and hearing the sounds of prayers emanating from the people of the land I was passing by. Standing for so long was a little challenging, but I was always inspired by love and faith in the Master, the certain knowledge that I had to find him.

Eventually I came to realize that by stretching out my sleeping bag on a luggage rack, lighting incense, and meditating, I could establish my identity as a *saddhu*, a worshipper, and have my place and general respect. Thus, in the midst of weeks of searching for the guru as he constantly eluded me, I was able to get a little rest on the luggage rack and meditate, undisturbed. For that prolonged period of train travel, this was the only home I had, and although it was challenging, there was also a great sense of beauty and peace.

As I remember it, there was no glass in the windows of the train. The train was just a metal structure, and we were traveling through the rolling plains, across rivers and by lakes, intimately close to the small boys on the backs of water-buffalo and the monkeys in the palm trees. In every town we passed through, I heard resonating within me the sounds of worship, the names of God, that were being invoked there. I was not a limited independent entity but was an interconnected part of everything. I was never treated by anybody I met along the way like a tourist or stranger. Wherever I traveled, I became part of the landscape.

In this way I continued to journey from one holy place to the next, where someone thought Maharaj-ji had been seen. On reaching each destination after days of travel, I found, again and again, that he was not there. Nobody knew exactly where he was, but maybe I could try the temple in Vrindiban, or the temple in one hill station or another. So, I kept on traveling, following one lead after the next. In each place, when I found that the guru was not there, I sat very still and waited until someone, often a child, would tell me that Maharaj-ji had been seen in one place or another. That was how I knew where to try next.

Such was my quest for the guru. I had no option but to pursue the path, however difficult it might be. I believed in the process, that it was in fact leading somewhere, although there was no external sign of this. As I can clearly see now, so many years later, everything was leading somewhere — leading through countless veils — ultimately to the path that is straight, to the Master, and to the Goal. Along the way, there were many things I needed to see and experience, to understand about the human condition and my own condition as a human being. That was really what the journey was about. It was not leading to the goal I had in mind but to the process of awakening itself.

Then, intriguingly, I received the message to go to Nepal. Harish had told me that I was in some way linked with Bhagavan Das, the American *saddhu* who had introduced Ram Dass to Maharaj-ji. I thought if I could find Bhagavan Das, that could be an important connection that could lead me to the guru. I had heard that he had been seen traveling a lot in Nepal and had been studying with Tibetan lamas. Not being able to find the guru, no matter where I went in India, I was pulled irresistibly to Nepal at this stage of the quest.

In the high mountain region of Nepal, I felt immediately at home. One of my underlying motives for leaving America was to escape from modernity with all its superficiality and consumerism. Here, in Nepal, I found the antidote to modernity. The beauty of the land and of the beautiful architecture of the ancient buildings and shrines was deeply satisfying to me. Everything seemed hand-made, hand-carved, handhewn. There were almost no traces of the modern world to be seen. The mountainous landscape was splendid and the culture full of color.

I wandered around Kathmandu following trails that had been trodden for centuries. I followed one down to a river and sat down to meditate. Sitting on the white stone steps leading to the banks of the river, I looked up and saw all around me huge, ancient, white, and grey stone temples. I wondered about these awesome structures, so old, so mysterious. Under what circumstances had they been built, and what had inspired the builders as they built them? They were no doubt powerful monuments but also somehow ominous.

Seated in the midst of these powerful ancient structures, I meditated. When I opened my eyes, I noticed a fire burning with people around it on the other side of the river. Was it another guru's campfire? No. I noticed, as I looked more closely, that a body was stretched out on a bier and was being consumed by the fire. The people surrounding the burning corpse were wailing intensely and inconsolably. I was astounded.

It was an overwhelming sight, but there was nothing to do about it, no one even to speak with about it. It was a tragic scene that deeply troubled my heart. So, I simply surrendered and then, I had to adapt. I chose to see the vision as a metaphor. I gazed upon the body in flames, imagining that it was my lower self, burning in the fires of purification. I sat there for a few days meditating upon this.

Thirty years later, I returned to this very spot, not searching for my Master, but traveling with him. This time, I had come to India, Nepal, and Pakistan with Sheikh Aly and four other disciples on a mission of peace, healing, and liberation. With greater clarity and knowledge, I saw the burning body not as a symbol of my own purification, but in its own actuality. It was the body of a person, being burnt to ash. From teachings received in later years, I had come to understand in the context of Islamic tradition inappropriateness of this practice, the anguish it imposes on the deceased. And I was grateful to have been led to the purity and simplicity, the sanity and dignity of the Islamic practices of burial.

After a few days in meditation at the burning *ghats* of Pashupatinath, I was inspired to get up and continue to follow the trails of Kathmandu. Next, I arrived at the beautiful Buddhist shrine called Bodhinath.

A distinctive feature of Buddhist shrines is that the base of the shrine is composed of prayer wheels. As the pilgrims make their circumambulation of the shrine, they turn the prayer wheels, thus activating the wheel of the *dharma*, the teaching transmitted by the Buddha. The turning of the prayer wheels is a sign of the turning of hearts in continuous remembrance.

The shrine of Bodhinath is a very large one rising up from the prayer wheelbase to a pyramid peak, which is an eye facing in all directions— the All-Seeing Eye. Stretching out from the peak in all directions are lines of colorful prayer flags, blowing in the wind. All around the circumference of the shrine are shops filled with colorful crafts painted chests, embroidered cloths and pillows, colorful clothing, paintings and prayer beads. In the center of this dance of life, this ever-animated three-dimensional painting, day and night, pilgrims are circumambulating the shrine.

I too walked around the shrine, feeling the well-worn path beneath my feet. As I was making this circular pilgrimage, I noticed another practice of the Tibetan Buddhists. For countless miles, I learned, they make their pilgrimage not walking, but in repeated prostrations. I marveled at this and at the fact that the way these people travel, by prostrating, becomes visible in the light shining through their faces and the warmth and compassion emanating from their hearts. After my sobering experiences at the burning *ghats*, I welcomed the shrine at Bodhinath, as a place of light and joy. This transformation of space and time, I thought, is what the liberation of the Buddha brought.

Born into the restrictive confines of the Hindu caste system, through meditation upon the nature of reality itself, through meditation upon the impermanent nature of illusory existence, and through the compassion for all beings that arose from his enlightened meditation, Siddartha Gautama Buddha transcended the limits of his karmic inheritance and transmitted this path of liberation to others. This atmosphere of liberation, equality, joyfulness, and peace was tangible at the Buddhist shrines to which I now gravitated.

At this point, I had come to understand that the journey I was on was nothing but a reflection of what I was ready to see, what I was ready to comprehend. So it was that I had to see the burning *ghat*, the Nepalese mountainscape, and the journey of perpetual prostration. All of these appeared before me, one by one, as a reflection and a teaching.

Circumambulating the Buddhist shrine, the *stupa*, was like going around the world. As far as we may go, we always return to the place we began, the point of our origin. The beginning and end of the circle are merged. This experience of the circle is one that I have returned to throughout my life's journey.

While circumambulating the stupa, I was reunited with a friendly girl named Vicki and a sweet and gentle young man named, appropriately, Foster Goodwill. I had met Vicki, who eventually became a Buddhist nun, while traveling east on the Orient Express. Foster, who spent a lot of time with me there at the shrine in Bodhinath, read my journal and knew of my love for Rumi. In subsequent travels, he would eventually come across Mary Bauermeister in Findhorn, Scotland and see, lying on a table in her apartment, my very dog-eared copy of the *Discourses of Rumi*. Seeing the book sitting there, he knew immediately that it was the very book I had loved so much and left with Mary when I visited her along the way. How wondrous is the divine plan!

Wondrous too was the simplicity of our life as we lived there in the rooms around the *stupa*. As I remember it, everything was white — the earth and the shrines formed of that earth. Everything was bathed in the bright light of the sun, and we were bathed in the light of meditation and the experience of pure *being*. It was a beautiful time and place, especially because our life was so simple and uncomplicated with no other focus than to *sit* as the Buddha sat.

Eventually I met someone who knew of Bhagavan Das, and I was guided to a little house in the mountains, where a friend of his told me that he had left Nepal some time back to go to the west. He then directed me to the Tibetan Lama, Kalu Rinpoche, with whom Bhagavan Das had been studying. He was living in Sonada, a hill station in the Indian Himalayas. At this time, my visa was running out, and I realized that it was time to return to India and continue my quest there.

I arrived at the monastery of Lama Kalu Rinpoche where small boys gathered in an open-air hall. They were Buddhist monks in training. They were turning around on a kind of turnstile, having the greatest time. Every one of them was laughing, everyone in bliss. I thought to myself, observing this, how joyous monastic life could be!

In another one of the vast halls, rows of monks in burgundy and saffron robes were chanting haunting harmonies. It was the reverberation of timeless being, invoking the endless source of compassion and wisdom. It was this chanting by monks who seemed so profoundly harmonized that prepared me to enter into the presence of Lama Kalu Rinpoche.

Eventually I was greeted by a more official-looking monk who guided me to the Lama. As soon as I entered the small wooden room where he was sitting, I was overwhelmed by his venerable presence. Lama Kalu Rinpoche's face was engraved with the most intricate lines, which revealed the profound journey of his lifetime. He did not speak out loud but whispered. I discovered later that this profoundly gentle, compassionate, and subtle being, who spoke so softly, had established fifty *dharma* centers in his lifetime. He was venerated by all who met him.

To be in the blessed presence of Lama Kalu Rinpoche was an initiation. One could feel immediately the mystic presence, as well as his profound humility, kindness and compassion. At that first meeting, he formally initiated me and gave me the name Karma Palden Dolma, *Mother of Compassionate Wisdom*. I knew that this was the spirit called by different names — Tara or Dolma, Maryam or Mary — which has always been with me, inspiring my soul in the awakening of enlightened womanhood.

With his blessed hand, he put his seal upon the unfolding process. After that, all speech was in Tibetan. There were a few western people in

the room who were fluent in Tibetan. I knew only a few words but was
receiving the powerful transmission of the Lama, the transmission of
compassion and wisdom.

Eventually, I was guided out of the Lama's room and into a great
hall with many *thankas* on the walls. *Thankas* are complex paintings de-
picting the cosmology of the worlds as taught in the teachings of Tibetan Buddhism. In the center of the *mandala*, the circular tableau, is either one of the Buddhas or Padma Sambhava, the father of Tibetan Bud
dhism, seated in meditation. Sometimes the central figure is a female
called Tara or Dolma. Surrounding the meditating figure are numerous
scenes, the many kinds of demons and, also, angelic beings one encounters on the spiritual journey.

These intricate paintings symbolize the central place of meditation in
the life of every being, male or female. The largest image, which is always
in the center, is of the person sitting in meditation, and positioned around
that central image are pictures of that person encountering many other
beings and situations, positive and negative. The impact of these paintings
upon the heart and soul of a spiritual person who sees them is to inspire
him or her to meditate and so gain the peace and wisdom to resolve all of
the circumstances encountered in life with equanimity and wisdom. The
Buddhist teacher, the late Dilgo Khyentse Rinpoche taught:

> *Our realization, our view, should be as high and vast as the sky.
> Once the awakening of pure awareness arises within the vortex
> of emptiness, conflicting emotions can no longer obscure it, but
> instead become its ornaments. The unalterable realization of
> this view, which has no birth, duration or cessation, is accom-
> panied by an enlightened consciousness that observes the move-
> ment of thoughts as a serene old man regards children playing.
> Confused thoughts cannot affect pure awareness any more than
> a sword can pierce the sky.*

Such is the beautiful state of mind transmitted by the teaching of the
Buddha. I saw it manifested symbolically in the *thanka* and experienced
it through the venerable presence of the great Lama.

From the transmission of this understanding, I received real and
lasting guidance. What is transmitted is a liberated state of awareness,

which can be accessed at any moment in the journey, no matter what path one is following. In light of this, I was very grateful to receive this valuable tool.

But I also understood immediately the complexity of the path of Tibetan Buddhism and felt that if I wished to truly study with the Lama, I must enter deep into this study and also learn the Tibetan language as well as the complex system of Tibetan Buddhism. I grasped in an instant that this was not the language I must learn or the path I was to follow. Still, simply to have met such an exalted person as Lama Kalu Rinpoche, to have sat in his rarefied presence and received an initiation from him, invoking within me the *Mother of Compassionate Wisdom*, was a great blessing.

I would have liked to sit forever in that tiny wooden room, filled with fragrance, filled with the blessings of compassion and wisdom. But, as always, I had to continue the journey. Now I was back in the Himalayas of India. Finally, after months of continuous travel, I returned to the hill station of Nainital, where I had begun my search for Maharaj-ji. Though this was his main center of activity, by this point, I did not know where I was at all. I walked into the mountains and collapsed.

For how long I lay there I do not know, but I was finally awakened by a man smiling broadly and wearing around his neck a sign saying, "I am Happy, Happy! How can I help you?" The sign was actually a wide flat bag in which he kept messages and things to give to people. He said that he was a disciple of Maharaj-ji and that Maharaj-ji was presently in his ashram in Nainital nearby, waiting for me. He told me that his name was Pakselieri, but everyone called him "Happy! Happy!" He also told me I was very yellow, from hepatitis, it appeared. Collapsed as I was on the hillside, I had not seen myself for a long time, or even begun to imagine in what condition I might be.

Immediately, he made a fire and cooked vegetables, which he fed to me. This food was incredibly delicious and wonderfully good for me. After so many miles of travel, this meal signified the beginning of my healing and the celebration of my arrival at last in a place where the guru actually was! After we had eaten and rested in that cool and beautiful Himalayan grove, he told me that he was going to take me to Maharaj-ji, but first he had to take me to the hospital. At the hospital, I was examined by a doctor. He pointed out that I had a severe case of hepatitis and that I ought to stay in the hospital for a month. I said, "Okay, but can I please see my guru first? I have been traveling for such a long time, and he is waiting for me." The doctor knew Maharaj-ji, Neem Karoli Baba, and said that he was a great saint. He agreed I could go to see him but said I should go back to the hospital after that.

Pakselieri took me to the ashram. When I entered the presence of Maharaj-ji, Ram Dass was there and also a group of western disciples I had known in California. They had all simply got on a plane and flown to India. They then drove directly to this temple in the hill town of Nainital and immediately found the guru. Hearing their description of their trip, I realized immediately that I was on a different kind of journey.

Although apparently a relatively small old man wrapped in a blanket, Maharaj-ji appeared at the same time to be infinite, unlimited, ancient, and formless. He greeted me like a long-lost sister or friend that he had been waiting for a very long time. He embraced me intensely. I was encompassed, enveloped by that blanket of grace. I felt that in reality I was being embraced by the love of God. Through this embrace, all traces of the hepatitis immediately vanished.

He described to me in detail many of the experiences I had just lived through. It appeared he had seen everything, been with me all along. He mentioned, for example, that one of his monks living at a certain temple had thrown me out of the temple, saying I could not stay there.

He scolded that monk and laughingly said he should not have done that but should have welcomed me with respect. I realized that he had the power to have made everything so much easier for me. He could have guided me to himself, as the others had come, but the difficulties of the journey were necessary for me and were blessings, deep teachings.

Maharaj-ji assigned to me a large beautiful room overlooking a lake, in the hotel where all the disciples were staying. After sleeping in wood piles and standing up on trains, I did not know what had happened, in what luxurious dream world I was now living. The view of the lake from the large picture window was radiantly lovely. But the dream was short-lived.

The next morning, someone knocked at the door and said that I had to move. I was given a tiny room in the basement, with no windows at all, next to the room where chickens were being slaughtered. Back to the wood pile! There I was interred, abandoned for several days. My visa was about to expire. I needed to see Maharaj-ji to get it renewed, but I was not able to see him at all. Having left everything behind to find him, I was now left in this small room to pray, weep, and be purified, to await *darshan* with the guru, spiritual communion with him.

Finally, after several days of such purification, I was told that he was waiting to see me. He told me that my visa could not be renewed, that I must go back, and that I must follow the path of love (*prema*). He told me that my journey was eternally linked with Jesus (Issa). And he said that he, the guru, and I were one. He told Ram Dass to give me the money he had in his wallet, and he blessed my continuing journey.

Maharaj-ji made me feel so much the sense of his oneness with me that I felt I had truly received what I had come for, and, after only a few hours in his presence, I could now continue, truly transformed.

At every stage in the journey with the teacher and the path, I have found that the teacher takes a different form and transmits a different level of teaching or understanding.

From every encounter with the teacher, we receive only that teaching we, in the course of our spiritual evolution, are ready to receive. We look into the mirror shining in the heart of the teacher and see our own face in that state in which we are capable of seeing. So, it was oneness —
"Sub eck! Only One!" as he said it, holding up his forefinger and smiling
— that I saw when I looked into the mirror of Maharaj-ji's heart. Having understood that, I was blessed to continue my journey in search of the Truth that would make me free.

Undaunted, renewed mysteriously in the depth of my being, healed miraculously and instantaneously from severe hepatitis, I returned to the open road. I had left everything, abandoning my life, as I knew it, to search for the guru. I had found him finally, after months of arduous travel, and had spent almost no time but an eternal moment in his presence, in which I learned that the teacher and I were one.

This knowledge alone was the treasure I had traveled hard to discover. This knowledge, which I felt he was transmitting to my heart and soul, filled my cup in such a way that I could return to the rigors of the solitary journey, full and satisfied, not empty and longing, not hopelessly wandering but deeply touched and inspired by knowledge of my connection to the teacher, *the spirit of guidance.*

Still, I did not know where I was going, but I knew by the guru's words and his penetrating transmission that I was following Jesus and traveling on the path of love. That, along with his presence within me, was a sufficient source of strength, energy, and inspiration to enable me to return to the cold, hard road very much warmed and relieved of fatigue. I was now returning to a still unknown life but with this secret knowledge — *oneness with the teacher* — glowing within my soul. Now, it was no longer longing for the form of the guru but the essential truth of the unfolding journey that was directing my steps.

Total truth is necessary. You must live by what you say.

~

Whoever works for God, his work will be done by itself.

~

It's better to see God in everything than to try to figure it out.

~

The best service you can do is to keep your thoughts on God.

~

Keep God in mind every minute.

~

You can plan for a hundred years. But you don't know what will happen the next moment.

~

Everything is impermanent, except the love of God.

~

Love is the strongest medicine.

~

Cleanse the mirror of your heart, and you will see God.

—Neem Karoli Baba

CHAPTER SIX

AN OASIS IN THE DESERT:

MEETING WITH A MYSTICAL SHEIKH

Discovering Islam in the Holy Cities of Tabriz
and Mashad, Iran, 1970

We will show them Our Signs in the horizons and in their own
souls, until it becomes manifest to them that this is the Truth.
—The Holy Qur'an 41:53

I had burned all my bridges to go to India in search of the Master, but now I was coming back. This was my first round, my first journey around the globe. By divine decree, the circumambulation of the planet would occur again and again in my life, every time yielding greater compassion for all lives and greater understanding and experience of the Way. This kind of travel — unlike any kind of tourism, vacation, or safari adventure— is called traveling *fisabilillah*, traveling for the sake of God, traveling in the way of God.

I have mentioned that I never followed a map. By this I mean that I did not plan a trip, I did not determine the course of my journey. In this journal, I have tried to recount the events that took place as accurately as I can remember them because each one had significance that was determined by the Planner of all. Just as I was led to India and to Maharaj-ji, so was I led back. Neither was Maharaj-ji nor India the real goal of my journey, and that is why, having endured so much to get there, it was so easy to leave. I had learned the lessons that I could learn at that stage, and now it was necessary to take the next step on the path of God.

We can see the signs of God in ourselves and in the horizons, in everything that occurs in our journey, both within and without. Often, I did not know in what town I was or how I had arrived at that place, but what I did know — what I did see — were the signs of my Lord continuously manifesting. And, I came to see more and more clearly that what was shining like the sun, through all the clouds, was the Truth, the Light of the One Compassionate Source of all.

Everything that happened to me on the journey was a teaching leading me through the veils, my own thought forms, toward the magnet that is the Truth.

Returning from India, I was let off the bus in another dusty town. I noticed people gathering, and, thinking that it was a religious assembly of some sort, I gravitated toward the crowd, only to realize that there was a conflict being fought between the people in the town.

Just as I was drawn into the crowd, some police officers pulled me out, rushed me up a staircase to a hotel serving as a shelter and quickly locked the door. Once upstairs, I was surrounded by people, most of whom were weeping. I had a bag of dried fruit and nuts, which I shared with them, and a zither on my back, which I took off and played, singing *La ilaha ill'Allah*, the meaning of which I did not really know. I simply heard it resonating within me.

The people appeared to be calmed by this strange phenomenon and said they felt an angel had come. I learned that the conflict in this little town was between Jews and Muslims. It had started when a Jewish man had spoken disparaging remarks about the Prophet Muhammad (saw).

Later that evening, someone gave me a small book about the Prophet (saw) which explained that he had come as the last of all the Prophets and Messengers (as) sent by God to bring unity, amongst all believers, and peace. I was trying to understand how these two pieces of information could fit together when I fell asleep, and I was still trying to understand the situation the next morning. If the Prophet Muhammad (saw) had come to bring unity and peace amongst the believers, why was this conflict going on? This question weighed upon me heavily.

I had no idea why, but I had an incomprehensible yearning to go to the Turkish bath. This turned out not to be a casual stroll through town but a guided evasion of periodic explosions on the roadside. I noticed this, but proceeded without fear, feeling with subtle certainty that I was being guided and protected.

Finally, I arrived at the baths, went in and bathed. When I came out, I saw a man who was encircled by children he was teaching. He called me over to join them. I do not believe I said anything to him at all. He said to me in excellent English, "What you were thinking is true. The Prophet (saw) did come to bring unity and peace to the believers."

The teacher continued to tell me many other things about the Prophet (saw). I do not remember the exact words he said but the way in which he spoke to me, the way in which he knew what I was thinking, and the way in which I was guided to the bath in that area to receive this information made me feel that this transmission came from God, Who directed that event. Because the teaching came to me in that way, I believed that what the man said was true.

I went back to the hotel and prepared to leave and carry on my journey. There were two young men from England that I had met in the hotel who were leaving on the same bus as I was. The prospect of actually traveling with others with whom I could speak, after being so long on the road alone, was overwhelming. I felt very much relieved, like someone who has been in the desert for a long time and comes at last to an oasis. I soon discovered, however, that this, too, was a mirage.

After we had traveled a short way and I had just begun to get used to interacting with these fellow travelers, the bus was stopped, and some officials got on and asked to see everyone's immunization cards. When they looked at my card, they said I was missing a cholera booster and that I must get right off.

I was taken to a hospital room and placed on a bed, where I wept. I said, *O God, do You want me never to speak with anyone again? Must I always be alone?* I knew that the love of God was so great a gift that I would have to give up anything for it, but the limits of my humanity were being tested.

It was not as if I knew those people and had become attached to them personally. It was simply the idea of traveling with anyone, conversing with anyone! That's what I had to give up, not knowing when I might ever have a companion again. So, I sat on the hospital bed and wept. As I was weeping, I realized that I was in the town of Tabriz, Iran.

I was in the town of Shams-i-Tabriz! I thought how much Rumi (ra) would have wept for joy to be here. Then, I began to think of Shams (ra) and Rumi (ra), to think of their love, and to weep from love. This love lasted long after Rumi's Master, Shams (ra), had disappeared and also long after Rumi (ra) himself departed from this world. Until today, it touches and inspires the hearts of the lovers of God everywhere. As a traveler on the path of love, seeking the Master who would so transform my heart, I felt great comfort and joy when I realized where I was, in the town of Shams-i-Tabrizi!

> *O lovers, lovers it is time to set out from the world.*
> *I hear a drum in my soul's ear coming*
> *from the depths of the stars.*
> *Our camel driver is at work.*
> *The caravan is being readied.*
> *He asks that we forgive him*
> *for the disturbance he has caused us.*
> *He asks why we travelers are asleep.*

Everywhere there is the murmur of the stars,
like candles thrust at us from behind blue veils,
and as if to make the invisible plain,
a wondrous people have come forth.

Mevlana Rumi,
The Divan of Shams of Tabriz

As I was crying with happiness, contemplating the mystery of my destiny, which had carried me here and that spiritual love which has continued to inspire seekers for so many generations, a hospital attendant came to me, and asked me why I was crying. I spoke of the love of Shams (ra) and Rumi (ra). He told me that he was a Sufi and would send me to the Sufis. This was the reason, he said, I had been detained there.

As soon as I had received the booster, the hospital attendant brought an old man to my bed. He said, "This man will take you to the Sufis. Go with him." So, I got on the bus with the old man, who did not speak English but who did know where the Sufis were. We traveled some distance and arrived in the holy city of Mashad. We came to the gate of a walled garden and knocked. The door opened and we were very warmly received.

Immediately, a bed was set up for me in the middle of this walled garden. When they learned that I was a vegetarian, they brought a beautiful meal of fruits, nuts, and vegetables. I was introduced to the people of the house, a very large family with many children, all of whom were disciples of the Sufi Sheikh. Everyone was very excited because the Sheikh was expected at any time.

Whoever we were waiting for, it was an extraordinary night for me. I rested on the bed, in a garden under the canopy of the illuminated sky. This was the second time, after the desert of Afghanistan, that I witnessed salat, the ritual of Islamic prayers, being performed. It seemed to me that this large family did not sleep. They alternately played and prayed throughout the night. Everyone in the family seemed to be getting along very well. They laughed and talked, ate and played together all night, except for the periods when they washed and stood together and bowed down together under the light of the starry sky.

It was a very beautiful sight in the moonlit night. The water they washed in was sparkling, like their laughter and their joy. The beauty of their life together, which was clearly divinely inspired, was visible to me on that illuminated night as I lay on the bed in the enclosed garden and watched this family repeatedly line up together to celebrate the praises of their Lord.

It was because Islam was introduced to me in real visions like this that I love and do not fear it. So, for me, the best word to describe the process of truly accepting Islam is always *"embrace."*

The next day, the family told me I was being moved to another home, that of a wealthy doctor who was also a disciple of the Sheikh. They were deferring to him because they were poor and he was rich, so they felt he could take care of me in a better fashion.

I was very sorry to leave that illuminated courtyard. But, in truth, it is a place where my heart has always remained, and, now, I have shared it with you.

When I arrived at the doctor's more opulent home, I found that his family and their friends were also engaged in waiting for the Sheikh. It appeared that nothing else was really going on. Various people came and went. We all sat in a room, we recited various *dhikrs* (zikrs) or devotional songs and prayers, occasionally ate, and more than anything else, were actively awaiting the Sheikh. He was expected at any time, but no one knew when, and no one wanted to miss that moment, so everyone had joined together in this prolonged wait.

Frequently, we went to the mosque — a very well-known and beautiful one. I do not remember actually going in, but rather standing in a certain place where I became the recipient of the flood of light that came flowing out of the mosque when prayers were over. I enjoyed standing in that place and watching as the venerable, ancient faces emerged radiantly beautiful from the mosque and I felt myself washed over by the light of their being as they emerged from prayers.

As I write about this experience, I do not know what I was witnessing, whether it was a heavenly or earthly congregation — probably both. But it seems to me that it was composed of very luminous eastern men, the heirs of ancient truths which, at that precise moment, they were somehow transmitting to a young American woman — me. I know that this experience, of beholding the light in the faces of the worshippers, was like the passage through a doorway in my discovery of Islam.

The first pillar of Islam is witnessing or *shahadah*. We bear witness that there is no reality other than the Reality that is God, and we bear witness that Muhammad is the Messenger of God. At that moment, being the recipient of the grace that was streaming out of that mosque, I began to witness these mysteries.

I want to share with the reader, here, how different it is to witness divine mysteries than it is to watch the news. It was only because I was brought into the state of witnessing and experiencing these subtle truths that I came to know about true Islam. That I had been guided to stand on the hillside facing the mosque in the holy city of Mashad, as people were pouring out of the mosque after prayers, was simply a step in the divine plan to make me see.

To begin with, I saw that the mosque was not at all a frightening, alien building where people were congregating who wanted to hurt me or to hurt others. I could see that it was an extraordinarily beautiful building, marvelously designed and crafted. I wondered who had designed it and what had inspired this beautiful construction.

Even more beautiful were the faces of the people as they emerged from their prayers. I saw the light of God shining through them. So, this is the way in which, step by step, I came to see the beauty of Islam and to learn more and more deeply about it in a way that is never shown on the news. However, I still had to truly enter the mosque to find out what mysteries were taking place within it.

We returned from the beautiful mosque to the doctor's house, and there we continued to wait for the Sheikh. After several days of waiting in the living room for the Sheikh, there was consensus among all those gathered that, since the Sheikh did not appear to be coming at exactly that time, I should be sent to a place in the middle of the desert with another old man in hopes that perhaps we might encounter the Sheikh there. Really having no doubt about the process and no fear, trusting in the unfolding of events, I got into a car with that old man I did not know and drove off into the desert.

As soon as he began to drive, the man began to weep. He was in a state of rapture, of overwhelming love for his Sheikh, and for his Lord, as he drove toward an inevitable meeting. He told me how much he wanted me to meet his Sheikh, who he called his Christ, and how much he felt I would love him. We drove on and on until we arrived at last at our destination, a tea shop with no walls in the middle of the desert. It was full of people. Everyone there was waiting for the Sheikh, so we joined them. We had many cups of tea and sat there for a long time, until finally the old man got up and told me it appeared that the Sheikh was not yet coming here. Instead, we were going to search for him in the place where he lived. Back into the desert again we went!

We followed a course that I would never be able to retrace. At last, somewhere in the middle of the desert, we came upon a large sanctuary enclosed by tile walls. Inside the walls were beautiful mosques surrounded by gardens through which a river flowed. I absolutely could not have believed that such a place existed in the middle of a vast expanse of desert if I had not been taken there.

I was ushered into a room with women. The men were outside in the garden, listening to the Sheikh. When the Sheikh came into the room where I was, all I saw of him was his feet. It seemed that all the women were touching his feet and weeping with joy. Then he was gone. We all went outside and sat on a terrace overlooking the gardens. They wanted to feed me, as all Sufis do, and brought a tray of beautiful food.

Dusk began to fall in this mystical garden. I was told that the Sheikh would like to see me in his home at three o'clock in the morning and I could spend the evening praying in the mosque. I took a walk through the beautiful grounds that led to the mosque. I looked up into the night sky and saw a perfect crescent moon with a star inside, a symbol of Islam that has many meanings.

Entering one prayer area that was filled with men, I walked through a corridor on the side of the mosque to get to the area where the women were gathered. As I passed through the corridor, I was amazed by the sound resonating through that sacred space, the sound of humanity singing beautiful songs to God.

I arrived in the place where the women were gathered. It appeared that there was a vast illuminated pearl tablet with calligraphy on it in the center, which was surrounded by women all dressed in black. I was dressed in white. I fell, prostrate upon entering; such was the power of God in that space. Eventually someone called my name and I rose up. The rest of the night was filled with remembrance of God and peace and grace until three in the morning, when I was led through the twisting lanes of the small town to the Sheikh's house. It was a very small house and simple, not at all fancy or pretentious.

I was carrying with me a very big book of paintings I had made of dreams and experiences I had on the journey. In the center of the book, which was dedicated to images found in all religions and paths, was a painting of a dream of a person of light I thought to be a symbol of the veiled Prophet. In the dream, angels were ascending and descending, a holy scripture was held in suspended hands, and the *kalimah*, "*La ilaha ill'Allah* (There is no deity but God)," was transmitted.

With his inner vision, the Sheikh knew about this page in the book and was very interested in it. He wanted to see it. He asked me many questions about my journey. I told him that my heart remained in India with Neem Karoli Baba, Maharaji-ji, and the teaching of oneness he transmitted.

He said to me that as far as I might travel all around the world again and again, I would not escape the *kalimah* but would come back to it. Though I was not ready to accept Islam there and then, I never forgot his words and came to realize more and more throughout my journey how true they were.

He told me that when I was ready, he would always be ready to receive me and to teach me the Sufi path but would want to teach me first, for forty days, about Islam. I would remember that offer many times in the future, but I had no idea either who he was or where this had all taken place.

CHAPTER SEVEN

SAVED BY GRACE

Iran, Turkey and Bulgaria, 1971

I had learned all that I could at that moment and had to move on. I had caught a glimpse of the beauty of Islam, but it was not yet time for me to fully embrace it. As Maharaj-ji had indicated, I had to find Jesus first. I was being carried along. Where exactly I was going or what lessons I must learn I did not know.

I took trains and buses until I reached Tehran, but by then, the money, which had been given to me from Maharaj-ji out of Ram Dass's wallet had almost run out. So, I went to a trucking company to see if I could find a trustworthy truck driver with whom to travel west. I knew of no other way to get back.

After some hours had passed, a representative from the trucking company told me that they had finally found someone they felt I could trust. They introduced me to a truck driver, a young man who told me that we would be traveling with his sister and her baby, that we would eat dinner and stay overnight in a hotel and then leave all together early in the morning. I accepted this proposed plan as that which was being provided.

A room was given to me, and dinner was served. I did not catch even a glimpse of the sister or her baby and wondered where they might be. As we were finishing the meal, I noticed that the trucker seemed to be looking at me in an inappropriate way. Throughout my journey, I had been absolutely celibate. My unrelenting certainty of my position was a great protection in this situation.

I looked at that man with such an intensely determined gaze that he instantly became terrified, got up and ran out of the room. I never saw him again. I have wished, in the years that followed, to master that gaze and address it to Satan, the dark seducer, in all the forms he has assumed so that he would run out of the room as fast as that trucker did.

The next morning, I went back to the trucking agency to try again, since that appeared to be my only option. We waited for a while for a reliable candidate. I studied the truckers who came in until I saw one who seemed clear and responsible. We talked about Islam. He said that he was a faithful Muslim, a believer, and he looked like it to me.

So, invoking the protection of God, the Merciful, the Compassionate, I climbed into the cab with him, and we set out. Long stretches in the desert and plains were punctuated by stops for refueling. We seemed to be riding parallel with another truck, which we encountered at every truck stop. Riding in that truck was a French hitchhiker. He and I spoke quite a lot and were looking out for each other in this potentially dangerous situation.

Dangerous it was when the trucks stopped at a café in the desert in the middle of the night. The energy was such that I felt I should bring my zither into the café and sing to God. This was an absolutely sincere call on my part, but also a reminder to these men that they were Muslim and should act like it.

I was sitting next to the hitchhiker from France. We noticed that strange things were happening in the café. The driver of the truck I was riding in was standing against the back wall of the café and was approached by another man with money in his hand. They were furtively glancing at me. My driver seemed to refuse several times. Then, he seemed about to accept the money.

Very slowly and steadily, the Frenchman and I got up and walked out the café. He led me to where my things were, I picked them up, as though I was clearly going somewhere, but truly we were in the middle of *nowhere*. A group of men came out of the café and were approaching us.

Suddenly, a Volkswagen van appeared out of nowhere. It was filled with a group of Europeans with whom the Frenchman had traveled in the past. He waved them down, and they stopped. He beseeched them, not to take him, but to take me, explaining quickly what seemed to be happening. They agreed.

I jumped into the van, pulling my things with me. They shut the door, and we zoomed off into the desert with a throng of men running after us. I managed to get all of my belongings into the van except a carved metal staff I was carrying which I had been told was to ward off evil. That was all that they could get from me. The van sped off into the night, crossed the border, and dropped me off in Bulgaria.

I certainly could not recommend this mode of travel to anyone. I would not encourage anyone — and certainly no young woman — to test fate like this. It was, however, important for me to pass through this test. I still remember, vividly, the feelings I experienced on that night and the way in which the Hand of God whisked me away from certain doom.

With so many clear signs, which have manifested directly in front of me, I do wonder why I continue, from time to time, to worry and fear, instead of being a constant witness to the Mercy, the Compassion, the living Presence, the Omnipresent Power of the One Who perfectly protects those who truly love Him, those who journey for His sake.

> *The Lord is my light and my salvation; whom shall I fear? The Lord is the strength of my life; of whom shall I be afraid?*
> —Psalm 27:1

CHAPTER EIGHT

WHO AM I?

IN THE CITY FLOWING WITH LIGHT

Amsterdam, 1971

Observe the wonders as they occur around you. Don't claim
them. Feel the artistry moving through and be silent.
—Mevlana Jelaluddin Rumi,
The Essential Rumi

Grateful to be alive and unscathed by this trial, I traveled from Bulgaria back to Cologne, Germany, from where I had originally set forth on the Orient Express. I called Karlheinz and Mary with whom I had stayed en route, but they did not answer their phone. So, the only place I was able to stay that night was on a steep hill. I had to fit my body between rocks into a position that resembled a cross and sleep in a semi-vertical posture. Faced with this particular circumstance, I found that this, too, was possible. From nights like this, I learned, for the rest of my life, to appreciate the wondrous provision of having a bed to sleep in.

The next morning, I crossed the border from Germany to Holland. Even the sky in Germany at that time seemed dark and foreboding, while the sky directly on the other side of the border was sunny and bright. I thought about how many Jews and other refugees had begun to taste the sweetness of refuge and release from their immense ordeal when they arrived in this benign land.

I, too, after the duress and fatigue of a long journey with no resting place, returned to Amsterdam with great happiness and found a place flowing with light and goodwill, such that simply setting foot on the land was healing. I went back to the home of a Dutch dancer with whom I had stayed during my travels.

It was very beautiful there in their quaint farmhouse on the emerald bank of the canal. The dancer had a lot of friends who visited, all of whom spoke Dutch, which I did not speak at all. After several evenings of listening to conversations in which I could neither receive nor give anything, I understood that there was no reason for me to stay there, so I packed my bags, expressed my deep gratitude to my hosts, walked down a path to the train station, and got on a train, having no idea at all where I was going.

I stayed on the train until the end of the line and then got off. As I was getting off the train, I heard someone calling my name. It was a young man named Jeffrey, who I had known in Berkeley.

He said he was waiting for me to get off before greeting me. There was someone he was sure that I should meet. I was pretty sure of this too, since I was waiting for a sign and had no other idea what I was supposed to do next.

Jeffrey took me to the apartment of a Dutch painter named Albert Jan, who, Jeffrey said, was a Sufi. When we entered the room, the painter, who had been sitting on the edge of a large bed, leapt up and ran over to embrace me. He greeted me like someone whom he had known forever and had missed for a long time.

He was very tall, very vulnerable and open, like a very large child. He spoke to me as if he had been in isolation for a long time and, had finally found someone to talk to. He spoke mostly about Sufism and his experiences in Jerusalem, but also about his experiences with the teachings of the great Indian Master, Sri Ramana Maharshi. Most of what he said was closely related to my journey and to what would happen to me in the future. I did not know this at the time, having no idea what the future would bring.

Now, in looking back at the map of my life's journey, I see where I was destined to go and receive the teachings waiting for me there. Those were the places of power that I had to visit, and all of this had been decreed. The Dutch painter who loved Sufism was simply one of the many kind beings I was destined to meet, through whom, stage by stage, I became aware of the path I was to follow.

He became for me an agent of divine mercy. He told me that he had created a prayer room in the attic, where he had no time to go, and that he would be very happy and honored if I stayed there and prayed there as long as I liked. That was a clear sign of where I was supposed to stay next, so I accepted with deep gratitude.

After so many miles of being on the road — often sleeping on the road itself, in wood piles and on the luggage racks of trains — what an experience it was to be in a room in which I could begin to contemplate what had unfolded in the months of continuous travel! Only in not having any place at all and no one to speak with throughout the journey, did I begin to sense the profound inherent blessing in everything.

During this part of my life — in which I did no business, had no idea of my identity or where I was going, and pursued no goal but the search for truth — I experienced a fundamental state of existence in which I had nothing and was utterly dependent upon the grace and guidance of God.

In later years, I was engaged in building and sustaining many things: a business, a family, houses, communities — but I never forget, in the core of my being, the experience I had during those years of travel, the experience of being invisible, indigent, and dependent for everything upon the grace of God. I had nothing to hold onto. It was not a vacation after which I would return to a "known" life. The life I knew I had abandoned. I had no plans at all. Every new step of the journey was revealed by the grace of God.

I believe that it was because of the purity, the poverty and absolute dependence of my state, the fact that "I" determined nothing, and I knew nothing about where I was going, that I was open to being clearly guided. As much guidance as has been given to me in later years, by the grace of God, the core experience of being, as it is described in Sufism, "a corpse in the hand of the washer," was revealed during this time and in this way. Many of the teachings I learned later from the teachers whom I was blessed to meet and study with were first transmitted during this essential journey when I was guided by nothing but the grace and love of God. Now, as I walked down the streets and along the canals of Amsterdam, the light of guidance was taking the form of the face of the illuminated sage, Sri Ramana Maharshi, and the guidance that he was transmitting took the profoundly simple form of a question, "Who am I?" This question, and the self-inquiry that is generated by it, was posed to us by the great sage, but truly arises from the depth of the mystery of our being. It is one of those phrases like *"Seek, and the truth shall make you free"* that is always relevant and must always be applied to the endless process of self-discovery and the search for truth.

While asking myself this question repeatedly, I found that all of the roles I had played in my life were not really who I was. So, the question remained, perpetually probing, evoking the mystery of existence, itself.

> *What is the means for constantly holding on to the thought 'Who am I?'. When other thoughts arise, one should not pursue them, but should inquire: 'To whom do they arise?' It does not matter how many thoughts arise. As each thought arises, one should inquire with diligence, "To whom has this thought aris-*

en?" The answer that would emerge would be 'To me.' There-
upon if one inquires 'Who am I?' the mind will go back to its
Source; and the thought that arose will become quiescent. With
repeated practice in this manner, the mind will develop the skill
to stay in its Source.

Sri Ramana Maharshi,
Ramana Maharshi, His Life

Engaged in this process of self-enquiry, seeking the source of my thoughts
and the knowledge of who was thinking them, I almost glided down the
streets of Amsterdam, not really focusing on the outer sights but on the
inner mirror of the face of the luminous sage, dwelling as I was, in the
process of self-inquiry he had proposed.

Although this advice was given to me by someone I had never met,
it was invaluable to me. Not defined within the context of any specific religion, as I saw it, it was a powerful psychological and spiritual tool, one
that helps the seeker to dispel the illusion of egotism, himself or herself.

It was a gift I was given, along with the gift of refuge, in the home
of the Dutch painter. Yet, even as we become aware that our thoughts
and perceptions are unreal in relation to the eternal reality of God, still
the thoughts and perceptions are there, like words on the page we are
reading.

From the time that we begin to be aware that there is a transcendent Reality, the reality of the true Self, we must observe this in contrast
to the illusory world of the ego. From this point on, we may begin to
perceive the counterpoint, the inner light of truth, the eternal light of
the inner sage, in contrast to the darkness of sorrows accumulating in
the illusory world.

I discovered after some time, that while I was enjoying the sweetness of inner reflection in the home of the Dutch painter, within the
home there were some deep problems. My gracious host, even while extending such kindness to me, was struggling with the dissolution of his
marriage, which was causing confusion, pain, and conflict in his family
and home. I tried to see if there was any way I could help but found there
was none, other than to pray for the peace of all.

Feeling that I must continue on the journey, not knowing where to
go next, I had one of a series of quest dreams that I had throughout the

journey. In each of the dreams, I began in a house with many rooms, often filled with light and warmth and a lot of people congregating, sometimes around a fireside, and I was told by a voice that I had to leave all this, leave world as I knew it, and make the journey alone.

The next part of the dream was a long, solitary trip, often through a desert or on a narrow mountain path. This solitary journey would lead to the next station of spiritual understanding or experience I was to reach. In the "quest" dream that I had in Amsterdam, I was in the very apartment where I was living with the family of the painter. They were struggling with the same problems I had sensed in waking life.

Again, I felt helpless to improve their situation. I was told by the voice to leave the world and return to my solitary journey, and I began to walk through the night. I walked and walked and came at last to a beautiful forest of large, bluish and grey-green fir trees against a luminous, pre-dawn, blue-grey sky. The voice said, "Here is He for whom you seek." I woke up from the dream but did not remember it until several days later when I arrived in that forest.

The next day, I heard the voices of monks singing a very beautiful eastern liturgy on a tape playing in an adjoining room. I was moved by this and inquired where the tape came from. Learning that it had been recorded in a certain monastery in Chevetogne, Belgium, I immediately went upstairs and painted a scroll on parchment paper to send to the place where this tape had been produced. I framed the letter with paintings of the Himalayas and a seeker traveling through them. I said that I was a traveler searching for truth. I had heard the sound of the monks singing and felt magnetically drawn by it — sensing that the journey was leading my soul to the monastery.

I sent this little scroll to the monastery in Belgium, and within a few days I received a response. One of the monks, Father Theodor, who was the doorkeeper of the monastery, told me that in a few days they would be celebrating the festival of the baptism of Christ and I was warmly invited to attend. The monastery was a famous gathering place of Christians of many denominations. It was so ecumenical that even a formless wanderer, a seeker of truth, a Jewish girl returning from the Himalayas, was definitely welcome, invited without hesitation.

As soon as I received the invitation, I accepted it and set out to locate the place from which that beautiful sound had emanated. I took a train from Amsterdam to Brussels, a bus to Namur and another bus to Ciney, where Chevetogne was located. Arriving late at night in the middle of a snowstorm, I got off the bus and could see nothing but snow, thick snow on the ground, snow flying in the sky. It was, as St. John of the Cross tells us, "*On a dark night, kindled in love, with yearnings, O happy chance! In the happy night, in secret, when none saw me, nor I beheld aught, without light or guide, save that which burned in my heart.*" In the darkness I could see nothing, nor could I be seen, but I was not afraid, because the light of faith and yearning was burning in my heart. Then, gradually, very faintly in the distance, I perceived a tiny light, penetrating the swirling snow flurries of the blizzard. Since that was the only sign I had, I followed it, up a hill, through the snowstorm to a small house.

There I found an old woman who indicated the direction of the house where the sisters lived, where I was to stay. It was quite a trek through the blizzard.

Finally arriving at the door, I was very warmly and sweetly welcomed by a nun, Sister Raphaelle, who was wearing a blue denim habit that matched her large blue eyes. I knew I had already seen her before, but in what world or dimension of consciousness, I did not know.

She took me on a tour of the sisters' house. It was equally familiar. Everything, it seemed, was hand-hewn and aglow with light. The interior of the house was made of golden wood. It was illuminated, by candles dipped by the nuns and decorated by icons painted by the nuns. I would be fed bread baked by the nuns and vegetables grown by them.

I was taken to a room where I was to stay that was very comfortable and aglow with the same light and warmth, not a cold and austere cell that we may imagine to be essential to monastic life. After a few hours' sleep, I was awakened and sent out on a path again alone, this time the one leading to the churches where liturgies were being sung. It was about four in the morning. There were two large, domed buildings, one where the Eastern rite was being performed and one where the Western rite was being performed. I was attracted to the Eastern rite in the Byzantine Chapel.

As I entered the vast, glowing church from the dark path, I was inundated with light. I had attended several churches in my childhood searching for a light I intuitively felt was somewhere in the church but found, instead, an atmosphere of darkness. Now, here it was, a church filled with light! There were candles burning everywhere and beautiful visionary icons on every surface of the arched cathedral, but the truly luminous dimension of the experience was shining within me.

I realized immediately upon entering that resplendent cathedral that the "man of light" I had seen so long within me was, it seemed, directly connected with Jesus (as) and the Master that he was serving. This is obvious to everyone who knows it, but until that moment, I had not grasped it. So, that moment — the entrance into that place of light to which I had been invited to celebrate the baptism of Christ — was, for me, an immersion in an ocean of light and understanding. This moment was revelatory for me in the sense that it was the first moment in my life when the inner light of my being was clearly aligned with the prophetic manifestation.

When the liturgy was completed and I left the church, a cool and radiant dawn lit up the forest through which I walked from the Byzantine monastery to the warm, glowing house of the Sisters of Bethlehem, where I was staying. I realized in the early morning light that this was the forest I had seen in my dream in which I heard the voice saying, *"Here is He for whom you seek."*

CHAPTER NINE

LIFE IN THE MONASTERIES

Chevetogne, Belgium and the French Alps,
1972

Lay not up for yourselves treasures upon earth, where moth and dust doth corrupt, and where thieves break through and steal. But lay up for yourselves treasures in heaven, where neither moth nor dust doth corrupt, and where thieves do not break through and steal. For where your treasure is, there will your heart be also.

—Matthew 6:19-21

Every morning before dawn, I would walk through the forest that I had seen in my dream. At one end of the winding path was the house where the sisters lived, and I with them, and on the other side of the forest were two large churches, one where the Western rites were being observed and one where the Eastern rites were being observed, several times a day. The church where the Eastern or Byzantine rites were being practiced was a huge, domed cathedral, the inside of which was covered with paintings of the saints and mysteries. In my generally altered state, I saw everything happening three-dimensionally in trans-historic time. That image which most attracted my heart and soul was the rendering of Jesus, arms outstretched, in the station of ascension.

I was strongly drawn to the Byzantine church and attended all the services held there. In the vast cool cathedral, full of mysteries, surrounding the central area where the priests performed their duties, there was a semi-circle of ornately carved wooden niches made of rich, dark wood. These were the niches where the faithful were invited to stand and celebrate the liturgy. Other than the three monks, I was often the only person present to respond to the divine invitation, and I felt perfectly at home, blessed and protected in that niche to which I returned day after day, many times a day.

Father Theodor looked like Saint Nicholas in a Russian Orthodox robe and was always giving gifts of kindness and love. It was he who had received my letter and welcomed me to come immediately. To this day, I am still struck by the quality of unconditional openness with which he received me. He was the manifestation of non-judgmental, universal acceptance. In addition to these meetings in the church, I met with him for one or two hours every day to discuss dreams, understandings and experiences which were arising within me in this holy place, all of which he seemed to welcome with interest.

I also met every day with Father Gabriel, who was another of the monks at the services. He was a towering figure with long red hair and beard and green light-filled eyes. In his long black robes and tall hat, with such grace, dignity, and mysticism, he was truly a man of my dreams. He was a deeply internal person radiating mystic presence. I sensed that he was directly linked with the Angel Gabriel, as with Jesus and Mary.

So, this is where Maharaj-ji was sending me, to this beautiful well-spring of Christian mystical life!

Every day, I traveled back and forth between the fathers, the sisters, and the liturgies in the Eastern Church. Then, one day, I began hearing that a very special woman was coming to the monastery. She was the Mother Superior in charge of the sisters who were taking care of the house and the community where I had been given refuge. She had given birth to a large order of sisters called the *Sisters of Bethlehem*.

I had already noted the special quality of the women I was living with. They seemed very happy, very open, fulfilled, grounded, creative, and at peace, not rigid or repressed, as stereotypes of nuns might suggest. Now, they were all awaiting the coming of Sister Marie, their spiritual Guide.

Since the monastery in Chevetogne was a well-known center of ecumenical assembly, there were always many people visiting. I looked at the women as they appeared, walking across the emerald grounds, wondering which one was the much-awaited Sister Marie. I saw various women with impressive-looking formal habits, but each time I thought, "No, that could not be Sister Marie!"

In the house of the sisters, which was called *Bethlehem*, the tables were placed in a circle for meals. We ate in silence, but beautiful music was played. I felt that the Holy Spirit was singing. One night, as the meal was unfolding, I noticed a striking woman. She was very tall with many deep lines engraved upon her face. She was dressed in the light blue denim habit of the order. Her habit, like her face, was well worn.

More striking than her appearance was the way she was standing over her food in prayer. It was a strange thing to behold the interiority of another person's prayer. I was powerfully drawn to her as she stood for a long time in silence before sitting down to eat. She was emanating a sense of deep worship, service, and submission to God. I felt that she was the foundation of this community upon which it was resting, not the "Mother Superior." She did not have the dress, the demeanor, or the attitude of a Mother Superior, but the demeanor of a servant of God. In her humility there was immense strength. I wondered who she was.

I finished my meal. As I was taking my plate to be washed, I felt a strong hand on my shoulder, and I was impelled into a small room. The door was closed. It was she who had led me there and sat down facing me, her face about two inches from mine. She said, "Jesus wants us to set the whole world on fire with the love of God! Mary is the Master of love! And the Father is searching for lovers! What does God, who is the Plenitude of everything, search for? Only those who truly love and worship Him."

She then told me the story of her life and mission. In her youth, she was living in a convent where many blessings descended upon her. She was filled with the love of God and deeply inspired. One day, she looked out of the window of her room in the convent and saw a barber on the street below. She wondered how she, enclosed in the convent, could be the recipient of so much grace, while the man below in the street might not have access to this grace. This perception catalyzed her mission.

She left the convent and went into the world. In various locations, she gathered people and asked them if they would give a year of their lives for the love of God. In each place, she formed a community composed of people consecrated to the church and also lay people, men, women and children living and working together. In this way, she built centers all around France and Belgium, all of which she called *Bethlehem*.

These communities of people dedicated to working together for the sake of God had become a great success. I saw how beautifully the experiment was working in Chevetogne. But the price she had paid for bringing forth these communities was that, in constantly traveling from place to place and working constantly with people everywhere, she had, to some extent, sacrificed the depth of her contemplative life.

When she saw me, she told me, she remembered the life of her soul. She told me that Jesus and Mary spoke to her about me. She was guided to give me refuge and also the spiritual freedom, as she said, to serve God and God alone. As she had been instructed, she must extend to me refuge and protection in all of her communities, but, unlike the other members of her communities, she wanted me to focus not on daily chores and interactions but solely on the path of contemplation, to learn to listen to and obey the voice of the Divine.

She took me with her to her community in the French Alps in a village called Les Voirons. The community assembled in the monastery was composed, like her other communities, of a great assortment of people. I was simply another one of the multi-colored threads in the beautiful tapestry she was weaving. Every day, we gathered in a circle to pray for everyone. Each person was invited to specify any individual or group of people to add to our collective prayer. Sister Marie was very touched by the fact that I was of Jewish origin, and every day at prayer time, she made reference to this fact, and, inspired by my presence and the fact that God had sent me to join their circle, she prayed for all the children of Israel.

That she prayed for me in this context and for all the children of Israel is significant in the context of this story, and it reminds me that I, as a journeyer through deserts in search of Divine Guidance, must not forget the original journey of my ancestors through the desert in response to the Divine Command. All the revelations that came later completed the revelations that came earlier. And this ongoing divine reality, remembrance of the people, throughout the ages, who have traveled on the journey guided by God, is what I felt Sister Marie was honoring when she brought the children of Israel into the circle of prayer.

Now, the feast of Easter was approaching. A Bishop was coming from Egypt to celebrate the feast in this monastery high in the Alps. Sister Marie felt that I should be baptized, by the Bishop on Easter Sunday. She said that she would be my godmother and I her spiritual child, although this was very unorthodox, since in general she would take this responsibility only for the sisters within her order.

Another unconventional aspect of this baptism was that I had received no catechism at all. Until today, I have learned almost nothing about the structure and the rules or dogma of the Church; I feel that I have been taught, only by the light, and the spirit of Christ.

But since she was functioning in the realm of truth, the realm of light and inspiration, Sister Marie was not concerned that I had not memorized the rules. Simply, the Bishop was coming, Easter was approaching, and my baptism, she said, had to occur at that time. She asked me what name I felt I should be baptized with. I said, "Miriam Arunati." "Arunati," a word I had learned in India, means, "full of grace."

Sister Marie, and all those brought up by her, transmitted a very powerful sense of the reality of Jesus (as) and his mother (ra), who, for them, were not idealized greeting card figures but absolutely revolutionary beings, courageous and fearless servants of the Truth. This was a very liberating and galvanizing approach. Jesus (as) was not as the world portrayed him. As dedicated and sincere disciples of the spirit of Christ and his teachings, the Sisters of Bethlehem conveyed to me how serious and great a spiritual Master he was and how profound a taskmaster, which I understood and experienced more and more deeply as I read the words he spoke to his disciples. What I began to understand, from the transmission of these followers of Christ, in contrast to what I had seen in Christian churches in my childhood, is the difference between Jesus (as) the man with his pure teachings, and the vast complex of Christianity, which evolved after he left this world.

Just as the Prophet Abraham (as) and the Prophet Muhammad (saw) were the greatest threats to people in the "idol business" in their times, Jesus (as), who sent the money lenders out of the temple, was the greatest threat to the worldly authorities in power because of his absolute purity and submission only to God. Yet he has strangely become the symbol behind which, for so many centuries, those worldly powers have rallied.

To a magnitude that defies comprehension, he who was free of egotism and idolatry had become an idol worshipped by multitudes. This is the great paradox apparent in every religion and the reason why the sincere seeker must go beyond all worldly appearances into the essence and the living truth, which all the representatives sent by God have brought. I loved the Sisters of Bethlehem because they took my hand and walked with me into the garden of the heart where Jesus (as) taught. They helped me to receive and experience the teachings that he brought.

On Easter Sunday, Sister Marie asked me to bathe as the disciples of Jesus (as) had bathed. I have thought about that request for the rest of my life. How did the disciples of Christ bathe? In retrospect, I see that this community, the Sisters of Bethlehem, it seemed, were living very much as the disciples of Christ lived, in the reality of his presence and his teaching. That was why I had been guided directly to them, to receive and imbibe this living tradition.

That night, we went out into the snow-covered Alps. There, a huge bonfire had been built. It was like a pillar of flame, reaching into the night sky. I was baptized in the snow, and then Sister Marie lit a very long, white candle, igniting it in the bonfire, which represented the light of Christ, and she gave the candle to me.

Having received the flaming torch and been baptized in the snow of Mount Blanc, the *White Mountain*, I went into retreat for forty days. Sister Marie was guided not to allow me to become distracted by house-work and social contact; the overpowering priority at this stage of my journey, she made me know, was to dedicate my life to contemplation of the Divine.

I lit the huge candle every day to remind me of the eternal light shining within me and within everything. Just as the light of the candle that had been placed in my hand was ignited by and drawn from the huge bonfire, so was the light of each soul ignited by and drawn from the infinite plenitude of the Light of God.

In the depth of that solitude, with nothing but the majestic whi te mountain to see, no one to speak with, nothing to do but to pray, I read the words of the Bible inwardly and experienced within my soul the story of the life of Jesus (as) as deeply as I could, dwelling upon his experiences in the wilderness and facing my own tests and temptations in the wilderness of my inner being.

When the period of forty days of solitude was complete, Sister Ma-rie sent me into the Alps every day with Sister Claire. Sister Claire had huge, shining, brown eyes and a brilliant, yet very gentle spirit. She was a maker of beautiful puppets and puppet shows, an artist and a poet. She was supposed to teach me catechism on our daily journeys into the Alps. In reality, all that we spoke about was Jesus (as) and Mevlana Rumi (ra). She shared with me the spirit of Christ, and I shared with her the stories and teachings of Rumi (ra) that I had been so inspired by.

Every day, we sat among those great white peaks and celebrated the presence of the people of God who in spirit sat with us. I never once contemplated the "Trinity" or Jesus (as) as the "Son of God" or Jesus (as) "suffering for my sins on a cross." All that we thought and talked about were the ever living, eternally inspiring and life-giving spiritual teachings of Jesus (as) and Rumi (ra), which, as we discovered, were interlinked. Such was *my* catechism.

Otherwise, under the direction of Sister Marie and her inspiration that I must focus principally upon the contemplation of God and the inner work, I spent most of my time in the monastery in a kind of retreat and then created a room for retreat in the monastery, which I heard later, was regularly used in the future by the sisters for individual periods of contemplation.

Sister Marie wanted me to stay forever with her and the Sisters of Bethlehem. I did not want to leave them, but one day I looked out into the courtyard of the monastery and saw a man, a woman and a child walking together. It was beautiful and compelling, and it was a message for me. I knew that I had to leave the monastery and continue my journey. My journey had more dimensions, which had to be fulfilled.

I sent this news to Lennie and Sophie, who immediately sent me a plane ticket. It was one of the very few times in my life I have ever traveled first class. There was only one other person in the cabin, and he was sitting next to me. He was a very refined, educated and devout person. He had a lovely face and manner.

We were served platters; it seemed a feast, of the most delicious fruits and vegetables. Throughout our journey through the heavens, celestial music came pouring through our earphones, a Magnificat to Mary, and other divine music. I felt that even these details of the journey home, were, it seemed, orchestrated by the Divine.

Chapter Ten

SHORT STAY IN AMERICA,

CULTURE SHOCK,

LONGING TO RETURN TO SANCTIFIED LAND

California, Colorado and New Mexico, 1973

Never look down to test the ground before taking your next step; only he who keeps his eye fixed on the far horizon will find the right road.

—Dag Hammarskjold

I returned to the America from which I had fled. Re-entry, with its culture shock, was softened by Sophie. When I had been living in the monastery in Chevetogne, Lennie and Sophie had come to visit. Lennie had insisted that he be in the church for all the liturgies, starting at four o'clock in the morning. Although he thought of himself as something of an agnostic, his soul was insisting that he not miss one time of prayer.

Sophie too had seemed to enjoy going into the church. After all, she was an artist, and the church was full of art. She was also amazed at the delicious food prepared by the *Sisters of Bethlehem*.

When I returned to America, it was through the gracious portal of the house of Lennie and Sophie that I entered. They were now living on a beautiful, wooded property near the ocean in Pacific Palisades. Adjoining the main house was a small glass house surrounded by trees. There, by hanging up the icons she had purchased at the monastery, Sophie created a small chapel in which I could live.

Whenever anybody, even people coming to work on the house, would come over, she brought them to this little chapel to meet me and played a tape of the monks singing at the monastery. Such was the nature of her acceptance, creative thinking, and religious tolerance.

Later, when I had embraced Islam, and I came home with Ahamad Kabeer, an *imam*, it was with equally great ease that, having invited Muslims from the neighborhood to join, he was able to perform the jumu'ah prayers (congregational prayers held every Friday) in the living room of Lennie and Sophie. That was just the kind of thing that you could imagine happening in their living room. I mention this in response to the often-asked question: how did my Jewish family respond to my embrace first of Christianity and then of Islam?

It was all like a river naturally following its course into the sea. It was as though my course was predestined. All that was to happen to me was already present within me from the time of my childhood, the time of my birth. Nothing at all that unfolded in my journey was surprising, shocking, or unsettling to my family because the sense of the unconventional, extraordinary things that were to take place in my life were present within me from the beginning.

It was very peaceful in the little glass chapel surrounded by towering eucalyptus trees, but I had to get on with my life and journey, whatever that entailed. I went back to Berkeley and moved into my brother Michael's house where I had lived before my travels abroad. This time, the glass lantern room, like all the other rooms in the house, was occupied, and there was only a small space available in the basement. So, I moved into one side of the dark basement. It was like living in a hole in the ground and also like being in a womb. I was gestating, processing all that had been revealed to me on my quest. Because the inner work was so strong and deep, I did not go out much.

After being in Berkeley a short while, I reconnected with Ram Dass and his community again. We had weekly *kirtans*, singing and chanting the names of God, and did a lot of meditation. With Ram Dass and a teacher of Vipassana meditation, we held a meditation retreat in the Santa Cruz Mountains. We also formed a band, *Amazing Grace*, and made an album. One song I remember from the album, written, I believe by Parmahamsa Yogananda, went:

> *Who is in my temple?*
> *All the doors do open themselves.*
> *All the lights do light themselves.*
> *Darkness, like a dark bird.*
> *Flies away, Oh flies away.*

The formless dimension of the meditation was very helpful to me. I entered into the practice of Vipassana meditation for sixteen hours a day, several days in a row. The practice is one of sweeping through the body with a current of awareness and dispelling all congestion, density, illusion or disease with the consciousness that all this is impermanent.

For me, this was an immensely effective practice. All of the confusion and pain, wherever it was lodged in the body, heart or mind, seemed to be dispelled by the current of consciousness that was passing through my body. For this practice, and its powerful cleansing and transformative effect, I was very grateful.

Otherwise, I found life in America difficult because of the lack of clarity, the lack of morality, the absence of guidelines being followed.

Eventually, many of the group went to Boulder, Colorado where Trungpa Rinpoche, a lama from Tibet who was quite westernized, was teaching his students. I had read his book *Cutting Through Spiritual Materialism* and found that it was brilliantly written. But I was baffled by the apparent effect of the teaching on the behavior of the disciples. This was an approach which taught, as I understood it, that the disciple could do whatever he liked, as long as he did it with "wisdom." Almost anything could be done, it seemed, as long as one was using "wisdom" and cutting through spiritual materialism while doing it.

Having been back in America only a short time and somewhat reintegrated into the "spiritual scene," as I observed the way teachings were often being transmitted, I was deeply unsettled by how loose and seemingly lawless the spiritual communities seemed to me to be. During my travels on the path overseas, I had become sensitized to and transformed by a completely different way of existing.

Although it was not yet revealed in its completeness, the path was now beneath my feet. In my heart and in my body, I knew that rules, discipline and spiritual guidance were fundamental and absolutely necessary for real spiritual development. At this very gathering, something did occur of great spiritual significance, but I did not know that it was happening, and I came to realize its great spiritual importance later, and this divinely inspired encounter will be explored in a later chapter.

I was profoundly homesick for the purity of existence I had experienced in the monasteries and throughout my journey. After only a short time in America, I wanted to leave again, to escape the cultural pollution and corruption that was seemingly rampant, even in the spiritual movements, and continue on the journey of my soul towards God. I had heard about initiatic orders in South America and was thinking about going there, when I took a side trip from Boulder, Colorado, to the Lama Foundation in the mountains above Taos, New Mexico.

There, I discovered my next step. The Lama Foundation, in the San Cristobal Mountain range, is built on elevated, blessed land, which stands like a high island surrounded by an ocean of space. The endless view, the space one breathes and beholds, is majestic and mystical. One gets the sense, as the Native Americans who were the first to make their homes here did, that one is standing on sacred ground.

I had passed through and lived for a while at the Lama Foundation some time before. Cooking in the round wood and adobe Lama kitchen with its windows overlooking infinity, was for me an initiation into cooking and service. With the hundreds of *chapattis* that we cooked there, it was the birthplace of my love of serving food and, after the house of Lennie and Sophie, as well as our collective tribal experience in the Floating Lotus Magic Opera Company, it was a real training ground in the beauty and sweetness as well as the challenges of communal living.

Now, as I was returning to Lama for a brief visit, I wanted to express my gratitude for the blessings I had received there, those blessings which were actually seeds of awareness growing within me. I visited the beautiful buildings of Lama, which were mostly domes built of wood and adobe and filled with light.

They were created to exist in harmony with the nature that surrounded them so that the light within flowed without obstruction into the luminous space surrounding each building and extending into the boundless vista. Walking through the buildings of the Lama Foundation was for me a lesson in sacred architecture and in the Tao, or effortless being, the natural state.

I walked over to the Lama garden. There, in the midst of the flourishing garden of organic green vegetables, was *the Green Man* himself, Nooruddeen Durkee. It was he, whose name means "the light of the way, the light of religion," who had built most of the buildings with his wife Asha and who had envisioned and facilitated the construction of each of the illuminated spaces I had just passed through. Nooruddeen, an impressive figure with long red hair and beard and green eyes, was standing in the greenness of the garden, wearing a green and white sarong and a red shirt.

I was carrying in my arms a huge tome, the journal I had made of my journey as I travelled.

Nooruddeen told me that he was preparing to go very soon with a small group of people to Jerusalem to write the fourth book in a series he had produced, working with a small group of people from around the world he called "*Companions of the Palm*." He was waiting now for whomever God would send to work on this project and at the same time preparing to go.

Arriving with my stone-covered journal in my arms, it appeared that I was one of the people he was waiting for, one of the members of the team. Since I was longing for the purity I had experienced in the monasteries, it seemed that a journey to Jerusalem would be the perfect next step.

We spent the next week together in a state of transcendent communication. This encounter was an oasis in the midst of the expansive desert of my solitude. On the second floor of a small, domed building filled with plants and sunlight, we met and shared much, so many dimensions, in one eternal week. I found in him a man of vision and action and light. It was the light of God that I saw in him that was guiding me to the Mount of Olives, where Jesus (as) had prayed, and to the grandfather (my first Sheikh) who lived near the tomb of Abraham (as) and to the embrace of Islam. When the eternal week in the light-filled dome was over, it was time to return to the road.

Nooruddeen and another brother who was going to work on the book, Abd'al Ahad, and I traveled by car across the country. From New York, I flew with Abd'al Ahad to Venice, and from there we crossed the shining waters of the Mediterranean to arrive in Haifa. We then found our way to Jerusalem and to the blessed Mount of Olives, on which we were to live for a sacred time.

CHAPTER ELEVEN

EMBRACING ISLAM IN EL KHALIL, THE PLACE OF ABRAHAM (AS)

Jerusalem and Hebron, 1974

And a voice came out of the throne, saying, praise our God, all
His servants, and ye that fear Him, both small and great. And I
heard as it were the voice of a great multitude, and as the voice
of many waters and as the voice of mighty thunders, saying,
"Alleluiah: For the Lord God Omnipotent reigneth."
—Book of Revelation 19:5-6

The day I arrived in Jerusalem, it so happened that my beloved spiritual mother, Sister Marie, arrived too. She had come to visit her mentor, an illuminated priest who was to give a seminar in a monastery on the Mount of Olives on the *Book of Revelation.* So that was where I spent my first week in the Holy Land, and it was truly a holy land that I was transported to by the priest as he made the Book of Revelation real for us, as it was for him.

I remember the subtle intensity of light in the room, the feeling of spiritual energy coming through him and filling the room as he read passages from the Book of Revelation. The priest never looked at us. He was facing another direction. I sensed that he was turned away from this earth and toward the Celestial Jerusalem. I was amazed at the rays of light I saw descending upon him.

In the normal world, if one was to give a seminar every day for a week and never look at his audience, he would lose his listeners, but this priest enthralled us with what was enthralling him. I went with him to the world of revelation and saw, to some degree, what he saw. As he described the images in the Book of Revelation and explained what they signified to him, exploring the meanings that they could have for a follower of Christ, I felt the Divine Presence manifesting through these images, a city of celestial peace.

That is how I entered Jerusalem, not as a militarized secular city which has endured centuries of conflict and strife, culminating in the present, tragic conditions but as a place of light in a plane of light, a place sacred to people of many religions — Jerusalem the Holy, that we the believers have yet to make real on earth.

When the seminar was over, I joined Nooruddeen and the others he had gathered together to work on the book on Jerusalem. We all lived in a large airy house on the Mount of Olives. I stayed in half of a long room, which I shared with Shahida, who would later become Noura Issa and also become the wife of Nooruddeen. We had nothing in that room but light and space. With barely a suitcase full of possessions, the basic necessities, and no possessiveness, I very much enjoyed sharing that space and light with her. It was a sign of the way in which our souls were linked.

As we assembled on the roof of the house on the Mount of Olives and were bathed in soft golden light at sunset, and as we walked upon the golden earth where the Prophets (as) had walked, I felt that I had returned home. Although I had been born as a Jew, it was not to a specifically Jewish homeland that I had returned but to a place of sanctity, holy for me and others.

Our life and research went on. The book was to be called *Jerusalem: A Garden in the Flames.* And, very much aware of the flames encircling the city, we were searching for the eternal garden which lay hidden in the heart of the city and its people. This being our intention, we were guided to the lovers of God of different faiths. We spoke to many people, recording interviews with Rabbis, Priests, Sheikhs (ra), and simply the believing people of all faiths. We were searching for and finding the common threads and fundamental truth. Many of the people, both Palestinians and Israelis, expressed that they had lived in peace with people of the other faith until outside forces, such as the British, had come in to foment conflict.

As my discovery continued to unfold, one day, wrapped in a large blue shawl that completely enveloped me, I was sitting outside Damascus Gate, waiting for Sister Marie. I was very much immersed in the inner space but little by little felt something drawing me out. When I opened my eyes, I saw a man with intense green eyes gazing at me, a very slim young man, but with a fervent spirit. His eyes were riveted to me. He said, "Are you Maryam from California?" I said, "Yes." He said, "My grandfather is waiting for you. When you are ready, I will take you to meet him."

The young man's name was Hassan as-Sharif, which indicated he came from the family of the Prophet Muhammad (saw). He came home with me that day, and we spent the rest of the day in our home on the Mount of Olives. We talked and talked and talked. I do not remember what we said, but I felt the beautiful, gentle, holy presence of his grandfather in some way entering my heart. I was also deeply impressed by something Hassan did. When he heard the call to prayer, he took everything out of his pockets and took his watch off, before he did ablutions and prayed. It was a teaching about preparation for prayer and prayer itself that I have never forgotten.

Probably a week later, when we were ready, I set out with Hassan, Nooruddeen and Abd'al Latif, a dear companion on the team, to go to the place where Hassan's grandfather was waiting for us. We traveled in an old, rickety bus from Jerusalem to Hebron, known as El-Khalil in Arabic. It is the holy city where Prophet Abraham (as) and several members of his family are buried.

The land between El Quds (Jerusalem, the Holy) and El Khalil, short for Khalilullah — friend of God, the title of Prophet Abraham (as) — is very beautiful, fertile land, sculpted into many-layered terraces. I strongly felt the presence of our father Abraham (as) during the journey, that he had not only walked on this land, but had also cultivated it and planted seeds in it that were still bearing fruit. If only his descendants could find this fruit and eat it together!

Something about the land was extremely familiar and healing. I felt, again, that I had been returned home. I was caressed by the care that had been shown to this earth and was greatly refreshed. But the peace that came to us as we traveled through this sacred land was disturbed when we arrived in El Khalil. In the bus station, many people were passing through and milling around, and one could instantly sense the tension and the strain of the inhabitants of this holy city.

We walked to the mosque, which is also a synagogue, the so-called "tomb" more accurately called *mazar* (place of the presence) of Abraham (as) and several of his relatives. It was a place of pilgrimage for Judaism and Christianity as well as Islam and was full of pilgrims of all three faiths.

Upon entering that place of power, I fell prostrate, not because I had heard I should do it but because it was the natural, inevitable thing to do. I arose eventually to find that I was surrounded by worshippers on all sides — angelic and human worshippers, it seemed, of different faiths and understandings but all descendants and heirs of one father, worshipping together in one sanctified space.

Blessed it was and deeply meaningful that I should enter Islam on the earth where Prophet Abraham (as), Khalilullah, Friend of God, had lived and was buried. He was the exemplar, the leader for all the people, and one whose descendants, God said, would be like the stars.

Feeling his presence so strongly here in *El-Khalil*, I wondered why all of us, the descendants of this great man, are not shining with the light of certain faith that illuminated his way and following the beautifully clear example he set for all humanity in his understanding of and surrender to the One God. I prayed that I might become a daughter worthy to follow in the footsteps of such an exalted father.

After bringing us to meet our one father, Hassan took us on a journey through the ancient narrow winding lanes, through many arches, doorways, and gateways to the *zawiyyah* (gathering place), where the grandfather was awaiting us. The grandfather, Sidi Sheikh Abdul Muttalib (ra) was one hundred and thirty-five years old, Hassan told us.

We entered at the level of the road and went far down into an amazing complex until we reached the zawiyyah below. Although it was considerably below street level, the zawiyyah seemed to be full of sunlight. Everywhere, there were beautiful plants, flowers and squash, incredibly healthy vines and creepers growing up and down the walls. Later, I saw the grandfather, although he was blind, lovingly tending them one by one. I came to realize that I too was one of the plants, which he would nurture and bring to life with the loving tenderness of his divinely inspired touch.

There were two sides to the zawiyyah. One was a cave-like room where the grandfather, the Sheikh (ra), lived with his wife, and the other was a larger room where he gathered every day with his disciples. We found the Sheikh (ra) with some disciples in the larger room performing *dhikr* (zikr), invoking the Divine Qualities. The Sheikh (ra) was ancient, venerable, and pure. He was wearing a white robe and green turban and an ancient long black cloak. In place of a shawl, he was wearing a towel.

I was utterly happy to be in his presence, feeling that I was reunited at last with my true father and friend. His being emanated not a trace of egotism but only great sweetness, kindness, and grace. The disciples were sitting in a semi-circle and welcomed us to join them as soon as we entered. We sat down with them and joined the circle. The fact that I was a female and that we were apparent strangers from another part of the world did not seem strange or awkward at all; our presence seemed to enhance what the Sheikh (ra) was doing, and we were integrated into their circle in the most natural and harmonious way, as though they had been waiting for us to complete it.

Sheikh Abdul Muttalib (ra) and his disciples were invoking the name of God, *Ya Latif, the Most Subtle, the Kind.* The *dhikr* went on and on, so gently and so deeply, with many subtle shifts and permutations. It was the most beautiful invocation. I have wished for the rest of my life that I had a recording of it so I could listen to it again and understand why it moved me so very much to hear them and join with them. But the recording was in my heart in accordance with the secret of that name, *the Most Subtle.*

It was a moment of initiation into that beautiful Name of God and the reflection of that Name as manifested in the actions, words, and resonance of the Sheikh, Sidi Sheikh Abdul Muttalib (ra), whom God had brought us here to meet.

After the *dhikr*, the Sheikh (ra) welcomed us very graciously and introduced us to the way of his tariqat (spiritual path). When our meeting was completed, we gave salaams and started to leave. Nooruddeen and Abd'al Latif were out of the *zawiyyah*, and I was at the doorway when one of the elder disciples stopped me and told me that the Sheikh (ra) wanted me to move in. I accepted this invitation without hesitation.

I went back to the Mount of Olives, got some things, and returned that day. I began living with grandfather and his wife in the cave. She sat on the floor in a corner and cooked the food over a small flame. He frequently placed the food in my mouth. Many blessings, which have come to me later in my life may be traceable back to the barakah, the blessing, of receiving and eating what the Sheikh put in my mouth.

The grandfather, Sheikh Abdul Muttalib, gave me his bed to sleep in. I came to realize that he did not sleep, but sat up the whole night, throughout which he blew on my head and prayed. I had a dream. I was living in a high mountain kingdom where there was a war going on between two tribes. I was making a spiritual retreat for forty days, alone in a cave, praying for reconciliation and peace.

One day, a man came to the cave and brought a rose. The next day, he came again and brought another rose. I never saw this man during my seclusion inside the cave, only the one rose he left each day at the entrance. This continued for days until the cave was full of roses. Finally, the man who had been bringing the roses told me that he was a messenger of the King. The King was asking for my hand in marriage. To fulfill the marriage, I would have to jump off a cliff. This offering or sacrifice, this *leap of faith*, would bring about peace in the high mountain kingdom where the two tribes had been warring for a very long time.

I told the dream to the grandfather. He said that the King was the Prophet Muhammad (saw) and that to fulfill the marriage, I must make *salat*, the ritual Islamic prayer. This, he said, was the leap of faith indicated in my dream.

Having been immersed in a "contemplative state," which I thought was continuous, I was not eager to get involved with the "exercise" of *salat*, so I had managed not to hear the command to make *salat* from anyone who had told me about it in the past.

But for the grandfather, the Exalted Sheikh, to tell me to do it in the context of the message delivered in the dream was as close to a divine transmission as could come in human form, I felt. The sweetness, kindness, and subtlety with which this blessed man invited me to surrender to the will of God engendered in me the deepest sense of happiness and peace I had ever experienced in my life. There was no doubt about accepting this invitation and no struggle at all. I felt I would join again with my ancient family and we would all worship together the One God, Most Merciful, who created us out of His Mercy.

If I had to jump off a cliff, it was into the unknown, but I felt in this secret holy enclave, to which I had been guided by the *"Hand"* of God, that the unknown realm into which I was now entering was the realm of God's infinite Grace. I had no choice and no desire but to surrender and enter.

And so, it was in this small, ancient and exalted congregation that I, a Jewish girl born in Hollywood, began to make *salat*. At each time of prayer, a small, lace curtain was hung in the tiny cave, separating the male side of the line from the female side. Standing close to the middle, I was at least fifty years if not a hundred years younger than everyone else in the congregation.

Although so small, it was a wonderful congregation composed of exalted beings. How could I fathom the mercy and loving kindness of the Guide who led me to discover the sweetness of prayer in such an assembly, full of blessing, hidden from the eyes of the world?

Now all of them have left this earth, leaving me alone the sole witness of what took place there. I know that everything I experienced in that cave, the purity of true Islam, the sweetness, kindness, harmony, and peace, all were manifestations of the Mercy of the One Who created us all and Who sent all the Prophets (as) bearing His message, to make me know that true Islam — Islam revealed by God to the people of God — is peace and light.

Every chapter of the Qur'an, except one, begins, "In the Name of God, the Merciful, the Compassionate." What a great irony it is that the word "Islam" has become so commonly linked in the media world with words such as "terrorism" and "fanaticism."

This media stereotype is certainly fueled and sustained by people who, in the name of Islam, do things which are condemned and forbidden in the Qur'an, antithetical to the way and religion of the Creator, Most Merciful. For example, the act of committing suicide in Islam is forbidden, as is the killing of women and children in war. In the clearly defined rules of war, fighting is only permitted in defense against attack, and even trees along the way must be protected.

In the present world in which people are committing, in the name of Islam, things that are absolutely forbidden in Islam, and some people in the media are amplifying and promulgating this falsehood, we are conditioned by the forces of darkness and ignorance, which want to keep us from the truth, to associate Islam with things that are totally forbidden in Islam.

But the lovers of truth, the seekers of truth, will find it, and the truth will set them free. It was unquestionably the magnetism of the truth — the magnet that is truth that led me to the grandfather, my first Sheikh, Sidi Sheikh Abdul Muttalib (ra), may Allah *subhana wa ta'ala* sanctify his secret. No map, no internet search could have led me to him, only the Divine Guide.

For, although I had encountered Islam several times earlier in my journey, it was only in the presence of such a being that Islam was revealed to me with such great sweetness, beauty, and integrity that I had no choice but to *embrace* it.

In embracing the message brought by the Prophet Muhammad (saw) there in the place of Prophet Abraham (as), I embraced all of the messages brought by all of the Messengers (as) sent by the One Creator of all. In embracing the tree and cherishing its fruits, I also found the ancient Jewish roots planted here in the Holy Land. All of these under-standings were transmitted to me, by the grandfather. He did not make me know or accept this through the force of his personality or the elo-quence of his words. Few words passed between us. Yet, he gave me so much.

I had dreamt of the ancient ones blowing upon me, blessing me, guiding, and inspiring me. Undoubtedly, that dream led me to him at whose hands I was to embrace Islam, and because that was the door through which I entered, I always have the most joyous, peaceful, and pure associations with the path I was guided to embrace. There was not a trace of compulsion, not a trace of politics, pressure or oppression. There was only sweetness, kindness, light and grace, manifesting in the form of a human being fully dedicated to the service of his Lord.

Because I was guided by the One Most Merciful to embrace His path at the hands of such a person, in such a beautiful way, this is the way in which I hope I can share it with others, as light upon light, love within love, truth within the heart, which loves the truth.

CHAPTER TWELVE

PRAYING IN THE DOME OF THE ROCK

JERUSALEM, 1974

Glory to the One who took His Servant by night from al-Masjid al-Haram to al-Masjid al-Aqsa, whose surroundings We have blessed, to show him Our signs. Indeed, He is the Hearing, the Seeing.

—The Holy Qur'an 17:1

Jerusalem is a city of many gates, many passageways, and many mysteries hidden in unexpected places and accessed by unexpected means. There is a garden hidden in the city, but one must pass through flames—centuries of conflict — to enter.

Having received from the grandfather, Sidi Sheikh Abd'ul Muttalib (ra), the beautiful gift of Islam and the practice of the *salat*, one day, when I had been making *salat* for only a few months, I was internally guided to go to the Dome of the Rock on Al-Haram Ash-Sharif and pray. It was not at a given time of prayer, but I knew that I had to do it then.

So, I strode through a gateway leading to the Temple Mount, without hesitation and without seeing the guards standing at the gate. They came running after me and with their bodies blocked my way. "You cannot come in here!" they insisted forcefully. "Only Muslims can enter." "I am a Muslim," I said. "I must go to the mosque to pray." They insisted that I prove this by reciting the fundamental verses of the Qur'an, which I did, not for their sake but for the sake of Allah *subhana wa ta'ala* who had asked me to pray. Still they did not want to let me enter.

I knew that I had to go in. I was being drawn by an irresistible force. They could not stop me from doing what I was going to do, nor could I stop them from doing what they were doing. Finally, the guards said, "We are taking you to the police." They took me to the police station on the Haram Ash-Sharif. When we entered the building, a man, who turned out to be the Chief of Police, saw me with them and said, "That is Maryam, you must take her to the mosque to pray. She has to pray." I personally never met this man and had no idea how he knew that or why he said it. But, *Alhamdulillah*, I was then escorted by the guards to the door of the mosque. So, I entered that amazing place, as I had known I must that day.

There is no adequate way to describe the rock around which the mosque is built. It is the place on earth from which the Prophet Muhammad (saw) rose on the night of his ascension. It is referred to in the Qur'an as the "Farthest Mosque." Upon entering, I beheld an extraordinary manifestation of grace. The rock from which the Holy Prophet (saw) ascended is immense, luminous, and appears to be in flight. It does not look like any other piece of earth I have ever seen. I saw it only that one time, and the memory of it is practically blinding. It is awe-inspiring. I realized then why I had to go there. Once you enter it, you do not leave; you have been there forever, and there you remain. It was a place I felt linked to, a place where I felt that I truly belonged.

This was the sacred realm from which the Prophet Muhammad (saw) ascended into the heavenly realms where he met with all the Prophets (as) and led them in prayer. Thus, was the unity of all the Prophets (as) and revelations they brought established on the Night of the Ascension, ultimately blessing this place forever.

On the day that I walked into the mosque, it appeared almost no one was there, and I walked straight to the *qibla*, where the imam leads the prayers, and prayed there. While I was praying in that holy spot as the Creator had willed, my soul was inspired to beseech the Lord to entrust to me a child that would serve him.

Many years later, my son Issa was born. Whether he is such a child who will serve his Lord, only Allah *subhana wa ta'ala* knows and will reveal. I continue to pray every day that my original supplication may be fulfilled, and in the midst of all the trials of bringing up a child in a world full of strife and corruption, I perceive subtle signs, such as his compassion and his deep inclination to serve, which indicate that my supplications may be answered.

In every blessed matter, it is only the will of Allah *subhana wa ta'ala* that is done. May the deepest intentions for goodness lead us on the path to realize the most exalted goals that He intends for us to attain.

Whatever may be the ultimate result of the prayer and supplication I made that day, there is a dimension of my soul that remains awestruck by the power, the majesty, and sanctity of that space and the opportunity I was given to enter it and find my place there.

I am also amazed, having witnessed and experienced that divine wonder that exists in the heart of the Holy City, when I notice that this sacred dimension is almost never mentioned on the news about the city. Yet, it is the resplendent secret of the garden hidden within the flames presently consuming Jerusalem, Darussalam, "the place of peace."

May the celestial Jerusalem, upon which such a name has been bestowed, become the place of peace for those who follow the Prophet (saw) on the path of ascension. And, as the inhabitants in the celestial Jerusalem unite in the realization of divine peace, may the rain of *rahmat*, the rain of God's grace, descend upon the earthly Jerusalem and extinguish the flames which engulf it.

While living on the Mount of Olives, we frequently ran into another Sheikh, Sidi Sheikh Muhammad al-Jemal (ra). We met him one day riding on the bus that goes down the mountain. From that point on, he came almost every night to our house to share teachings with us. These were Sufi teachings, which very much interested us all.

The time came for Nooruddeen, Shahida (Noura Issa) and the others in the group to return to their homes in America and Europe. By this time the grandfather, Sidi Sheikh Abdul Muttalib (ra) had transmitted Islam to me, but very little verbal communication was possible between us.

So, at this point I moved into the *zawiyyah* of Sidi Sheikh Muhammad (ra) to receive more of these teachings. Sheikh Muhammad (ra) was able to speak enough English and I was able to understand enough Arabic for there to be ongoing communication between us. Sidi Sheikh Muhammad (ra) often gave the Friday sermon in Al Aqsa Mosque, and he spoke frequently about many interesting subjects. Because these subjects intrigued me, I felt inspired to remain in his *zawiyyah* for a time to learn more about Islam and *tasawwuf,* the Sufi path.

The *zawiyyah* was a very large, empty basement on the lower level of the house of the Sheikh (ra). The door opened onto the desert, and the desert wind would flow in. Because there was almost no furniture, all sounds resonated beautifully in that cool open space. It was a very good place in which to recite surahs and do *dhikr.* It was here that I began to enter into the resonance of the Holy Qur'an and the prayer.

One beautiful gift the Sheikh (ra) gave me was the blessing of my first *khalwah* (guided spiritual retreat). He put me in a room with a beautiful set of five hundred prayer beads and instructed me to visualize the name of God in Arabic written in light and not to sleep through the night. That was for me a beautiful night journey, the first of many I would be blessed to make.

For the most part, I lived alone in the *zawiyyah*, though from time to time, someone would come to stay for a while and then leave. Often, the sweet children of the Sheikh (ra) would come to visit. The real quality of my experience at this time, however, was in solitude and in the sense that I had been here centuries before and that my soul had returned home.

On certain days in the week, I took the bus down the Mount of Olives to Jerusalem where I taught English in a school called *Dar'ul Awlad*, the Place of the Children. The children were orphans of Arab origin from the streets of Jerusalem.

Given their challenging life conditions, they were wonderfully bright, open, and untroubled. It was a blessing and a delight to get to know them and share with them. It was also always a joy and spiritual education to explore the narrow, winding lanes of the Old City after school and discover what treasures lie within the shops and within the hearts of the people. In this way, I continued the work on the project, interviewing the people of the city and continuing to discover and explore the garden within the flames.

On certain days I went to the Haram Ash-Sharif (Noble Sanctuary) to pray. One day, I was walking there and ran into an old friend named Aaron who was studying to be a Rabbi. He wanted me to meet the Rabbi with whom he was studying. I met with the Rabbi. He wanted to know why I, a Jewish girl, was studying with a Sheikh (ra). I told him that the Sheikhs (ra) were transmitting to me deep mystical teachings about prayer and life, things that I very deeply yearned to know and to put into practice.

I asked him if he could teach me what the Ba'al Shem Tov, a very illuminated Rabbi, taught his disciples. He told me that he could not teach me. He arranged for me to meet with a Rebbitzen, a female Rabbi, or the wife of a Rabbi. It did not appear that she knew anything at all about the spiritual knowledge I was yearning to learn.

This, then, was the answer to the Rabbi's question. I was studying with the Sufi Masters because they had the knowledge of the journey to God and were very willing to share it.

On the other days of the week, I walked along the ancient mountain paths to Bethany, where Lazarus was brought back from the dead. There I had a job working with handicapped children. It was not in the Holy Sepulchre or in the designated tourist sites where I felt the presence of Jesus (as) most deeply but on these walks on the mountain paths between the Mount of Olives and Bethany. I had the strong sense that he had walked along the same paths, and he was walking with me.

How had he lived here? I asked myself, as I walked along those ancient paths. By what means, by what power, did he give life to the dead? How does a human being, living and walking upon this earth, become the instrument of the One and only Being Who can give life to the dead? Then, how can I and each of us become an instrument for that life-giving Power?

Such were the questions inspired in my soul by that journey back and forth between Bethany, where I learned about the healing power of love, and the Mount of Olives, where I learned to pray. I had received a great candle lit from a bonfire on one mountain, there for the purpose of understanding who Jesus (as) truly was and what message he truly brought to this earth. Now, I was walking on another mountain where the presence of the prophetic manifestation was even stronger.

I felt, as I walked, his humanity, his love for the poor, and his willingness to go everywhere to find them and do everything to feed them and heal them. I did not envision him hanging on a cross or dying for our sins but truly and eternally living that we may follow his example and live eternally in the presence of God. He, who was the pure servant of the Eternal One, did not die, I felt, so that our sins may be forgiven; he overcame all the temptations of Satan, thereby conquering sin and evil, and he taught all of his disciples, all of us, that in following him we must do this too.

Jesus (as), *"son of man,"* as he humbly called himself, went ahead, along with all those sent by God as our Prophets (as) and guides. We must walk on the same path behind them and be judged for what we do, not for what they did. For, as the Holy Qur'an tells us, on the Day of Judgment, we will each see every atom's weight of good that we did and every atom's weight of evil. The scales of our judgment are balanced by our own deeds.

Walking on the path behind Jesus (as) was, as I was experiencing it, powerful, dynamic and profound. As I walked in those hills where I felt, certainly, somehow, I had walked before, always, I saw signs that the teachings were alive.

What made the Holy Land holy? I asked for inner understanding. Not only Jesus (as) but so many of the Messengers (as) of God were sent to this land. I asked myself why, as I walked upon the narrow pathways, along the red-gold cliffs, which were then as they had been when the Prophets (as) walked there. What about the words they said, the words they were commanded to speak? How were those words to be fulfilled? How had the Prophets (as) been received, as they came one by one, bearing the divine treasures to humankind?

As I walked through the olive trees in the Garden of Gethsemane, where Jesus (as) had walked and taught his disciples, where he stayed awake while others slept, and as I looked down from the wall on the Mount of Olives over the extraordinary view of the city of Jerusalem with the Dome of the Rock in its center, I contemplated the terrible, bloody history the city had endured and the wondrous divine mysteries contained at the same time within its walls.

Gazing upon the panorama of the walled city with its stone gates and ancient dwellings, I pondered how many references had been made to it in scripture and how many Messengers (as) had been sent here carrying both good news and a warning, directly from the Source.

Yet, time after time, age after age, they were persecuted, rejected, and denied. The Prophets (as) looked down upon the city, upon the condition of humankind, and wept in lamentation. They knew where things were leading, the repercussions of the choice made by the majority of the people to whom the message was addressed.

All human beings are inhabitants in the city of God. Why have we persecuted and denied the Messengers (as) who came to us with the honorable task of bringing to us the living *Word* of God? Why have we not honored the One Who sent them, and heeded their advice?

The grievous condition of the world today, I thought then, with the divided city of Jerusalem at its epicenter, is the inevitable outcome of the rejection of the Messengers (as) of truth, and the Truth, *al-Haqq*, which sent them. Nevertheless, the Scriptures tell us that the situation is not irreversible. The redemption is also foretold by the One whose promise is eternally true.

In the center of the city is the mosque wherein lies the rock from which the Holy Prophet (saw) ascended. If only we listen to our Creator

Most Merciful and do what He is telling us to do, we can rise up through the flames and be united with His peace that transcends all wars.

I, a daughter of Zion, from the tribe of *Bani Isra'il*, to whom, I have heard, the greatest number of Prophets (as) had been sent, had come to the Holy Land to perceive these things. In the cave of the grandfather, the *zawiyyah* of the Sufi Master, I had a dream.

I dreamt there was a war in a high mountain kingdom, and I entered a cave to pray for peace. One day after the next, a man came to this cave and sent in a flower, a rose from the King. When the cave was full of roses, a proposal was presented. The King was asking me to marry him. For the marriage to be completed, I would have to plunge off a cliff — sacrifice myself — so that there would be peace in the kingdom.

The kingdom was Jerusalem, the kingdom of the heart, the city of God. The warring people in the high mountain kingdom were the Jews, Christians, and Muslims, all children of one great father, the Prophet Abraham (as). "Why must this war go on between the children of this great man who served and worshipped nothing but the One God, Most Merciful?" I asked myself. "How can I make an offering of my life so that it may become an instrument of peace, an instrument of the reconciliation of the children of Abraham (as)?"

The grandfather, Sidi Sheikh Abdul Muttalib (ra) told me in the softest and strongest possible way that what God wanted me to do was to bow down. The Sheikh's (ra) communication to me was strong because as softly as he spoke, there was no way I could refuse the message he transmitted to me.

In bowing down in submission to the one and only Lord of all, the Jew within me, follower of Moses (as), the Christian, follower of Jesus (as), and the Muslim, follower of Muhammad (saw), were all perfectly reconciled. There was no conflict at all, only one Message, one Truth.

Many years later, what I had sensed then about the Messengers (as) and the One Truth was explained with beautiful clarity. The prophetic Message that Truth brought to humankind by all of the Prophets (as) is like a glass. At first, the glass was empty. Then, Prophet Adam (as) put water in it. After that, every Prophet continued to fill that glass with the water of the teaching he was charged by God to bring. When the Prophet Muhammad (saw) came and put the Revelation of the Qur'an into the glass, the glass became full and no more could be added to the water in the glass.

What is most important to realize is that all the teachings brought by all the true Messengers (as) of God are now merged in the water in the glass and cannot be removed or separated in any way from each other. The unity of all the divine messages and the absolute necessity to bow down and pray in accordance with the commandments of the One Lord of all were amongst the great gifts bestowed upon me on my journey to the Holy Land.

Now that the knowledge had been implanted, I knew that I must return to America. I had maintained contact with Nooruddeen and Noura. They were building the Intensive Studies Center at the Lama Foundation and working on the Jerusalem book there. After all, I had come to Jerusalem to work on this project, and it was time to go back, reunite with the circle, and help to move the work along.

As I was heading back to America, on a long ride across Europe, the train stopped in Bulgaria, where it was delayed for several hours, and there I began to experience the impact of what I had received in the Holy Land. The time for prayer arrived. I did not begin to think about where I was. Simply, knowing that the train was not going to move, I went onto the side of the train tracks, laid out my prayer mat and prayed.

When my prayer was over, and I gave salaams to the right and the left, so many people came running from both sides, weeping, to embrace me. We were, after all, in a Communist country, where praying, it was said, was illegal. Regardless of what religion these people were, they were overjoyed and profoundly moved to see and feel someone praying.

CHAPTER THIRTEEN

BUILDING THE ADOBE MOSQUE:

WATERING THE SEEDS OF ISLAM PLANTED
IN THE HOLY LAND

LAMA FOUNDATION, TAOS, NEW MEXICO,
1975

Standing, Bowing, Prostrating, Kneeling. Rising and falling... It was perfect, complete. I marveled even more how this act transformed my landlord and his son... I was utterly moved at that moment, and equally I knew... that this was the best and most perfect action I had ever seen in all my travels across the world... it was obviously something that had come down from the realms of perfection — a complete and holy providential provision.

—Shaykh 'Abdullah Nooruddeen Durkee (ra),
Book of Exile, Embracing Islam

The beauty of sajda is you whisper down on the hearth and it's heard in the heavens.

—Imam Ali (ra)

I returned to Lama with a bundle of Bedouin clothes and a bag full of transcriptions and tapes. There, I continued transcribing the tapes as I had been doing in Jerusalem. This was work I had to do, but it was also my therapy. It was a way I could continue to hear the voices of Jerusalem, continue to feel, blowing upon my face, the softness of the desert air. My soul was still there, walking on the path to Bethany and back.

At the same time, slowly, my body was habituating itself to the earth of New Mexico. Earth it was that I found in my hands many hours a day, as it was in the earth that we needed to plant the sacred seed. On my return to Lama, I discovered major building going on. The Companions of the Palm, having transmigrated back to Lama, were now building, out of adobe, the Intensive Studies Center.

The I.S.C. (Intensive Studies Center), to be distinguished from the Basic Studies Center of the Lama Foundation, was a five-minute walk away from the large dome and many small houses. It was a semi-circle of rooms built of adobe surrounding a central gathering space. This was to be a center for intensive spiritual work, and all of these rooms were in the process of being built when I arrived.

Sculptor that I was, with the love of clay forever in my hands, I threw myself into the "mudding" to such a degree that I became known as the "holy mudder." Nooruddeen was a focused taskmaster. We worked many hours a day, "no ifs, ands, or buts." It was very helpful training for which I am indebted to him. Having tendencies to space out and dwell on other planes, I learned from him how to live on earth and to work with it.

I was assigned to cell number five in the semicircle and given the task of adobeing that room, as well as others. The other rooms were heated by wood-burning stoves. There was no electricity at Lama. So, when it became cold, especially in the very cold, snowy winters, we greatly appreciated and needed our fires.

With the help of Henry Gomez, the son of the great Native American elder Grandpa Joe Gomez, I built a traditional Southwestern rounded fireplace and spent a great many nights sitting beside it, often in his company. I appreciated very much the purity of sitting with Henry and the subtle way that the Native American tradition he had inherited was transmitted just by sitting in his presence in silence and looking at the fire.

Having sculpted it as I wished, caressed the curves, and brought the sculpture forth, I was happy to live in my adobe cave. Lying in my bed and gazing at the fire under the skylight, through which I could see the star-filled sky, I felt a kind of ancient peace. There were also, I confess, many nights in which I felt lonely, filled with longing. The room I had sculpted was the kind of romantic space — so simple, unadorned, and of the earth itself — that I would have loved to share it with "my beloved." But where on earth, was he?

Such was the test of solitude, a desert I traversed for years upon years. However, although it was difficult to cross alone, the desert was not arid and barren but filled with gems and treasures — the treasures of awakening to the knowledge of being and the jewels of gratitude for exactly what God, in His mercy, had given me to live through on the journey leading to Him. For, once our life becomes consecrated to Him, if He wills for us extended solitude, the treasures of His love can be found within that, and if He wills for us marriage, the treasures of His love can be found within that. Everything unfolds in precise accordance with His merciful Decree.

Although I passed, in my adobe cave, some lonely nights, it must be remembered that we were living in cells for the purpose of intensive study. It was not a romantic vacation. We were in a school, to learn how to focus, how to become disciplined, how to work. I see now that the real goal of our study was to come to know, to understand, and experience the great, multifaceted treasure that we had found in the Holy Land and brought back with us — the way of Islam. The words of Shaykh Nooruddeen (ra) that introduce this chapter are precious to me because they express what I was experiencing. When I say I was embraced by Islam, it was through visions, experiences and transmissions like the awe and clarity and certainty in which the light of Islam was transmitted into his heart and soul simply as he beheld his landlord and son performing the salat. This, as we came to understand it, was the completion of the way of life and worship transmitted by all the Prophets and Messengers (as) throughout time. This was what I felt in the garden in Iran where I beheld the family praying and in the blessed zawiyyah of Sheikh Abdul Muttalib (ra). That I was guided with Nooruddeen and Noura and our small circle of companions to the Holy Land, there to embrace Islam, then back to New Mexico to plant the seeds in our hearts and souls in that soil was the precious gift of Allah *subhana wa ta' ala* that we forever share.

Surrounded by the individual cells, the central area of the Intensive Studies Center was the place where we all gathered. It was constructed of wood and adobe, like all the buildings at Lama. On one side of the building was the kitchen and table where we ate, and on the other side was the place where we prayed.

So, as God willed it, Nooruddeen, Noura and I, who had memorized *Surat'ul-Fatihah* (the opening chapter of the Qur'an) at the same time while walking on the Mount of Olives, now grew in our love and understanding of Islam in this humble, rustic, hand-built mosque. Thus, does the light of true Islam, the way of God transmitted by all His Prophets (as), spread from the Source of knowledge to open spaces — open hearts — in which the seeds of knowledge, can, by God's will, germinate and bear fruit.

It was very appropriate for true Islam, that peace which comes with submission and surrender to the will of God, being the natural state (al-fitrah), to grow within us in the midst of nature. I sensed within our tiny congregation and with our very initial efforts the purity of the first mosque built by the Prophet Muhammad (saw) and his companions (ra) in Medina. It was the purity of the love of the truth of God, the beauty of the revelation, as it was being born within us.

It was like that in those days and nights at the Intensive Studies Center, fires burning in the middle of the brilliant cold winter, the men in their row and the women in their row, pressed together, shoulder to shoulder on the large *kilim* prayer rug upon which we all prayed, with the love of the community, the love of the Way that was dawning within us, an even greater source of warmth.

I remember this time with great fondness and nostalgia because the Islam we were discovering was independent of any political or worldly context. There was no cultural or political overlay. We had been searching for the Way, the path of truth, for union with the Divine. Our Creator had answered our yearnings and supplications by revealing to us the Way that all the Prophets (as) had followed, each in his own time, in accordance with that time. How does the light of truth travel, but as God wills, from open heart to open heart? As Sheikh Bawa Muhaiyaddeen (ra), whom I was soon to meet, would later explain:

> *Faith alone can capture another heart. Faith alone can rule the world. The qualities of God that exist within the heart of one with determined faith must reach out, enter the heart of another, and give him comfort and peace. It is seeing God's compassion, His equality, His tranquility, His integrity, His honesty, and the manner in which He embraces and protects all lives with equal justice, which can bring a person to the state of harmony and compel him to bow in unity. It is these qualities that can conquer people and nations. They begin by capturing the hearts of a few, then they reach out to all those in the village, then the city, and eventually these qualities reach out to the entire population of the country.*

That faith had been transmitted to our hearts in the Holy Land. We were traveling in the current of the divine transmission. As it had been decreed for us to receive the seed of Islam in Jerusalem, so it was decreed that we continue the journey, guided to different places of training in which the seed was to be cultivated. Nooruddeen and Noura were guided to Mecca, where they were to live for several years. Upon returning to America, they formed communities of sincere seekers both in New Mexico and in Virginia. They were and remain to be beacons of light spreading the eternal Grace of Islam, while writing and sharing with the world many illuminating books of the transcendent teachings, including a beautifully clear translation of the Holy Qur'an, which I, as well as so many others around the world have greatly benefited from.

∽

May I acknowledge, with deep respect, the passing of our beloved companion on the sacred journey, Shaykh 'Abdullah Nooruddeen Durkee (ra) who returned to Allah (swt) on October 8, 2020, *inna lillahi wa inna ilaihi yarjiun* (to Allah do we belong and to Him do we return), Alhamdulillah. He has imparted to us a living legacy of profound love for Allah (swt), wisdom and deeply dedicated service.

∽

As for my unfolding journey, in order to fertilize and cultivate the soil in the garden of the heart, thus enabling the pure seed of faith to grow, I was guided to Sheikh Muhammad Rahim Bawa Muhaiyaddeen (ra), in whose company I was blessed to live for several years, until he passed from the world in 1986. And I have been blessed to be guided by the living truth of his legacy ever after.

CHAPTER FOURTEEN

ARRIVAL IN THE PRESENCE OF THE AWAKENED ONE

PHILADELPHIA, 1979-1986

Allah is the One who creates, protects and sustains. He is the one treasure for all of creation: for the earth, the sky, the sun, the moon, the body and the soul. He is the one treasure for life, for love and for goodness. He knows the needs of every life and feeds it accordingly. He is the supreme power who gives the milk of grace to all lives. That power called Allah is an ocean of grace that never diminishes, no matter how much is taken from it. He is an ocean of bliss, wisdom, love and compassion. He is an ocean of divine knowledge, or 'ilm, from which each life can take whatever it needs for the freedom of its soul in all three worlds: the primal beginning, or awwal, this world of earth, or dunya, and the hereafter, or akhirah.

—Sheikh Bawa Muhaiyaddeen (ra),
A Mystical Journey

During the week or so I had spent at Lama before going to Jerusalem, an enigmatic, impassioned, determined person turned up on Lama Mountain. He was a man with a mission. His name was Ahamad Muhaiyaddeen (Jonathon Granoff), and he was inspired with great fervor to speak to me about his teacher, Sheikh Bawa Muhaiyaddeen (ra). Before he left, he gave me a book by his Sheikh (ra).

I carried the book with me from that moment on, along with the knowledge that such a person, an ancient sage, was living in Philadelphia and transmitting to the people there, teachings of great value. Thus, I became aware deeply within my heart that there was an ancient Sufi Master living in Philadelphia and that one day I would meet him.

It is interesting to note that in later years, Ahamad Muhayadeen told me that he had arrived at a gathering at the Naropa Institute in Colorado to deliver a message from Bawa Muhaiyadeen to Trungpa Rinpoche, the teacher at that gathering, well known at that time for his book entitled *Cutting Through Spiritual Materialism*. I had arrived at this gathering in the mountains of Colorado to share a course in these teachings with my friends from Berkeley: Ram Dass, Bhagavan Das and Krishna Das, etc. after returning from India and life in the monasteries.

I was only there for a few days but felt quite out of place in a world in which almost everything was permitted as long as you did it while *cutting through spiritual materialism*. Although it was good to see my old friends, I did not really feel comfortable there and did not know what I was doing there. Now, so many years later, I have come to understand exactly what I was doing there, when Ahamad Muhaiyadeen told me that he saw me there and knew that he had to bring me back to Bawa Muhaiyadeen (ra).

When I left to go to Lama Foundation in the mountains of New Mexico, he asked someone where I had gone, and then he hitchhiked in the back of a pickup truck from the mountains of Colorado to the mountains of New Mexico to place in my hands Bawa's book and transmit the call to bring me to the Sheikh (ra). In this way, Bawa (ra) called me to join with him in his mission. And, it is important to note also that Jonathon Granoff, my spiritual brother and friend on the sacred journey, is now the head of Global Security Institute, working tirelessly for world peace.

In 1979, the Jerusalem book, *Jerusalem, A Garden in the Flames*, had evolved to such a degree that we thought it could be submitted to a publisher. While Nooruddeen and Noura had left the project and gone to live in Mecca, I continued to work on it with a small group of people in Santa Fe, and now I was going to take the fruits of our labor of love to the East Coast to begin looking for a publisher.

From a Sufi teacher named Reshad Field with whom I had spent a little time in New Mexico, I received some names of people of the path that it would be good to see on the East Coast. One of them was Abdul Azziz Sayyid, a Professor at American University in Washington, DC. I called his office and went to see him as soon as I arrived in Washington. There was a couple sitting in his office at the same time as I was — Walter and Vicky, who lived in Philadelphia. Walter was a Sufi student of Professor Sayyid. I mentioned that I had heard about a Sufi Master living in Philadelphia and would like to meet him. I hoped to interview him for the book on Jerusalem before going to the publishers. They kindly invited me to stay with them while I was in Philadelphia. Walter, it turned out, was the connection between Bawa (ra) and Professor Sayyid. Bawa (ra), at this time, was writing letters to President Jimmy Carter. Walter would pick up the letters and deliver them to Professor Sayyid, who would pass them to the President.

We went to Philadelphia, and Walter took me to the Fellowship. While I was sitting in the meeting room downstairs in the Fellowship house, waiting to meet Bawa (ra) in his room upstairs, many Fellow-ship members greeted me. I mentioned that I was working on a book on Jerusalem and would like to interview Bawa (ra). Because of this, I was treated *temporarily* like a "media person," someone who was coming specifically to interview Bawa (ra).

Then I was led up to Bawa's (ra) room. He was seated on his bed. He was a very ancient man but with a very young, beautiful, eternal face. Though he was physically very small and very humble, his pres-ence was great with the light of purity and wisdom. Bawa (ra) was speaking in the Tamil language, and his words were being translated into English. While I did not know Tamil, his words affected me di-rectly and intensely.

He did not treat me like a media person at all. That mask was quickly discarded. He addressed other aspects of my identity — *who* I thought I was and what I thought I was doing with my life and jour-ney. Very quickly he penetrated many veils and left me nowhere to stand comfortably or sit. Thus, did he reveal to me, behind the romantic veil, which was stripped away, the deep, hard, fundamental work of which the real spiritual path consisted.

Bawa (ra) looked, not at me but through me, with the laser beam of divine wisdom. He was not politely engaging various aspects of who I thought I was but powerfully penetrating veils, discarding whatever could be released, and showing the way to the goal: "*La ilaha ill'Allah.*" The *dhikr*, "*La ilaha ill'Allah*," was the powerful medicine and tool of transformation. The way that we become liberated from all our illusions and all the negative qualities we have been often unconsciously sustain-ing within ourselves is by contemplating, with the breath, that only Allah *subhana wa ta' ala* truly exists.

The Sheikh (ra) spoke for a long time and said many things about my life and journey. One sentence that I remember is, "You have read many books, but you cannot cook a paper squash." This statement led me to wonder what real squash he was referring to and what *real squash* he was, even now, giving me to eat.

I was overwhelmed by the intensity of this encounter. It was cer-tainly not that he spoke loudly or forcefully, but his words were deeply penetrating through at least some of the false identities I had been at-tached to. For the next several days, I could barely speak or move. It was like the tip of the sword of *al-Haqq*, the Truth, was pressed into my heart and I was paralyzed, awaiting the Grace of God to resurrect me in the next dimension or phase of my journey. There being no reality but the Reality that is God, I was in the process of comprehending that my existence and the continuation of my journey were totally contingent upon the Reality, which is God.

I was wearing a long maroon skirt and shawl at that first meeting. I was so much stopped in my tracks by the reality of meeting with the Master and the profound challenge that was being posed that I was unable to do the simplest things such as change my clothes. So, I wore those same clothes, day after day. I was staying at Walter and Vicky's. He would drop me at the Fellowship, and I would remain there for the day, simply waiting for the words of the ancient sage that would guide me to the next step.

On about the third day, in the middle of a discourse, Bawa (ra) said, "You are like a person who has worn the same clothes for three days." I was shocked into awakening by the words. He was not looking directly at me, but suddenly I realized my condition and felt certain that he was speaking to me.

Then he said something so extremely helpful that I have never forgotten it but have understood its application to so many situations in my life and in the lives of others: "You need to put these clothes in the washing machine and wash them." From this teaching, I understood that I (relating to the soul within) was not dirty; only my clothes were dirty. All I had to do was to remove them and wash them. It was like that also with the veils, which were covering over my soul. They too could be removed. The soul was pure.

I came to see many times later in life how often I, and others, become attached to negative energies such as guilt, regret, unworthiness and other garments and veils that are covering up the purity of the soul as though they are inseparably attached to us and, therefore, if they are dirty, so, inevitably, are we.

But what Bawa (ra) revealed to me at that moment, which I often remember and sometimes unfortunately seem to forget, is that all of these "clothes" can be taken off and cleaned. Only the soul is eternal, the essence of reality, and that cannot be "taken off." As soon as I understood this, I was able to let go of my attachment to who I thought I was and begin to tune into the pure and powerful transmission that was coming through the awakened Sheikh (ra).

Within the first few weeks of meeting Bawa (ra), I had three powerful dreams. The first was the dream of *the emerald child*. In this dream I found myself surrounded by children at a fair in the yard of the Fellowship. They led me to a big field full of flowers. In the middle of the field was a large bed with a baby sitting on it. The baby was sitting in an erect posture. His skin was translucent, and he was composed of emerald light. All of the organs and inner workings of his body were visible, light within light.

People were saying the baby had no parents. It was clear that he was a most unusual, beautiful child. From the distance, he saw me and bowed to me, and I bowed to him. When I approached him, he was somehow drawn to my heart. He came into my arms then entered my body and disappeared into my heart.

The next day, when I gave the Sheikh (ra) salaams, I remembered the dream and felt the presence of the emerald child within me. I told him about it. Bawa Muhaiyaddeen (ra) said:

> Whoever can raise that child with love is the one who must raise him. All the other children you saw are children who have parents, but that child that you saw, from that time until today, is an orphan. For the person that can bring up that child, hell and the difficulties of life will be very, very far away. To be able to rear that orphan child, you need to show lots and lots of love. You must take care of him like your own life. If you nurture him like that, that child will grow. Otherwise, he will leave and go to play with the other children.

> The other children that you saw playing in the yard are children, no doubt, but this wonderful child, is the gift of God. Whoever raises this child in this world, in the world of souls, and in the kingdom of God, will have happiness. They will see the victory of their lives and hell will be very, very far away. God's grace, God's light, and God's blessings will be with them. If you can bring up this child properly, if you can keep it where it has to be kept, and then rear it, that will be very, very good.

My second dream was the dream of the mosque of Mankumban. In the dream I entered into a building, a holy space that was vast and empty, filled with awe and wonder. There was a great silence, but also an intense battle was going on invisibly. All the molecules in the air were charged.

The power was so intense it took a great effort to walk from one side to the other of that building. You had to be deeply immersed in the state of remembrance to access the strength to make the journey. I entered the sanctified space and made salat. Some people came to me and asked if I would teach them how to make *salat*. I said, "The *waqt* (allotted time) is over; we will meet at the next *waqt*." Then, I began to walk through the mosque. It was a very demanding journey just to get across the vast room.

Along the way, I passed by some people who were speaking about *dhikr*. Although a few people were there, there was a great sense of emptiness in the mosque and also fullness in regard to the unseen realms. I came to a stairway and began to ascend. It required great energy to take each step. When I approached the top, I saw a very tall, very beautiful woman, veiled in light, standing and making *salat* at the top of the stairs. She was a powerful presence, completely cloaked in light in a very majestic way. Sheikh Bawa Muhaiyaddeen (ra) explained to me, "*This is a real secret, a real mystery. That is Maryam (Mother of Jesus).*"

I had sensed that the majestic, luminous woman I saw praying at the top of the stairs was her, and Bawa (ra) confirmed this mystical awareness. He then went on to speak about his deep relationship with her and the building of God's House, the mosque he built by the ocean in Jaffna with the help of many of his disciples from America. This mosque is, as I had seen in my dream, a place of great power, mysticism, and light. I was very blessed to have visited it in my dreams, and later to go there and pray in that radiant space in waking life. It was, as Bawa continued to describe it, in response to the dream I had just shared with him:

> *Within that mosque there are so many spiritual beings who are protecting it. All the Prophets and Awliya (friends) of God are there. The person you saw praying and another person are always there praying in that mosque. Although it is a small mosque, it contains many, many secrets. In two and a half months we completed the work that should have taken two and*

*a half years. That lady you saw praying — that is Maryam. It
is the eleventh place for the Qutb (the pole) to rest. You visited
that place. So therefore, there is some connection for you also
there. It is because of that connection that you have come here.
You have had that search and you have had that connection
and that is why God has brought you here.*

Sheikh Bawa Muhaiyaddeen (ra)

My third dream was the dream of the man of light in the mirror. In this
one, I was in Jerusalem in the tunnel which goes beneath the Haram
Ash-Sharif. There is a stream which flows there called Silhuane. The
Prophet Jesus (as), it is said, healed people there. In the dream, there
were people sitting in wheelchairs who needed to be healed. It appeared
that the spirit of Issa (as) stood up (within me) and began to move quickly and powerfully down the tunnel alongside the stream. A white shawl
dropped into my hand. I put it on my head and looked into a mirror that
suddenly appeared. I saw the face of Christ looking back, his beautiful,
glowing eyes shining through. His face appeared in place of mine and I
looked deeply into his gaze.

Some of the people of Jerusalem, in biblical dress, walked by. I looked
away from the mirror so they wouldn't see his face in the mirror, feeling
it might be too much for them to bear. They left and I looked back into
the mirror. After some time, the man of light continued to move down
the tunnel. He returned to the healing spring. Two men were attempting
to urinate into it. He said, "This is the pure spring. You should never do
anything like that here." I woke up at four in the morning, with body, heart,
and soul shaking. Sheikh Bawa Muhaiyaddeen (ra) commented:

*Very, very good. The mirror. There is no other mirror. God alone
is the mirror. Only His 'eyes' are the real eyes. We have to have
faith in Him. The water is His rahmat, His benevolence. That
benevolence is the light of the Qutb, which is divine luminous
wisdom. That is the water, which is called the rahmat (mercy)
of God. It is by drinking that pure water, the water of pure rahmat that you can make yourself pure, and through that you can
establish the firm iman of certitude. It is only that water that
can quench the thirst.*

That mirror is the mirror of God, which has no form. What we see in that mirror is Him... If we look in the mirror here, all we see is our own figure, and all that we see in that mirror is like urinating in the purity. Only the rahmat of God can heal. All that we do, saying we are doing it, is impurity. What we do is that we urinate into the purity. We bring the differences of 'I' and 'you,' 'my religion' and 'your religion' and put these things into the places of purity. No one is worthy of worship other than God Most High.

We must go and die in God. That is what you saw. Everything else — and you — all differences are removed. When one goes and falls into it, that is the purity. You must become that light. That is what you saw. All other things are things that make the purity impure, the differences of 'I' and 'you.'

Jerusalem, from the time it came into being until today, has been a battlefield. All the Prophets came to clear this place, which is the central spot, but still it is the battlefield where the Prophets were killed, and people were made to suffer. All this happened in Jerusalem. It is the battlefield, and from then until today, it has been flowing with blood. 'Yeru salam' in Tamil means 'fire-water.' Whoever wants to grab that place, as his own, will get burned. They were all destroyed.

In truth, that place belongs only to God. Peace and equality are there. In Jerusalem, you can (also) find earth, fire, water, air,and ether. The people you saw urinating into the spring are the ones who wish to grab Jerusalem as their own. But you can also find there, the arsh'ul muminun, the throne of the believers, the throne of God.

So, let us clear the Jerusalem that is within us, the place of purity, paradise, heaven. Let us organize this house within us. If we can organize this house within us, that will be good. The other Jerusalem is just burning water.

Bawa's (ra) first name for me was *"Jerusalem Poullai,"* or "Jerusalem Child." He said that I had spent seven years (considerably more than I had actually spent in physical time) in Jerusalem, and it was a very profound experience for me. He himself was engaged in speaking about Jerusalem a great deal, which I was aware of from the time I arrived, but when I asked him about the book we had planned to publish, he said clearly not to publish it.

Imagine, he explained, that we were to take out a full-page ad in a newspaper in which we put passages of the book. We say that we want peace in Jerusalem. We put quotations from the Scriptures and from people of different religions, advocating peace. We put our telephone number at the bottom of the page.

Then, imagine if people called and asked for advice about how to make peace in Jerusalem, we would not be able to tell them how to do it. He then said that instead of publishing the book, I should build Jerusalem, the place of peace, in my heart. He told me, further, that if I could build the holy city within myself, honey would develop there, and then, many bees would come to get that honey.

I understood. I knew that I could not bring peace to the outer Jerusalem but must first bring peace to the inner Jerusalem as he had indicated. I knew that I had no choice but to surrender to this guidance and, God willing, learn from him as much as I could about building the inner place of peace.

After working for many years on the Jerusalem book, I knew I had to simply let it go and then focus upon what the Sheikh (ra) was showing me about the world within: how to get all the money-lenders out of the place of prayer, the place of peace, and how to look into the mirror of God and be healed by the water of His benevolence, rather than urinating into that pure spring.

I knew that I had no choice but to do the inner work that was being demanded and that there could be no real success without real purification. It was as the Qur'an tells us, *"He will be successful who purifies it (the self)"* (The Holy Qur'an 91:10).

But I had not come here prepared to move in, only — I thought — to get an interview with the Ancient Sage. In fact, as the media person that I temporarily appeared to be, I had not had the opportunity to ask him even one of the questions that I had planned to ask. Not knowing that I would have real spiritual work to do in Philadelphia, I had left all of my somewhat humble belongings and a certain amount of unfinished business in New Mexico. I needed to go back and put things in order before I could really settle into the work that had to be done here.

So, I went back for a brief visit, hoping to resolve what remained unresolved, and found in New Mexico that whatever I hoped to find, I would have to climb up through thick snow to get it. I went directly to the Intensive Studies Center and, after being warmly welcomed by some very dear old friends, took refuge in one of the cells. Somehow, I had to regroup, re-establish my inner balance, find the center. I had to ask again, "Who am I? I am not this, nor this, nor this."

For example, I was attached to a style of living and a concept of myself within that style of living. I would never have wished to leave the mountains of New Mexico to go live in a city. But how could I deny the truth that was beckoning me to move forward and choose instead to hide in the mountains or in "the "book," as if these things had any inherent reality, any verification by the Divine.

All the things I had identified with had been real for me and spiritually valid only until I had entered into the presence of the Awakened One of Wisdom who was now directing me towards another goal. He was guiding me through the veils toward the realization of greater and more subtle dimensions of the spiritual path. As always, it was time to let go and move on, but I needed to come back to the mountain in order to let it go.

There, by the fireside, in the middle of the dense snow, I made one final retreat. I made peace with the mountain, made peace with the past, left behind what could be left behind and took with me a small bag of external possessions, and some more internal possessions, which were still coming along with me into the life to come. Then, I made the journey from the mountain of earth to the mountain of spiritual transformation, which Bawa (ra) referred to as Mount Sinai, the mountain, which every spiritual seeker, following the prophetic example, must ascend.

Now, I began to settle into the life of the community, in Philadelphia, but it was not quite a simple, natural fit. Appearing in the Fellowship meeting room in Bedouin clothes, which were still covered with the dust of Jerusalem and New Mexico, I felt like someone from another generation, someone who had been sleeping in a cave for hundreds of years and then woke up one day and walked into the modern world. Even the currency I carried in my pocket was money from a different world.

Although I did not quite fit in to the apparent picture of life at the Fellowship, there was a reason that I had to be there. I had to hear and deeply imbibe the words that came flowing through the mouth of the Sage.

Sheikh Bawa Muhaiyaddeen (ra), although he was very, very old and often in fragile health, at this time in his life, spoke abundantly, morning, noon, and night. He was "unlettered," so the knowledge he transmitted he had not acquired through reading. It was knowledge transmitted to and through the Sheikh (ra) in his profound experience on the path of God.

At various times of the day and night the word would spread throughout the house and community that Bawa (ra) was speaking. Immediately the students came running from wherever they might be and assembled around his bed. The words flooded through him like a current. No one, listening to the discourse, could remember everything that he said. Of the rain of words, which fell upon us, each caught what he or she could catch and understood only what he or she could understand at the time.

Within the flood of the teachings that came pouring through, there were also some that might appear contradictory to others. This ultimately caused some of the students to understand the teaching in a different way than others.

Dusty traveler that I was, having wandered so long in the desert, I stood with arms outstretched in the rain. Listening as one in love with the light and beauty of Islam, I was amazed to hear the inner explanations of so many of the dimensions of Islam. Day and night, the Sheikh (ra) was speaking about the profound and wondrous mysteries and truths of Allah *subhana wa ta'ala* and His Messenger (saw) and the light of the Revelation sent by the Creator through His Messenger (saw).

Yet, it was time to pray, and no one was making salat. I turned to God. What should I do? The message was unequivocal. "This is My House. So you must pray!"

I put down my prayer mat in the Fellowship meeting room and prayed at every time of prayer. I was not aware of it then but have heard since that many people, seeing this sight for the first time, were stunned. They thought that I was simply crazy to think that I could do such a thing in the Fellowship meeting room. But for me it was the simplest action, the fulfillment of my covenant with my Lord. It had nothing to do with anyone else, and so I was unaware until many years later of the response of some people.

Now, as I am writing this, many years after the Sheikh (ra) left this world, a beautiful mosque exists, which was built by his order and explicit direction, a place where many people gather daily to pray, confirming the message I received — "This is My House. So you must pray!" But, at that time, it seemed it was a message that I alone had received.

During my first month at the Fellowship, when all sense of self-importance was being clearly annihilated, and I was permitted only to clean the bathroom if I was lucky enough to have any duty to perform, I saw people walking around with large manila envelopes, which contained discourses that they were working on.

When I saw those envelopes, I realized how much I yearned for the chance to work on a book again. Then I found out that I could volunteer to type discourses. Every time I was given something to type, it happened to be one of the earliest discourses Bawa (ra) had spoken to me, always annihilating my sense of self-importance. That was a very necessary phase.

Then, suddenly, about a month and a half after I had arrived at the Fellowship, the Sheikh (ra) called me into his room. He said that since I knew some Arabic, he would like me to edit a book that he had dictated in the sixties. I had heard from many of the people of the Fellowship that it was a great work.

The Sheikh (ra) told me further that he would soon be going to Sri Lanka and he would like me to go, too, and work on the book with him there. As he placed this book in my hand, entrusting it to me, he said, "Every word has seventy thousand meanings. If you change any one of them, the *blood* will be on your hands." How staggering and impossible a task he had given me!

The transcript I was working on often consisted in many parts of solid text with no paragraph divisions. A whole page could be one sentence, with concepts building upon concepts, made into a sentence only by a small phrase at the bottom of the page. What did these words mean?

I began to read and read. I entered into the text and attempted to decipher it. It was not at all like other books. It could not be grasped with the intellect. It was like an ocean, and one had to dive completely in. It created its own universe, and you had to be within it in order to comprehend its spiritual logic and meaning.

In accordance with the Sheikh's (ra) instruction, I immersed myself in this ocean and began to think with a "new" mind. I continued to swim in it, discovering the pearls within it as God permitted me to, and doing the best I could to edit it, which really meant that I was being *edited by it*, for the next many years.

With this mysterious book in my arms and a foam bed rolled up upon my back, I arrived at the airport in Philadelphia and set off with a small group of people to join the Sheikh (ra) in Sri Lanka. Ready for whatever was to unfold, I was so happy to be back on the road again and going to work with the Sheikh (ra).

CHAPTER FIFTEEN

THE RESONANCE OF ALLAH,

THE EVER-DEEPENING EXPERIENCE OF PRAYER

COLOMBO, SRI LANKA AND PHILADELPHIA, 1980-1982

*My children, if the truth contained in the resplendent expla-
nations that come from God's grace could be made clear and
printed in books, and if you wanted to understand it, you
would need the wisdom of the resplendent Qutb which is God's
grace. My brethren who have been born with me, it is with that
wisdom that you should delve into these books in order to learn
and understand what is contained within them.*

—Sheikh Bawa Muhaiyaddeen (ra)

Arriving in Sri Lanka, I was picked up at the airport by Doctor G., the translator with whom I would be working on the book. The first thing he said was, "Bawa has been waiting for you so we can get started on the work." What a wonder, I felt, that such a person would be waiting for me! Now, this work was going to take place in Sri Lanka, an island beneath the lower tip of India. In the past, this island had been called Serendip, and Bawa named the community he had formed here the *Serendip Sufi Study Circle.*

The island of Sri Lanka is, like every part of the holy creation of God, blessed with unique mysteries. One of these undoubted wonders is the majestic mountain called *Adam's Peak.* It is venerated, by Christians and Muslims, who believe that this is the place where Prophet Adam (as) first set his foot on the earth, as well as by Buddhists, who believe that the footprint of the Buddha is imbedded on the mountain peak. The mountain is a place of pilgrimage and the small island, a place of peace and refuge for many, as I found that it was for me, as soon as I set foot upon the blessed land.

We left the airport and began to drive through a relatively undeveloped expanse of light-filled jungles. I sensed the presence of the ocean, although I could not see it. The air was warm, soft, and welcoming. Once again, I felt that my consciousness was being rearranged. I was so happy to have arrived and, as we drove along, I tuned into the land, the light and the energy of Sri Lanka as well as the joy of arriving at the next stage of my journey, a profound joy, I came to discover, which arises from working closely with the Sheikh (ra).

One of the miracles of traveling across the earth in the way of God is that one becomes a witness to the miraculous artistry of the Creator as it manifests in His creation in such wondrous diversity.

It is amazing to behold His vision that manifests before us: that He willed there to be jungles, deserts, mountains, oceans, all kinds of climate, all kinds of animals, all the colors and kinds of flowers, and all the colors and shapes of human beings which arose in the context of all of the different climates He created in which human beings were to live.

We learn as we travel that we do not belong only to the small piece of earth where we were born. For that piece of the earth is connected to the piece next to it and that piece to the one next to it. As you see more and more of the pieces, you experience more and more profoundly that the earth is one. It is round, not flat, and when you come to the edge of the country you call your own, you do not fall off. All national frontiers and borders are artificial, not inherent.

Every life we encounter as we travel through the lands is a mirror in which we see our own life reflected. I took my father's early advice, about which he so often sang, literally, and journeyed to so many different points on the map, everywhere finding only human beings just like me! No matter what the color of their skin, what their language, nationality, or culture, I see all the living beings I am blessed to meet as I travel as my brothers and sisters, members of my own family, all children of Adam (as), the *family of man*. For our Creator has not revealed to us any divisions that should be acknowledged between the children of Adam (as), except for in their states of the awareness of the Divine. He has told us that He made the creations diverse intentionally, and no creation is superior to another except in regard to their degree of *taqwa* (consciousness of Him).

Therefore, when arriving in a place I have never been, I do not consider it a foreign land but the next dimension of His creation that the Creator is unveiling to me.

And now, it was the island of Sri Lanka, to which I had been invited by the wondrous Guide Bawa Muhaiyaddeen (ra), which was the next dimension for my soul to discover. As Allah says in the Holy Qur'an, *"Every moment, We manifest a new creation"* (55:29). Whenever you arrive in a new place in this state of mind, you too are *new*. You are ready for the next dimension of your own unfolding, ready to see what you can see and to learn what you can learn. This is especially true when you are working with Sheikh Bawa Muhaiyaddeen (ra).

I felt the soft tropical jungle air wafting through the car window, sweet air filled with peace and blessings, as we drove through the gentle lands en route to Colombo and the house of Dr. Ajwad and Amin Macan-Markar, where Bawa (ra) was staying with the disciples.

As I was working on this chapter many years later at the end of 2004, we had just witnessed in the news the beautiful island of Sri Lanka and its people covered by a tsunami, a devastating tidal wave. We were all stunned by what took place. Much of humanity was profoundly moved and united, at that moment, in a common concern. As saddening as this was to behold, it was inspiring to see people uniting in charity and prayer, inspired by compassion for those members of our human family who, on that day, were taken back to their Lord and those who remained on earth, the survivors after the flood.

We have learned from all the Scriptures and the great teachers that natural disasters such as these earthquakes and floods are a warning and a call for humanity to return to the Way of Truth. Have we not learned from the story of Noah (as) to listen to the message and follow the directions of our Lord before the deluge covers the earth, before death, in whatever way it is destined to come, overtakes us? How can we truly respond to the immense magnitude of the events shaking the earth, challenging in so many places and ways our hopes that life on this earth has any kind of lasting stability or permanence?

I know that the beautiful earth that Allah *subhana wa ta'ala* showed me in Sri Lanka will never exist in exactly the same way again. Nor will the beautiful lands and cultures of Afghanistan or Kashmir or Tibet or Syria or Yemen ever exist exactly as they did before each was tried, invaded or possessed and inevitably changed.

We are witnessing the transformation of our world, before our eyes and before the eyes of our heart and the eyes of our soul. As the signs continue to unfold, we see that the whole earth is in radical transition, and the only place whose beauty, safety, and peace are our certain refuge, not subject to devastation and destruction, is the land of God, the Divine Presence, and that is where our real journey must lead.

We need to receive the guidance of the Prophets (as) and the saints (ra), that is — the guidance of Allah (swt) — in order to learn how truly to prepare, how to die before death, how to cut our attachment to the destructible, perishable, illusory aspects of our being, before destruction

and death strike us. I knew that it was for the development of this training, and not for a holiday in an earthly paradise, that I had come to the
island of Sri Lanka.

We arrived at night. Bawa (ra) was sitting on his bed awaiting us. I
felt as if I was meeting him for the first time and also that I had known
him forever. Bawa (ra) often addressed his disciples, "Jeweled Lights of
my eyes, you who were born with me," confirming for me the sense that
I had been with him forever.

In Philadelphia, there had always been so many people and so
much of the institution present that I was only able to see Bawa (ra) from
time to time, and there was a certain formality about our meetings. But
in Sri Lanka, at this time, there were only a handful of Americans, and I
had come here to work directly with the Sheikh (ra) at his request. This
kind of close interaction of the spiritual seeker with the Sheikh has an
especially transformative impact, as Bawa (ra) describes:

> There is a power in the face, in the beauty, and in the words of the
> Sheikh. That power, Allah's Qudrat , and His Light, will fall in front of
> the Sheikh. When that falls, and if you are in the front row when you
> are reciting the dhikr with that yearning and that tenderness, then
> that light will also fall on you. When it falls on you, some of what is in
> your qalb will be burnt away. Some of your illnesses and your diseases
> will be burnt away. If the Sheikh is a true Insan Kamil, and if you look
> into his face as you are doing the dhikr, then the light in his face, the
> rahmah that is Allah's grace, will shower upon you as it falls from him.
> If it does, then it will cure you of your illnesses and your diseases. It
> will remove your difficulties. Because of that, some of your darknesses
> will be removed. Therefore, when you are with a Sheikh, those of you
> who have that love, must make an effort to come to the front. Accord-
> ing to your effort, you will receive the benefit and the gain.

So, from the very moment I arrived in his room, there was a kind of
intensity, a sense that the corn kernels, which had been sitting in heated
oil, were about to pop.

The next morning, I was sitting on the floor in Bawa's room, when
the call to prayer for *fajr*, the early morning prayer, echoed from the

nearby minarets. At the Fellowship in Philadelphia, when I prayed, I was downstairs in the meeting room, while Bawa was upstairs in his room. At that time, I was not in a relationship with him in which I could ask him if I should pray. I had to have the courage to make that decision apparently "on my own."

Now, in Sri Lanka, I was sitting in his room, in his presence, looking at him, while listening to the call to prayer. I believe I said nothing out loud but asked him internally what I should do. He said to me, "Yes, of course, you should pray. Amina Hannum will show you the direction to turn, and others will follow you."

I was guided in the right direction, did my prayers outside Bawa's room on the second floor of the house, and, as he said, people started gathering behind me. Through the love of Islam and dedication to its practice that the Creator had instilled in me, I was thus used as an instrument to activate this practice in the community of Sheikh Bawa Muhaiyaddeen (ra). That was an honor and blessing. But for me, truly, it was simply the most natural thing to do — perform the prayer when it was time to pray! Of course, as a woman, I could not be the formal *imam* of the ritual prayer. I was simply performing the prayer and then joined by others; an *imam* was needed.

In addition to Amina Hannum, who was an elderly woman and the wife of one of Bawa's (ra) translators, I noticed someone else praying in the corner of the living room. He was one of Bawa's (ra) children who had been with him for a long time. He seemed to be very close to Bawa (ra) and was always sitting at his feet, making talismans for people at the Sheikh's (ra) request and doing other kinds of prayers and blessings as Bawa (ra) directed him. He spent many hours doing this work and seemed to be intensely focused, without distraction on accomplishing these tasks, as the Sheikh (ra) was asking him to do. He generally wore a white sarong and a white shirt. He seemed unusually untouched by worldly influences. His name was Seyed Ahamad Kabeer, and he was often called Ahamad Kabeer or just Kabeer.

After some weeks, I mentioned to Bawa (ra) that I had noticed Ahamad Kabeer praying. Could he not take over the duty of *imam*? Bawa (ra) called Ahamad Kabeer in and asked him to do this. He resisted at first but finally surrendered and became the *imam* of our tiny burgeoning congregation.

It is important to mention here a little more about the history of Ahamad Kabeer with Sheikh Bawa Muhaiyaddeen (ra) to get a better sense of how he came to be so close to Bawa and engaged in so deeply serving the Sheikh (ra). He was from a lineage of blessed spiritual teachers and came from several generations of bards of spiritual litanies. He also was an heir of the family of the Prophet Muhammad (saw).

He went to Sri Lanka as a teenager to find work. While working as a pearl diver, he became a part of a group who went to visit Spiritual Masters. With them he went to visit Bawa Muhaiyaddeen (ra). Kabeer would visit often, and his visits kept increasing. Bawa then told him that he should stay and live in the Ashram where other spiritual seekers resided under the Sheikh's guidance.

Also, as the Sheikh (ra) was travelling extensively between communities of disciples in different regions, he asked Ahamad Kabeer to travel with him on these trips. On these long trips, Bawa (ra) would ask him, "Kabeer, are you sleeping? Let's sing instead." And they brought copies of books of "Gnana Oli Malai" (A Radiant Garland of Divine Wisdom) and other songs by Bawa that had been written down earlier, which they sang together throughout the long journeys. In this way did Ahamad Kabeer become the heir of the living legacy of Bawa's songs and the grace and wisdom and beauty that they contained.

He was also trained extensively in many other profound spiritual practices transmitted in the direct presence of the Sheikh (ra), as Allah *subhana wa ta'ala* had ordained. I later learned that Ahamad Kabeer spent much time learning from the Sheikh (ra) while praying and singing with him in caves. Contemplating this vision of their shared journeys singing together through the realms and meditating together in caves gives us a little idea of why and how Kabeer was always sitting so close to Bawa's bed and became the instrument of the Sheikh's (ra) transformative teaching in many ways. Of course, there are so many mysteries in this that we may feel but do not really comprehend.

At a certain point, now in Sri Lanka in the 1980's, both Ahamad Kabeer and I went to India, he to visit his family, and I, along with some other disciples, to renew my visa. After we left, Bawa (ra) scolded the men and implored them to learn how to lead the prayers. Several of the brothers then learned, and when we came back, everything was put into balance in the correct configuration, and thus the mysteries of the prayer continued to unfold.

Bawa (ra) asked me to teach classes about prayer. Many more people from America had come, and Bawa (ra) wanted the knowledge to be shared.

This was a challenge, because in order to share the information, it was necessary to face and, hopefully, help to transform the resistance that many people had been developing all their lives against their conception of Islam and its practices.

For the first seven years of his mission in America, Sheikh Bawa Muhaiyaddeen (ra) transmitted the very essence of the remembrance of God through the *kalimah: La ilaha ill'Allah*. From the time he came to America in 1972, he had been transmitting to his disciples the awareness of perpetual prayer, exhorting them to focus on the *dhikr* (zikr) with the breath so they might abide in the state of remembrance, prostration, and submission with every breath. He was teaching the disciples to breathe out all falsehood and illusion on the outbreath and breathe in the light and grace of God.

There were several years in the mission of the Holy Prophet (saw) also before the actions of the *salat* were revealed and taught, transmitted as the practice of salat was, on the Night of his Heavenly Ascension (Al Mi'raj). Following the prophetic model, Bawa (ra) now introduced the *salat*, the formal Islamic prayer, to his disciples. He also began to transmit and explain the significance of the other obligatory duties *(furud)* and other dimensions of Islam. Those years in Sri Lanka, the last years of Bawa's (ra) life there, were filled with the transmission and explanation of the inner and outer meanings of the way of Islam and the multi-dimensional practices of prayer.

Our days and nights were filled with prayer and instruction. We usually had three two-to-three-hour sessions of *dhikr* a day, the last one from eleven at night to two in the morning. Then, we would awaken a few hours later for awwal-fajr (pre-dawn) and fajr (dawn) prayers and get ready for the next day of prayer and teaching about prayer. Sitting directly in front of or next to the Sheikh, we were truly engaged in a course of intensive studies with the Sheikh (ra), the goal of which was to make every dimension of prayer as vitally alive as possible.

There were many of Bawa's (ra) children who were surprised by this course of events, by the way in which Bawa (ra) was now teaching specifically in regard to the integration of the practices of Islam. Yet, what I came to understand, as I listened deeply, is that what he had been teaching from the beginning was the essence of the path of pure Islam.

He spoke about this in the context of the evolution of the human being *(insan)*, explaining that all religions existed at different levels within the body of the human being, and Islam, or the Criterion *(furqan)*, was at the level of the head, the crown.

When Bawa (ra) returned to America in 1982, this deep teaching about prayer and the practices of Islam led directly to the building of a mosque behind the Fellowship house in Philadelphia, a mosque of light whose building he overlooked and supervised down to the last detail.

Bawa (ra) taught extensively on so many different levels, no one could grasp or summarize the depth and extent and significance of his teaching. Some of the things he said seemed contradictory to others. As a result, there is a diversity of understandings among those who followed him. What I am reporting is based upon exactly what I saw and experienced. Coming to the Sheikh (ra) as a devoted Muslim, my experience and practice of Islam was very much deepened and strengthened by the teachings I received through him. Bawa (ra) provided insight into the heart of Islamic practices through explanations like this:

> *Allah says: My children, please think about this. Come forward and perform the prayer. I have given this message to every Prophet. Faith, the Kalimah, iman (faith), salams (greetings of peace), salah (prayer) , sadaqa (charity), nombu (fasting), and hajj (pilgrimage) are for you to correct your qualities. The salah (prayer) is for bringing about unity, affection, and one love. When all of you join together and pray as one congregation, there will be no battles, enmity, divisions, wars, or fighting. When you live as one brotherhood, as the children of one Father and Mother, you will create peace. Peace and tranquility are Islam.*
>
> Sheikh Bawa Muhaiyaddeen (ra),
> *Prayer*

Others among his disciples did not seem to hear what I heard. Not all of Bawa's (ra) disciples embraced Islam. He spoke to each in accordance with the level and capacity of that person's faith, understanding, and wisdom.

While people of all religions, and even, no religion, were powerfully drawn to him, to the light of wisdom that was manifesting through him, he did not build a temple, a synagogue, or a church. By the decree of Allah *subhana wa ta'ala*, he left as one of his great legacies a mosque, which is truly an inheritance and pure transmission of light.

Through the *kalimah*, he transmitted the wisdom that, filtering and filtering, led us to the Source of purity. And every aspect of the obligations *(furud)* of the practice of Islam was explained in the context of the fundamental role of the *kalimah* to absolutely transform the consciousness of the sincere worshipper.

Thus did the holy seeds of Islam, which had been planted by the grace of Allah *subhana wa ta'ala* within the garden of grace within me, continue to be nurtured by the blessed Hand of the Master of all the worlds, as He intended and decreed.

I worked continuously throughout this time in Sri Lanka and altogether for a period of many years in America, as well, on Bawa's (ra) book, *The Resonance of Allah*. This was the powerful transmission and esoteric explanation of many dimensions of prayer, the true state of the human being, and the soul's journey to God. In this deep treatise, words regularly understood in Islam in a simple, direct way such as *shariat*, *ilm*, and *iman* were presented as multi-dimensional mystical realities, containing meanings within meanings.

With a translator I sat with Bawa (ra) for many hours each day penetrating very deeply into the words and teachings embedded in this amazing text that no one could truly understand as did the Sheikh (ra). It was a great blessing to be able to explore these deep meanings, in order to translate them as accurately as possible, with the Sheikh's guidance, in his exalted presence.

Doors of understanding and experience were opened for me by being in close proximity with the Sheikh (ra) day and night and committed to fulfilling the work he had asked us to do. Day after day, we were able to ask many questions about the book and its treasury of meanings, so I received much knowledge and understanding directly. The extensive sharing of questions and answers, filled with blessings, ultimately became the footnotes of *The Resonance of Allah* when it was printed.

This dialogue with the Sheikh (ra) did not only continue throughout the day; very often I continued to ask him questions and receive explanations while I slept. People told me that I would often sit bolt upright on my sleeping bag and say, *"Alhamdulillah!"* and have a lively, lengthy discussion with the Sheikh (ra) in my sleep. This was a sign of the depth of the engagement of my psyche or soul in the dialogue with the Sheikh (ra) on the project.

I once had a dream that I discovered all the chapters of the book separated and out of order, on yellowed pages, tied up in packages in a dark, dusty attic. I was deeply troubled to see this great book in such disarray. Then a powerful, clear voice spoke to me and said, "Do not worry. This book has already been encoded in your DNA."

Bawa (ra) told me on more than one occasion that the reward for the selfless effort I had put into this work would be given in the hereafter, not in this world. I have come to realize again and again that no valuable gift is given to a seeker in the way of God that is not also a test and purification and, through this, an elevation.

Having received the blessing of working so intensively on this project with the Sheikh (ra) while he was alive, I had to give it up completely after he left this world. After Bawa (ra) passed, there was a complete restructuring of the project in which I and others who had been working on it for many years were replaced by others.

After the book was published, a small film was also produced about the process of accomplishing it. My involvement was never acknowledged in any way. This was a blessing for me. I came to understand more and more clearly what Bawa (ra) had been telling me. Whatever had taken place in the process of my working on this project, whatever part of my service to this work was pure and good, the reward was not to be found in this world but solely in the world to come.

When we realize that the reason Allah *subhana wa ta'ala* created us is most importantly that we may worship and serve Him, we must cut away all thoughts and intentions that have been grafted onto the original intention and thus dispel within our consciousness the illusion that we are here to get our reward in this world. This is what I came to understand and experience from what Bawa (ra) told me and from all that I went through attempting to fulfill the assignment he had given me.

Another situation arose during the time spent with Bawa (ra) in Sri Lanka that, like everything else on the path to God, was a lesson and a test. From the beginning, through the prayer, Ahamad Kabeer and I were connected. What touched me about Kabeer, was his piety, his simplicity, and his devotion to the Sheikh (ra). This was the wealth and knowledge that he had, no worldly wealth.

He once showed me a trunk in which he had all his treasures. He had saved every small gift, down to the tissues, given to him by the disciples of Bawa (ra) visiting Sri Lanka. I was touched by his unspoiled attitude. During this period of his life, at Bawa (ra)'s request, he had stopped doing any work in the world so he could focus entirely on his service to the Sheikh (ra). He was thus at the mercy of God, the Sheikh, (ra) and the disciples for every material thing he received, and he seemed very grateful for the smallest gift.

Understanding that Ahamad Kabeer had a very close and unique relationship with Bawa (ra), in the context of this holy situation, what really brought Kabeer and me together was the prayer. Having started to do the salat upstairs outside Bawa (ra)'s room, where I had been originally guided to pray, we had now moved to the large living room downstairs because more people were coming. Sometimes there were several people in the congregation, and sometimes just he and I and one or two others. Our connection was thus established in the congregational prayer and in communication about prayer.

Relationships which are meaningful, in the way of Allah (swt), are those that bear fruit, and that fruit, when eaten, brings people closer to Allah (swt). Thus, our joining in the prayer was useful in the way of God, as He had decreed, since more and more people came to pray together, following that example.

There was another fruit also destined for us to bear. This was revealed, like so many of the unfolding mysteries of my life's journey, in a mysterious way. On the trip to India, where we went to renew our visas, I had the pleasure of meeting Kabeer's holy mother. Her name was Maimuna Umma, but we called her Babicha (grandmother in Tamil). She was one of the ancient ones that I have been so blessed to meet on my life's journey. I felt the sanctity, holiness, in her soft-skinned hands like in the hands of the other ancient ones I was graced to meet. You feel that this ancient hand has touched no impurity, and you are so blessed that it is now caressing you. As soon as she met me, she took hold of me, held me, and prayed over me for a long time.

Though nothing had come to pass that would indicate marriage between Kabeer and me, I seemed to sense that she was praying for our offspring. Kabeer had never been inclined to marriage at all. It seemed that this was the one and only chance that she might see his progeny. I felt the intensity of her embrace and knew that there was a blessing in it. It was not for nothing that she lived her entire life in a state of prayer and purity. What she intended would come to pass, but not right away.

The meeting with Kabeer's mother was deep. The intensity of her desire made me realize that I, also, was in some way inclined to that union and especially to the fruit that it would produce.

When our visas were ready, we returned to Sri Lanka. Bawa (ra) knew about the subtlety of what had taken place in my meeting with the mother of Kabeer. He called me into his room and spoke to me for more than an hour explaining why, specifically and in depth, I should not think about marrying Kabeer. It was an intense discourse that nearly made my hair stand on end.

As he spoke about so many details I could not possibly know, I realized again that the Sheikh (ra) knew what I knew not. Once again, I had no choice but to follow his direction. And then, entering more deeply into the teaching, I asked myself: *What is he really saying to me? And how can I be truly obedient with my heart and soul and understanding to what he is teaching me?*

To begin with, I needed to control the mind, desire, and imagination. This was the real inner work, the most fundamental and necessary level of submission to the Divine Will, but also the most difficult to achieve. Who I am to marry, when, and how — all of this is in God's Hand. *The* destiny is already written. Why should I attempt to project any fantasy I may have into existence? It is much better to let the story unfold by itself.

Bawa (ra) then showed me that I did not know, really, who Kabeer was. I saw how much we project our mind and desire onto others and do not know who they really are. Such is the power of our mind and desire to make us see what they want us to see, but the Sheikh (ra) wants us to see something else and to see in a different way.

It was an intense communication with the Sheikh (ra), as he exposed to me these forces within myself and the tendency that I had to project them onto others. Once again, he placed me in a state of shock.

Bawa (ra) often spoke about the state of metal, which needs to be transformed by the blacksmith. As long as it is in the heat of the fire, it is malleable and can be reshaped, but once it is out of the fire, it becomes fixed and cannot be molded. On that day, he kept me in the heat of the fire for a long time, and when I came out, I wanted nothing but to let go of any idea I may have had and surrender deeply to the Divine Decree. For the following year that I was in Sri Lanka, as carefully as I could, I followed the advice Bawa (ra) gave me that day. I regarded Kabeer respectfully at a distance and spoke to him infrequently.

Approximately a year later, however, two weeks before Bawa (ra) left Sri Lanka, I walked into his room wearing a green sari outfit. He said to me, "Green Maryam, are you dressed for your wedding?" He then told me to prepare for the marriage to Kabeer, which would take place in about twenty-four hours.

I had barely looked at or spoken to Kabeer for the past year in obedience to the Sheikh's (ra) instruction. Once he had cut the attachment in me, I was able to look at the situation much more objectively. Kabeer barely spoke English and had no training to work in America, nor would it be easy for him to integrate with the culture and life there. I felt the weight of that responsibility. I sat in front of Bawa's (ra) bed, absorbed in this awareness, hoping for some kind of clarification or reprieve. The fantasy had long before been dispelled. Now I was facing reality.

Nevertheless, there did not seem to be anything to discuss. The Sheikh (ra) told me to get ready, and that was all. I believe that this was so — that he did not ask me what I thought or felt about the idea — because it was a thing ordained. Kabeer had to come to America to serve Allah (swt), the Sheikh (ra) and his community, and Issa had to be born. On that day, when I realized that I had twenty-four hours before the destiny would be fulfilled, Lennie and Sophie called and said that they were in China and would like to come visit in Sri Lanka in a few days. Our wedding was the last one ever performed by Bawa (ra) in Sri Lanka. The house was packed with people, people sleeping everywhere, even on all the steps of the staircase, since everyone knew that the Sheikh (ra) was leaving soon. In reality, he would n (in physical form) return.

When Bawa (ra) performed the wedding ceremony, the room was filled with imams. Bawa's (ra) discourse was powerful. He said that all the responsibility would rest upon me. He said that everything rests on the earth, so the earth must not shake, or everything will fall. He told me not to expect anything in the marriage, from Kabeer, but to take responsibility for everything myself.

When I saw how our life unfolded in later years, I understood the truth in his words. As heavy as it sounded, that was how it was. But, as I have learned again, again, and again, in all the circumstances of my life, *surely* with difficulty comes ease. The very fact that I had to bear so much responsibility made me learn how to take care of many things, and I became independent as a result of this marriage and able to take care of almost everything by myself. It's also important to appreciate how many prayers and sacred services Ahamad Kabeer performed for us and so many, many others throughout the years we shared on the sacred journey. His contribution to our household and extended spiritual family was more valuable than any financial offering! In truth, the deeper and ultimate realization learned through all that occurred was that Allah (swt) Alone was taking care of me and of everything! That was part of the ever-unfolding blessing that I was receiving, stage by stage, throughout my life. So, all that we can truly say is: All praise be to God, for all the lessons we learn and all the challenges and blessings we meet!

The next day, my parents arrived as well as the Ambassador to Sri Lanka from Pakistan and his wife, friends of Bawa's (ra) close disciple, Fuard Utteman. Fuard, my parents, the Ambassador and his wife, and Kabeer and I went off into the tea country in the hills of Sri Lanka to celebrate our honeymoon. Bawa (ra) specified that this trip could not last longer than two and a half days.

Once we were out on the road and traveling up into the mountains, true to form, my father started to sing. Several times, he sang the call to prayer. I do not know where he learned it, but he was definitely inspired to sing it on that trip. Then he sang his old favorites, such as:

If we could consider each other
a neighbor, a friend or a brother,
it could be a wonderful, wonderful world.
Oh yes! It could be a wonderful world!
If there were no poor and the rich were content
If strangers were welcome wherever they went
If each of us knew what true brotherhood meant
It could be a wonderful world.
Oh yes, it could be a wonderful world!

If each little kid had enough food each day
If each working man had enough time to play
If each homeless soul had a good place to stay,
It could be a wonderful world.
Oh yes! It could be a wonderful world!

The wedding was done, the honeymoon was a group adventure in the hill country of Sri Lanka, and what was really being celebrated was the wonderful world that could exist if true brotherhood reigned.

When we returned to Bawa (ra), he asked Kabeer what had happened on the trip. Kabeer said, "My father-in-law sang many songs," and he attempted, with some help, to sing a song that Lennie had sung. Bawa (ra) laughed and laughed and said that was very good. Soon after, he went back to America, and Ahamad Kabeer and I followed about a month later.

We arrived in America in the middle of winter. When he saw that all the trees had no leaves, Kabeer, who had always lived in a tropical climate, where the trees do not lose their leaves, was shocked. He thought that a great fire must have devastated the land, and, out of respect and sympathy for us, he did not want to say anything about this disaster.

He only told me about his initial perception much later. We arrived in Philadelphia and before too long rented a room in a house down the block from the Fellowship. All the work, the focus on prayer, the building of the mosque in the heart, which had been galvanized in Sri Lanka, continued to develop in Philadelphia. Kabeer and I were actively engaged with the work. He was leading prayers and performing blessings; I was teaching classes of all kinds — prayer, Arabic, and so on. All of the activity, of course, was centered around and directed by the Sheikh (ra).

Day and night, Bawa (ra) would give discourses revealing the light within true prayer, Islam, and the Qur'an. For example, he said:

> *Our house is Allah's house. If our state is correct, our heart (qalb) will be Allah's house, His kingdom, His justice, love, compassion, and unity. Preparing for this state of beautiful peace and unity to come, we need a place in which to meet, unite, understand, think, and reflect every minute and second, establishing relationships of unity and peace. Instead of wasting time in the world, we can go to this place five or six times a day to do prayers and worship. We can gather in Allah's house, focus on Allah, think about Allah, pray to Him, and remember Him. It is for this purpose that we are building this mosque.*
>
> Spoken on March 10, 1983

The words coming through the Sheikh (ra) day and night upon his return from Sri Lanka galvanized the community step by step into the building of the mosque, both within and without. Bawa (ra), who was not strong enough to go downstairs, was informed of every step of the building process through videos and guided the process, moment by moment. The labor was done almost entirely by members of the Fellowship.

It must be acknowledged that both before and while the mosque was being built there was resistance to it in certain members of the community. Bawa (ra) had been teaching for so long the necessity to transcend religious differences, saying, "That which separates us from our fellow man is that which separates us from God." He taught that all the religions represented stages of the development of the human being and that all these levels of development were united in the true human being. He also taught that the true place of worship is not an outer building but the innermost heart *(qalb)*.

But along with the repository of inner teachings, he also left, as part of his eternal legacy, the mosque and an abundance of teachings about the mosque, about true prayer and the Holy Qur'an. For example, in explaining how to perform *dhikr* and the daily prayers *(salat)* with the deepest sincerity, Bawa (ra) said:

Children, precious jeweled lights of my eye, when you make the intention to do tasbih and pray to Allah, you must have certitude of iman. With certitude, you must place that iman in your qalbs and focus intently on Him. When you do tasbih (dhikr) to Him, that certitude should be focused within your qalbs. That intention, that concentration (niyyat), that determination, and that iman must be there at every waqt (time) of prayer. This must spread throughout the entire body and qalb. This point must be fixed before starting the dhikr. We must strive to bring the qalb to one point. Once we have done so, we can begin doing tasbih to Allah.

Sheikh Bawa Muhaiyaddeen (ra),

Prayer

In speaking of the mosque, he described to us so many marvelous mysteries related to its spiritual origin and subsequent physical manifestation, and he also shared with us that the mosque was filled with exalted beings praying there twenty-four hours a day. The presence of this unseen congregation, we are often very much blessed to feel praying with us, Alhamdulillah!

For me, there was never any choice but to go deeper and deeper into the state of prayer and submission. All the Sheikhs (ra), all the teachings I have encountered, have guided me unfailingly in this direction. This is what our Creator, Most Merciful, created us to do and explains in His words when He says, "*And I did not create the jinn and humans except to worship Me*" (Holy Qur'an 51:56).

So that is, I believe, why Sheikh Bawa Muhaiyaddeen (ra) left a mosque as a legacy: to enable those who came after him to understand and experience the meaning of this beautiful ayat as well as all the verses of the Holy Qur'an.

The mosque was completed and opened in a ceremony, just before Ramadan in 1984. Sheikh Bawa Muhaiyaddeen (ra) left this world, at a very old age, in December 1986. I have not heard of anyone who could say that he or she knew exactly how old he was. The extent of his life, and the mysteries it contained were known only by Allah *subhana wa ta'ala.*

At the moment that he passed, for a fraction of a second, there was an intense cry uttered by a few, but it was immediately overpowered by powerful *dhikr* that filled the house and, I sensed, the universe. What I felt was not sadness that he had left but the great blessing that he had come. A few days earlier, while sitting at the doorway of his room, I had felt his spirit speaking blissfully within me, "Do not be concerned; I am simply taking off the shirt."

On the night of his passing, I was blessed to sit at the head of Bawa (ra)'s bed and play Qur'an tapes, throughout the night. There was a beautiful, gentle, peaceful smile on his face and light and peace emanating from his form and filling the room. People came circling around the bed throughout the night, including many children. I saw no fear or distress in the people coming through that night. There was a transcendent sense of peace covering over everything.

Bawa (ra) left so many beautiful gifts as his legacy, a vast ocean of teachings yet to be received and realized. As much as I profoundly respect and love the Sheikh (ra) and feel his illuminated presence radiating and resonating within my heart and soul as a powerful living transmission, I felt that my journey was not complete and I needed further training and transformation, more experience in the journey through the stages of the Way, in order to attain complete realization and liberation that he taught us about and that he himself embodied. It is interesting to note here that my story, "the journey through ten thousand veils," was not finished. In this endless tale there were more chapters to come.

Shortly before he passed from this world, we asked our beloved Sheikh (ra) where we could find him after he had made his passage. He told us, "Find me in your heart." This profound truth and spiritual access point have sustained us all, both while he was physically present, and after he left this world, Alhamdulillah!

To discover that great treasure within my heart, that Divine Treasure he left with us, I had more miles to travel on the mountains and in the valleys of the spiritual path. And, once again, it was a journey that I had to make alone.

My marriage to Kabeer was truly not an earthly matter. We were married to the Sheikh, the teachings, and prayer. When our Beloved Sheikh (ra) left this world, we were each guided to accomplish many tasks separately — I, through many trips to West and North Africa, and he, through many trips to Canada.

But, although these journeys across the earth were awaiting us in-dividually, there was still one important thing we had to do together. It was one of two things that Bawa (ra) frequently asked me about. These were two "in-jokes" or spiritual secrets that we often shared, and they were part of the personal legacy he left to me. First, very often he asked me, "Maryam, how are you?" Whenever he asked me this question, im-mediately I felt that I was in the Divine Presence, that God was gazing upon me and asking me this question. Every time this happened, I was overwhelmed by love and awe and gratitude and said, "*Alhamdulillah, Bawa! I am very well!*"

The Sheikh (ra) never asked me the question when I was even a lit-tle disturbed, or too far away from contemplation of the Divine to know that God was gazing upon me. He was targeting the state of divine joy, the plenitude of contentment in the Divine Presence.

Then he would often say about me that whenever he asked me how I was, I always said, *"Alhamdulillah (All Praise be to God)!"* In this way, he trained me to know that this is what I must always say, that this was the state in which he wanted me always to abide. And I extend this blessed invitation, with all my love, to you, dear reader.

Another thing that Bawa (ra) said to me almost every time he saw me was, "Maryam, where is Issa?" He asked me this so many times that all I could do is smile and say, "You know, Bawa." Then, one day, he asked me if I had any questions. I said, "Yes, Bawa, where is Issa?" He said, "Issa is the light of the soul."

He gave a very beautiful, exalted discourse about the light of Issa, *ruh'Allah,* the soul of God. So, this was one of the dimensions that he was referring to when he asked me the question. But he was also referring to Issa, our son, who was to be born. He said some very deep things about him and then kept asking me where he was. I really did not know. I too very much felt his presence and his nearness, but I could not seem to bring him in.

The Sheikh (ra) had given us instructions about how to conceive a child consciously in the state of prayer. We were following them scru-pulously, targeting the correct times, and then following the protocol, but Issa was existing comfortably in the world of souls and not ready to come in. I miscarried six times. In all of the miscarriages, I did not feel that a child had come and left. No, the same child was there, but he was not ready to come. I had to go through the doorway six times so that my intention could be purified and my faith strengthened. But after the sixth time, I did wonder!

Bawa (ra) had asked about Issa so many times, but by the time that he left this world, still Issa had not come. Where, O God, was Issa? On the day of Bawa's (ra) burial, I laid my head on the ground near his grave and placed the matter of Issa entirely and absolutely in the Hand of God. I had tried as much as I could, but I could not bring him in.

That was on December 8, 1986. Soon after, I became pregnant for the seventh time and the due date for the baby was December 8, 1987. Issa was born, however, one week later on December 15, 1987.

His personality and energy were very noticeable, even when he was in the womb. This was especially so during the twelve days in which we celebrated the *mawlid* (birth) of the Prophet Muhammad (saw) and during the month of Ramadan. It was as though he was doing flips and somersaults for joy, or maybe he was praying. Then, as it was decreed, he came into the world quite easily with a four-and-half hour labor and no complications.

Since the journey in the way of God was such an important and valuable part of my life, I could not, but share it with my child. He began to travel with me when he was eight months old and we went to New Mexico. Many short and long trips followed. In general, he was a very happy traveler.

When he was four and a half, Issa, Kabeer and I went to the south of India so he could get to know his father's family, and to the north of India to visit my friends in Kashmir, from whom I had been importing tapestries. Issa fell into the arms of everyone in Madras and merged easily with his cousins, uncles, aunts and beloved grandmother, Babicha, whose prayers had now been answered, as well as with our beloved friends in Kashmir. That was the first of many international journeys that he, the son of a much traveling mother, would make.

CHAPTER SIXTEEN

THE VALE OF KASHMIR, DEEPLY BLESSED AND DEEPLY STRESSED

Srinagar, Kashmir, 1992

Did you think that ye would enter Heaven without Allah test-
ing those of you who fought hard (in His Cause) and remained
steadfast?
—The Holy Qur'an 3:142

Soaring mountains, limpid lakes and gardens enhance its aes-
thetic appeal. This is the place, which boasted of a wealth of
flora and fauna, beauty and serenity and attracted great saints
and rishis. Today, alas, it is desperately struggling for survival
and peace.
—Partha Bannerjee

The journey of descent into the Vale of Kashmir is breathtaking. As we flew down, the pilot was inspired, flying like a cosmic dancer up and down and around the magnificent, amazing sculptures of snow. This could only bring forth, in the beholder, awe and contemplation of the inspiration of the Sculptor, Himself. There are rare moments in our life, when we are permitted and blessed to see such things — all awesome signs of the grandeur of the Creator and that which He created — all signs of His wondrous Creative Grace. As we descended further between the snowy peaks and entered the valley, we passed through layer upon layer of emerald light. The spectral beauty of the land, with its intensity of color and light, was awe-inspiring.

I have descended by plane into many lands but none more radiantly beautiful. In addition to the elemental beauty of this magical valley, the spiritual energy was intense. Upon landing in this realm, I felt as if the top of my head flew off and was replaced by highly charged, luminous air. From the moment of arriving in this energized sphere, my heart was seized by a kind of ancient nostalgia. I do not know in what way, but in some profound way, I was connected with this place.

The land and the people were extremely familiar. They recognized me instantly, as I did them, and so deep was the attraction between us that, during most of my stays in Kashmir, I remained consciously inside the house because I felt if I went out, even into the marketplace, the love and longing inspired by being in the midst of these people would be more than my heart could bear.

The political situation of this remote yet strategic valley is, itself, heartbreaking. In stark contrast to the great natural beauty of the landscape and the luminous intelligence and warmth of the people and their wondrous artistry is the darkness of the force of occupation that oppresses this land. It reminds us that although we can see an image of it, paradise has not yet been attained on this earth.

The Kashmiris, who were given the right to self-rule by the United Nations in 1948, until now have not been able to exercise that right. On the contrary, these noble and gifted people have been severely oppressed, and, in a sense, held hostage in their own land. While Kashmir is, as we were told, a tourism-based economy, much of the time tourists cannot get into the country, and a major source of its income has thus been cut off.

The people have endured so many ordeals that there is no way we, who are not living through this with them, can truly fathom their trials and their suffering. This must not be forgotten, even while we appreciate the beauty of the land, the people, and the unique artistry of Kashmir.

On our second trip to Kashmir, we were vividly aware of this. We sat in an airport in London, waiting to take off to fly there.

Although we were told that a strict curfew was being imposed and no one could get in, we continued to wait, like those who know that the sun is hidden behind the clouds on a very cloudy day and that it will inevitably shine again. Only a short while before our plane was scheduled to take off was the curfew lifted, and we were able to fly under that black cloud cover of oppression and to land in our beloved imperiled paradise. We were met at the airport by two large families, our original suppliers, and those with whom we were currently dealing in tapestries, all of whom we loved very much. They were now very politely vying with each other for the blessing of hosting us and, no doubt, for our business also. We went home with our present suppliers, an elegant, princely man, kind and lovely, named aptly Jelaluddin As-Sufi and his beautiful wife, Shahnaz, who became my dear friend, as well as her brother, Yousuf Shah, with whom I would have the pleasure of continuing to do business with for many years in the future.

Traveling the relatively short distance between the airport and their home was an experience fraught with danger. One could feel a confrontation, something oppressive, taking place nearby, and it turned out that some violence had occurred five minutes from their house that night. Our hosts knew the parties involved and were very much concerned by the news. They knew also that the people injured could, at any time, be themselves.

I looked at these beautiful people, drank in the sight of them, and appreciated their presence deeply. I understood that just because they lived there, they could be injured or killed. I prayed that these wonderful people, my gracious hosts, be protected from the darkness which surrounded their beautiful land and that the light I saw shining so clearly through them would guide them through all this to the ultimate Goal.

I also knew that I was there to witness, even to the small extent I could, what people have to go through and then understand and bear witness to what I had seen. As a contemporary American, one is taught to avoid dangerous situations like this at all costs when traveling abroad, but I am indebted to the Creator that He permitted me to be there and to share the danger and difficulty with my relatives in the human family. If we are not with the people who are suffering, feeling even a little of what they feel, how can we truly understand the human condition, experiencing it as our own condition?

Although it was no doubt dangerous to visit their land, under those circumstances, for me to share that experience with the people of Kashmir was a blessing I cannot forget, a knowledge that has been embedded in my heart. One of the most important gifts of traveling through the world on the spiritual journey is the ever-deepening realization and experience that all lives are interconnected. We are all embodiments of the one creation made by the One Creator. In respect to the absolute oneness of our Source and Ultimate Reality, we come to realize that every being that we meet is a manifestation of this sacred truth.

Whatever Allah *subhana wa ta'ala*, the Divine Guide, has willed me to see, that is the story I have to tell. It is my profound hope and dream that somehow, through telling the stories of the beautiful beings I have met along the way, I will, God willing, find some means of helping. After our somewhat perilous trip through unknown danger, we arrived at their house, which was so large and full of rooms and people that I could not immediately make sense of it. One room was filled mostly with the elders, some rooms with mostly children of various ages. One room was the active kitchen, and one was a vast cathedral-like room in an attic with rays of light descending into it — the showroom where rugs and tapestries were stored.

As in all the Sufi houses we have visited in our travels, Issa disappeared and was assimilated into the local life. In the days that followed, when looking for four-and-a-half-year-old Issa, I would find him happily ensconced and merged in the activities of one or another of these rooms, blissfully intermingled and entertained, as though this was all a delightful show put on for him. He would usually be in someone's arms, hugging or wrestling with someone, as though he had been born there and always lived there.

Since traveling in the way of God has played such an enlightening role in my life, I could not, but wish to share this with my child, and I am very grateful that he had the opportunity, as his world view was forming, to know and experience his intimate connection with these people and many other members of the human family. The awareness of the universal family is one that I began to learn about in my father's house. From that point on, I have always had a community awareness. I have always known that the "family" was not nuclear but universal, inclusive, and, in fact, the *"family of man."* The houses of the lovers of God are like this. This is the manifestation of the Way.

Another sign of holistic community and the natural manifestation of the human family that we discovered again and again in our travels, as we did in this house of many chambers, is that the children and the elders are always together. The elderly are given the respect due to their age, experience, and accumulated wisdom, and they are integral to the fabric of the family, thus transmitting their knowledge to the generations that follow them in a way that is absolutely natural and holistic. Issa knew this and that is why I often found him in their arms.

Another place to which he gravitated was the third-floor magical chamber, the vast vaulted room on the top of the house into which rays of light descended in a spectral pattern. When I could not find him elsewhere, I would go up and often find him there sitting alone, silent, transfixed, with rays of soft light falling upon him. Filled with tapestries, carpets and light, it was the room where we most often prayed and also where we did our business.

As I was passing through it, the whole experience was like a manifest dream. I had dreamt all of this and now I was living it. Our gracious host had given us a very cozy room, one which was almost entirely filled with a huge bed. When I drew the curtains and looked outside, I was completely transported to another time, another dimension of being.

The view was mesmerizing, an ancient scene I knew I had seen before somewhere in my consciousness — the ancient wooden buildings in front of snow-covered mountains, people walking by from absolutely another epoch than contemporary mall traffic. All this I remembered, had longed for and had now found my way back to. The entire situation filled my heart with peace yet, at the same time, a kind of intense longing and excitement. I looked out at that scene and did not know in which world I really existed. I was deeply inclined to go outside and throw myself into that other existence. But, for a time, I consciously resisted.

We went to sleep in the cozy room and were awakened before dawn by the beautiful sounds pouring through the valley from minaret to minaret. In all Muslim lands, when the call to prayer goes out, it echoes and resounds from minaret to minaret to minaret. All time and space, one's heart and soul, are enveloped by this resounding echo. From hilltop to hilltop, all sounds and energies are intercommunicating, ricocheting, relaying the same message — calling us to remember our Lord.

Having lived in and traveled through many Muslim lands, I had become accustomed to this beautiful resonance filling mountains and valleys at the times of prayer. But, pre-dawn, in the mystic vale of Kashmir, the resonance of the sound filling the valley was beyond extraordinary. Broadcasting from all the minarets, echoing from one to the next, was not only the call to prayer but extended profound *dhikr* (zikr), remembrance of Allah (swt), one after the next, the words we love most, the words we were inspired by our Sheikhs (ra) to say, the words that express the love in our hearts, from and for the One of Infinite Splendor, the Most Kind and Loving One who created us, echoing throughout this elevated valley. We felt as though the prayers of our innermost heart were resounding throughout this realm.

I also realized at this moment that whatever political oppression had imposed itself upon this land and people, it could not silence or inhibit the power of their prayer. (As I am in the process of revising this book, so many years after writing this, with the situation in Kashmir so much more deeply challenging and oppressive, all our prayers for this beautiful people and land are so deeply called for.)

After some days of retreat, in which we discovered these and other mysteries of Kashmir within our souls, our hosts told us that they wanted to take us out to meet the artisans who make the tapestries and to show us the beauty of Kashmir.

So, we ventured forth into an ancient world of extraordinary sights and sounds, a valley of crystal lakes, hand-carved wooden buildings and houseboats bordering the lakes and floating upon them, a land of terraced hills, and fruit orchards surrounded by huge snow peaks. The air had a crystalline clarity and was filled with the aromatic odors of fires burning everywhere.

There is a Kashmiri custom in which each person carries a basket of coals inside his or her beautifully embroidered garment. When you meet someone on a path, if you are not already carrying such a basket, the other person will give theirs to you. This is their way of greeting each other and sharing the warmth.

Our hosts took us on a tour of the town of Srinagar, past the intricately carved houseboats, to a small boat docked at the shore of Dal Lake in which we were to ride across the lake.

Our journey across the vast lake was bittersweet. We learned that we were the first visitors to ride in this boat in many months. Since very few people were able even to get into the country, the tourist industry had plummeted, and these ferry men had no people to transport, no way to make a living. They told us that some of them had even resorted to eating poisonous roots because they could not cope with the hopelessness of their situation. Our lovely trip across the lake was undermined by this awareness.

Then, our hosts continued the tour of the land with its celestial gardens and orchards and crystal lakes surrounded by the towering snow peaks which frame the picture that is the beautiful valley. We passed through the marketplace and met the merchants in their colorful old stalls. I was deeply touched by their beauty, refinement, and intelligence. Even the children there seemed to speak many languages with eloquent ease. Our tour culminated at an ancient mosque. I was guided to a carved wooden deck outside where I was to pray. It was built of dark rich wood, which had been prayed on so many times that it had become as soft as velvet, smooth and cool. Going down in prostration, I wished never to get up again. So much light, understanding and love were flowing through me, as I remained prostrated there. I felt that, within the prostration, within the surrender, within the love, a door opened, and blessed knowledge was given.

From the moment I had embraced Islam, or I could say, more accurately, from the time that Islam embraced me, I was moved and inspired, such that, whatever small amount of understanding or knowledge came to me, I wanted to share it. Whatever life-giving water was poured into my cup, I wanted to share it with those who might be thirsting. So, it had been very natural to teach, that is, to share the knowledge about prayer, Arabic, the Sufi way, the way of true Islam.

It was at this moment in the blessed vale of Kashmir that I was told that the words I had been speaking were not mine. They were the words of God, the words of the Creator, Most Gracious and Merciful, Most Loving and Kind, that He had given to me to give to others, so that all of us may turn again to Him. This understanding came to me while I was prostrating on that dark, cool, ancient wood.

When I sat up at the end of the prayer and turned to my right, I saw that sitting next to me was a very elderly, holy woman gazing and smiling at me. It seemed that she was there as a witness and participant in this divine encounter.

With that final message, our time in the holy valley of Kashmir had come to an end. The snows were coming with force, and we had to fly out before we were snowed in for the winter. As we were leaving, we were told that there were many Sufis in the mountains whom we should meet. I deeply felt that I would love to come back, and, *insha'Allah*, find our ancient companions there.

In the context of the present profound challenges facing the Kashmiris, I am waiting for any moment that curfews may be lifted and I could travel there to go and visit the beautiful souls assembled there to express my appreciation for them and deeply share our love and healing prayer.

CHAPTER SEVENTEEN

MECCA, MEDINA AND
THE MOUNTAIN OF LIGHT

Saudi Arabia, 1996

Behold! We gave the site to Abraham of the House, saying: "Ascribe nothing as partner unto Me, and sanctify My House for those who compass it round or stand up, or prostrate themselves. And proclaim unto humankind the pilgrimage.

—The Holy Quran' 22:26

Precious children, jeweled lights of my eyes, within you there is a house just for God. That is the Ka'aba. That is paradise. All the prophets, all the good ones from this world and the world of souls are there within it, praying and glorifying God. The sounds of their constant dhikr, their salaams, and salutations on the Prophet, the call to prayer, and their prayers are always heard.

—Sheikh Bawa Muhaiyaddeen (ra)

There are certain places to which one cannot go without an invitation. The Holy House of Allah *subhana wa ta'ala* in Mecca is such a place. I had been a Muslim for twenty-two years, hoping very much to make the journey to Mecca and Medina, but the invitation did not come until the destined time, the time when *Allah subhana wa ta'ala* willed to send it. He leads to His light whom He wills, when He wills, as He wills.

In my case, I was standing in the shoe room of the Fellowship, waiting to use the phone when I happened to see a little casting notice for a play that was going to be presented at the Fellowship. It was being directed by my dear friend Abdal-Hayy, with whom I had shared so much of the adventure of *rite of passage* theatre in the Sixties.

One of the characters in the play was a representation of the great Sufi saint, Rabi'a Al-Adawiyyah. The little note was a sign for me. I was seized by the sense that I had to play that part. I called and discovered that it had already been cast. They had been intending to ask me to play it but thought I was too busy to have time for rehearsals. It had been thirty years since Abdal-Hayy and I last worked together in the Floating Lotus Magic Opera Company. Now this opportunity had surfaced, and I told Abdal-Hayy and his wife, my beloved friend Malika, that they should be aware, at least, that I was ready if they needed me. Within a few days, they called to say that the woman playing the part had suddenly dropped out.

I did not have much time to learn the part and integrate with the total flow of the company and the play, but the character and what she said were so deeply relevant to my being that they caused me to enter another world, that is, a totally different yet somehow deeply familiar state of awareness. One line that she said and that I related to profoundly was, *"Lovers are with their beloveds now, two by two by two, but I, unseen by all of them, am alone, Allah, with You."* The play dramatized the legendary story of Rabi'a (ra), in which since she was unable to go to the Ka'aba on pilgrimage, the Ka'aba came to her. As the Ka'aba approaches her, she says the words that all pilgrims say on encountering the Holy House:

> *I am here, O Lord, I am here.*
> *I am here. You have no partner. I am here!*
> *Surely all praise and blessings are Yours — and dominion.*
> *There is no one who is Your partner.*

As I spoke these lines, it was a case of art inspiring life, of art and life becoming one in the moment of truth. At the very moment that I spoke the words on the stage, I knew that this was not an act in a play. The words were the absolute truth of my being. I was saying them sincerely to the One to Whom they must be expressed. This was my invitation to make the journey, and I must go as soon as possible.

It was mid-October. I inquired without delay and discovered that a group of pilgrims from the Fellowship was traveling to Mecca on 'umrah (the lesser non-obligatory pilgrimage) in December. Suddenly, it became absolutely clear that Issa and I would be amongst them. With lightning speed, since the Divine willed it, all of the details of preparation fell into place.

With fifty other people, many families with children, we set out on the first stage of our pilgrimage, the journey to the airport. There were televisions on the bus, on which we watched the movie *The Message*. I had watched this movie many times with Bawa (ra) in his room in Sri Lanka. Now, the Sheikh (ra) was guiding us into a new dimension, walking in the footsteps of the Messenger (saw) of Allah. This movement would galvanize and transform the rest of my life.

We spent a few hours at JFK airport. There were many kids in our group, and Issa thoroughly enjoyed himself as he is inclined to do. I found a spot in the airport and prayed freely and joyously, knowing that the journey was sacred and that all the world was a mosque or place of worship.

With this intention and abundant energy, we flew. Arriving in Saudi Arabia's capital, Riyadh, we found that passing through the gate was not so easy. The guardian at the gate, inspecting my passport, noted that I was married. Where was my husband? How could this be? How could a mother and a child travel without a man? After Bawa's passing, increasingly feeling that the marriage was lacking vital force for me and and sensing that I had many miles of the journey to travel alone, I had asked for a divorce. The process took about five years to finalize, but by this time, we were separated, and he had given me a note that Issa and I had his permission to make this journey.

After a few minutes of confusion, the guide of our group turned up with the paper signed by Kabeer, giving us permission to make this journey. He explained the situation in Arabic for several minutes, and finally we were allowed to pass. This was a sobering experience we often encountered in Saudi Arabia, this attitude of the "gatekeepers." It contrasted with the bliss of our immersion in the light — the wide-open space of our journey — the dimension that is not and could never be controlled or restricted by anyone.

Having made it through the gate, we began our journey into the desert. Like most things on the pilgrimage, the encounter with the land in Saudi Arabia is extremely powerful and intense. There are vast expanses of desert and areas of the earth where immense volcanic activity has taken place. One experiences directly that the land and the people of Allah *subhana wa ta'ala* have undergone great ordeals here.

It is not a breezy tropical paradise but a land of ultimate encounter. One can sense powerfully how the pilgrims, gathering on the plains of Arafat under the scorching sun, are living on earth before they die, the mystery of the souls rising up on the Day of Judgment, the Day of Reckoning. The passages in the Qur'an that describe the Day of Judgment and what will inevitably come to pass are so powerful it makes sense that they were revealed in a landscape like this, which is absolutely unyielding, which does not give comfort or solace in itself, but forces one to turn in a direction other than the earth for things that people in other lands have in abundance and take for granted like water, ample vegetation, coolness, and shade.

Our trip through this desert went on for hours and hours in a bus packed with men, women, and many children. The children were amazingly quiet and submitted to the entire process and in peace. The blessing in the intention of our pilgrimage was carrying us along, and everyone was behaving differently than they would on any other kind of trip. We finally arrived, after many hours of traveling through the volcanic expanse, in the proximity of Medina. Having traveled through the night, we arrived in Medina, the city of the Prophet (saw), *Medina al-Munawwarah*, the city of lights, just before the dawn or fajr prayer. We went to our room to bathe and were cleansed and refreshed in time to hear the call to prayer echoing from the minaret, flooding the city of the Prophet Muhammad (saw) as it called the faithful to assemble.

I looked out the window, and from above the veils and robes of the women and men, mostly white, were merging one into the next in what looked like a stream of light flowing down the road. It appeared to me to be a vision of the people of paradise being transported as a current of light to the throne of Allah *subhana wa ta'ala*. We watched this pure and radiant river flowing so beautifully toward the mosque. Then we went down and became immersed in it.

Beautiful breezes were blowing as we were carried along toward a complex of illuminated buildings bathed in and emanating turquoise light. The towering, commanding structures were surrounded by a vast expanse of shining marble, which shimmered like crystal.

Along with the sea of believers with which we had merged, we were gliding along on the marble toward the mosques when suddenly my prayer beads, a set of bright turquoise crystal beads, broke apart and sped across the marble in every direction, like luminous tears. That was the end of my life as I knew it and the beginning of the next cycle, as the Lord was revealing it in this *city of lights*.

Issa went with some of the men into the mosque where the men assemble, and I went into the women's mosque. The interior of the mosque was even more amazing than the exterior. Being within it was like being within a jewel of infinite dimensions with infinite passageways.

Having entered the mosque and adjusted my eyes to the light, I found my place within the sisterhood. There were rows upon rows of sisters from everywhere, tiny babies to ancient women, assembled beautifully in clusters in their native dress. I found my place as a female in this great gathering of women, but, even more than that, I found my place in the vast assembly as a servant of *Allah subhana wa ta'ala*.

There was a great sense of unity in the midst of tremendous diversity. Everyone, it seemed, was moving together in submission to divine harmony. However individual a person might think she is, in the midst of the vast inspired divine movement, these individual characteristics were absorbed like bubbles in the ocean. One does not lose the bubble but gains the ocean.

In celebrating this profound sense of unity of all believers united in these holy precincts, united by the one light of the teachings of Divine Revelation, let us include in this memoir the message shared with humanity by Malcolm X, Malik El Shabazz, who himself was so deeply moved and transformed here. For someone like me who grew up in a family passionately devoted to racial equality and who then was so deeply guided on the spiritual journey towards union with Allah *subhana wa ta'ala*, these words, expressed by our dear brother, fellow pilgrim on the sacred journey, resonate as treasures of grace within my heart and soul:

> *Never have I witnessed such sincere hospitality and overwhelming spirit of true brotherhood as is practiced by people of all colors and races here in this ancient Holy Land, the home of Abraham, Muhammad and all the other Prophets of the Holy Scriptures. For the past week, I have been utterly speechless and spellbound by the graciousness I see displayed all around me by people of all colors...*

> *I have been blessed to visit the Holy City of Mecca, I have made my seven circuits around the Ka'aba, led by a young Mutawaf named Muhammad, I drank water from the well of the Zam Zam. I ran seven times back and forth between the hills of Mt. Al-Safa and Al Marwah. I have prayed in the ancient city of Mina, and I have prayed on Mt. Arafat. There were tens of thousands of pilgrims, from all over the world. They were of all colors, from blue-eyed blondes to black-skinned Africans. But we were all participating in the same ritual, displaying a spirit*

*of unity and brotherhood that my experiences in America had
led me to believe never could exist between the white and non-
white...*

*America needs to understand Islam, because this is the one re-
ligion that erases from its society the race problem. Throughout
my travels in the Muslim world, I have met, talked to, and even
eaten with people who in America would have been considered
white — but the white attitude was removed from their minds
by the religion of Islam. I have never before seen sincere and
true brotherhood practiced by all gathered together, irrespective
of their color.*

The Autobiography of Malcolm X

(Feeling so deeply grateful for the realization of the transcendent sense
of the unity of the human family in the Divine Presence that had brought
us all together here, expressed so beautifully by the sharing of Malcolm
X above, I return now to the description of our unfolding journey in
Medina.)

After the prayers, I reunited with Issa, and we glided back to the
hotel. The next days in Medina were timeless. I do not know how long
we were there but only that the beauty and sweetness of the Prophet
Muhammad (saw) and the presence of Allah *subhana wa ta'ala* filled all
time and space.

This was Medina, the city where the Holy Prophet (saw) and his
community went to seek refuge when they were exiled from Mecca because their belief in the One God threatened those who controlled Mecca at that time and whose livelihood, prestige, and position, depended
upon the people worshipping many gods, many idols.

This was the Medina where the Prophet (saw) built the new community, founded upon the principles of the unity and absolute sovereignty of the One Creator of all and upon the equality in the fundamental rights of all of His creations. It was the place where this inspired
community of believing people developed in piety and love for God, receiving the wealth of the divine revelations, memorizing them, and then
manifesting them in action.

All of the divine mysteries and truths that had taken place here were somehow alive in this blessed realm, accentuated by the remembrance, in the hearts of the worshippers assembled, of the words and events which had been revealed here.

Sensing this accumulated grace and blessing, we were flowing along in the state of love, worship, and oneness, with almost no ripples on the surface of the infinite sea.

This sense of the continuity of undisturbed peace was interrupted by one trial. At every time of prayer, I let Issa go with some of the men we were traveling with into the men's mosque. Then, one day, the time of prayer arrived, and we could find no one to accompany him. He very much wanted to go by himself. I was hesitant. We had always prayed together, but now he was nine.

I could not take him with me and also did not want to deprive him of the chance to enter into that wondrous space and pray. I had to put the matter in the Hand of Allah *subhana wa ta'ala* and let him go. He went in and, after prayers, much to my maternal relief, promptly appeared in the place he was supposed to meet me.

The next day, however, he went in but, when the prayers were over, did not appear in the designated spot. I sat there waiting and waiting to see his beautiful, sweet face, his form, but he did not appear. This was agonizing. It was a test of faith, and, it seemed, I failed.

I waited and waited but to no avail. Finally, completely stricken with concern, I got up and went back to the hotel and sat on a bench, bemoaning my plight. Where could he be? In what situation could he be? I knew that he was in the place of Allah *subhana wa ta'ala*, but had I failed in my responsibility to him in letting him go? The sense of concern was overwhelming my heart and even my body, when, suddenly, he walked in the door. I have no idea how he found his way, but here he was! My precious boy! The one entrusted to me!

Of course Issa was going to come back. He was, in fact, on his way back, but I understood in that eternal moment of his absence the immeasurable importance of the responsibility entrusted to me, and I beseeched Allah *subhana wa ta'ala* to enable me to fulfill the trust. It also helped me to experience, to some extent, the anguish of those parents whose children are lost and do not return.

Having passed through that trial, we were ready to continue our journey and draw nearer to the One who created us, the One who had given us to each other as a trust and placed us together as pilgrims on His path.

We had prayed for a timeless time in the cool oasis of Medina, the turquoise-emerald jewel, and now our pilgrim caravan returned to the vast desert, barren of almost everything but the blessings of the Revelation which had descended upon it and oil within it, which had brought the betterment and also the corruption of the inhabitants of this land.

As the bus pulled out onto the road, I felt the immense magnetism of the Ka'aba. We were traveling with many people who had already been to Mecca and seemed to know what to expect. For me, however, Mecca, the Ka'aba, was something utterly unknown, an immense mystery that was very powerfully pulling us toward it. It pulled us through the black night, through the desert of black rock, through our own personal veils and fears towards its mysterious presence. We traveled in this way through the night.

We entered in the depth of the night. This revealed to us, as we entered Mecca, that the Ka'aba never sleeps. As we approached the hotel where we were to stay, we drove through a tunnel formed of volcanic rock, and it was clear we had entered sacred space. We got off the bus, performed our ablutions, and passed, all together, through a gateway with very high walls leading into the sacred grounds that surround the Ka'aba. The walls were immensely thick and high, and our group of about fifty entered the holy precinct with great force, singing intently all together the prayers designated for us to say as we were making that passage. Immediately, in the middle of the night, we were inundated with light. The Ka'aba is always illuminated, filled with prayer and enveloped by prayer. Being a symbol of the unity of the Divine Presence and the focal point of worshipful intention for all those in whom the light of Islam has dawned, it is like a heart that is constantly beating with the heartbeat of the prayers flowing into and out of it, penetrating throughout all time and space.

For this mysterious symbolic manifestation there is no night or day. There is no cessation in the turning of the cosmic sea of praise and worship that flows around it or in the flow of the bloodstream — the divine remembrance — passing into and out of that heart.

Whatever else may take place in the world of Islam, there is no separation between men and women or children in the movement circulating around the Ka'aba, the earthly manifestation of the throne of God. Like blood cells clustering in the bloodstream or heavenly bodies traveling together in the galaxies, different groups of people — travelling together as families, tribes, or spiritual orders — move together as units, each reciting in its own way the words that Allah subhana wa ta'ala has given to humankind through which He wishes to be remembered in this holy place.

Issa and I were traveling with a group of truly good friends and acquaintances, yet I felt deeply at that moment the longing to be with the most intimate companions of our soul. In that brilliantly illuminated space, exposed to the gaze of God with no hiding my state, I felt strangely alone yet filled with the profound longing for realization of the soul's purpose and reunion with its innermost companions. I knew that I was not ready, not *completely* present. This was an introduction, a preparation, an opening of the door.

There are supplications we make with our tongues, with our hands, our thoughts, our intentions. This one arose involuntarily from the depth of my soul and being. Our prayers are not answered as we wish or when we wish, but they are heard, and everything that happens from that moment on is a response to the supplication. My soul spoke to my Creator in that moment in the midst of that powerful manifestation of His Presence, and from that moment on all my life has been a revealing or an unveiling of how that prayer is being fulfilled.

Allah says in the Qur'an, *"And when My servants question you concerning Me, then surely I am nigh. I answer the prayer of the supplicant when he cries unto Me. So let them hear My call and let them trust in Me, in order that they may be led aright"* (2:186). That moment was a glimpse of the fulfillment, a vision of all souls hearing the call and inspired by the trust, gathering in the Presence of God, in the Light of God, in His Love, His Radiance, His Mercy. All of us, all humanity, turning around the Light of our Lord, are being drawn into that Light, to be consumed by it. At least we have received the invitation and the powerful call, and on whatever level and wherever this occurs, our life is a response to that call. After we made tawaf (circumambulated around the Ka'aba) seven times, we went to the *Spring of Mercy* to make our ablutions in the water of *zamzam*. This abundant wellspring of God's mercy, which appeared in the middle of the most barren desert, is the symbol and embodiment of the response of the One Most Merciful to our prayers and supplication.

It was in order to discover and receive this plenitude — the water of life — not only for themselves but for all lives, that Hagar (ra), the second wife of Prophet Abraham (as), and their son Ishmael (as) were sent into the most barren of lands with nothing but faith to sustain them.

I was considering deeply the overwhelming hardship and challenge faced by the mother left in the midst of that most barren of deserts, running from one hilltop to the other, in search of that water necessary to save her child's life. How utterly profound was the trial faced by that mother and her child and even more amazing was the solution provided by the One Most Merciful to the grave plight of His creations, who are so intensely beseeching His aid.

Now, I was here, drinking this life-giving water, on the spiritual journey with my son, contemplating these deep sacred teachings. It may appear to us that we are abandoned in the desert from time to time in our life's journey. Sometimes we reach the point of desperation and hopelessness.

But the difficulty and severity of the trial, we may come to realize, is the pressure that must be imposed upon our heart and faith to make the supplication arise, which is so profound and sincere that it brings forth the water of God's Mercy. There, in the midst of the desert in which we may feel we have been deserted, when we come to the point of true prayer, true submission, the rain of Allah's grace pours down upon us and our cup is filled.

Imagine the miracle of an ever-flowing source of water appearing in the midst of the bleakest and most barren desert. That is the true miracle of Allah's grace that manifested for Hagar (ra) and Ishmael (as) between the hills of Safa and Marwah, yielding water that has continued to quench the thirst of pilgrims ever since. It is a great sign of hope for us all, reminding us that the endless Source is there. And, we can access this plenitude, which will satisfy all our hunger and thirst, all our needs, only through our deepest prayer.

Here I was, a single mother with my son, making the journey between the hills of Safa and Marwah, realizing that we were as much in need of the help of Allah *subhana wa ta'ala* as Hagar (ra) and her son had been. Hagar (ra) was a humble servant of her Lord, apparently abandoned in the desert with her small son, but how often, how deeply, and in what a blessed sense she is remembered, and solely because of the sincerity of her prayer and the miraculous way in which Allah *subhana wa ta 'ala* answered her prayer.

It is by the sincerity of our prayer and supplication that the value of our life and journey too will be determined. We cannot accomplish the purpose for which we came here; we need to turn to our Creator with all that we are and all that we have and ask Him to fulfill all of our needs, just as they did. In our daily prayers we say, *"You alone do we worship, and You are our only help."*

Whatever we may be searching for, thirsting, hungering, or yearning for, our provision is with our Lord, the One who created us all. That is why the Ka'aba is a central focus for all the people who have come to know it. It is not simply a focal point of worship for Arabs or for those born Muslim. As the last of the long line of Prophets (as) sent to earth with His message, the Prophet Muhammad (saw) was sent by God (as He has told us) as a mercy to *all* the worlds.

When you are at the Ka'aba, you know this. You are enveloped by humanity, engulfed by all the tribes. It was when he came to the Ka'aba that Malcolm X realized that Islam could never be claimed by people of one color, for it is the path of the submission of all lives to the Source of all life.

Thus, the journey that we make in *tawaf*, the journey around the Ka'aba, is a journey we make with people of all nations, all tribes. All of us come to stand in the place where our father, Abraham (as) stood. We can see his immense footprints and almost feel that we are walking in them. He is the guide, example, and inspiration for all of us, an especially powerful role model for those of us who have grown up, called within by the power of the One God, in a world filled with idolatry.

He found the strength to follow and serve the One God, Allah *subhana wa ta'ala* with all of his being, no matter what the people were doing around him. This is also what we must do. He was unwilling to carry on the family business of idol selling, and so must we be. Having been guided by God to the *Haqq*, the Ultimate Truth, Abraham (as) fearlessly proclaimed it through everything that he did, and as many sacrifices as he had to endure to manifest the truth under all circumstances, for him, *fire, itself, became cool.*

Through the power of his faith, manifesting in constant submission to the Divine Call, Abraham (as) became the *Friend of God and the perfect example, the leader for humanity.* The Holy Qur'an states, *"And when His Lord tried Ibrahim with His commands and he fulfilled them, He said 'Lo, I have appointed thee a leader for humankind'* (2:124).

It was here in Mecca, close to where the zamzam water sprang forth that Abraham (as) and Ishmael (as) were directed to build the House of God. Describing their connection to this sacred place, the Holy Qur'an says:

> And Ibrahim said, "My Lord! Make safe this territory one of peace and security and preserve me, and my sons from worshipping idols. My Lord! The idols have indeed led astray many of humankind. But whoso follows me, he is verily of me, and whoso disobeys me still, Thou art Forgiving, Most Merciful! Our Lord! I have made some of my offspring to dwell in a valley without cultivation, by Thy Sacred House, in order, O our Lord, that they may establish regular prayer. So incline some hearts of men toward them and provide them with Your bounties so that they may be thankful.
>
> The Holy Qur'an 14:35-37

Now, we who are making the *tawaf* are among those whom *Allah subhana wa ta'ala* wished to compass the House which has been sanctified by the Messenger (saw) who came as decreed to rebuild the Ka'aba with the light of Revelation. Whatever may have been the tradition of our fathers, we stand in the presence of our Lord and prostrate.

We are amongst those who have been purified by the Revelation brought by the Prophet Muhammad (saw), which was the completion of the message brought by all the Prophets (as). Everything has come to pass as the Qur'an revealed. Such is the significance of our journey, and the journey of everyone who has heard and responded to the call of Allah *subhana wa ta'ala* to make the pilgrimage to Mecca.

So many have responded, coming from all nations and all corners of the earth, that sometimes it is difficult even to make the tawaf because so many people are moving around the Ka'aba at the same time. This was a challenge for me as a single mother with a son, since in the midst of that ocean of humanity when the call to prayer came, Issa had to go pray with the men, and so he was not right at my side. He also looked so much like all the boys of Mecca and, even, of the world. I placed on his head a shining golden cap so that I could identify him in any crowd.

Still, it was very unsettling to let him go into that massive assembly, and I was stricken from time to time by attacks of anxiety, which were tempered and quelled only by my faith in God.

Then, very fortunately, we learned that we could go up a spiral stair-case and pass through large classes of Meccan children learning Qur'an to a balcony overlooking the Ka'aba where men, women, and children in families and extended families can all pray together in a very peaceful and protected way. This discovery was a great blessing for us, and we regularly went there.

From the balcony, I was able to see the Ka'aba and all the activity surrounding it from a new perspective. I could see that the vast numbers of people gathered together at the time of prayer were assembled in per-fect symmetry. This symmetry allowed more and more people to enter into the divine configuration, yet the symmetry was always perfect.

I thought that this beautiful configuration was a sign of the sanc-tification of Islam as the completion of all the stages of Revelation that preceded it. If we were to see an aerial view of any other gathering of people on earth, I do not believe that we would be able to see such sym-metry and harmony, in which all the people assembled are bowing down to the One God who sent all the Messengers (as), all the books, all true religions.

While we were praying on that peaceful balcony, Issa made friends with people, as he always does. One day, our dear friend Malik told me that Issa had made friends with one of the guards of the sacred precincts. The guard gave Issa a beautiful Qur'an and took him and Malik on a tour of the inner realms of the *haram*, the sacred grounds, including a jour-ney in an elevator to the top of a minaret overlooking the Ka'aba. Thus, while other children his age were going up in roller coasters, Issa was blessed to rise up in a different vehicle, blessed to do and see things that are not usually done and seen.

Our hotel was less than five minutes from the Ka'aba. We both knew how close we were to all the light shining there, and neither of us could easily sleep. So, we would quietly get up, take the elevator down through the bookstore, and then walk out into the ocean of light that was circulating around the Ka'aba. On the night before my birthday, as we were heading towards that ocean of light, Issa bought me a Qur'an in the bookstore, one of the many great gifts I received from Allah (swt) on that birthday. How great was the gift of the light that we shared on that night! As a mother and nine-year old son traveling together, however, not everything was always totally clear between us. We did have our issues to work on. And our being together in that amazing place and situation provided us with the opportunity to share and transform our relationship deeply. We had some very interesting, serious talks in our hotel room and worked on some of the fundamental struggles of our relationship and life. Finally, we wrote a treaty, which dealt with everything we were going through in our life together and we signed it, with witnesses, on that sacred earth and in the presence of Allah *subhana wa ta'ala*.

From the time that we signed that document as a heartfelt expression of our commitment to God and to the betterment of our relationship, we've seen how deeply our life and journey have been, albeit through ongoing challenges, clarified, guided, and blessed. Such are the wonderful results of traveling for the sake of God. I am especially grateful that I have been able to share this holy transformative journey with my child.

There are many dimensions of journeying for the sake of God, and one of them is that sometimes you must go through challenges and difficulties, yet still you continue to travel. Then, the difficulty leads to a spiritual opening. When we had been in Mecca for several days, I became extremely ill. For a few days, I could barely move.

During this time, I heard about several people who were planning to climb the Mountain of Light to the cave where the Prophet Muhammad (saw) went into seclusion and received the revelation of the Holy Qur'an. I heard that it was a struggle for many people to climb the mountain. I wanted to climb the mountain and go to the cave very much, but I was very ill and thought it would be impossible for me to make the journey since at that point I could barely move.

The illness, I thought, was part of the purification of the pilgrimage, and I simply had to accept and endure it.

Then, when we were about to start on our second *'umra* (leaving the holy precincts temporarily in order to repeat pilgrimage rites), suddenly, a kind friend offered me medicine. I realized instantly that the medicine was from Allah *subhana wa ta'ala*, as well as the illness, so I took it. By the end of the *'umrah*, I was amazingly well. Then I knew that I must climb the Mountain of Light, no matter what, *insha'Allah!*

I went with four old and dear friends in a car to the base of the mountain. Immediately, one could see that this was an extraordinary place. Even in the village below, there are incredible rock formations. I felt that the mountain itself was somehow ablaze with vital energy. It was also very rugged and challenging to climb. A fellow pilgrim had led me to think deeply about the devotion and strength of Khadijah (ra), the beloved wife of the Prophet Muhammad (saw), and how she climbed this mountain every day to bring him food. In light of her profound devotion and the service that she rendered to the Messenger (saw) and his mission, I began to climb.

I bear witness that, after a few steps, I made no effort at all. I was carried up the mountain, exerting no energy of my own. This carried me up to the top of the mountain very quickly, much faster than my friends were able to go. I know that this was not at all due to physical strength or training. I was not in shape at all and had only the day before been extremely sick and weak, barely able to walk.

It was a gift from Allah *subhana wa ta'ala,* the Most Merciful, showing me that the ascent to the sanctified place, where the revelation is given, is empowered solely by grace. Climbing that mountain, I knew that the power of Allah (swt) had taken me, and I had not gotten there by my strength at all.

Close to the place of the cave where the Prophet Muhammad (saw) had stayed, I waited for the others, feeling greatly exhilarated and liberated from the physical body, the limited mind, and the force of gravity. I had never in my life felt so extremely healthy and strong.

When they arrived, we walked together, approaching the holy cave. There was a large group of people assembled there, worshipping in a loud and energetic way. They completed their worship and then continued on their way, allowing us to enter the cave in complete silence, stillness, and peace. Once you are at the entrance and in the cave, everything else ceases to exist. All sounds of people are silenced.

In this tiny cave, where there is only enough room for one person to stand and one person to sit or bow down, there is only the sense of the presence of the Messenger (saw) immersed in the Presence of Allah *subhana wa ta'ala*. One is led to contemplate what took place here and the huge significance for all the universes of what occurred to one man, hidden from the sight of the world, in the privacy of this tiny cave. This tiny space is, as I understood it, the epicenter of sacred space, that place where God and man, Master and servant, met and united, for the sake of bringing mercy to all the worlds.

As a child in elementary school, hearing the little that we did about the Prophet Muhammad (saw), all that I could envision was a man on a horse riding into battle with his turban flying in the wind. We did not hear or know about the man called by all *"Al-Amin"* (the most honest and trustworthy), who, perceiving the great darkness of idolatry, injustice, and cruelty enveloping the world around him, entered this cave and remained here, meditating, contemplating, and supplicating for years, as he was being prepared to receive the mantle of his prophethood.

We did not hear about this great mystery as we were growing up in America. Nor did we hear about how the Revelations of the Almighty descended upon him with such power that he was absolutely overwhelmed and profoundly shaken.

We did not hear about how the revelations of which the Qur'an is composed descended upon the Messenger (saw) verse by verse, as he sat in this cave or how he shared these with his Companions (ra) so that each of them memorized and absorbed every verse of the Qur'an as it was revealed. One of those verses states, *"If We were to send down this Qur'an upon a mountain, the mountain would be ground to dust"* (59:21). So powerful it was! And yet this powerful Revelation descended upon a small but growing group of humble, vulnerable human beings, and with the strength that God gave them, they were able to endure it and to become living embodiments of the words that the Creator was revealing to them and, through them, to us all. I did not hear about these things as I was growing up in Southern California, but the yearning for true knowledge was burning in my heart, and it would not let me rest anywhere, compelling me to travel from country to country, from mountain to valley, from shrine to shrine, cathedral to mosque, until finally I entered this cave.

Many holy sites have monuments built upon them. Underneath the marble and all the embellishment is the earth where one of the Prophets (as) or friends of God lived and prayed. Very often shrines have been constructed over the places they were buried. But nothing artificial, man-made, or modern has been built inside or around the cave where the Prophet Muhammad (saw) prayed. It is as it was when he sat there, when the power of the Revelation came upon him.

I felt the awesome honor and blessing to be praying upon the earth where he prayed, at the exact spot. I sensed so strongly that he was with me, within me, and that the same Lord that guided him to pray there also guided me to pray there.

As deeply inspiring as it was to go there, it is not the cave that is important but what took place there. This is what is to be celebrated and proclaimed, especially in light of the fact that it has been hidden from the view of so many human beings whose right it is to know the truth about their Creator and what He has revealed.

This book is my loving endeavor to share with the reader whatever I can of what has been shown to me so that the right of every one of us to discover His Liberating Truth may be fulfilled. Every step in this journey has been motivated by this intention.

As Allah *subhana wa ta'ala* willed so that I could draw closer to Him and come to know Him better, on that day I was carried by light into the light on the Mountain of Light. It was a pilgrimage to a place where there was nothing but purity and light, a shrine built and preserved for eternity by God.

I also bear witness, through the ever-continuing miracles of my life and journey, that the Messenger of Allah (saw), the servant of Allah *subhana wa ta'ala*, who was chosen in his purity to be the vehicle for the last revealed Message of Allah *subhana wa ta'ala*, is our beloved friend. The more we love him, invoke his presence, and long to be in his company, the closer we come to that radiant Light, the very same Light and Truth which guided and manifested through all the Prophets (as) who came before him, the Light of Allah *subhana wa ta'ala*, which dispels all darkness, illuminating the path that leads directly to Him, the One of infinite Grace.

Chapter Eighteen

RETURN TO THE CONTINENT OF ORIGIN

Senegal, West Africa and the US, 1999–2001

Did We not open wide your heart and lift your heavy load from
you that was breaking your back?
And have We not exalted your remembrance?
Truly with difficulty (comes) ease,
Truly, with difficulty ease.
So when the load is lifted, then rise up and to your Lord, strive.
—The Holy Qur'an 94:1-8

From the moment I made the supplication at the Ka'aba, I felt that I was being pulled through all of the layers in my being toward the light of the Messenger (saw), the light of Allah *subhana wa ta'ala*. I had caught a glimpse of it. But I needed to be purified, clarified, and deeply realigned in order to become the true servant that Allah *subhana wa ta'ala* created me to be. I needed to find my place in the divine universe and more deeply come to appreciate the true companions of my soul with whom I could reunite with the Divine Presence in completeness.

We can imagine the goal, even catch a glimpse of it, but to reach the destination is a very deep complex process. As the title of this book suggests, there are so many veils to penetrate. I have referred to them as *ten thousand* only as a figure of speech. Sufis often say that there are seventy-two thousand veils to pierce through.

The reality is that the light within us is covered up by many things, and to realize the true purpose for which we were created, to become who we truly are, we need to be liberated from attachment to these attachments. The divinely guided journey is the means by which we learn to let go, one by one, of each thing we have become attached to other than our connection to the pure light, which is the light of the Divine within us.

I have seen that the veils are pierced, penetrated, and lifted in different ways. On all the different levels of our experience in this life, both the difficulties that we have to endure and our release from these difficulties can become a means by which we are purified and brought closer to the reality of our true existence, that is our relationship to the Reality, which is Allah *subhana wa ta'ala*.

Marriage, childbirth, child-raising, earning a living, simply interacting with other people, caring for and serving the creations of our Lord, pursuing the path of purification and transformation under the guidance of a Spiritual Master, and through all this, striving to be a sincere servant of the Master of all — all of these can be annihilating and purifying experiences that we may have to go through to get to the Goal.

Simply being alive in the time in which we live and experiencing, to any degree, the suffering that so many people are enduring is a deep test both of our faith and our commitment to serve. But, as the Qur'an tells us in Surat'ul Inshirah, *"Truly, with difficulty comes ease. Truly, with difficulty comes ease"* (94:5-6). This is a passage of the Qur'an that explains so much about what all human beings must go through in our life on this earth and in our journey to God.

Many of us recite this *surah* many times a day because of its profound relevance and power to remind us of the intimate and intrinsic relationship between difficulty and ease.

As these complex experiences unfold, one after the next, we come to see that whatever difficulty we may be facing there is an ease, mercy and blessing that comes with it, if, only in surrendering to the Source of mercy, we can perceive and access it.

In contemplating the meaning of this surah and the significance of this formula given to us by our Creator, we must reflect upon the circumstances in which the surah was revealed and the great difficulties faced by the Prophet Muhammad (saw) and his companions (ra), which they endured solely for the sake of Allah (swt) and the manifestation of His will on earth.

The Prophet Muhammad (saw) was sitting in the Cave of Hira when the Divine Command was addressed to him through the mediation of the Angel Gabriel: *"Iqra! Read!"* Muhammad (saw) was unlettered and could not read. He was being asked to read and recite, receive, behold, witness: the Divine Revelation as it was being transmitted to him.

On the first occasion, the power was so immense that he went to his wife Khadijah (ra) totally shaken and asked to be covered by a blanket to calm him, so utterly powerful and overwhelming was the experience. From the very beginning, his task was immensely difficult, as was the task of all the Prophets (as), to deliver to a humanity often unwilling to listen to the message that God willed to send to His creatures.

What they had to endure, of hardship in fulfilling the mission bestowed upon them by the Creator, is far beyond our capacity to know or comprehend. But we know that they accepted whatever was given to them in a state of submission to the One who had decreed them to go through all this, and it was through this state of profound surrender to the Divine Decree that all the difficulties they endured led them to the highest victory and success, that highest level of victory for a creation, which is to accomplish what the Creator wills it to do. This success cannot be attained without the journey through many different kinds of challenges and difficulties.

So, following the Prophets (as), who are our guides, and the examples Allah *subhana wa ta'ala* has given us, revealing the way a true human being should be, we each realize that we must go through difficulties in our search for the truth and in manifesting that truth if we find it. This is clearly stated in the Holy Qur'an, when Allah *subhana wa ta'ala* asks:

> *Or do you think that you shall enter the Garden without such trials as came to those who passed away before you? They encountered suffering and adversity and were so shaken in spirit that even the Messenger and those of faith who were with him cried: "When will come the help of God?" Ah! Verily, the help of God is (always) near.*
>
> The Holy Qur'an 2:214

This, I believe, is a crucially important passage of the Qur'an. It tells us, first, that we cannot reach paradise, the garden of nearness to our Lord, without undergoing hardship and adversity, and that even the Holy Prophet (saw) and his Companions (ra), the most noble and blessed of all the creations, in the midst of what was decreed for them to go through, cried for the help of Allah *subhana wa ta'ala*.

And, finally, Allah *subhana wa ta'ala* gives us the key, the solution to every problem, when He reminds us that His help is always near. We need to become aware, no matter what we are going through, that He, who has the solution for all our problems, is always unfathomably near. The difficulty is simply something that we have to go through so that we may come to realize, through calling the One that is always present, that His help is always near.

Consider all the hardship, oppression and plagues endured by the Children of Israel in Egypt. Then behold how the Holy One parted for them the sea, enabling them to walk through on dry ground while Pharaoh and his people drowned. Surely in this situation, as in all, He revealed that along with the difficulty, on the path that leads to Him, comes the ease.

The utility, for the seeker of nearness to the Lord, of difficulties encountered along the way, is that they are indeed the context in which we turn to God, our Divine Source, for help. To this end, it seems that each one of us has a unique configuration of tests and trials to go through as we are journeying to our Lord. But no matter what difficulty may be given to us to experience and endure in the way of God, Allah Most Merciful has told us that there is an easing, an opening, an expansion or liberation and a blessing and teaching that comes with it.

However intense the contraction, it is not a permanent state, but will give way in due time to the next stage of expansion, the next stage of growth, the next door opening into the next station of our journey. It is a reward from our Lord, of mercy and knowledge, for each sacrifice that we make, each difficulty that we endure for the sake of drawing closer to Him.

And when we arrive at that opening and the pressure of the trial is released, as the burden is lifted from our back, with all the energy that has been liberated from the difficulty, the Qur'an tells us we must stand in the presence of our Lord and strive to rise in the celebration of His praise.

It is not possible for me or for anyone telling the story of their life and journey in the way of Allah *subhana wa ta'ala* to describe the number of times such a passage has taken place or the repercussions and the blessings and gifts that emerge from this process of labor, this process of dying and being resurrected by the grace of Allah. When we give birth to a child, the pain is as intense as we can bear but not more.

Allah *subhana wa ta'ala* tells us in the Qur'an, "*We do not give to the soul a burden greater than it has the capacity to bear*" (7:42). Whatever it may be, it is not greater than we can bear. But, sometimes, it does seem to be as great as we can bear. It is great because it pushes us beyond our limits, beyond our fears, prejudices, conceptions, and attachments. When you are in the midst of labor (as in the process of dying), you do not worry about what you look like or what people think or say about you. You are busy. You are completely involved in the process until it comes to completion and the fruit for which you have been laboring is manifest.

Being able to bear the pain of childbirth earns for us the reward of the beautiful baby that comes out of that labor. Being able to bear the pain of child raising, if we do this in the way of Allah *subhana wa ta'ala,* earns us the reward of seeing a beautiful human being emerge.

As we continue to travel in the way of Allah *subhana wa ta'ala,* we come to realize that we are the child and the beautiful human being that is emerging, but nothing can happen without the labor! In order to be born, truly, to be born again as a true human being, we have to die, again and again, so that everything within us that is not truly consecrated to the work of the Eternal passes away. The process of growth, evolution, and transformation inevitably demands real change.

The Qur'an tells us that surely what is coming is greater than anything we have known before: *"Assuredly what comes after will be better for you than what has gone before"* (93:4).

God willing that we are traveling on the path that leads directly to Him, we will realize what these words really mean. As we travel towards that end, we must continuously let go of what we have previously known and unconsciously become attached to in order to attain the greater reality that we are journeying toward. This requires true fearlessness, trust, and willingness to surrender to the ultimate Guide who is leading us through all the stages of our development.

After the passing of our beloved Sheikh, Bawa Muhaiyaddeen (ra), I was inspired to continue to travel on the journey of purification and transformation, to bring to fruition all the seeds that had been planted within me. I was next guided to meet Sheikh Abdoulaye Dieye (ra) of Senegal, West Africa. Sheikh Abdoulaye Dieye (ra), I believe, came into my life to continue to accelerate the process of my purification, leading to the ultimate Goal. He guided me in a direction in which I had to face many challenges and psychological hardships, ultimately enabling me to penetrate many veils in the quest of becoming who I truly am. He exposed to me the shadow world of unworthiness, fear, doubt, and pain so that these very tendencies within me, all based upon illusion, could be dispelled. He came to break the earth, so plants and flowers could grow in it. He appeared in my life as a catalyst because I *needed* to continue to grow.

From the moment on December 8, 1986 when Sheikh Bawa Muhaiyaddeen (ra) left this world, I had remained in a holding pattern, honoring the deep practices he had established, such as the inner *dhikr* (zikr), the outer *dhikr,* and also the formal prayer. I continued to work on the editing of books, as he had asked me to do. I had the child, Issa Muhaiyaddeen Kabeer, about whom he had spoken to me so many times before Issa was born. And I proceeded to travel around the world with my son. All of this was deeply important and meaningful, but there was a sense in which I knew that I needed to continue to dynamically travel on the spiritual journey, so Allah *subhana wa ta'ala* placed in my path another catalytic force to propel the seeker through the veils towards the Goal.

A few years after the passing of Sheikh Bawa Muhaiyaddeen (ra), I met Sheikh Abdolaye Dieye (ra) from Senegal, West Africa at a Sufi Symposium in San Francisco. He was one of the presenters at the conference. I met him in the suite we had organized in which we served food to the participants in the conference.

Immediately upon meeting me, he spoke to me about Senegal and invited me to visit there, which I did a few months later. Then he expressed interest in Bawa (ra) and said that he would like to come with some of his disciples to Philadelphia. I invited them to stay in our house which was then, as it always has been, a refuge for wayfarers on the path. The Sheikh (ra) and several of his disciples, most of whom were from islands in the Indian Ocean, happily accepted the invitation, just as I very happily welcomed them. It is always an honor and blessing to receive guests *fisabillilah* (for the sake of God), in the way of Allah *subhana wa ta'ala.* Seeing the disciples camped out all around the house made me feel that this was what the house was all about.

Upon his arrival in Philadelphia, Sheikh Dieye (ra) said to me that he had come to pour water on seeds planted by Sheikh Bawa Muhaiyaddeen (ra). It did seem that he poured water upon the earth within me in which the seeds were planted and also turned the soil so that it could be aerated and receive the water.

He knew things about me that I did not tell him. He acknowledged the potential within me to serve God and indicated to me that he could and would develop that potential. That was what interested me in this relationship --the possibility that he could help me to develop my potential as a servant of God. I wanted most deeply to continue to develop in the capacity to truly serve, and I hoped that, in whatever way, this connection could help me to progress.

The Sheikh (ra) frequently expressed what he was teaching through diagrams. I mentioned once that I wondered why, although I had been married, I had not found my true mate. He drew a picture of a pot covered with a lid, an image that Sheikh Bawa (ra) also often used in speaking about marriage. Sheikh Dieye (ra) said that I had such a large pot that it was difficult to find a lid large enough to fit it.

The image he had drawn made a deep impression upon me, and I could understand its possible relevance. But as time went on, I also attributed to it a different significance. It seemed to be, in another dimension, an illustration of the transformative process I was undergoing in the presence of the Sheikh (ra). The covered pot was a crucible in which an alchemical transformation was taking place. It was as though, throughout the work which unfolded between us, he had placed a cover on the pot, which was my process, and fire below, causing whatever was in the pot continuously to boil. In the course of our deep sharing, he bestowed upon me the mantle of Sheikha, and as the mystery unfolded, he taught me how deep that initiation really was.

From the time I met Sheikh Dieye (ra) until he left this world, suddenly, at the age of sixty-three, I traveled with him and whatever small group of disciples was traveling with him, frequently. This was definitely a journey through worlds which demanded, most of all, spiritual and emotional stamina. His own life was often threatened by various extreme health conditions. Nevertheless, regardless of any illness or condition, he traveled ceaselessly with the intention of accomplishing his mission.

He was like a candle burning at both ends and blazing in the middle. The intensity of this energy was contagious and activated a similar intensity within me. This is why I say that for me, traveling and working with him was like being in a crucible whose lid was almost never lifted. Wherever we were in the world, in whatever colorful locale or gathering, he led me on the path of purification. It seemed that so much within me that needed to be purified and thus transformed was, by the process of traveling with him, constantly being addressed and alchemically cleansed.

Once again, the attachments, illusions, and impurities were burning, while the gold, the pure essence of truth, was being cleaned and purified.

This training, in cutting the attachment to the ego — the illusory identity — purifying the sincere servant within to serve purely, was often so difficult and intense at the hands of Sheikh Abdoulaye Dieye (ra) that sometimes I imagined longingly how simple it would be to just get up and walk out of whatever house we were in and back into the "free" world, where I would not have to continue to endure this process of continual purification. But, in reality, I was, for all the time that I knew him until I was released during the last week, undergoing a kind of profound psychological surgery on the operating table, and I could not get up and go anywhere until the operation was done.

Once in a while, he gave me a clue and a sense of hope, the sense of a light at the end of the long, dark tunnel, by saying very quietly to me in the middle of the trial, "I am only doing this to perfect you." Such messages gave me the strength to endure the very difficult process of purification and transformation.

Along with all the difficult contractions, there were two deep gifts of expansion which Sheikh Dieye (ra) also gave to me. He guided me back to Africa, the great continent of origin, and, he introduced me to the teaching and the noble example of Sheikh Ahmadu Bamba (ra), the Sheikh of his Sheikh (ra), and one of Africa's great Sufi Masters.

I had come to experience the mysteries of Islam and the Sufi path in many countries of the world, stage by stage and step by step. Knowledge is always revealed in stages. In Afghanistan, I saw the beautiful vision, as the buses stopped in the middle of the desert, of all of the passengers getting out and laying their prayer mats out in the desert to pray. That vision continued to evolve and deepen throughout my life and journey.

I saw the family praying and playing joyously together all night in the garden under the starry sky in Mashad, and I beheld people of light pouring out of the mosque in that holy city.

I saw the ancient grandfather, Sidi Sheikh Abdul Muttalib (ra), his wife and disciples bowing down in a sacred cave. Then, suddenly and naturally, I too bowed down and became a part of the congregation. This is the organic process of embracing Islam — entering into the reality of Islam.

First, you see an image, which slowly attracts you profoundly. Although it may be the first time you have seen it, this image — like the people spreading out their prayer mats in the middle of the desert and praying — stirs up a deep sense of spiritual awareness.

Although it is apparently the first time you have seen it, this image reminds you of something you have known before in your distant past, something within you that you are longing intensely to reconnect with and reclaim.

You are, at first, like a person on the shore of a great ocean, contemplating its beauty. Then you jump in, you become immersed, you become a part of and inseparable from that beauty.

Like that vast ocean is the assembly of the believers, called the ummah. Though there are impurities within the people in the ummah, the ocean itself, the assembly of souls gathered to worship the Creator, is pure.

From the moment of entering into the *ummah,* the community of true believers, I have continued to travel around the world, finding that this assembly, this gathering of the believers joined together to praise and worship the One and only Creator, is taking place in countries and assemblies around the world.

The Creator has told us that the whole world is our mosque, the place in which we bow down to Him, and "*Whithersoever you turn, there is the Face of God*" (The Holy Qur'an 2:115). And this is what I have observed taking place everywhere the journey has led me. It is a universal reality totally transcending any cultural differences. As we continue to travel on the way that leads from God to God, with each real step, more knowledge and understanding is given to us about the path we are traveling on.

In every country, in every village, in every mosque, in every assembly of the faithful, and in the presence of every Sheikh (ra), I received more knowledge and more understanding of the meaning and experience of Islam and the path of *Tasawwuf,* the Sufi path. Then, to continue to gain the ever-deepening understanding of the teaching, I was guided to *Africa!*

Since the time that I first went to Africa, specifically to Senegal, West Africa, I have been drawn back sixteen more times. What ultimately drew me there so many times is a great mystery that I have been compelled, from the first moment I set foot upon this land, to penetrate and, stage by stage, come to understand.

Nothing among the landscapes of Senegal that I saw on my visits was so interesting and beautiful as to cause me to return so many times.

So, why was I compelled to return again and again? What was compelling, irresistibly magnetic, was the knowledge of the Divine, the gems and treasures of Divine Knowledge, the mystical dimensions of Islam, that lie beneath the surface in the vast deserts of West Africa. It is also compelling because of the open heart of the people and the uniquely powerful way in which the *dhikr*, remembrance of Allah *subhana wa ta'ala* is pouring through that open heart and spreading throughout the land.

The first time I went to Senegal was with Issa in the month of May to commemorate the *Maggal,* the exile of Sheikh Ahmadu Bamba (ra). For the followers of Sheikh Ahmadu Bamba (ra), the most important event in the life of the Sheikh (ra) is the time when he entered into an extended period of exile, ultimately thirty-three years, imposed upon him by French colonialists.

It is not the time when he was liberated from this oppression that is celebrated but his entering into the trial. The exile and all the tribulations that he endured on the path of God for the sake of God were for Sheikh Ahmadu Bamba (ra), as he said, the source of blessing, and that wealth of blessing is what is celebrated.

Our intention to learn about the life of Sheikh Ahmadu Bamba (ra), and all those who endure hardship for the sake of serving and drawing closer to God, brought us, also, some difficulty, and with the difficulty, as always, came the blessing.

We arrived at three in the morning, the time we always arrived and parted from Senegal. We were greeted by Sheikh Dieye's driver, Sheikh Babu(ra). Since there was not enough room in the car, Issa went first, and I followed on the next trip. As soon as he arrived at the Sheikh's house, Issa was offered a tall glass of water, which he readily drank, being very thirsty after the journey. That was the beginning of his trial.

I was picked up several minutes later, and as the wind from the desert blew in through the car window, I felt the great peace of coming *home* again. Sheikh Dieye's house was about fifteen minutes from the airport, enough time to begin to get acclimatized to the land, the air, the energy. I went into the mode of attunement and knew that in some way I had certainly been here before.

As the Sheikh was an architect, his house was very thoughtfully designed and very spacious, yet with a minimum of furniture. I went to pray in the appropriate corner of the large prayer and assembly room, and I felt and heard the resonance of prayer pouring through me, and, filling all the worlds. I remembered praying in the *zawiyyah* (prayer space) on the Mount of Olives and in so many other empty rooms filled with light. I was so happy to be in the place of prayer, in a room filled not with a lot of furniture but with the sound of prayer.

The next morning, extremely early, everyone was awake, preparing to make the journey to Touba, the city founded by Sheikh Ahmadu Bamba (ra) as a spiritual center in which the teachings he had been transmitting could be manifested. Issa and I were in the back of the Sheikh's car in a kind of hatchback where we could fit only by lying tightly tucked in next to each other. We traveled for many hours like this. Although we were packed in and squeezed, we were comfortable simply to be traveling together in the way of God.

The journey to Touba is extraordinary because on one single road there are so many cars, trucks, and buses packed with people, often standing for hours on the sides and roofs of these vehicles — all of these heavily laden vehicles making the pilgrimage all at the same time.

That so many people travel, in any way possible, often under extreme physical duress, to get to Touba, is a sign of the deep impact that Sheikh Ahmadu Bamba (ra) had upon the people of Senegal. He, who had been so greatly tried and had transformed every difficulty into ease and victory for the sake of God, became a beacon of light and a symbol of hope for people suffering and struggling in so many ways.

For the hope that he represented to transform their difficulties into the light of grace, a great many people are willing to undergo hardship to make the pilgrimage to Touba. The road leading to Touba in the time of the Maggal is so packed it is almost impossible to move — a massive traffic jam on the way to God. Sheikh Babu (ra), however, was tremendously creative, fearless, and resourceful, and we soon learned that driving with him was often very much off the beaten path and paved road. So, when the cars were all lined up on the paved road, we often left the road entirely and drove over hill and dale, venturing across the natural terrain. What a journey!

We arrived late at night in the countryside surrounding Touba and were received very beautifully and sweetly by many people making *dhikr* (zikr), disciples of the Sheikh who had been preparing and waiting for hours to surround his car and welcome him to Touba with love and honor.

On the pilgrimage to places of power in the presence of people of light, Touba is one of the power points, one of the centers of mystical energy, a place consecrated from its conception by Sheikh Ahmadu Bamba (ra), who invoked with its name the Tree of Touba, a tree planted by God in Paradise and referred to in Sufi literature. As Ibn Sirrin wrote in *The Interpretation of Dreams*:

> When a man dreams that he is sitting under the tree of Touba, he gains the best of both worlds, since God has said, "For them is blessedness and a beautiful place of return" (*The Holy Qur'an* 13:29). If he finds himself in its gardens, he gains faithfulness and perfection of religion. If he eats its fruits, knowledge equivalent to the fruits he has tasted will be given to him. Equally, if he drinks from its water, its wine and its milk, he will be given wisdom, knowledge and riches.

It was to this mystical ideal that Sheikh Ahmadu Bamba (ra) dedicated the city he built, intending and beseeching Allah (swt) that the sincere seekers who made the pilgrimage to it would gain such benefits. Issa and I had now arrived at this station in our pilgrimage, ready to learn what God wished to reveal to us.

The procession moved to an enclave of tents set up specifically for this holy occasion. With the beautiful *dhikr* surrounding us, we went to sleep for a short while under the tents and woke up with the sun burning so intensely that we could barely move. I have never experienced such heat before or after that day.

The heat was so strong we were barely able to sit up. We were literally pressed to the ground. When we were able to barely get up and walk to the ablution area, we found only a tiny trickle of running water. Yet, this holy place, hotter than any place I could imagine, had been an oasis of cool refuge for Sheikh Ahmadu Bamba (ra) when he had finally arrived here after so many years of exile.

The heat of Touba, along with the water, which he had drunk immediately upon arriving, now made Issa very sick. He went to visit the Sheikh (ra) in his tent and immediately released the contents of his stomach on the Sheikh's bed. The Sheikh accepted this graciously, had the bed cleaned, and kept Issa near him, hugging him. He later said that this was an initiation for Issa, in which he released many of the veils and difficulties of his past, preparing for the next, wide-open dimensions of his life.

Our arrival in Africa was, for both of us, the opening of the door into a very significant process and spiritual homecoming. Issa has returned to Africa seven times so far. In the summer of 2003, when he was fifteen, he went alone to pursue his study of the Qur'an and experienced another rite of passage, this one almost on his own.

When he arrived at the airport in Senegal, for some reason, he was not able to find his ride. Since he had the address of the school, he simply found a taxi and got there on his own. On his return trip, when he arrived at the airport in Paris, again, no one was there to meet him. Actually, they had gone to another airport in Paris to meet him. He waited for a day and a half at Orly Airport, without doubting his destiny or losing the peace and light of the Qur'an that he had gained. When he was finally found, those searching for him said that he was sitting, patiently, with no sign of stress or distress, like a little Sufi Master. So, that was a sign of the progress on the journey of his soul, he had made, from the time he first arrived in Africa.

I believe that it was also significant in his unfolding life journey that from the early years of his life in Africa he did abundant dhikr, such as hundreds of thousands of the powerful prayer called Salat al-Fatih, as well as pursuing his studies of the Qur'an. These processes, in which he was engaged in the early years of his life, established a spiritual foundation upon which, I pray, he will be able to build in later years in a variety of ways.

My own relationship with Africa remains a great and deep mystery to me, but it is a mystery slowly and surely being unveiled. It is the mystery of the attraction of Adam (as) and Eve (ra), the black and the white, the East and the West, the apparent polarities powerfully attracted to each other by the power of absolute Oneness.

It is not only an individual quest but the quest of humanity, the creation of the Creator Most Merciful, for reconciliation and union. This movement toward ultimate integration and unity, spiritually, humanly, and globally, along with the intention for healing the wounds of separation, is what compelled me, one born ostensibly "white" to go to Africa so many times.

Sheikh Abdoulaye Dieye (ra) was not my ultimate guide in the path of reconciliation, healing, and union. He was a catalyst for my process of growth, a teacher and friend on the way, an expander of my horizons. One major way in which he did that was by inviting me to come to Africa.

He said that he had come to Philadelphia to pour water on the seeds planted by Sheikh Bawa Muhaiyaddeen (ra). The teaching of Bawa's that he activated most for me was, *"You must love all lives as your own."* All the lives that I must love are not in the Fellowship house. They are not in my house or the house next door or the house down the street. A fundamental blessing of meeting Sheikh Dieye was that in traveling with him and then continuing to travel with his Successor, Sheikh Aly, I met so many people and came to love so many more lives as my own. In this way, the Sheikhs did water the seeds that Bawa had planted in my heart and made this love and knowledge grow.

Sheikh Dieye (ra) was a member of the Senegalese Parliament and also a candidate for the Presidency of Senegal. Several times, I had the very interesting experience of traveling with him and a group of disciples on the campaign trail. That was a fantastic experience that is completely different than anything we, in the West, could imagine, a totally different kind of campaigning.

Wherever we went, into whatever town, village, or area of bush, great numbers of children came running and surrounded the Sheikh's (ra) car, exclaiming *"Allahu Wahidun! Allahu Wahidun!"* *"God is One! God is One!"* They were the Sheikh's (ra) supporters. Large groups of children and some adults would run alongside his car for many blocks, exclaiming *"Allahu Wahidun!"* This is what he was called everywhere; his own name was never used.

One day he said, "We are going to a political rally. Get ready." As we were traveling, I was trying to visualize what kind of rally it would be, based upon my past experience of political rallies. We drove for hours and went deep into the bush. There was nothing like a street sign anywhere, no sign of any kind indicating where we were. There was only the desert and the bush.

Once in a while, a horse-drawn cart would appear in the desert and our driver would ask the driver of the cart for directions. I thought to myself, "What kind of rally is this?" Thinking that many people would be gathering together from many different places, I wondered how they could even find this place.

We went from unmarked desert into thick bush. The car was surrounded by dense vegetation. Finally, we arrived in a clearing at a tiny village and all got out. We went into a small house and met with some of the Sheikh's people. We all greeted each other. Then, we went outside again and were told that the meeting was about to begin. Several straw mats were laid out under a tree, and everyone sat down. A beautiful newborn baby was placed in my lap.

One mat was filled only with children. In fact, the majority of people at this "rally" were scantily clothed children. The Sheikh (ra) addressed his discourse to them. He was speaking in Wolof, so I could not understand what he said. But I saw that he was speaking to the little children, and they were applauding his points, responding with great enthusiasm.

When his discourse, or *campaign speech,* was completed, he turned to me and said in French, *"The whole world has forgotten these children. You must not forget them."* In this sentence was the essence of the teaching that was given throughout the journeys and the kind of experience we had. He then told me that these children very much needed clothing and blankets and that we must gather and send them these supplies.

This message so deeply affected me. Both before and after I heard these words spoken, I have intensely wished to help the children of the world, the needy and indigent. When we had returned to America after this trip, we went to the Friends Meeting at the Quaker School Issa was attending.

When I told this story to those gathered in the assembly, they too were moved, and, within a week, many blankets and clothes were gathered to send to those children in Africa. This was so easy to do: to transfer even a tiny amount of the excess of resources that we have here to people who have so little and appreciate everything so much. I hope and pray that in my lifetime I may not forget the lives in need but may serve as a conduit through which aid is delivered (not only materially).

My travels throughout Africa continuously inspired a deeper and deeper sense of love and connectedness with living beings. From one village to the next, one gathering to the next, I met countless African children, many of whom had never seen a "white" person before. All of them wanted to touch my hand, as I wanted to touch theirs and hug them. All of them were people I could not forget. They are all our children, and whenever I hear or see on a bumper sticker, the slogan, "God Bless America," I can only affirm with all my heart what I truly believe: *God bless the world. God bless all the worlds that He has created out of His love and His light.*

I had always intuitively known these truths, the truth of the oneness and interconnectedness of all lives. Being in Africa deepened the knowledge and experience. When you are in the middle of a desert in a large gathering of children who have almost nothing but are shining with light and love and joy, the consumer world, with all its glitters and attractions, all the things that you have personally owned or wished to have, fades away into the distance like a mirage, an illusion with no reality.

The reality that you see and feel, taste and experience, is that you are one with all beings, all of these children are your own, all lives are your own. When you hold these children in your arms and feel the warmth of their bodies and their hearts, you know that politics, power, and possessions have no intrinsic reality or benefit. What does have reality and importance among the things we encounter in the world is the preciousness of every living being that we meet. They are all uniquely precious and intrinsically valuable, being created by the One of Infinite value, power, and grace, and He has created nothing in vain.

Those who, throughout the ages, truly believe in, seek, gain, and wield political and mercantile power cannot afford to consider the value and preciousness of all living beings. As much as they speak about God and in the name of God, they are servants of the force whose express goal is to destroy the beauty and truth and unity of God's holy creation. But the Messengers of God (as), the people of God, those truly submitted to the only true Power, have come to earth again and again, appearing in every time and to the people of every nation, to purify the places of purity and protect and guide the pure of heart. As Jesus (as) did, they throw the money lenders out of the holy places and ask for the children, the pure of heart, to come forward.

They are the people who serve only God and speak only as God guides them to speak. Never do they speak as the corrupt leaders of the world guide them to speak. Sheikh Ahmadu Bamba (ra), who rose up out of the soil of Africa at the end of the nineteenth century to fight against the forces of oppression and corruption with the light of unwavering faith, was such a person.

Following the example of the Prophet Muhammad (saw), the last of the long line of Messengers (as), with deep love and scrupulous dedication, he, along with other great servants of the One, living in Africa at this time, inspired the light of the pure teaching of the One God to shine for people of Africa and, ultimately, the world. This was the second gift of expansion given to me by Sheikh Abdoulaye Dieye (ra), which he gave me simultaneously with the gift of return to Africa.

CHAPTER NINETEEN

WALKING IN THE FOOTSTEPS OF THE
FRIENDS OF GOD

Dakar, Gabon, Lambarene and Mayumba, 2000

Ye have indeed in the Messenger of Allah a beautiful pattern (of conduct) for any one whose hope is in Allah and the Final Day, and who engages much in the praise of Allah.
—The Holy Qur'an 33:21

"My religion is the love of God."

"Allāh led me to Muḥammad (saw). Muḥammad (saw) can lead me back to Allāh."

"The only weapons I will use to fight my enemies are the pen and the ink that I use to write my poems in the glory of the Chosen One (saw)."

"When they put the chains on me, Allāh opened the doors of mystery for me."

"The motive of my departure to exile is the will of God to elevate me and to make of me the mediator between my people and the Prophet (saw).

—Teachings of Sheikh Ahmadu Bamba (ra)

For many weeks, I had seen the word Gabon popping up in French emails sent to us by organizers of an historic pilgrimage to be made by a group of people including Sheikh Mourtada (ra), the son of Sheikh Ahmadu Bamba (ra), for the first time in many years to a remote island in equatorial Africa called Mayumba, as well as to other locations in the region where Sheikh Ahmadu Bamba (ra) had spent many years in exile imposed upon him by the French Colonialists. This proposed event sounded to me like something formal and "official" and therefore not too compelling to my independent nature.

Then, the word *walking* appeared — walking in the footsteps of the Sheikh (ra). This definitely drew me. I felt these messages pulling on my feet.

By the grace of Allah *subhana wa ta'ala*, I had been blessed to pray in the cave where the Prophet Muhammad (saw) received the revelation of the Holy Qur'an. I had prayed in the garden of Gethsemane, where Jesus (as) had prayed with his disciples and walked along the path from the Mount of Olives to Bethany, where I sensed that he had walked. On my first trip to Senegal, I had prayed in the prison cell where Sheikh Ahmadu Bamba (ra) had been imprisoned. Because all of these experiences had affected me so deeply, when I saw the words "*walk* where he walked," I was moved to go.

Why is this? It is because I know that this life is a sacred journey, a pilgrimage leading to greater knowledge and experience of the Divine, and, therefore, when, by the decree of God, the way opens to walk in the footsteps of the people of light, automatically my feet will go there.

The people of light are those upon whom God's grace is perpetually falling, those whose entire existence is a pilgrimage, those whose sole intention is to worship God alone, those who turn to Him alone for help. They are those who do not go astray. Therefore, they are our blessed guides, our *imams,* and our intention is always to follow them.

From the time that I learned *Surat'ul-Fatihah*, and even long before that, I knew that I wanted to travel in their company and to go the way that they were going. It was not to worship them, to say how great they were, but to go the way that they were going — to follow the Path that they were following.

This is the real reason that I went on the journey to Gabon and to other places where Sheikh Ahmadu Bamba (ra) had spent many years in exile and endured many trials for the sake of Allah *subhana wa ta'ala* and the love of His Messenger (saw). My purpose for going to these places was to access and develop within myself the qualities that I perceived in him, such as profound faith, determination, fearlessness, acceptance and contentment with the Divine Decree. These were all divinely inspired qualities that enabled the Sheikh (ra) to live through the tribulations he experienced with ever-increasing faith, gratitude and joy.

What does it mean to walk in the footsteps of the *awliya,* the *friends?* of God? For me, it does not mean to wear a photograph of the teacher around your neck and thereby define yourself as his disciple. Nor does it mean to create a tight, close-knit community, like a fortress, that will exclusively protect the teachings of the teacher.

The Truth can be protected and preserved only by the Truth. The friends of God, the beings of light that we stand behind and walk with, are those immersed in the unlimited ocean of Divine Consciousness. The only way that we can really follow them is to dissolve in that ocean of God's Truth as they have, through God's grace and His guidance.

This is not an organization we can join and then claim that we are great because we are members of it. The transformation, the process of purification, dissolution, immersion, and merging does not occur quickly or easily; we have to persevere in the journey and go through many stages and stations, *insha'Allah,* to reach it.

I was guided, at this time, to walk in the footsteps of Sheikh Ahmadu Bamba (ra), not to worship him, or to serve his family, or to become a member of any exclusive group, but to study profoundly how he lived, how he stood directly behind the Messenger of Allah (saw), and how he served Allah *subhana wa ta'ala* with great dedication, following the example of the Prophet Muhammad (saw).

The history of his life is significant because in the course of fulfilling his mission, Sheikh Ahmadu Bamba (ra) faced extreme hardships and tests, all of which he transformed into victories for the sake of Allah *subhana wa ta'ala.*

I had been studying the life of Sheikh Ahmadu Bamba (ra) and learned that he was a devout child born of a very pious mother and erudite father who was also a religious leader serving the King. The young Ahmadu Bamba amazed those around him with his knowledge, his nobility of character, sense of ethics and justice and detachment.

He rapidly surpassed all his fellow students as well as his teachers in Qur'anic studies and mastered the teachings of the Sufi orders predominant in Senegal, the Qadiriyyah, the Tijaniyyah, and the Shadhiliyyah, until, as he expressed it in many *qasidas (poems of praise),* he was standing directly behind the Prophet Muhammad (saw).

Being empowered by the light and the presence of the Prophet (saw), he accepted and submitted to no other authority than the authority of God. Thus, he could not be controlled by worldly powers, and for this reason he became a threat to the authorities of the world, especially the French colonialists, the imperial force of that time that was controlling and oppressing Senegal. It was not only his own state of liberation that threatened the colonial forces which were oppressing his country and his people but the power of God within him that could liberate others.

Sheikh Ahmadu Bamba (ra) had profound love for the Prophet Muhammad (saw), and it was by this love that he was elevated so quickly and powerfully out of the framework of this world. It was also through his nearness to the Prophet (saw) and his pure devotion to God that he had to endure many trials. These tests were apparently imposed by the colonial forces, who wished to destroy the threat he posed to them, but at the same time, as he stated in many qasidas (devotional songs), they became the means enabling his spiritual ascent.

We had been learning about the inspiring story of the life of Sheikh Ahmadu Bamba (ra) from Sheikh Abdoulaye Dieye (ra) who was now requesting our participation in the pilgrimage that would take us to the places where the Sheikh (ra) endured some of many tests. Now, in response to this invitation to deepen our knowledge and experience of the spiritual journey, two friends and sisters in the Muridiyyah Tariqah, Nasiha and Jariatullah, and I flew to Dakar.

When we arrived at the airport, however, we discovered that our flight to Gabon had been cancelled. And we did not even know when the next plane would be operating. The pilgrimage had begun! This was the stage of acceptance — surrender to the Will of God. We remained in the hot, dirty, disorganized airport for nine hours waiting to discover what we were to do next.

This was a time in which to purify our intention and focus our inner prayer, with really nothing else happening, a time in which to realize that the journey to God is not what we expect or wish it to be. It is what it is, a school in which we are formed and developed, in which we grow in understanding in proportion to our submission to the Divine Will, which is manifesting through exactly what is happening.

Finally, after nine hours of being suspended in this state, we were released from the airport and given vouchers to stay in a hotel for the next few days until the next plane might leave for Gabon. We took a taxi to the hotel, which was quite a lovely one, surrounded by a beautiful garden of exotic trees on the shore of the ocean, a breath of earthly paradise after our confinement in the hot and dirty airport. This, in itself, was a gift from God, a reminder of His beneficence and confirmation of His words, *"Truly, with difficulty comes ease."*

A few days later, we went to the airport, the plane was running, and we flew to Gabon. We were greeted at the airport in Gabon like celebrities, the American pilgrims who had traveled so far to make this historic pilgrimage and then could not get a plane. Everyone had been waiting for us. There were cameras everywhere and flashing lights. It was strange indeed for pilgrims on an inner journey of the dissolution of the self, to be received like movie stars.

We met with Sheikh Dieye (ra) and the assembled disciples in the morning. Immediately, he spoke to me and asked me to tell the story of my life — how I had embraced Islam and what I understood about the "women of God." Then, he told me to prepare to speak to a huge assembly that evening. It was a gathering dedicated to the women of God: Jariatullah (ra), the mother of Sheikh Ahmadu Bamba (ra) whom my friend was named after, Maryam (ra), the mother of Jesus (as) whose name I share, and other blessed women, may God be pleased with them all.

He mentioned a long list of fascinating topics and told me to prepare a talk about them and have it ready as soon as possible. I was somewhat floored. I went into a room and wrote and wrote about all the things he mentioned, all relating to women on the spiritual path. I was, to some degree, overwhelmed by the assignment and the fact that I would soon have to address a huge audience on such a huge subject. But I was doing my best to hang in.

With my raggedy pile of papers, I went to see the Sheikh (ra). He was working with a number of people. In the middle of all this, he had me read my speech to him, which he kept questioning, adding to, and cutting back. By the end of the expansion and contraction of that speech, I did not have a clue really what I would say or how to make it through that particular test.

At this point we were told that one of the many descendants of Sheikh Ahmadu Bamba (ra) was offering us his house to stay in. So, we were all transported from the hotel over to that house. We had been given a house for the remainder of our stay here. What a gift, I thought!

When we entered the house, we discovered that it was a different kind of a gift than we expected. It was absolutely filthy, cockroaches and all. Jariatullah and I thought of the clean hotel and wished we could run back.

When I saw how the more seasoned *murids* (disciples) approached the situation, however, I realized that that lesson was the real gift. They did not hesitate for a moment but simply dug into the cleaning process.

The value of the situation and location was its capacity to be transformed. Only after everyone had worked together for several hours, did we have the house that we would live in and receive so many guests in for the next several days.

In the evening, dressed all in "pilgrimage whites," we were transported to a huge tent. Dressed in the whiteness of the purity of the path, I felt tiny in the immense, regal gathering but also empowered with the grace given to us by God to focus the energy of that beautiful assembly.

Nasiha very sweetly sang a few verses from the qasida called *Sindidi* that Sheikh Ahmadu Bamba (ra) wrote for his mother, Maryam Boussou (ra), and the people in the audience were overwhelmed with joy. I spoke, then, about the women of God. I looked out over the vast field of human beings and beheld a great sea of love and grace, and we were sitting in the center of it.

After all the writing and rewriting of that speech, the most important thing was not the words that were spoken, but the experience of being in the center of that gathering of energy, that assembly of love, dedicated to the women of God.

I was one of three white women in this ocean of brilliant black, this immense garden of exquisitely beautiful flowers. What was most overwhelming about the experience was the sweetness and the power of the love directed toward us and focused upon us.

At that moment, I was struck profoundly by the awareness of a contrast. We had arrived in the heart of Africa and were accorded the warmest welcome and deep respect. We were given the place of honor and became the focal point of a great amount of love. If only our African brothers and sisters arriving in our "civilized" land could have been given such love, honor, and respect, instead of being chained, enslaved, raped, and lynched!

The awareness of this deep imbalance and injustice has brought forth within my heart many questions that are not easily answered. A great debt needs to be paid and a deep wound healed in the body of humanity. As I travel back and forth between America and Africa again and again, I ask the Divine Healer to reveal to me whatever part I may play in healing this wound through the very love, respect, and unity manifested so unconditionally in Africa, the land of our origin.

The next morning, we set out on the pilgrimage. There were many red vans filled with pilgrims setting off in a column on a winding road heading into the lush equatorial jungle. The vegetation in this part of the world around the equator is spellbinding.

Imagine the most dense, intricate vegetation that could be found in a rainforest anywhere else, and then multiply it many times over. There are layers upon layers of ferns and other leaves, banana plants, palms and other wondrous trees. As we drove deeper and deeper into the jungle, it was as though we were entering a new universe, blazing with the vitality of organic life.

In our caravan of red vans passing through the vibrant green jungle, we traveled for several hours. Beautiful qasidas by Sheikh Ahmadu Bamba (ra) were sung throughout the journey. Although we were from opposite sides of the earth, there was nothing but unity and love amongst all the travelers as we focused on the journey of the Sheikh (ra), intending to follow the way he had cut through these jungles, with the power of his illumined faith.

But while we had the luxury of riding in vans, driving along paved roads, he had walked through those jungles and been exposed to continual dangers, challenges, and profound tests. It was the power of the light of his faith, his God-consciousness *(taqwa)* that had carried him through all difficulties. He was unimpaired — on the contrary, spiritually strengthened — by every challenge he faced and surpassed. In this sense, he is an excellent role model for all of us who are facing challenges and tests. Further, we must never forget that it was the Prophet Muhammad (saw) who was the inspiration for all that the Sheikh (ra) did and was, just as he is the primary example for us all.

What amazed and inspired me most about the qasidas that the Sheikh (ra) wrote in the midst of his tribulations in exile was that these experiences, oppressive as they may have been for another, were celebrated by him. All that he wished to express, no matter what was happening, was gratitude to the Lord:

> *[O Lord!] Impart to me Righteousness and Thy Guidance, protect me from blame and grant me Worthiness by the Grace of the Prophet.*

~

> *Allah, the Creator, has guided me [on His Path] and has led*
> *me to Him through all kinds of wonders. The Matchless Lord*
> *has freed me from anything but Him and has led me [on the*
> *Right Path].*
>
> Sheikh Ahmadu Bamba (ra)

How wondrously inspiring, then, is the revelation of the Holy Qur'an, which came through the vehicle of the Prophet Muhammad (saw), even as he and his Companions (ra) were being so thoroughly and continuously tried.

Our caravan arrived in Lambarene, the village where Sheikh Ahmadu Bamba (ra) landed when he was exiled to this region by the French. We sat on the shore of the sea, where the boat in which he traveled had docked. We prayed, recited the Qur'an and the qasidas, and contemplated what had taken place here.

Sheikh Ahmadu Bamba (ra) followed the example of the Prophets (as), specifically the Prophet Muhammad (saw), who endured for the sake of God and the transmission of His message difficulties and hardships that we cannot imagine.

Our hardships do not compare to theirs, but they are the ones that God has given us to face, those upon which our own judgment rests. To follow these great men, our *imams* and guides, to the best of our ability, we have to face our challenges and tests as they did, penetrating whatever darkness we may encounter with a heart empowered and illumined by faith in the All-Powerful Lord. It is not our strength, but the strength of our connection to the Power, which heals the sick and gives life to the dead, which carries us through, test after test.

This is what those guided by the light of the One Most Luminous have come to realize. And this is what gives us all the strength to transform any hardship to ease. Having contemplated the trials, the Sheikh (ra) had endured here, all of which, it seemed, strengthened his faith, we got back into the caravan of vans and returned, on the winding roads that had brought us here, reaching our little house late at night.

The next morning, we went with all our fellow pilgrims to a very small airport from which we flew, in a tiny plane, to the island of Mayumba. When the plane landed on the island, we were greeted by an amazing sight and given a beautiful reception. It appeared that the whole population of this tiny island had assembled in an immense circle on the tarmac to welcome us.

Each segment of the circle was dressed in a different beautiful indigenous clothing style, each group singing a different song, performing a dance, or making another unique offering as a way of truly welcoming us and honoring the memory of Sheikh Ahmadu Bamba (ra) and the wondrous events that had occurred when he was here.

I felt that we were being received as royalty and that they were royalty also, as we made our way around the great circle greeting each of them. When I came to the end of the circle, I saw Sheikh Dieye (ra) standing under a small overhang and went to stand next to him. He was in a state of intense joy, speaking about the great mysteries of this island, Mayumba, and what had happened here.

He explained that, here, on the island of Mayumba, Sheikh Ahmadu Bamba (ra) had been exiled for years. The French colonialists had sent the Sheikh (ra) here, certain that he would die, as had the other prisoners they had sent here. Every night, the waves rose up and flooded the island so that almost all of the people who had been sent here were drowned.

But Sheikh Ahmadu Bamba (ra) was not one of them. As he described in his qasidas, he spoke the powerful words of Allah *subhana wa ta'ala* to the waves, and they submitted to the power of Allah *subhana wa ta'ala* and were subdued. Many miracles have been attributed to Sheikh Ahmadu Bamba (ra) by those who honor his memory. However, what happened is only truly known by Allah *subhana wa ta'ala,* Who was the real Witness of these events.

But I believe certainly that the true miracle that manifested in the life of Sheikh Ahmadu Bamba (ra), which gave him the ability to do whatever he did, was the Holy Qur'an and the love of Allah *subhana wa ta'ala* and His Messenger (saw). All of the qasidas he wrote unconditionally testify to this profound truth. All who follow him should thus follow what he followed. May we all be guided on the Path that is Straight, protected from ever going astray.

Of the array of gifts, I received from Sheikh Dieye (ra) that he had to share with those he met along the way, the gift that was, I believe, most loved by Sheikh Dieye (ra) was his love and respect for Sheikh Ahmadu Bamba (ra), his teaching and the way in which he became the example of the teaching. This was the strongest transmission I received from him in the time allotted for us to know each other.

The last time I saw Sheikh Dieye (ra) was on a trip through Southern California focused on the Inner Directions Conference in La Jolla. I remember this last week with a depth of feeling because it was the last week. Once again, I am struck by the importance of realizing the preciousness of every life that we encounter. We have no idea how long we will have to come to know, understand, and love each being sent to us on our path, before that being returns, often suddenly and without warning, to the Source.

At the same time, even as we begin to appreciate and sense the preciousness and magnitude of every life that we encounter on our journey — every teacher and friend who appears on our path — we cannot get attached to any form, precisely because, at any moment, that form can disappear.

It is, thus, very important to realize, as one after the next of the friends and teachers Allah has willed us to meet on our journey to Him returns back to Him, that Allah *subhana wa ta'ala,* Alone, is our only Friend that lives forever, our only Beloved, who never dies and never leaves us. And it is His Teaching, His Guidance, and His Acceptance, none other, that we truly seek and need.

From time to time, Allah *subhana wa ta'ala* places in our path a person who has a certain amount of information to give us, which will help us to proceed in our journey. Then that person, as all lives must do, returns to the Lord, in exactly the time and the way decreed by Allah.

There is nothing we can do about this but surrender to the Decree of Allah *subhana wa ta'ala.* We must, certainly, pray for the soul as it makes its journey beyond this world. And then, let us look, see, pay attention: What information did he or she give us? What legacy did they leave us that will clearly guide and illuminate our own journey back to our Lord?

These were understandings I became more deeply and intuitively aware of during the last week I spent with Sheikh Dieye (ra). It was an intense week because the soul of the Sheikh (ra) was already transitioning, and the sense of the *Hand* of God upon us was very strong. One wall of the apartment was glass overlooking nothing but the ocean. It seemed as though the ocean, alternately very peaceful and very turbulent, always full of light, was in the room. Just as the waters surrounding the island of Mayumba were subdued and illuminated by the words of God, which had been addressed to them, I prayed that these waves, too, within and without us submit and be illuminated by the powerful truth of our Lord. Sheikh Dieye (ra) was transported, speaking intensely, often almost transfixed. I was translating most of the time. The Sheikh (ra) was deeply kind, respectful, and caring to me. He spoke to me about the time that we had spent and the work we had done together. He expressed his gratitude for all the work that Issa and I had done with him, transmitting to me the importance that we had in the fulfillment of his mission. I felt that my journey with him had come to a place of peace and clarity and light. The struggle was over. And this, I sensed, was a result of the intense therapy I had passed through in his company. The Sheikh (ra) had been simply mirroring the very deep process I had to go through in the time I had to journey with him before he left this world.

It was a therapeutic process of learning to accept everything that unfolds on the path of God, learning to accept ourselves as we are, without avoiding anything, accessing what we hide in the depths of our being, and bringing it forth so that, exposed in the light of day and submitted to the mercy and grace of God, everything within us can be healed, transformed, and illuminated.

Only by fearlessly accepting the very things within ourselves and others that disturb us most can we begin to be healed, transformed, and liberated. I am indebted to Sheikh Abdoulaye Dieye (ra) for inspiring and encouraging me to do this.

The Sheikh (ra) left this world on March 21, 2002. We heard that a car in which he had been traveling had been in an accident and that the others in the car were minorly injured, but he was the least injured. The next day came the shocking news that, as a result of an aneurysm in his brain triggered by the accident, Sheikh Abdoulaye Dieye (ra) had passed away. The deep legacy he left is in the heart of each person that he touched. I can bear witness, with gratitude, only to the gifts and lessons I received. Of the true meaning of all things, Allah *subhana wa ta'ala* alone is the Knower:

> *So Glory be to Him in whose Hand is the dominion of all things and to Him will you all be brought back.*
> —The Holy Qur'an 36:83

CHAPTER TWENTY

THE THERAPY OF LIBERATION,
A JOURNEY OF CONSECRATION

Senegal, Mauritania, Morocco and Mauritius,
2003

*And on earth there are signs [of God's existence, visible] to all
who are endowed with inner certainty, just as [there are signs
thereof] within your own selves: can you not, then, see?*
—The Holy Qur'an 51:21

Sheikh Dieye (ra) did not leave this world without having prepared a
successor. For many years he had been training Sheikh Aly N'Daw, who
was also born in Senegal but was eventually sent by Sheikh Dieye (ra)
to Reunion Island in the Indian Ocean to build a spiritual community
there. Sheikh Aly traveled extensively, following the example of Sheikh
Dieye (ra). While Sheikh Dieye (ra) was alive, Sheikh Aly, his successor
in training, manifested in the humblest way.

When Sheikh Dieye (ra) and the disciples first stayed in our house,
Sheikh Aly came with them. However, while Sheikh Dieye (ra) stayed on
a bed upstairs, Sheikh Aly stayed on the floor downstairs. He attracted
no attention to himself but was extremely kind to everyone, a very warm
and loving friend to us all.

Following the passing of Sheikh Dieye (ra), I had the blessing of traveling with Sheikh Aly and a small group of disciples to various parts of the
world. Throughout these journeys, teachings, which flowed as effortlessly
as the breath, contributed to my basic understanding of the integration of
spiritual teaching within the experience of life. This began with a healing
process that he has called the "therapy of liberation." Explaining this therapy and why it is needed by those on the path to God, he said:

*The therapy of liberation is a way to help people, through the
experience they have had, to find their way back to God. The focus is on the transformation, not the elimination, of any aspect
of the personality. The question is how to transform. It is based
upon our very own life experiences, and comes through the exercise of forgiving, as opposed to judging and finding fault. This
is the transformation that God refers to in the Qur'an, when,
again and again, He invites us to pardon. When you look closely, you see that whatever teaching God is giving in the Qur'an,
at the end of it all, He comes back to this idea of forgiveness. The
aim of this work is to help people grasp the idea that they can
transform themselves.*

Whatever is happening, it can be controlled and must be trans-formed.

At what moment do idols become established in our heart? How does this happen? At puberty, the child starts becoming judgmental about what he sees his parents doing. It is at this moment that the child opens himself to problems, because he has started to judge. How did pride arise in Iblis? It is because Iblis judged Adam, and, from this, sprang pride. Where did jealousy spring from? It came because Iblis judged God in His creation of Adam. So this is the danger in judging...

It is not a surprise at all that we have problems now, and that these problems have become, in fact, our life's priority. As long as this is not resolved, we will never be able to assume our role as the servant of God. We will not be able to truly assume the position that the Lord has created us for, that of His true repre-sentative on earth...

So, how do we put an end to this? It is by the prayer of asking for forgiveness. Why must we do this? Because the Lord did not create anyone in vain...

Each one of us can be an instrument of the Divine Will. All of this leads us back to the teachings of the Prophet, our Master Muhammad. And this is what allows us to give religion its true value, its true dimension...

As has been stated in a hadith of the Prophet, 'All humanity constitutes a single family, and the one who is most loved by God is the one who is most useful to this family.' The Prophet showed us this when he delivered the last sermon. Everyone was there to bear witness that he had fulfilled his mission and that, in fact, he was the most useful person to humanity...

We see that all of this is related to service. The state of being a slave, or servant of God, revolves around service and also around love. So, in this way, we come to understand that our relationship with God is linked with the relationship that we have with others, and the relationship that we have with the Master himself. And the contract that we have with the Master is thus linked with the original contract that exists between ourselves and God...

Sheikh Aly taught that, in order for each of us to become healed and transformed in such a way as to become a true representative of God on earth, we need spiritual formation:

This formation unfolds little by little. Our character is thus formed to the end that we become the instruments of God. And the formation is nothing other than the way in which we arrive at the state in which our heart is pure, loving, and completely concentrated upon the Lord. One arrives at this state by participating in these various activities...

Because from the time God called Muhammad (saw) to be a Prophet, it was within the call that God formed his character. And it was thus that he became the Seal of the Prophets...

When he met people who didn't like what he did, the Lord told him what to do, how to behave. When he met people who were opposed to his mission and plotted against him, the Lord told him how he should behave. The Lord said: Pardon them and forget, until the decision of your Lord intervenes...

Thus it is through these encounters that the formation of each person occurs. So the work on the terrain, in the field, is very important and we must know that it is in the middle of the situations of life itself that our formation unfolds. And separating ourselves from others is not the way that has been indicated...

In each situation, there is a behavior that the Lord has shown. And that behavior is dhikr (remembrance of God). There is the external dhikr in which we gather together in a group and sing together, but there is also the internal dhikr, or remembrance, which arises in the middle of all these different situations and guides us to the right conduct...

The Prophet (saw) met certain people in his life. The goal of some of the people was different than the goal of the Prophet (saw). What did the Lord say to him? He did not tell him to throw these people out, but to treat them in a very beautiful way, so that tomorrow, they could return. And this will make it easy for them to return to God...

We must arrive at this nobility of conduct; we must see this nobility of conduct in the work that we have to do.

The example of the Holy Prophet (saw) interacting with all those that he encountered on his path and the fact that the teachings of the Qur'an were revealed in the very midst of these interactions is a constant reminder that the exercise of living and interacting with other beings is a sacred exercise. It is a continual test to see if, in the midst of the challenges and vicissitudes we must inevitably face in our daily lives, we are able to put into practice the realizations we are gaining deep within.

Traveling with Sheikh Aly was always the context for learning about healing and becoming liberated from debilitating patterns. It was always the context for the formation of character, with the goal that each one of us would develop truly noble conduct and, with the completion of our formation, become a true representative of God on earth.

As humble and hidden as Sheikh Aly was when his Sheikh was alive, as soon as Sheikh Dieye (ra) had departed from this world and the responsibility fell upon Sheikh Aly to carry on the work, he manifested his strength. Immediately, he called together all the disciples who could come to gather in Senegal for the next Maggal to visit the city of Touba, to visit the tomb of Sheikh Dieye (ra), and to travel together to Mauritania to visit the tomb of Sheikh Sidi Ahmad Ismouhu Deymani (ra), the disciple of Sheikh Ahmadu Bamba (ra) and Sheikh of Sheikh Dieye (ra).

When Sheikh Aly and many of the disciples arrived at the airport at three o'clock in the morning, "perpetual Senegal airport time," Sheikh Aly himself picked up almost every piece of luggage and loaded it onto a luggage cart. I saw that his sleeves were rolled up and he was going to serve the disciples, not wait to be served.

The next morning, we were told that we were all going to a memorial for Sheikh Dieye (ra), which was being held in a huge hall in a newly built cultural center five minutes from the Sheikh's (ra) house. With almost no notice, I was informed that I was to speak to a large, quite august assembly. I had brought some photographs of the Sheikh's (ra) visits to America, mostly of him embracing children, expanded to a large size. I took them to the gathering. I really did not have anything prepared to say, just a deep feeling in the heart.

The huge auditorium was packed with illustrious people of Senegal, including many dignitaries. For me to speak correctly to this assembly in French, having nothing prepared, was a spiritual challenge. I knew that there was no way that I could do it by myself, and I was completely dependent upon Divine Grace.

When I was called onto the stage and went up to the podium, I felt like I was walking into the wide, open space without any plan of what I was going to say. Invoking the grace of Allah, I recited *Surat'ul-Fatihah*, the opening chapter of the Holy Qur'an. The power of the *Fatihah* filled the auditorium. I felt that it was the grace of God that was resonating throughout the hall and through the hearts of the people. So, I did not have to speak myself. That was an immense relief!

I then held up the pictures to show how the Sheikh (ra), throughout his travels, had embraced children. I spoke in French but felt that I was not speaking; the words, activated by the power of the Fatihah, were pouring through me. The heart was communicating with the heart. I saw many people in the audience weeping, it seemed, not with sadness, but because their hearts were moved. The power that I felt was manifesting was from God alone. It was the awareness of the divine love, the divine embrace, as that love itself had manifested through the life of Sheikh Dieye (ra) that moved the audience to tears.

Then, in celebration of his memory and living legacy, we went on a journey to many places that we had visited earlier with Sheikh Dieye (ra). As well as those places of power and peace in Senegal that we had visited often and now visited again on our pilgrimage, this time we crossed the river on a barge and entered the land of Mauritania. We were greeted on the barge by tall, princely men, all dressed in white robes with light blue outer garments similar to togas that rolled up on their shoulders like wings. They were extremely kind and extended to us the warmest welcome.

It was dusk as we crossed the river, and the water was dark and glittering. Our gracious guides led us to a configuration of beautiful, hand-embroidered tents, under which we assembled. We were graciously welcomed by the local Sheikh (ra) and the whole village, which had assembled in the tent, singing and dancing their traditional songs and dances and reciting poetry in praise of the Prophet Muhammad (saw). After this beautiful welcome in the amazing tent, we sat in the remembrance of God, in *dhikr* and prayer throughout the night.

For me, it was a night of deep memories. I had the profound sense of having sat through nights of *dhikr* and remembrance, in tents such as these before. The tents were immense, chambers upon chambers of billowing hand-embroidered cloth. I could not imagine how many hours went into the creation of this beautiful cloth.

Of his exile to Mauritania, Sheikh Ahmadu Bamba (ra) had said that it was a journey of consecration, and that was the feeling I had in the tent that night. We were on a journey of consecration.

Whereas Gabon, to which Sheikh Ahmadu Bamba (ra) had been first exiled, was a spiritual wilderness, Mauritania, to which he was exiled later, was a land whose people had been prepared to receive spiritual teaching through generations of development. It is a land of spiritual elevation, of deep Qur'anic study and training. Sitting in the illuminated tent, I felt the presence of Sheikh Ahmadu Bamba (ra) and other great African Sheikhs gathering in huge billowing tents such as these. I felt the power of the teaching and transmission that had taken place and was continuing to take place in this blessed land.

Outside the tents, large campfires were burning, and the desert sky was brilliant and cool. I slipped out of the tent from time to time during the night, so that I could experience the beauty and the vibration of the land and its people. Once outside the tent, I came across a group of boys from the village. Their large, beautiful eyes were glowing. They spoke to me about their Qur'anic studies, and I saw the light of the Qur'an shining through their faces, their comportment, and their words. Every time that I meet children who are developing in this way, shining with the clarity and peace of the prophetic way, uncorrupted by the rampant chaos of the modern, misguided world, I believe that there is hope for humanity.

The Holy Qur'an, like all of the revealed scriptures, describes to us the end of the world, but that is not the end of our story. In a saying of the Holy Prophet (saw), God says, *"My Mercy precedes My wrath."* Allah *subhana wa ta'ala* tells us again and again, for those who obey His commandments, pray regularly and do righteous deeds, there will be gardens with rivers flowing beneath, wherein they shall have no fear, nor shall they grieve. To find this kind of peace and security in this world and the next, we need to study the words that Allah *subhana wa ta'ala* has sent to us and to make them the reality of our life.

So, when I meet, anywhere in the world, children like those I met in Mauritania, I feel that there is real hope and a real future for those of humankind who truly turn to the Creator for guidance that becomes the very substance of their life.

The next morning, in the beautiful, cool light of dawn, I sat outside the tent on the blessed earth of that village and recited Surah Ya Sin and Surat'ul-Waaqia for the people of this consecrated land, may the consecration ever continue.

Then, after sharing breakfast with all, we set out on a pilgrimage to the tomb of Sheikh Sidi Ahmed Ismouhu Deymani (ra), the Sheikh of Sheikh Dieye (ra). We traveled for hours through the desert and mountainous terrain. It was a rugged drive and many of the brothers were squeezed together, standing up in the trucks as they bounced along the very rocky trails. Such are the rigors of traveling for the sake of God, and every sincere effort and sacrifice made for the sake of God brings with it a hidden reward.

From time to time, we would stop at an oasis in the desert and drink at a watering hole. At one of these oases, a great number of camels, donkeys, and other animals were also drinking. The higher we went up into the barren, rocky desert, the more animals we found assembled at the watering holes. I was amazed to see such a menagerie of animals of all sorts gathered together in perfect peace.

So peaceful were the gatherings of the animals at these oases that even the presence of many people and trucks could not disturb them. I noticed especially one long row of donkeys, standing in a perfect line with each donkey resting its head on the back of the donkey in front.

What a beautiful vision of the natural condition of creatures living together in harmony and balance! It was one of the signs from God on the path, transmitting an understanding about how human beings, too, could travel and live together in harmonious interdependence and peace. We traveled further and further up into the wild mountainous desert. At another oasis where we stopped in our rocky ascent, I received another message. I heard, "Speak. Tell the story. Tell people about the things you have seen and experienced."

I had the sense that I was to go to places like colleges, organizations and spiritual assemblies and speak about my experiences in Africa and throughout the world, talk about the experience of being united with African people and people of all the world. I heard in the depth of my heart this message to speak to people, wherever their ears were open, about this ongoing pilgrimage on which all differences — such as those of race, color, and culture — are completely dissolved in the oneness of community in unity.

When we had traveled very far into the desert, we finally arrived at the tomb of Sheikh Sidi Ahmad (ra) and prayed there that the work of Allah *subhana wa ta'ala,* through all of us, be fulfilled. The tomb, so many hours into absolute desert wilderness, was well hidden from the world, one of those secret places that is just what it is, with no external artifice at all adorning it. We had traveled so far to find this holy spot, which was truly only seen by the "eyes" of God.

The next morning, we were more than graciously received in another tent by the descendants of Sheikh Sidi Ahmad (ra). Then we returned on the ferry to Senegal.

When our collective pilgrimage was completed and all those who had come together from countries around the world left to return home, I was drawn magnetically to Morocco, which is actually on the opposite side of Mauritania from Senegal.

I went to Morocco ostensibly to investigate business possibilities, but, in reality, there was a much deeper reason I had to go there, and that was a stage of the pilgrimage. Just as West Africa was a part and reflection of the mysteries of the soul, so too was North Africa another dimension. In the architecture, the art, and the mysticism of Morocco, I felt there were keys to my awakening that I needed to find.

Morocco is a land flourishing with multi-dimensional manifestations of art and beauty. Even the airport is an artifact of beautiful tile-work. As I witnessed the spectacle of exquisite artistry, the question posed itself: what inspired these people to be so creative? This creativity was a mirror, and I saw, in the walls of beautiful tile mosaics, a reflection of my life and journey, which is, itself, like every life, a mosaic composed of many amazing tiles, arranged in an amazing way.

May we each be able to perceive the configuration of the mosaic of our life, appreciate its beauty, and decode the meanings encoded in the complex arrangement of tiles.

We landed in Casablanca but then began to drive through the rolling hills and gardens, the beautiful verdant landscape, to the ancient city of Fez. Fez is a city where great Sufis have gathered throughout the centuries, and the prayers of all who have gathered there to pray and receive knowledge of the Divine still, I felt, are tangibly present.

So that is why I, too, like multitudes of others, had to come here: so that my prayers, supplications, and contemplations, inspired by this accumulation of blessed energy, could unite with theirs, that is, unite with the One to whom all supplication is addressed in a place where He has been deeply remembered.

The journey to places of power in the presence of the people of light is one in which every place that you visit and every person that you meet along the way is a mirror to your soul, and once you have seen and experienced this, it becomes a part of you.

When people ask me, "Where do you come from?" the answer I give is: *"From all the places that I have ever been."* What we each are is a composite of all the people and places that we have visited and deeply embraced. Such is the mosaic of tiles of which our life is composed. And these are the experiences in which the story of our soul is told. And now it was, in the city of Fez, that the mystery of the soul and its timeless story was revealing its multiple dimensions. I want to describe this beautiful, ancient city because it is a place that I would like the reader to visit, as we travel together on the journey of self-discovery.

The old city of Fez is encircled by huge walls, within which is a fantastic beehive of creativity. Everywhere, in every nook and cranny of the outer edge of the old city, artisans are humming. They are making fine grillwork, pottery, embroidery, leatherwork, woodcarving, hand-painted furniture, and practically every other craft one could imagine. The outer circumference of the old city is one extended multi-media craft workshop which, with so much woodwork going on, smells like a shrine filled with freshly ground sandalwood and cedar.

On the next level, going in, in concentric circles, from the studios where this plethora of crafts is being created, one finds the colorful and also fragrant shops where the crafts are being sold.

In the center of the configuration of the holy city of Fez is the illuminated, sanctified space of the *Kairaouine Mosque*, in the center of which is a beautiful courtyard, in the center of which is an ever-flowing fountain.

All of the beautiful, intricate tiled doorways into the immense mosque are thus leading into the empty illuminated space in the center, which is filled with prayer, and in the center of that space is the fountain, which, for me, was a symbol of the abundance of the Divine provision that is always flowing.

With the open, sanctified space of the mosque in the center of the city, all that is taking place around it seemed to me to be blessed and balanced. I felt that the configuration of the city was inspired, and I very much sensed the spiritual presence of the awliya (ra), the friends of Allah *subhana wa ta'ala*, who had lived and prayed here throughout the centuries.

When I saw people gathering in circles in the bright open space in the center of the mosque courtyard, I felt, *the great ones have assembled here; the great Sufis have gathered together here. The lovers of God have celebrated His Praise abundantly here.* And I felt that I was sitting with them, all of us united in the love of the Divine, in the light of the open space in the middle of the Kairaouine Mosque.

The Holy Qur'an tells us of those who have died in the way of Allah *subhana wa ta'ala*, that they are alive, though we see them not. They are present in the Presence of the One, who they love — the Inspirer, the Teacher of all, the Living, the Eternal. The great Sufis who gathered here are eternally present as long as the Beloved is loved here.

In earlier times, such as the times of the great Sheikh, Sheikh'ul Akbar, Muhyd'din Ibn al Arabi (ra), so many more people lived in the awareness of the Divine, gathering in holy places like this and sharing the divine mysteries. As the stories of his life tell us, his journey through life was profoundly mystical, greatly blessed. Wherever he went outwardly and inwardly, he met, and deeply interacted with the *awliya*, the illuminated ones.

From those times to today, the spiritual landscape has changed. And what was abundantly revealed in the time of the Sheikh'ul Akbar (ra) is now hidden. But, although this great mystery may be hidden to the eyes of many, it continues to be alive for those who truly seek the manifestation of Divine Grace revealed in assemblies of souls such as those that have gathered here throughout the ages.

"Please count us among them," I beseeched the Everliving One as I sat in the illuminated courtyard of this ancient mosque, where so many great souls had prayed. "Please count us among them!"

The next stop on the journey of the soul in pursuit of *taqwa* (consciousness of God) was the island of Mauritius. I went there the following summer with Issa, as soon as he was finished with his school year. We went to visit there with many people of the community of Sheikh Dieye (ra) who we met when they came to stay in our house and who we had met again and again in Senegal. Now we were going to get to know our friends even better, by staying and praying with them in their homes.

The airport in Mauritius was, like the airport in Morocco, full of light. You know as soon as you enter the airport that you have arrived in a wonderful place. It was completely decorated with murals and other works of beautiful, whimsical art. Right away, as soon as you have landed and set foot in the land, you feel that you have arrived in a country with a *heart!*

Reuniting with dear friends, we got into the car and began to drive into the lush, fertile terrain, the verdant fields and hills, great mountains, marvelous waterfalls, palm trees and exotic tropical vegetation.

But, as lovely as the island of Mauritius is, we had not come as tourists on a holiday. We had come to gain more knowledge and understanding of the way of God, and, in accordance with our intention, the gift that we received there was greater in its beauty than the most beautiful landscape. This gift was to perceive the beauty of the circle of the believers and then experience how the circle *works*.

There were many families in the spiritual circle activated by Sheikh Dieye (ra) and Sheikh Aly around the Island of Mauritius. Our trip was arranged so that we would not stay with a single family but would travel from home to home and thus become closer to everyone.

What I noticed immediately in every home was that there were big piles of highly activated and much used prayer beads. This was another sign of the activated remembrance of God, that touched and inspired my heart.

In the home of my dear friend Ruqayyah, where we stayed the longest, the community gathered almost every day and prayed extensively for everyone in need. In addition to a large dinner served to the poor and needy every week, these prayers were going on continuously for people in the community itself.

This is the way to build real spiritual community, I deeply felt. We must not judge or gossip about each other, but pray for each other, not superficially, but deeply. To pray with deep focus and intention for another is a very effective way of implementing the practice of forgiving and dispelling judgment. The more you pray for someone, the less you will be likely to judge that person, and the more likely you will be to truly intend the best for that person.

It was the regular, daily practice of this community to pray for each other, whatever the need may be. So, if someone lost a job, or had to take an important test, or was ill, or getting married, or going into labor, or needed prayers for any other reason, the whole community would pray extensively for him or her.

For example, they would say *"Bismillahirrahmanirrahim"* (in the Name of God, Most Merciful, Most Compassionate), invoking the Mercy and Compassion of the Creator 16,000 times for that specific purpose. I felt that this was a wonderful way of thinking about each other, holding each other's best interests in our hearts, and supplicating the Creator on behalf of this person.

During our stay in Mauritius, a tragic accident occurred which brought to light the importance of the circle of prayer even more deeply and poignantly. A young girl who was a part of the community was, shortly after she was engaged to be married, in an automobile accident with several other girls. For a week, she was in intensive care. Then, by the Decree of Allah *subhana wa ta'ala,* she passed away. May Allah bless her journey back to Him and also give His comfort to her family forever.

The week that this young woman was in the hospital was the week that we happened to be in Mauritius, traveling from family to family, house to house. The prayer circle was activated everywhere. Even in houses filled with young children, everywhere the prayer beads were moving. Everyone, including the young children, were engaged, more than in anything else, in praying for those families in their difficulty.

I, as a traveler, there to learn as deeply as possible about the life of the community and how the circle works, was blessed to participate, again and again, in the circle of prayer as well as to go to the hospital and sit with the grieving mother. How can I convey the experience of sitting on a wooden bench next to that dear woman and embracing her, as she had to pass through an inconceivably profound trial?

A few days later, the young woman passed, and we gathered with the large extended family to honor her life and pray for the journey of her soul, as well as to express our deep solidarity with those who were suffering so deeply the loss. As sad as this gathering was, it was also inspiring because the power of prayer, the power of the solidarity of the community, the power of the human family itself, was also undeniably evident.

All of this was the deep gift that Allah *subhana wa ta'ala* gave to us on our pilgrimage and learning journey on the island of Mauritius. As I and two of the sisters were riding together on a bus back from the funeral prayers, we looked up into the sky and saw a huge, brilliantly clear rainbow descending vertically directly from heaven to earth. It was a sign of the direct descent of God's Mercy to the earth, confirming acceptance of the beautiful teaching we had learned in our time here, of the importance for each and every one of us to deeply care and pray for one another.

CHAPTER TWENTY-ONE

TRAVELING ON A MISSION OF HEALING AND PEACE

India, Nepal, Bangladesh, Pakistan and
Kashmir, 2003-2004

And your Lord shall give to you and you shall be satisfied. Did He not find you an orphan and provide refuge? And did He not find you wandering and guide you? And did He not find you without means and provide sustenance? So as for the orphan — do not oppress him. And as for the beggar — do not drive him away. And as for the grace of your Lord — proclaim it.

—The Holy Qur'an 93: 5-11

May I become at all times, both now and forever,
A guide for those who have lost their way
A ship for those with an ocean to cross,
A bridge for those with rivers to cross
A sanctuary to all those in danger
A lamp for those without light,
A place of refuge for those who lack safety
And a servant to all in need

—Shantideva

At the end of 2003, Sheikh Aly told me that he was planning to go on a mission of peace and solidarity to India and several surrounding countries and was searching for those inspired to come. With so many valuable and meaningful memories of traveling *fisabilillah* (on the path to God), how could I really refuse the call? Each time that *providence* presents to us such an opportunity, how can we refuse? Since I had been for so many years doing business with Kashmir, I could also add this dimension to the journey, so it was clear that this was the next step in my pilgrimage. *This mission of peace and solidarity* was to be undertaken by a small group: Sheikh Aly, four of the women we had stayed with on the island of Mauritius, and myself. It was very well organized by Djamila, who had been doing graduate work in the field of social work and had come to know people in different countries who were dedicated to helping others. To her list of contacts, I added mine, and so God provided us with a beautiful itinerary composed of visiting people committed to the cause of doing good in many countries.

Almost every place we went was imperiled in one way or another. The people were enduring trials, and the situation was dangerous. Sheikh Aly was never deterred by news of the difficulty or danger in a region. When we were warned that we could be approaching a situation of conflict or danger, he said that it was a place in need of peace, so we must not avoid it but must go there and bring peace. He said that if there was difficulty, that was why we must go there, to share with people struggling and in need of support, our love and faith in the Source of all healing. The amazing scenes we beheld of people helping one another was itself truly healing and inspiring to my heart and consciousness.

Our journey to India and other nearby lands was a continuous witnessing of the transformation of darkness into light. We saw people, oppressed and tried, who were so filled with the light of hope and commitment that it seemed they were able to achieve anything. In every country, in every village and city where we traveled, we found the righteous ones activated by the power of God to change the world around them, people inspired to give with all their heart, not truly expecting anything in return.

We visited places and people assaulted by political oppression, poverty, illness, and strife, but what we found in every crucible was *gold*: the transformative power of love. It is by the love of God that we are brought back from death into life, and it is His compassion implanted in the hearts of His servants that inspires them to bring hope and life to those who might die without it.

We began our journey in Lucknow, India at the City Montessori School, a wonderful, extraordinary school dedicated to peace, nonviolence and unity, founded by Jagdish and Bharti Gandhi. This school began with five students in one family. Now, with twenty-seven thousand students, it had become at that time the largest school in the Guinness Book of World Records. As large as it has become, the school remains passionately dedicated to manifesting these noble principles.

The students in this unusual school have created an international congress of world governments, to set an example of real justice for the adults in the world. In response to their many extraordinary efforts, these students were awarded a peace prize by UNESCO in 2002. So, with this beautiful vision of what people of any age can do to change the world, we began our journey.

On all of the buildings of the school are engraved teachings of universal truth, such as a quote of Baha'ullah: *"The world is but one country and mankind its citizens. Every child is potentially the light of the world.*" So, where there was nothing, a small city has been created, with twenty-seven thousand students, each of whom is potentially a vehicle through which can shine light that illuminates the world. Every one of those students going out into the world may become the catalyst for another school, community, or activating principle of peace, non-violence, and unity.

While Sheikh Aly and I traveled throughout this school of peace, we shared the vision that Issa should attend this high school, which was deeply connected to his spirit and vision. This was definitely a prophetic impulse. While he did not come to Lucknow to attend this wonderful school, he was destined to receive an education in peacemaking throughout his unfolding life in many amazing ways to be explored later in this book.

Next, we went to a leper colony in the countryside. There, in emerald fields well cultivated by the leper community, the Sheikh embraced the people. It was a vision of light, not one of hopeless despair. The women of the community, dressed in beautiful saris, were working in the fields, and the men were sitting in clusters, upright, with a kind of stillness and purity and grace. I saw in those emerald fields, not fear and misery but peace and dignity in the people — the light of submission — and that light dispelled so many preconceptions, stigmas and fears I had been unconsciously harboring about our brothers and sisters who are afflicted with leprosy.

Back in the city of Lucknow, we met with a group of children who had been living on the street, but who were now living in a shelter with a very loving priest. Each boy showed us, smiling from ear to ear, with great joy and pride, his bedroll and the rice that the boys had just cooked. For they who previously had nothing, those small things inspired so much pride, contentment and joy.

Then, we went into the countryside and met with a group of poor children who had been left behind by the Indian educational system, until a small group of kind and loving people created a school for them. We met with these rescued children in their stone schoolhouse and shared with them their joy at being given the chance to receive an education.

The same compassionate caring people guided by Dr. Sumita Gandhi, who had organized this school, had also created a system of literacy that enabled people to read and write in six months, and this system was spreading around the world.

Next, we went to Kathmandu, Nepal. There our host, Som, was in charge of four orphanages. We visited one of the orphanages where a great many children were sheltered together in an extremely warm and loving environment. There was a sense of solidarity and real fellowship in this home. We could feel that the power of love had created a real experience of extended family so that the children were saved from isolation and despair by the sense of belonging, the joy of having a warm and loving home and a great family.

This brought to my mind and heart the many passages in the Qur'an in which the treatment of orphans, as well as of the needy and the destitute, is of paramount importance. As Allah *subhana wa ta'ala* tells us in the Holy Qur'an 2:215:

> *They ask you what they should spend. Say, "Whatever you spend on good (let it be first) on your parents, and your near kin, and the orphans, and the destitute and the wayfarers." And whatever good you do, surely God knows.*

In light of the importance of the welfare of orphans, as well as the destitute and needy, revealed to us by our Lord, we needed to visit the orphanage, to take these children and those lovingly helping them into our hearts and prayers, as this mission of solidarity continued to unfold.

After taking us to visit the children in the orphanage, Som took us on a walk around Kathmandu. This was very significant for me. I was retracing the original steps of my journey. I was back again at the burning ghats where I had sat and meditated thirty years before. But now I saw things in a totally different way. I was walking along the same well-worn paths, past the same ancient buildings as I had passed in the beginning of my quest for the Master and the way of God. But now I was walking with the Sheikh (ra) and others, appreciating, with deep gratitude, all that God had revealed to me of His path since I last walked here.

Som took us to the shrine of Bodhinath, which I had circumambulated in my early journey. And as we were walking around it behind two young girls who were making their circumambulation in prostrations, Sheikh Aly said to me, "You have completed the circle. You have come back to where you started, and the circle of your life is complete. Now you are ready to rise."

After Nepal, we went to Bangladesh. In the town of Tangail (pronounced "Tanguy") we were hosted by a dedicated person named Tuhin Islam, who works for an organization committed to transforming the condition of every sector of disadvantaged children in the community, including children of ethnic minorities, child laborers, and the children of prostitutes.

Shortly after we arrived, he took us on a tour to meet with these children in so many different shacks and rooms where they had been assembled to be educated and trained so they might have a real chance to make something of their lives.

The most troubling place on the tour was a brothel that was a village in itself, consisting of about three thousand women and children. It was deeply shocking and saddening to me to see to what degree the principles, laws, and safeguards offered by the One Most Merciful had been abandoned in the formation of this sad vision.

And yet we saw these very principles of mercy and righteousness, manifesting through those who went in to help and rescue the souls from that tragic fate. We walked down the long lanes of this village and saw our young sisters, our aunts, and mothers lined up, their faces masked with bizarre makeup, endless lines of young women gazing into stark emptiness. We saw the rooms where they live and work, the beds under which their children have been growing up. Imagine the miserable plight of a child growing up under the bed of his mother as she engages in her daily and nightly work.

The project aims to save the children and their mothers, too, if they are willing and able to become liberated from their patterns. For the children, who truly wish to be free, a large home has been built in the countryside where they are educated in every way. They are removed from that space beneath their mothers' beds that was the only home they have had and transported to a beautiful estate in the countryside built for them.

There, many children are being educated academically, religiously, and culturally. In addition to all academic subjects, they are being trained in cottage industries, agricultural skills, martial arts, and traditional arts.

Most importantly, they are given the opportunity to become reha-
bilitated from those patterns into which they were born and live a pro-
ductive, free life. In contemplating the blessing granted to the children to
become free of their inherited oppression, we prayed that we too might
be liberated by the grace of God Most Merciful from the inherited legacies that have been imprisoning us.

We were invited to spend a day at the children's home. It was so
lovely there. Most beautiful of all were the children themselves. We
prayed with them, played with them, and saw the bright large rooms
where they now live. During the day, we saw them practicing karate,
and, in the evening, they performed for us a marvelous, very profession-
al program of traditional South Asian dance. As we were finally leaving,
walking to the van, ten or so children were holding onto each of my
hands and I to theirs.

My primary instinct was to stay with the children. I felt that my
body and heart were merged with them, and I wished never to leave
them. I experienced again the exhortation, "You must love all lives as
your own." Each child I saw was a reflection of both the child within me
and the child I could have borne.

Meeting, caring for, and embracing all the children we met and,
at the same time, accepting and embracing the child within myself, I
found that the journey was continuously educational, deeply touching,
and therapeutic in many ways. I was very grateful to be witnessing, in
the midst of an often apparently heartless world, the power of love and
compassion made absolutely manifest.

The next morning the Director of all the programs, Mr. Hamid,
took us out to the fields that had been cultivated by his organization. The
produce from the fields funds all the projects, including two hospitals
where all the people in the community can get healthcare for free or for
almost nothing

Mr. Hamid told us he wanted to take us to the source and inspiration for all this, that which had motivated him to work for the sake
of God and His creation without cease. "It must be your mother!" I
said.

We followed a little winding path into the jungle and came at last
to a light-filled village shack. There we met, sitting on a large bed, Mr.
Hamid's mother. Her hands, her face, her fragrance, and her vibration

were like those of the venerable Sheikhs I have been so blessed to meet along the way.

When we left her presence, I wanted nothing but to return and stay with her longer. But that was not possible. A few months later, she departed from this world, leaving a great and growing legacy.

Before completing this remembrance of the selfless, noble servants of the Merciful that I was blessed to meet in Bangladesh, I would like to contemplate and celebrate the wonderful work of Muhammad Yunus, a native of this beautiful land. What he, himself, has done in creating the Grameen Bank, an extensive structure of micro-credit banking, is proof that every human being is capable, with the grace of God, to make an immense difference in transforming the condition of his fellow beings.

He began his experiment with micro-credit banking observing a group of very poor people who were forced into a corrupt system based on usury, because they had no other way to get the funding to develop their small businesses. Because they were poor and had no collateral, they were unable to get funding from any bank.

When he counted up all the money that these people needed to pursue their goals, (as we have been told) it was a total of twenty-seven dollars! Lacking these twenty-seven dollars, this group of people who could not get this money from any established banking system was forced into usury, a practice forbidden by the One Most Merciful.

Muhammad Yunus, acting on behalf of the Merciful, gave this group of people the small loan that they needed to develop their businesses. This worked very well, and he continued to help other groups of people like this.

Thus he began his practice of micro-credit banking which, now, so many years later, is empowering more than seven million people, mostly women, to fund their businesses and take care of their families, helping them to rise up out of the depths of hopeless poverty to become truly independent and successful. This is a miracle of God's Grace made manifest in absolutely tangible action.

As much as we see that the land of Bangladesh has had to endure intense poverty along with so many natural disasters and their aftermaths, let us consider the greatness of spirit, which has manifested there — how most extreme poverty has been transformed into abundance and great success.

This is indeed a tremendous inspiration for every one of us and a message for the entire world. We cannot each help seven million other fellow beings on the planet, but every person we can help, every loving thought and action, truly counts. May we each search for the many ways that we can do this.

As we were driving away from Tangail into the lush landscape of Bangladesh, rich with rice paddy fields both blessed and deeply tried by the abundance of water, tears flowed from my eyes in streams. What overwhelmed me most deeply was the comprehension of how much capacity one person has to help another. And the acts of true charity are yet greater and more exalted when they are addressed to those most helpless and most deeply in need.

All of this was the manifested teaching of the Messenger (saw) of Allah subhana wa ta'ala and of all the Prophets (as) who preceded him, the teaching of Allah subhana wa ta'ala, the One Creator who sent them all. As our Creator, Most Merciful, tells us in the Holy Qur'an, "*Repel evil with what is better.*" He tells us that good works and good words lead directly to Him:

> And whose speech is better than one who calls others to Allah and does good deeds, and says, "Surely I am among the willingly surrendered ones." Good and evil deeds are not equal. Repel evil with what is better. You will see that the one with whom you had enmity will become, as it were, your dearest friend.
>
> The Holy Qur'an 41:33-34

Whatever difficulty, whatever evil we or our fellow beings face, with the Grace of God, may we not be discouraged, frightened, or upset, but may we repel it with what is better. The light from one small candle can illuminate a huge dark room. This is the divine teaching that we saw manifesting in action, everywhere that we went.

Imagine what would happen to the condition of the world, the human condition, if we all followed this divine advice? Such an approach taken by one after another of the inhabitants of this planet, would, person by person, extinguish the fire fueling all the conflicts, all the wars, all the pacts of revenge!

This, as simple as it is, is the most powerful teaching. May every one of us who hears and comprehends this message from our Creator discover the way to implement it in the multiple contexts of our life.

Let us start with ourselves, take these words to heart, and see how they transform the situations we encounter in our life!

Next we were led to Lahore, Pakistan, to the shrine of Al-Hujwiri, who was known as Data Ganj Baksh, the *bestower of treasure*. He had written the great Sufi book, *Kashf al-Mahjub,* or *The Unveiling of the Mystery*. It was one of the first Sufi books I had ever read. Early in my development, I had read this book, and it had a deep impact upon me.

The first words that we read and hear about the reality of God and the path that leads to God are so profoundly beautiful to the soul because they are like its first food, its first life-giving water.

> *The Sufi is he who speaks truth. In his silence all parts of his body give evidence of his absorption in God. This means that when the Sufi talks, he relates truth and the knowledge of God. His speech is according to his spiritual state. When he is silent, his silence declares his absorption in God. He is an example of detachment from this world. His discourse is about truth and his conduct is complete detachment. In other words, his speech is pure truth and his actions are pure absorption in God.*
>
> Al-Hujwiri,
> *Kashful Mahjub*

They are not simply words on a page; they are our vital connection to another realm. So, they are precious and beloved to us, like valuable gems we find on a road that came from another world! We have no idea where they came from or how they got there, but we feel that they have special meaning for us, and although we do not really know what they mean, we keep them near us, feeling that they are a sign of great treasures we are destined to receive.

Al-Hujwiri's book was like that for me when it came into my hands in my late teens. To this day, I remember the feeling of holding my wellworn copy in my hand and of carrying it with me everywhere. It was a link to the unseen, containing clues relating to my real purpose in life.

I cannot remember when that precious book fell *out* of my hand. But, somewhere, in the course of traveling I had lost the book amid all the vicissitudes of my life, and had not seen it again all these years until this moment when, in the library below the mosque, we were handed the book written by the saint who was buried here. It was like mysteriously finding again a love letter that I had lost thirty years before. It was not the letter that was so precious to me but the One who sent it, the One who had been with me forever and, was ever continuing to send His messages and the signs of His Presence, His boundless Love.

This was another sign that the circle was coming to completion. Subtly, in the midst of all the outer events, I was witnessing: the deepest supplications for divine knowledge that had been made throughout my life, from the time I first set out on the journey of the soul, were guiding me powerfully towards the Goal.

In the beginning, the One of Infinite Grace *called,* making me know that the purpose of my life was to journey in quest of His Truth. Now, as the veils were lifted, I was coming home to realize the beautiful completeness of the message He had been sending from beginning to end, and the end was, in fact, *endless.* Further, I bear witness that the power of what was coming was infinitely greater than anything I could have imagined or asked for.

The sense of the presence of the Beloved and the power of His Love were very real as we stood in the library beneath the shrine of the great Sufi saint. I felt that, step-by-step, I was being drawn closer to the understanding of the divine plan for my life and the lives of others.

We called it a *journey of peace,* and truly this was the goal, but I realized as I traveled that, to get closer to that goal, I had to wage a war (of clarity, wisdom, and inner strength) with those elements within me that were still not at peace, which truly had to be exposed, then healed and transformed.

The journey was like an ever-unfolding rite of passage. At every stage, in every country, I had to pass through some kind of deep illness, physical, emotional, and spiritual. As much as I was learning from our beautiful meetings with the people of the world, I was also being tested, purified and transformed.

This was often dramatically demonstrated. One day, for example, I was stricken with a fever and could not move for a few hours. When I got up and took my laptop out from its carrying case, I found that the screen was shattered. This reflected something that was shattered in myself. I had to accept all the pain and trauma I experienced, in order to finally release it, before I could be liberated from the circle of the life I knew to rise up to meet and embrace what was ultimately destined for me to realize on the journey to my Lord.

It was through accepting my own pain, limitation and joy that I could feel the pain, limitation, and joy of everyone that we met and, through the power of humility and submission, pray for the redemption, healing, and liberation of all. Every child released from the terrible prison where she had lived beneath her mother's bed was, I felt, myself. Every leper sitting upright in the courtyard with his brothers and sisters and accepting his destiny courageously and peacefully was a manifestation of myself.

The joy of every orphan finding a home and brothers and sisters to live and grow up with was my joy. Each of the young boys proud to have a bed roll and rice that he had cooked was also expressing the joy and gratitude I felt to have exactly what I had been given, that joy of having made it through so many challenges and difficulties and still being alive to take the next step!

Deeply, I was experiencing those lives as my own, my life and love also mysteriously reflecting theirs. That was why we were drawn together and did not want to separate. These were the teachings I needed to learn on my journey toward peace, solidarity, and liberation.

This is, I believe, part of what Gautama Buddha learned when he left the opulent palace of his father, the king, and went into the streets of the world, to encounter and learn about the many dimensions of the suffering of the human condition. Traveling on the path, we experience that liberation and union with the ultimate Reality does not come without suffering.

From conscious suffering arises compassion, which leads to deep contemplation of the oneness and interconnectedness of all life, and this inspires the yearning to serve in the process of transformation and liberation. This is the understanding and energy that leads us to accomplish real change in ourselves, as well as in the conditions of the world around us. There is not one problem that we face that cannot ultimately become fuel in the process of personal and global transformation. But we must turn in the right direction to get the answer to all of our problems and the cure for all our diseases.

In order that we could learn more about this process and participate more deeply in it, as the final step in our mission of peace, we went to Kashmir, to unite with a community of people who had been gaining mastery, for so many years, in the art of responding to what is evil with what is better.

As I mentioned in the earlier chapter dedicated to these wonderful, noble people — what amazed us most about them is that whatever hardship they had to endure, such as years of occupation, danger and oppression, their *dhikr* (remembrance of God), their faith, illumined intelligence, inspired artistry and boundless generosity always seemed to increase, becoming deeper and stronger, no matter what adversity they had to face.

The believers are asked in the Qur'an if they think they will enter paradise without being tested as those before them were tested. Certainly, the noble believers of Kashmir understand this *ayat* deeply. For so many years, they have been tested in so many ways.

And every time I return to their beautiful land, I find that they are more kind, generous, positive and faithful. I pray that all of the sincere people of this land (and all lands) be rewarded for their steadfast faith in Allah *subhana wa ta'ala,* which they have manifested under all conditions, and that all their needs may be satisfied in a paradise that is far greater and more enduring than anything they may have lost in this world. Descending once again through the radiant skies and then the magnificent snow peaks crowning the Vale of Kashmir, my heart was deeply moved by all that I had experienced and all that I knew of this land and its people. I felt, certainly, that I was coming home again to one of the places on earth that I love most and pray for most deeply.

We were welcomed, upon landing, with great love, sweetness, and, as usual, immense hospitality, by Yousuf and Nedeem Shah, my dear friends, who had been supplying me, for many years, with tapestries. From the moment that we arrived at the airport, we felt that our Kashmiri hosts rolled out a beautiful tapestry beneath our feet and it was that which we walked upon, throughout our stay in Kashmir. In truth, it was their love, generosity and respect unfolded before us, upon which we journeyed through their land.

The first day, they had arranged for us to stay in a rustic hotel over-looking Dal Lake, with rugs and tapestries everywhere, a very Kashmiri kind of lodge. This was the beginning of winter in Kashmir, very, very cold, and there was a metal drum filled with fire in the Sheikh's (ra) room, around which we sat through the night, singing a beautiful dhikr (zikr). It was another ancient, eternal night in which the *dhikr* sang itself and resonated throughout the universe.

The next day we were transported in small boats to an exquisite, hand-carved houseboat with beautiful stained-glass windows and hand-made adornments of many kinds, moored in the middle of the lake. There, encompassed by peace and beauty, we stayed for the rest of our visit. We would travel back and forth to land in small boats.

While on land, we went on a journey from mosque to mosque, the great mystic mosques of Kashmir, mosques high in the snow-covered mountains, majestic *masjids* on the lakes. I saw, experienced, and felt the way in which the Creator was being praised in this elevated land and understood that this deep worship and love of the Creator was what was giving these people the strength of spirit to respond to darkness with light. Everywhere we went, we were connected, heartfully and soulfully, with the people. I longed to speak with them, to deeply support them, and to understand their real story.

Then Yousuf arranged a meeting at his house. He said he had only invited members of his family, but the large room where we all gathered was packed with extraordinary, venerable, light-filled people of all ages, from very young children to elders, all of whom were members of Yousuf Shah's family.

Sheikh Aly gave a beautiful heartfelt discourse to this exalted assembly. He began by addressing the congregation saying:

> *It is a very great pleasure to be in Kashmir among you. We have been introduced to this part of the world only through the media and through books of geography. We have heard that the people here are fighting a war and we have heard about the actions of the government of India. We knew that there were many Muslims living here. And even though we were not here, we were very moved because we knew that our Muslim brothers were here. And we felt concern about what*

was happening in this part of the world. We felt that your
suffering was our suffering.

I appreciated this introduction very much. I realized again what I have
experienced so many times in my journey — that what we hear or see in
the media can never convey to us fully the reality of the lives of people.
So often, *the news is heartless.* Thousands of people in a region undergoing one kind of oppression or disaster or another are dismissed in thirty
seconds.

That is why it is a great blessing to travel, to live with people and
see how they live and in what ways they are facing and surmounting
their difficulties, as well as to begin to comprehend their pain and their
struggle.

By coming to know the people of the world one by one, we realize
the preciousness of every life and then seek for any way that we can truly
share with that living being. This is one way that the great disorder of the
world can begin to be healed, balanced and corrected.

This description of our trip to Kashmir was written several years
ago. As of 2019, the situation for these noble people, which had been
profoundly challenging for so many years, had become intensely more
difficult. Their internet and phone service had, almost entirely, been cut
off. A fierce curfew or blackout was being imposed. For the most part,
they could not really leave their homes, and, as we have heard, many
were being imprisoned and killed. Words cannot express the grief and
concern we feel for all who are undergoing such trials, and we pray with
deepest love for the liberation, not only of the Kashmiri people but for
the restoration of the sacred land of India, itself, where so many saints
and truly good people have walked and prayed.

In regard to our trip there in 2002 and the sharing of knowledge
with our spiritual companions there, we had come to Kashmir on our
journey of peace and liberation certainly as much to learn as to teach.

Back then, Sheikh Aly spoke to the gathering at Yousuf 's home
about Islam in the life of the Prophet (saw) and the journey of the Prophet (saw) from Mecca to Medina. The discourse was simple and direct,
targeting the very essence of the point of spiritual transformation that I
had been coming to understand with greater and greater certainty:

When we reflect again upon the shahadah, the profession of faith, La ilaha ill'Allah, we see that it means that there is no god but God, no divinities but God. And we see that the struggle of Muhammad (saw) in Mecca was a confrontation between God and all the 'divinities,' a confrontation between the Creator of the universe and all the idols, the weaknesses, the vices that the people were attached to...

We must not forget that the mission of the Prophet (saw) was to take the people from the darkness and lead them to the light. When we make the shahadah, we say that there is no god but God. The ilaha is not Allah, only God is eternal, everlasting. The entire message of Islam is how to move from the ilaha to only Allah. And all of the work that the Prophet (saw) did was to purify the Ka'aba of all the idols within it, consecrating it to God, the One God. This was not only the transformation of the Ka'aba. It was a transformation of the population...

To leave "Mecca" [in this context] also meant to leave the qualities... [of certain] ... Meccan people. At this time, such Meccans did not believe in one God. The values of the society were tribal values, racial values, cultural values, values according to wealth. In that culture, according to these values, from the time of your birth, your destiny was fixed...

But, in Medina, the Lord gave the Rasul (saw) a place to put into practice that message that he was spreading. And, in this place where he was spreading the message, he taught other human values...

It is very important to see the way in which... [certain] ... Meccan people accepted to leave Mecca and, go to Medina. The Prophet (saw) showed them the concept of freedom in the choice that they made to leave Mecca and, go to Medina...

Although the Prophet Muhammad (saw), proposed this choice to all those around him fourteen hundred years ago, as did all of the Prophets (as) before him, the Truth is eternal, and exactly the same choice is being proposed to us today...

We must make the choice, make the total paradigm shift. We cannot serve our fear, pain, unworthiness, anger, arrogance, pride, desire, attachment to worldly wealth and power, and all the countless idols with which we have packed our inner ka'aba, our inner heart and, at the same time, be free to worship our Lord, the Unique One, to celebrate His Praise and enjoy His eternal peace with all our heart and soul.

Such was the message that Sheikh Aly left with the people of Kashmir, as we left this blessed and beautiful, yet deeply challenged land. Having returned from Kashmir, we accompanied Sheikh Aly to the airport in New Delhi and watched him, smiling and waving, disappear into the crowd. Many useful and beautiful teachings, experiences, and understandings had been shared in my travels with this wonderful Sheikh, and yet I had to continue to travel on. As he had indicated to me, walking into the unfoldment of my destiny, I was to rise, to discover the next unfathomable dimensions of the journey.

***

But before moving on, I must bear witness to the unfolding events which took place shortly before I was to send the revision of this book to the Publisher. After we shared deep salaams at the airport in New Delhi, our beloved companions on the sacred journey, Sheikh Aly N'Daw, and his representative, Sheikh Aly Peerbocus, did come to stay with us and to visit Temple University where Issa was working on a PhD. Our sharing together was deeply beautiful as ever.

Then in early 2021, I was given Sheikh Aly's phone number in Pout, Senegal, where he had been digging wells and providing many villagers with water and other necessities. For some reason I did not have his number until this moment and this was the blessed moment to call. When he realized that it was me calling, he seemed to be overwhelmed with ecstatic joy as I was overwhelmed with love for the Divine who had brought us together to share such sacred moments and blessed steps —

manifest teachings on the journey back to our Beloved Source (swt). We had that one more truly wonderful meeting, acknowledging together the blessings that we had shared. A few weeks later, on February 17, 2021, Sheikh Aly (ra) returned to Allah (swt), *inna lillahi wa inna ilaihi raji'un.* We pray that all the blessed service he did and all the love and wisdom he shared are now welcoming him, as a wealth of Grace in his blessed abode in akhirah.

***

One week after I returned home from the trip to India, a few hours after we had recited *Surah Ya Sin* in honor of the passing of Kabeer's holy mother, Maimunna Ummah (ra), who had left this world at ninety-three, I was stricken with pain from one side to the other, pain that did not cease, no matter which way I turned.

When an attack of such unabated intensity occurs, unlike anything you have ever felt before, you have no idea what is happening. The experience goes beyond any point of reference you have. I could not imagine what was happening or what to do about it. My friend Sara standing next my bed and tuning in to my condition, said, "You had better go to the hospital." My brain was not functioning enough to think of that. But I understood that what she said was right and, with the help of the people in the house, particularly Issa, made it to the Emergency Room.

There, I waited for what seemed to be an interminable time for a room. The intense pain did not, at all, abate. Finally, I was given a bed in a small room. It was only when I lay down on the bed that I was able truly to let go and let Allah (swt) and the doctors take over. From that moment on, the peace came and covered me like a blanket of light, and the pain was irrelevant.

At about three in the morning, after the test results were back, I was diagnosed with acute appendicitis, which can be very serious and even lethal if not treated properly at the proper time. As usual, how great was the blessed protection of Allah (swt) that this condition did not become acute, until I had returned home from the dangerously rough and rugged route, where we were often so many miles away from any hospitals or any health care systems that we could have known about, and I was now five minutes away from our local hospital. This acute condition was clearly the culmination of all that I had been suffering on the trip ripening into its full intensity here.

The appendicitis was diagnosed at three in the morning, and at the time of the *fajr* (early morning) prayer my appendix was removed through laparoscopic surgery. I remained in the hospital for a few days more and was released.

But I was not really well. Deeply something was not quite right. When I returned to the hospital to see the doctor for a checkup, it seemed that not all the material had been removed, and a large abscess had formed. He ordered more tests, and the next day I was readmitted, urgently, to the hospital.

The second hospital stay was profound. Hooked up to tubes and subject to invasive procedures which occurred throughout the day and night, intravenously fed powerful antibiotics which had, for me, extreme side effects, with nurses and doctors passing through so quickly and impersonally that they barely had time to say hello, much less give a healing prayer or caress, I began to experience the painful plight of the many members of our human family: brothers and sisters, fathers and mothers, aunts, uncles, and children everywhere who are confined as prisoners to hospital beds, from which many of them may never again get up.

As much as I possibly could, I felt them and the very difficult life that they must endure, and, as difficult as that was, I then began to sense the pain of those who could not even get to the hospitals to get help and were suffering in so many places and ways.

These people, too, are lives that are a part of this story. All the people suffering in hospital beds, in their own beds and in the streets, mountains, or valleys where they may lay, are a part of this story. Because this is not only the story of one person's journey; it is interconnected with the journey of all creations in search of the meaning of existence and a blessed return to the Source.

And we cannot reach the goal without sacrifice, suffering, purification, transformation, and our inevitable meeting with death. I had spent only several difficult days in the hospital. What about the people who spend weeks and months and even die in the hospital?

Most sincerely we pray that wherever our fellow beings are, they may receive comfort and solace in the presence of the Lord, the comfort of His presence in whatever difficulties they are facing, as at the time of the transition from this life, peace and salvation in His Eternal Existence in the life to come.

The room in which I stayed to receive this teaching in the hospital was two doors down from the hospice room, where our brothers and sisters are sent when they are in transition into the realms of death. It was not yet my time to go to that room, to make that journey yet. But I had to come to this room two doors down to make a passage, profoundly to give up my life as I had known it.

As I left the hospital room and walked slowly out of the hospital, I had to consider deeply that I had been blessed to leave alive and that, with the gift of life, came the responsibility to fulfill this life's potential, that potential Allah *subhana wa ta'ala,* created it to fulfill. Every step and every breath remaining are, by His Grace, another chance to gain and deepen knowledge of His Path, to serve and surrender more deeply, to receive and surrender to true guidance, to send real provision to the hereafter, and draw closer to the Ultimate Goal.

CHAPTER TWENTY-TWO

IN THE TIME ALLOTTED BEFORE WE MUST GO, MAY WE ATTAIN THE GOAL

Out of the Context of Time and Space

Blessed is He in Whose hand is the Sovereignty, and, He is able to do all things. Who hath created life and death that He may try you, which of you is best in conduct; and He is the Mighty, the Forgiving.

—The Holy Qur'an 67:1-2

What is the duty of the time in which you live? It's the thing that the era in which you live calls upon you to do. It's the action that will alleviate the suffering and therefore please the Lord. It's the action that only you can do. The only thing that will make us happy and fulfilled today is our alignment with the duty or the obligation of our time, and so the question now is: What does Allah want from us? And what would be incumbent on us in a time like this?

—Shaykh Hamdi ben Aissa

I had been told that the circle of my life was complete, and I was ready to rise to another real dimension in the journey to my Lord. Within a few weeks, I was in a hospital, connected to many tubes, two doors down from the room where terminal patients are sent to make their journey back to the Source. I had just returned from a mission of peace and solidarity in which I witnessed how noble and great are things that a human being, with the grace of God, has the capacity to do for others. I was experiencing, in difficulty and ease, the blessing in every step of the way. What was the message coming through all that was unfolding? And where was it leading?

As I walked slowly and tentatively out of the hospital room and down the long corridor, I knew that my life had been created, and also preserved, for a reason and a purpose.

A short while later, I was sent again to this hospital, this floor, this corridor, to the room two doors down, the hospice room, to recite Surah Ya Sin for a neighbor who had just passed away.

By the Decree of Allah, her time in this world was up. She had not one more chance in this life to say a prayer, think a noble thought or perform a loving deed. Whatever of good and evil she was able to do in this life, the pen was lifted and the ink was dried.

But what about you and me, dear reader, and all the other beings who are still alive, still full of the potential either to worship and serve the One Creator of all or not? Consider the sacred opportunity that we have!

In the precious time remaining, what are we going to do? This is the great challenge posed to all the children of Adam (as). We are told that, on the Last Day when we are standing in judgment in the presence of our Lord, every atom's weight of good and evil will be seen.

We do not seem to realize the importance of what we are doing here, what choice, what challenge is being presented to us, every moment of our lives. If we did realize the ultimate importance, repercussion and result of every action, would we not want to make each action — and the thought and intention that lead to the action — truly good? It would be very helpful to us now and in the future if we could consider this deeply while we have the chance to improve. How can we become truly good so that our scale, in judgment, will be heavy on the side of the good actions and the true purpose for which we were created by our Creator Most Loving and Wise may be fulfilled?

In the course of coming to understand what causes us to incline to goodness, we must also understand what could make us incline toward evil. So, let us consider what our Creator tells us about the contrasting dimensions of our human condition:

> By the Fig and the Olive. And by Mount Sinai. And by this city of Security. Surely, We have created man in the most exalted form. Then We brought him down to the condition of the lowest of the low. But those who believe and do good deeds, for them, there is an unending reward. What then causes you to question the judgement? Is not Allah the wisest of all judges?
>
> Surat Tin, The Holy Qur'an 95:1-8

And also let us consider this very important, connected surah:

> By Time,
> Verily Man is in loss,
> Except those who believe and do good works,
> and enjoin one another to truth
> and enjoin one another to patience.
>
> Surat'ul 'Asr, The Holy Qur'an 103:1-3

Knowing that the time is limited in which we have to learn our deepest lessons here, let us contemplate these words of our Creator, seeking to understand in what exalted form we (humanity) were created and how we then descended to such a low state. Through understanding the way in which we were brought down, we can also understand the way in which we can rise to attain the exalted station that He intended for us when He created us.

Having fallen through ignorance and disobedience to the Divine Guidance, from the original state of grace, may we rise by means of divinely inspired knowledge and obedience to the realm of the One of infinite grace.

With direction from the One who is the Knower of all, may we come to understand from what world we descended and to what world we came and discover how, with His Mercy and clear Guidance, we may rise in the journey of returning to our exalted Source.

One descent we made is to the earth itself, this world *(dunya)* of material, emotional, and mental density. Before we came to incarnate in this dense world, we had existed in the world of souls, in realms of light, in proximity to and in remembrance of our Lord.

According to the words of the Holy Qur'an in pre-existence, before we came into this world, there was a great assembly of the souls, gathered in the presence of God, and this assembly was addressed by Allah, *subhana wa ta'ala,* who said, *"Alastu bi Rabbikum? Am I not your Lord?"* In response to this, the souls expressed their recognition of the Sovereignty and Divinity of the Lord, pledging fidelity to Him alone:

> *When your Lord took out the offspring from the loins of the Children of Adam and made them bear witness about themselves, He said, "Am I not your Lord?" and they replied, "Yes, we bear witness." So you cannot say on the Day of Resurrection, "We were not aware of this."*
>
> The Holy Qur'an 7:172

Some of the souls, we have been told, made this response of affirmation more quickly and some took more time to affirm, "Yes, You are our Lord!" in accordance with the speed and certainty with which we responded to the question addressed to us by our Lord in *alam'ul arwah,* the world of souls, we came into this world with greater or lesser certainty about this knowledge and the affirmation of it.

We did not want to leave that world and come here, but we were told that we had to come here to learn certain lessons and eventually be given an examination. The results we received in that examination would determine exactly where we would go from here, for, indeed, this world itself is a temporary stop on the journey to our Lord.

After we have been in this world for a while and become implanted or entrenched in this dense realm, we may or may not have any recollection of where we were before we came here.

To have forgotten this: where we came from, who we really are, and why we have really come to this world — is a cause of great confusion and suffering for us, wasted time, and misdirected thought and action. May we come to realize the truth before, suddenly, it is time to leave this world and we have not accomplished the purpose for which we came here.

As a small child growing up in my mother's house, like many young children, I seemed to have an awareness of the other world, the other realm, and it was an extremely different reality than the world into which I had incarnated. This is why I wondered what I was doing here and felt deeply nostalgic, yearning for knowledge about the world from which I had come and the mysteries of the Divine Source, which no one around me seemed to have knowledge about.

On the contrary, life here was organized on entirely different principles. The things that were being discussed and sought after were very different than the things that my soul yearned to know. The questions I had, about the origin and end and real meaning of existence, could only be answered by one who had knowledge of these deep matters, and that was something that I would have to search for and find. The profound inner longing to make the journey in search of real knowledge was already activated within me as a child, so, even at the age of twelve, I received the mandate written on a scroll: "Seek, and the truth shall make you free."

What does this mean? To "seek to be free" indicates clearly that we are in a prison from which we seek to be liberated. What is the nature of the prison in which we are apparently entrapped? As we have all been encountering, consciously or unconsciously, throughout our journey through this life, it is a psychological prison that was constructed, layer by layer, veil by veil, from the time that we arrived on this earth and had to deal with the various trials appearing in the life of this world.

And the very unique challenges that we each face present us with the deepest, most difficult obstacles that we have to overcome in order, ultimately, to pass the test presented to us by the Divine Examiner, realizing the purpose for which we were created and the mission that we have to fulfill.

By facing these specific difficulties and challenges, we hopefully gain the discernment to know what is right from what is wrong and develop the strength of character — faith, determination, and certitude— and also the tools that we need to transform darkness into light, ignorance into true knowledge.

We each have the capacity or potential to alchemically transform everything that is dark and heavy in our lives into gold, that is, into light. But we can do this only with the grace of God, the power of God, and the guidance of a true Master who is totally surrendered in the service of God and authorized to transmit the knowledge of Allah *subhana wa ta'ala* and of the journey that leads to Him.

As I did, many of us had a recollection of the beauty and light of the vast realm from which we had come, and in contrast to this was the tiny table at which I was now sitting, so small that even I alone did not fit.

I felt that my clothes were too small. They could in no way fit the vastness of the soul I sensed within. The part that I seemed to have to play, a part that step by step was formed by the accumulating veils, was an identity that was hiding the light of the soul, its origin, and its destination.

Thus, by the contrast of the identity I was assuming in the world and the truth of who I really was, a fundamental conflict emerged, and, in response to that conflict, a structure of limitations composed of accumulated veils was created in which I became somehow imprisoned.

I speak to you, O heart and soul of the reader! Whatever prison you and I may have consciously or unconsciously constructed around ourselves — reacting as we did to the sometimes stressful, hurtful, and challenging circumstances of our unfolding life in this world — that artificial structure is hiding from ourselves the light of our true nature, that nature which is inherently inclined to lovingly serve and ultimately unite with our Beloved Lord.

Let us make the intention to find true guidance, exchange falsehood for Truth, and thus find the way to deconstruct the prison walls so, without a door or lock and key, we can dispel the illusions and be free to become who we truly are — who the Creator Most Merciful intended us to be.

For this we need tools. We need the blessing and the guidance of the One who created us in the most exalted form. We need to ask, to beseech Him that we may learn what the Divine Intention was when He created us and how His intention can be fulfilled in us.

To come to know ourselves, so that we may know Him, is a course of mysteries and challenges. It is a process of deeper and deeper unveiling. One by one, each of the illusory identities that we have acquired must be discarded, recognized as unreal. To do this, we need to know the difference between what is unreal and what is real.

The statement in Arabic experienced as the first pillar in Islam, *La illaha ill'Allah wa Muhammmad ar-Rasulillah,* if we understand its true meaning, will be our greatest aid. This statement bears witness that there is no reality other than the Reality that is God, the One Creator of all, and that Muhammad (saw) is the Messenger of Allah *subhana wa ta'ala,* the last of all the Prophets and Messengers (as) and the Seal of the Prophets (as) who came before him.

This is the most powerful tool we have been given by the One who created us in the most exalted form. This realization is the holy fire and the light for the alchemy of our transformation. We must realize that nothing exists, that nothing truly exists other than the reality that is God. The true reality, the true nature of our being, is as is stated in the Hadith Qudsi (a saying of God in the wording of His Prophet Muhammad), *"I was a Hidden Treasure and longed to be known. Therefore, I created the creation that I might be known."*

Then what are these other multiple realities to which we have become attached and with which we have become identified — the fearful, depressed, ailing, arrogant, rebellious, jealous, lustful, angry, unbelieving aspects of the self that is inherently false, that is, illusory? These are the aspects of ourselves which, veiling the light of the Reality within us, need to become transparent, must be transformed. But how?

On the path of Tasawwuf, (the Sufi Path) we learn of the stations of the self, heart, and soul through which the seeker must pass on the journey of ultimate transformation.

All of the complex aspects of our being that have been thriving on unrest, separate from the Source of Peace, are guided, station by station, to the Source of Peace and the other Divine Attributes. This is a deep spiritual science which is understood and can be implemented only with the guidance of a true Spiritual Master.

Like this, is the journey of the seeker for the Divine Qualities and for the station of awakening to the Divine Presence within guided by the Divine Guide, with the direction of the authorized teacher (Sheikh) until the nafs (self, soul) is totally surrendered, purified, and transformed.

This journey leads the nafs (self) through the stations of nafs ammarah (the self prone to evil) and nafs alallawama (the self that blames) to the stations of nafs'ul mutmainnah (the soul at peace), nafsur-radiah (the content soul), nafs'ul mardiah (the satisfied soul), and nafs al kamil, (the perfected soul). Such are the places, the stations, the realms that we pass through, with the Grace of God and the guidance of the Sheikh on the journey to our Lord.

It is when the transformation is complete, when the nafs (the self which is now at the level of the soul) has reached this station of true ultimate peace that it is invited by the Creator to enter the garden:

> *O Soul at Peace Return to your Lord*
> *Pleased and well-pleasing*
> *Enter the ranks of My worshippers Enter the garden.*
> The Holy Qur'an 89:27-30

To even hear these words and imagine our Lord speaking them to the soul within us is amazing, inspiring of hope. But how, in truth, can we attain that eternal station of peace?

In this and many other passages in the Holy Qur'an, our Creator, Most Merciful, invites us to enter the garden and guides our souls, through this life's challenges and tests, on the path to get there:

> *And vie with one another to attain to your Sustainer's forgiveness and to a paradise as vast as the heavens and the earth, which has been readied for the God-conscious who spend [in His way] in time of plenty and in time of hardship, and hold in check their anger, and pardon their fellow beings, because*

> *God loves the doers of good; who, when they have committed a*
> *shameful deed or have [otherwise] sinned against themselves,*
> *remember God and pray that their sins be forgiven — for who*
> *but God could forgive sins? And do not knowingly persist in*
> *doing whatever [wrong] they may have done. These it is who*
> *shall have as their reward forgiveness from their Sustainer, and*
> *gardens through which running waters flow, therein to abide:*
> *And how excellent a reward for those who labor!*
>
> The Holy Qur'an 3:133-136

To become the truly righteous, those who are God-conscious *(mut-taqun)*, those who continuously forgive and seek forgiveness and who are continuously giving of the bounties they have received — to become those who are thus invited to enter and dwell in the gardens of nearness to their Lord — we must understand how our original parents, Adam and Eve (as), fell from that state of grace. Whatever caused them to fall from the state of paradisal innocence and purity is exactly the same force that is dedicated to making us descend over and over again. Our Lord tells us again and again that Satan is our avowed enemy. And, we are told that we have no enemy but that primordial enemy who caused our parents to go astray.

In Surat'ul A'raf, Allah warns us:

> *O Children of Adam, do not let Satan seduce you, as he caused*
> *your parents to depart from the garden stripped of their gar-*
> *ments exposed to their shame! Surely he sees you — he and his*
> *folk — from a place where you cannot see him. Surely We have*
> *made the evil ones to be allies of those who do not believe.*
>
> The Holy Qur'an 7:27

The qualities and aspects of ourselves — those false identities to which we have become attached that cause us to surrender ourselves to anything other than the light and grace of God's Qualities — are, it would seem, allies of Satan and his community who are waiting in ambush to catch us in their entrapments, as we are traveling on the journey, and deter us from reaching our noble Goal.

This is what the seducer would have them do. For Satan has said, as the Qur'an tells us:

> *[Iblis] said: "Now that You have caused me to err, I shall lie in ambush for them along Your Straight Path. Then I shall fall upon them from before them and behind them and upon their right and upon their left. And You will not find most of them to be grateful."*
>
> The Holy Qur'an 7:16-17

Understanding the forces and tendencies within ourselves that, allied with Satan, are lying in wait to ambush us and learning how not to be entrapped by them are essential parts of our therapy and cure. We each have to fight the Great Struggle *(Jihad al Akbar)* within ourselves against everything within us that turns us away from the Divine Reality, which is our Exalted Source and End.

The inner war was called *Jihad al Akbar* by the Holy Prophet (saw) when he returned with his Companions (ra) from fighting a battle and told them that it was time to fight the greater war, the war within. From this we learn about the intensity and importance of the war that we have to fight within ourselves.

But how do we fight this war? Not with guns and bombs, not with hatred and aggression. We need the Grace of God, skill, and subtle wisdom to see through and thus overcome the ruses and tricks of the tempter, the seducer, the one who is our only enemy, no matter what form he is hiding behind.

The arrogance, unworthiness, fear, jealousy, sadness, anger, desire, pain, and so many other states of being we have become subconsciously identified with are veils behind which that force is operating, with the express purpose of undermining our commitment to reach the Goal.

We need to become aware of this, as we are engaged, moment-to-moment, in this battle against illusions within ourselves. This war is fought with understanding, with love and forgiveness. It is a war of awakening and transformation, not of destruction, in which darkness is dispelled by light and fear and hatred are dispelled by knowledge, peace, and love. No doubt, every one of us who came from the vast pure realm of God's Presence into this world of limitation and testing has suffered different kinds of wounds. From the first days of our life here — especially in worlds where, often, money, power, sex, egotism, and brutal warfare are worshipped and pursued with much greater determination than the path of the True God — we began, in these early years, to hear words that were not true and suffer their impact upon us.

Can we begin to remember the moments in our childhood when falsehood, fear, and unworthiness were first injected into our hearts and consciousness, pulling us away from the state of purity, trust, and submission that we experienced as babies? Can we remember the shock of that encounter and the way that poison entered our bloodstream?

That pain and fear and confusion that began to flow in our blood in our earliest years may continue to subtly corrupt and undermine our awareness throughout our life until, God willing, with the power of faith in the Truth and surrender to the Truth, with real spiritual guidance, we can truly dispel those subconscious tendencies which make us doubt ourselves, our Divine Source, and the sanctity of our existence.

We need to access and retrieve the state of grace we originally had to find and reconnect with the purity of the inner child intact, the believing soul, subtly living within ourselves. Then we may be able to clearly see how that purity and fundamental trust became covered up and almost completely hidden from view.

In Arabic, the word for covering up is *kufr*. Allah *subhana wa ta'ala* tells us that this is one of the most serious diseases in the heart of man. What, then, is humankind covering up? This word is most often used to describe the way in which so much of humanity has rejected and denied the messages sent by Allah *subhana wa ta'ala* through His Messengers (as).

What a profound loss it has been for humankind to reject the great gift from God and cover up the light of revelation with the darkness of ignorance! But, the light, the reality, and message of Allah *subhana wa ta'ala* have also, more importantly, been placed within our hearts. The human heart, as it was created by the Lord Most Merciful, has a vast capacity. The words of Allah *subhana wa ta'ala* tell us, *"The heavens and the earth do not contain Me, but the heart of My faithful believer contains Me"* (Hadith Qudsi).

Our Creator, in the very act of creating us, has placed within us, within this heart, Himself, His light, His treasure that He wished to be known. It is this light, this Divine Reality within us that becomes covered up in the course of our interactions in the world until we may not even know that it is there!

As we faced, one by one, the challenges of becoming conditioned to life in this world, reacting to the shock of one after another perceived attack or challenge, we built layers of protection over our heart, attempting to defend and protect it. Thus was the essential purity and trust in our hearts, veil by veil, covered up.

Allowing ourselves to feel again the heart of that pure, open-hearted child, we may be able to remember how, where, and when that child, the believing soul, withdrew and went into hiding and then denial.

Now, as we are reviewing this material, our life story, we have the choice to make the paradigm shift. And we must do this if we want to be truly free.

Imagine if we could see goodness in the place of evil, truth in the place of falsehood, if we could see, with wisdom, the circumstances of the people who seemed to oppress us and forgive them, forgive ourselves, and become free of the endless cycle of aggression and oppression and depression, moving from the world and paradigm of darkness into the world of light. That is how the therapy works.

When we become aware of the love and grace of our Creator that brought us into existence, this is the medicine that can heal whatever wounds we seem to have suffered in this temporary world that we have come to in order to be tested, purified, and transformed.

We need to see, with wisdom, that our Creator, who is the Best of Planners, determined that we should be born in such and such a place with exactly the parents that we had. This was not an accident but part of a plan. All of the details — where we were born, under what circumstances, through what parents, where we grew up, what inspirations arose within our souls — all of these things are messages to us from our Lord, messages ultimately leading back to the One who created us, messages that we need to accept and come to understand.

There is a much greater plan at work, a much greater dimension to the story of our life than we can initially see, and that is why we need to access and imbibe the medicine *(ash-shifaʾa)* of Allah's light and grace and mercy to penetrate the veils, showing us the way to heal our deep karmic illnesses (repeated unconscious patterns of behavior).

Inspired and guided by this light of grace — wishing to truly understand and forgive in the process of seeking the truth that would make me free, invoking the mercy and guidance of the One who had truly given me life, my real Source, Sustainer, and Nourisher — I turned with compassion toward my mother.

When I say that the table in my mother's house was so small that I felt that I couldn't fit, this means that I felt that somehow it seemed that there was no place for me in her world. My thoughts, understandings, feelings, and longings were not understood or valued by her in the context of her worldview.

This was the source of my tendency to feel that, somehow, I was unworthy, unappreciated, and unloved. It is not that the worthiness wasn't there; it is only that she couldn't perceive it. Living within the world that she did, constrained as she was by her level of understanding, she simply could not see these things.

As an essential part of the healing, the forgiving and understanding, I realized how important it was for me to thus see with the eyes of wisdom, love, and compassion, simply that she did not have the benefit of seeing all that I saw. She did not have access to the knowledge that throughout my life was being revealed to me, and that is why she did not understand or appreciate who I really was. Such was the nature and size of the limited table she set in her house, the limited state of her awareness and understanding.

My father and Sophie had a table that was very big and usual ly surrounded by guests from everywhere. I felt very comfortable there, knowing that anyone might come to the door from anywhere and be welcomed, just as I was, free to express my unfolding being. That was an expanded space in which I was able to grow in my formative years.

So, this was a dynamic contrast which formed me. These expanding and contracting influences created a dynamic tension; all of these forces were necessary to keep pushing the baby, the awakening soul, through the birth canal. And there would be no birth or movement without all of these energies and forces being activated.

There was also another table of which I was aware and from which I received the greatest nourishment. That was an unseen table, the table of divine provision. It was at such a table that (Mary) Maryam (ra) was eating every time the Prophet Zakariyyah (as) came into the temple to bring her food:

> *Allah received her with gracious acceptance and caused her to grow in a gracious manner under the protection of Zakariyyah. Every time that Zakariyyah came to her in her sanctuary, he found her provision before her. He said. "Oh Maryam, how does this come to you?" She said, "It is from Allah. Truly Allah provides for whom He wills without accounting."*
>
> The Holy Qur'an 3:37

And it is this continuous source of provision of and love coming from the Source that is, by far, the most powerful element in every stage of sustenance, healing and spiritual transformation. Therefore, at whatever table I am sitting, I am certain that the real provision is always coming only from Him, our sole Sustainer.

All of these dimensions of the table were significant in the forming of my character and the challenges I had to overcome. Since all of the elements are necessary and useful in one way or another, we must be truly grateful for each and every gift we are given on the path that leads us toward union with our Lord. By being truly grateful for everything that has been given to us, we defy Satan who said, *"And most of them are not grateful"* (The Holy Qur'an 26:19).

Finally, I saw, at the end of my mother's life, how the therapy was working. This was revealed in a very graphic way when I went to visit her in the last few weeks of her life. I had been told that she was very weak and could barely move. When I entered her apartment, she sat up, bolt upright, blazing with life.

She said, "I have been waiting for you! Where have you been?" She then spoke to me, it seemed, for twenty-four hours straight. She spoke to me only when no one else was in the room and was a completely different person when anyone else was around. To others, she may have appeared to be intolerant, cantankerous, impatient, and extremely para-noid. But, when they left, she became like a rapturous radiant young girl, joyful, poetic, full of love, and very humorous.

There were certain things that she had to tell me and could not leave the world without, somehow, passing on to me. She said, "I have thought a lot about it, and I have decided that you are the one who can carry on the work!"

I truly did not know what work she thought that it was that she wanted me to carry on. Only as I am writing this now do I begin to sense what she wanted to pass on to me. And that was love. She had not discovered the love of God. We had several talks about this, and it was something we could never agree upon, since it was an awareness that I had come into this world with and one which, until the end, did not apparently dawn within her to the extent that she really knew what it was.

Yet, she was impelled to transmit to me a legacy of love that she had for me. All that she could wish for me was the best of what she had herself experienced deeply. What she had experienced, which had the greatest meaning for her, was the love of her husband. This was the highly cherished treasure of her life, the greatest thing that she knew. And that, I believe, is what she wished to give me and what she wished me to carry on. (I did accept to carry on the legacy of love, but not in a way that she could have imagined or fathomed.)

Sitting on the television near her was a photograph of herself and her husband Kenny, gazing at each other, smiling with intense adoration. On the wall of the room that she was facing were beautiful photographs of my brothers and a painting of me, painted when I was about ten years old. It was a very pensive portrait that, I felt, looked thoughtful and somewhat inward and hidden.

She looked at the painting and then looked at me, sitting close to her bed, and seemed astonished. "Who is this beautiful woman?" she asked gazing at me. The pensive child had grown into another being nourished by the love, guidance, and beautiful, all-merciful parenting of God — and this she clearly perceived in our last meeting.

This was the first time that I felt she truly saw me, that is, saw the essence of the divine beauty within me. And this moment between us was the moment of liberation and real sharing. She said, "I have lived my life and it is complete. Now live yours! Do not make a memorial for me. Live your life completely! That will be your memorial to me."

I have no doubt that this is what she wanted me to know: that I should live my life to its completeness. The significance and impact of her words — her intention for me, and the fulfillment of my life — went far beyond her comprehension.

From the beginning of my life to the end of hers, she wished and willed for me the gift of freedom, to find the truth for myself, and the gift of courage to live by the truth I had discovered to the point of completion. In accordance with the true intention she held for me, I pray that all the blessings which have descended and will descend upon me in this quest for truth and completion aid her and my father in their journeys in the next world.

As much of a blessing as it was to be seen, even a little by my mother as she was preparing to leave this world, her inability to see this until that time was also a gift to me, one of the most potent catalysts to my journey and growth.

Although the gift of freedom was given, the love that I yearned for so deeply from my mother was not given freely and easily. If it had been, I may have been inclined to stay at home and take refuge in my mother's loving arms, in the loving warmth of her abode.

But the love that I truly sought could only be found through leaving my mother's home and searching profoundly, sacrificing myself again and again to gain it, stage after stage, in many places and many ways.

On the journey of the soul to attain its liberation, nothing occurs without sacrifice. At every stage of the way, we have to give up life as we knew it, to discover the wealth of treasure, the wealth of understanding that lies behind every closed door waiting to be opened.

When we begin to perceive the dynamism and inclusiveness of the path of self-realization, we see that everything, if we allow it to be, will be catalytic to our growth. Therefore, without any regret or dissatisfaction, we must thank our Lord, Most Generous, the only true Giver of all, for all that He has given to us to know and experience on the path which is our life.

Because I could not find everything I was seeking at home, I set out on the endless journey and found my home everywhere in the vast universe while finding that vast universe within myself.

From the moment that I was released from my mother's hold, released subconsciously by her from her jurisdiction, I was the leaf carried by the wind of the Divine Will. Whether or not she could accept the "concept" of the Divine, from the time that I was very young, she had released me into the jurisdiction of the Divine Hand, by which I have been guided for the rest of my life.

As I came to see and register the immensity of what I saw, I sent my parents parchment scrolls with burnt edges, upon which I had etched out ecstatic messages from all corners of the globe. One day, a large bagful of these messages that I had sent to my parents throughout the years came back to me. I poured them out of the bag and saw the mass of energy inscribed upon those pages.

I wondered if the letters had ever been read and what my parents could possibly have thought about these strange messages if they had read them. I was like an explorer who, in traveling, had discovered an *entirely new world.*

It was only in the final moments with my parents that I felt that they may have begun to see what I had been seeing in me. One was this moment with my mother when in her last request she bequeathed to me love and a life fully lived. Another was a very beautiful moment that I was blessed to share with my father.

Several years before he left this world, my father, Lennie, suffered a stroke while driving a car. Thus began the last phase of his life on earth. From that time on, he suffered a number of debilitating illnesses until, at last, he was bedridden permanently.

At a certain point in this progression, he expressed a strong desire to go the *mazar,* the shrine of Bawa Muhaiyaddeen (ra). Although he was ill and it was difficult to travel, he made it to Philadelphia, traveling with Sophie, and we all went to the mazar. It was a beautiful sunny day. Lennie laid down on the ground in front of the mazar and went to sleep for quite a while. When he woke up, he said that he had a wonderful rest and that seven years had been added on to his life.

The last seven years of Lennie's life were, in truth, a testament to love. During these last years, when Lennie could no longer get out of bed or even sit up by himself, Sophie took care of him with great love, peace, and happiness. And this love, which she continuously manifested, this love, which always existed between them, was a legacy for me and for all who witnessed it. When he was no longer able to say anything else, still he could say, "I love you." I felt that this was a period in his life in which he was surrounded by peace and able to resolve within himself many things even though he could not tell us about it.

Almost the last thing he did tell me, while he could speak, was a description of a very deep dream. I had been sitting at his bedside reciting Surah Ya Sin, the surat referred to as the heart of the Qur'an, which I had the blessing of reciting many, many times for him. After reciting the surat, I left the room. Several minutes later, I was called back into the room by the person taking care of Lennie at that time, who said that Lennie had a dream that he wanted to tell me about.

Lennie told me that he dreamt that he was in heaven. First, he said, he was doing penance for things he had done in his life that were not clear.

Then, he said there was a huge feast being served with delicious foods of all kinds. He told me that it was very, very beautiful there. Also, he saw many books there, written in many languages, and he could read them all. Those were the last words that my father really spoke to me.

It was wonderful for me to contemplate that my father, who introduced me to the outspread table, might be served a beautiful feast in paradise and that he might be nourished by the feast of divine knowledge there.

Now, both of my parents and several of my blessed teachers and friends had left this world. And I knew that it was time for me, still living on earth, to take the baton, run the marathon and, with the grace of God, fulfill whatever legacies had been bequeathed to me. I was aware, deeply, of the passage of time, knowing that just as their time on earth had come to an end, so would mine.

This time we have left on earth to fulfill the purpose for which we were created and sent here is profoundly precious. May we realize the importance of every moment and treat it with respect. Every remaining moment is the opportunity to serve our Lord with deeper and deeper sincerity. May that faith to which He is referring be awakened and established deeply within our hearts. And, may that divinely inspired faith express itself in truly righteous deeds.

We are also instructed in this short but immensely important message about the passage of time that we must encourage in each other truth and patience. In order not to be in a state of loss, as the time is passing by, we must encourage ourselves and one another to drink, to imbibe knowledge from the wellspring of Divine Truth and develop patience, steadfastness, and contentment with whatever the Divine decrees.

It is true patience and acceptance of the Divine Decree that dispels the anxiety that makes us feel, often even with desperation, that we are responsible to make things happen in the way that we think is best. Inevitably we will fail to achieve anything when driven by the anxiety born of lack of faith in what God wills.

Instead, we need to access the Truth and accept its decree in every situation in which we find ourselves. To have this deeply focused awareness and acceptance of the Divine Principle as it is manifesting in our life is the way in which we can avoid wasting or losing our time, but will, instead, find ourselves traveling, moment to moment, in the journey to ever greater nearness to our Lord.

CHAPTER TWENTY-THREE

SURELY, WITH DIFFICULTY COMES EASE

Behold the signs of Allah in the horizons and in yourself.
—The Holy Qur'an 3:190

All that is on earth will perish. But will abide (forever) the Face of thy Lord, full of Majesty, Bounty and Honor.
—The Holy Qur'an 55:26-27

In order for us to gain understanding of the human condition and our life in the universe, the Qur'an tells us to travel the world and behold what has become of those who reject the truth. As powerful and indomitable as a civilization or a person may have appeared to be in the height of glory, we can see what has become of them all. Behold the ruins! Contemplate the graves! Surely nothing created lasts forever, and that blast, which transforms everything, comes in an instant without warning, as the Qur'an tells us in Surah Yasin, *"All it will take is one blast whereupon they are summoned before us"* (36:53).

I remember, as a child in school, hearing about the destruction of Pompeii. I saw a picture of a stone table with dishes on it, on which the people had laid out their meal, not knowing that Mount Vesuvius would erupt the next moment and their whole world would be destroyed before they could eat the meal they had just prepared.

What we see on the news every day makes us know that the startling tale of the destruction of Pompeii is, not only a legend of the past. Wherever we look in the contemporary world, we can see the signs, the proofs, that life on earth is impermanent and subject to destruction. Many of us across the country and the world witnessed the news that a huge apparently well-constructed bridge, without warning, crumbled into pieces. What does this tell us about the rest of the seemingly dependable infrastructure that we rely upon?

As I was completing this chapter, Southern California, the land of my birth, was being consumed by fire. Fires were burning out of control, followed by devastating mudslides. So many beautiful homes that had taken so much time and money and effort to build were destroyed, one after the next, on a single day. Now, as I finish the second edition of this book, over a decade later, fires have continued to ravage California, Australia and lands around the world bringing incalculable loss to humans and wildlife. Tragedies that they are, with so many suffering the consequences of these disasters, what are they telling us?

Then we have seen the floods once again sweeping across the landscape of Bangladesh, testing, again, the forbearance of these long-suffering people.

We have also witnessed, in our very lifetime, man-made disasters which stagger the human imagination, break the human heart, and stun the soul. In Darfur, Rwanda, Kenya, Somalia, Uganda, Tibet, Iraq, Afghanistan, Pakistan, Syria, Yemen, Sri Lanka, Kashmir, Turkestan, and in many other lands, as in the streets of most American inner cities, we behold the great suffering that has arisen as a result of untold abuses in a very uncivilized world, "civilizations" gone radically astray.

Certainly, we see in all of these situations the signs that man is, indeed, in a state of loss. Witnessing all of this, we are led to deeply inquire what is the underlying message of these cataclysmic events. And how, as we witness tragic merciless acts taking place throughout the world, can we be among those who, accessing the Source of mercy, become conduits of that mercy and healing grace? We need to see, behind all these phenomena, signs from the Unseen and learn to see all that is unfolding with wisdom from the Divine.

Then, as we behold daily the continuous series of natural and man-made disasters, when we look with wisdom, we can see without doubt that there is nothing we can truly count on in this impermanent world. This is a very important concept to grasp.

The ephemeral world is, as we gaze upon it, crumbling, dissolving, and burning before our eyes. This perception itself is an invitation, a call to awakening. The signs of destruction manifesting all around us are messages urgently directing us to turn towards the Eternal.

How do we shift our consciousness from identifying with the perishable to identifying with the Eternal?

As we behold that the world is, in one place or another, breaking apart before our eyes, how do we detach from the destructible world and unite with the Eternal Source, that which never perishes or dies?

How, in the time allotted, can we make this shift of awareness? How can we detach from the perceptions and concepts promoted in this world and affirm our fidelity to the original covenant we made with our Lord? How can we — each and every one of us — find out what we came here to do, what assignments we have to fulfill, and proceed to accomplish these tasks?

My journey through ten thousand veils is one in search of the answers to these fundamental questions. I have come to see that, in the middle of the apparent chaos of the breakdown of this world, there is a way that leads to eternal peace. Our Beloved Lord, who created us out of His Love and His Mercy, has sent us with instructions, things to do and not to do.

We need to read that manual, understand these instructions, and follow these directives so that we may come to know the One who sent them and live our lives in harmony with His will and in accomplishment of His will. This, in truth, is our way out of the conflict, crisis, and destruction that we see critically imperiling the world in which we are living, albeit temporarily. Following the way that leads us to eternal peace, in Islam there are steps prescribed that guide us to levels of deepening understanding and experience.

Based upon the principles clearly stated by the Creator in the divine messages sent down, they are guidelines that lead us on the path of self-transformation and realization and thus help us to solve the mystery before, in the blink of an eye, we return to our Source. The state of *Islam* (based upon the word *salam*, which means peace) is the state of surrender, submission to the Divine Will. It is not a religion sent, for example, to the Arab people. It is a state in which each one of us created by His merciful intention comes to realize the Infinite Greatness and Sovereignty of the One who created us and surrenders to Him in accordance with the guidance and the signs He has revealed and is still revealing to us. It is a structure built upon five pillars, each of which is a dimension of the practice of worship, realization, and charity enjoined upon us by our Creator so that we may live a balanced, loving, and fruitful life.

The state of *iman* is a state of deep knowledge and faith. We come to see, with this resplendent inner knowledge and experience, the meaning, the inner life, of the commitment we have made. It is the inner state not only of faith but of determination and certitude. We experience with certainty that we have chosen to affirm the best, what is most real and eternal in existence. When we have attained this state, our faith is secure, and we cannot turn back to faithlessness. This is something we come to know for ourselves that greatly blesses and inspires our life and our journey.

But the knowledge and inspiration that have come to us and are established in our heart must manifest in our actions. The state of *ihsan,* which comes from the word *hasan* — meaning beauty, goodness, and perfection — is a state in which we manifest, through clear and consecrated action, the knowledge and faith that we have come to realize as travelers on God's path.

The state of *ihsan,* manifested as the path of Tasawwuf, the true Sufi path, is not simply the perfection of deeds. Our actions will not be pure if our consciousness, feelings, thoughts and intentions are not pure.

And for the purification of all the dimensions of our being, of the heart and soul, we need, according to the path of Tasawwuf, the direction of the spiritual Guide, one who has attained the perfection of the state of *ihsan* and can clearly lead others to the completion of the way.

I had, by the Grace of Allah, been blessed to set foot on the path and travel upon it, guided by very blessed teachers, for many miles. Yet, I knew deeply that I was still in process, had not attained the goal, and more steps on the endless journey of the ultimate transformation were still ahead.

Having experienced the passage of my parents in a state of peace, my therapy was moving along. But the essential question was burning, time was passing, and I was still not correctly aligned to be a representative (servant) of God in my designated place.

Both of my parents and, more deeply, all of my teachers had left me with a legacy of love, but how was I to fulfill it? And far greater than this was the legacy of love given to me and to all of us by our Creator when He created us. How was this potential to be fulfilled?

I had seen, in a dream, that a man of light was approaching me. He was immense and powerful, liberated, bounding with energy, with dark yet luminous skin and green light pouring through his eyes. He was altogether emanating light. He was eternally young and immensely creative.

He placed in my hands a book composed of three-dimensional visions, the history of all of existence. Then he said, "I am the one who has known you forever and loved you forever." And he embraced me so completely that I dissolved in that embrace.

In the next part of the dream, I saw that gathering places had been created all around the world, the size and visibility of convenience stores, where people came to be spiritually guided, inspired, and regenerated — totally transformed. In reality, they were places of prayer and training.

Written upon each of these way stations were the words, written in multicolored flowers, "ACT NOW!"

This dream of the man of light kept me going through all the years, all the mountains and valleys of intense, arduous travel. By visions like this, I was sustained through so many years of solitude, nourished by light and hope and faith in the ultimate fulfillment. But now, as the second half of the dream indicated, was the time for real action, action that was the manifestation of that divine love, the time for bearing the fruit of the blessed tree.

The dream was significant both as a sustenance and encouragement to the heart and soul, revealing that, no matter what we have to go through, we will, God willing, reach the Goal, be embraced by the Beloved, dissolve in that embrace, and then become the manifestation in action of that love. The being in the dream was not a human being but a light being coming to me with love from the Beloved Lord. It was an ocean of eternal love and knowledge that embraced the soul, the light within me, and in that meeting, that merger, I was dissolved. In the Arabic language, this state or station is called *fana,* the annihilation, of the limited being. The drop dissolves in the Ocean. Only if our individual beings are dissolved in the vast Ocean of Divine Love will we be able to assume our true responsibility on this earth, to transform both ourselves, and others, until we become purified and true servants, acting in every moment for the sake of the One Alone who is worthy of praise, the Most Loving, Merciful Lord of all.

For us to be freed from the limitations of our own "bubble" and merged in the ocean can in no way be determined by the bubble. Everything has been decreed, by the Divine Will, written on a *preserved tablet* before time existed. What was magnetizing and calling us from the beginning is that which we find, awaiting us, at the end.

In the beginningless beginning, thousands of years before anything had come into existence, the light of Muhammad (saw) was bowing in adoration before the Lord of Majesty and Glory. It was through this extended act of pure worship that all things came into existence. That is why the purest natural inclination of all beings is to worship and praise the One of Infinite Grace who created them.

Unfortunately, some creations, especially those in human form who have the greatest capacity to worship the Lord, have lost contact with that natural state of love and praise. But the light of Muhammad (saw), which existed before anything else had been created, continues to exist and shine within us all, whether we realize it or not.

As we discover this light within us which dispels the darkness, per-petually loving and serving the Creator of all, we come to know with ever-deepening certitude that this light is the source of our salvation and the means of our spiritual ascent.

With this ever-increasing knowledge growing within us, as much as we invoke and welcome the light into our heart, we experience, with increasing clarity, the Divine Presence within our lives, within our be-ings. We realize what it is by what it does, how it transforms us, how it enables us to see what we never saw — what we could not even imagine seeing before.

As this light, which we call *Nur Muhammadiyyah*, continues to dispel the darkness and obscurity, veil by veil, within us, revealing to us the illuminated path that leads us to our Lord, we realize how hidden a mystery in our world is the truth about who Muhammad (saw) really was and what he truly brought to humankind. Until this light is revealed, people may say whatever they like about who they think the Prophet Muhammad (saw) is and do whatever they like in his name. In reality, the atrocities we are beholding being committed in the name of Islam today are the absolute opposite of the Mercy that he came to bring.

But the One of Infinite Mercy and Love leads to His Light whom He wills. And we deeply thank Him for blessing us to be among those He has guided to discover the Truth that is hidden like the sun behind clouds. And since that brilliant sun has revealed to us, even some of the rays of its Divine splendor, we too bear witness to its illuminating radi-ance, along with all those who this light has illumined.

I speak to you, dear reader, not as one born Muslim, proud and defensive of my religion saying to you that my religion is better than your religion. No, I am writing to you only to share with you my experience of light dispelling darkness, the light of wisdom illuminating realm after realm, as the journey proceeds in the direction of its Goal.

When I was young and read the stories of those who set out on the spiritual journey, I was thrilled and amazed to contemplate that a human being could make such a journey and, overcoming so many obstacles and ordeals, reach the Divine destination. It was in this way that the Unseen caught my attention and laid claim to my life.

Now, what a wonder, so many years of traveling later, that I am the person writing the story about the spiritual journey and all of the obstacles and tests that I have had to face and overcome! Perhaps, God willing, someone reading this book will be inspired to make the journey. That, indeed, would be another great wonder. It is in such a way that seeds, distributed by the wind, fall into fertile ground, souls are invited to return to their Lord, and the message is spread.

Wherever you may be in the course of your search, I encourage you, O traveler, to keep traveling. Seek true guidance and never cease to yearn and work to attain the Goal. Know that surely, with difficulty comes ease. And the ease, which will sustain us through any difficulty we may have to face, is the love of the Creator that created us and wills us ultimately to unite with His Infinite Bounty. It was that Bountiful Grace that called and guided me. I set out knowing nothing about where I was going, impelled only by the deep instinct to seek for the path of Truth.

As I was moved from one place to the next, assuredly, I did not choose to go where I went, to see what I saw, or learn what I learned. I did not write the script for this rather amazing story. The itinerary of both the outer and the inner journey was revealed to me. Even the writing of this book has been a most unusual experience in which the teachings — the points I am to share with you — come forth on the page. I do not choose what to write. I think about a certain day in my life, and everything seems to fade away except the teachings — the shining points of knowledge that were given on that day. So many things about my life I have forgotten, but this is what I truly remember — these points I have been sharing with you — these understandings that unfolded for me along the way.

In sharing with you this array of points, I do not want to make you believe what I believe but only for you to contemplate the possibilities! When I say that I was guided by light from God, which led me through many realms, I truly did not know what to call it as it was guiding me. I came to know and then define it in accordance with my level of understanding at each stage of the journey.

When I arrived at the monastery, I experienced that the man of light whose presence I felt within was connected to the Prophet Jesus (as). In El Khalil, the place of the friend, where the Prophet Abraham (as) and many members of his family are buried, I felt that the light within me was connected to the Prophet Abraham (as) and that I, too, was truly a member of his family. Then, when I prayed on Jabal Nur, the mountain of light, in the blessed cave where the Prophet Muhammad (saw) had meditated, prayed, and received the revelation of the Holy Qur'an, I understood and experienced that the light that had been guiding me through all the states and stations was the Nur Muhammadiyyah, the light of the one who is praised and is the one who is most deeply, perpetually immersed in the celebration of God's praise.

What was revealed stage by stage was not a comparison or competition between religions but one continuous revelation of the Divine Truth. There is only one Light — one Divine Reality that sent and guided all the Prophets (as) — all the people of God. As the Holy Qur'an tells us:

> *The Messenger believes in what has been revealed to him from his Lord, as do the men of faith. Each one (of them) believes in Allah, His angels, His books, and His messengers. "We make no distinction (they say) between one and another of His messengers." And they say: "We hear, and we obey. We seek Thy forgiveness, our Lord, and to Thee is the end of all journeys."*
> The Holy Qur'an 2:285

Bringing to completion all of the messages brought by all of the Prophets and Messengers (as) who came before, the Prophet Muhammad (saw) is *called Khatimil Nabiyyin,* the Seal of the Prophets. He was sent by the One Who sent all who came before him to complete the messages they brought, not to deny them.

This realization in itself is the key to a great paradigm shift for humanity. After so many centuries of bloodshed in the name of "my religion is better than your religion," would it not be wonderful if we could realize that there are not many religions but only a continuity of the Revelations of One Truth?

In the course of moving through the stages of understanding, this is what was revealed to me. This is what I came to realize with certainty. Having come to this realization by means that are beyond my own fathoming, I offer it to you. Please investigate this understanding and see what you find, yourself.

CHAPTER TWENTY-FOUR

A PROPHETIC LEGACY IS REVEALED

The story continues, dear reader. Having come to realize, with certitude, on deeper and deeper levels of awareness, that the Prophet Muhammad (saw) was the Last Prophet, the Seal of the Prophets, who brought the completion of what was brought by all the Prophets (as) who came before him, I deeply wanted to understand and experience what it was that he brought to us as the *Bounteous Gift* from God.

To the best of my ability, I studied the Message he was sent to bring from the Lord, following the commandments and avoiding what was forbidden, always yearning to understand more deeply what these words meant and what real bearing they had on my life and the lives of others. I had studied for years searching for the meanings of this Message — what the Creator was saying to us, His creations, and how to manifest the reality of these words in all the dimensions of our consciousness and life.

I yearned to know the inner meanings of these sacred teachings and the secrets that they contained. From all of my blessed teachers, I have received the transmission of the profound mystical science which awakens the inner knowledge of the meanings of the Quran, those meanings which would guide me directly to the One who sent this message to his Creation. However, this knowledge was not yet fully awakened within me, and I longed to reach that blessed ocean and become fully immersed in it.

Shortly before I went to India on the mission of healing and peace, I was guided to attend a conference celebrating the Birth (Mawlid) and Ascension (Mi'raj) of the Prophet Muhammad (saw) in Columbia, South Carolina. As soon as I saw a flier for this conference, which somehow appeared on a table in our living room, I had the deep sense that I must go and participate in it. There was no doubt about this. As ever, the Hand of the Merciful One was moving me.

I boarded the train and felt, as the train gently rolled down the tracks, that I was being carried to the next dimension of understanding and knowing. I went to sleep and had a very beautiful dream. In the dream, I was told, "Tomorrow, you will meet the people of paradise."

I arrived in Columbia at three o'clock in the morning and was greeted by a lovely person named Sheima who took me to her apartment to stay. Some hours later, the organizer of the conference, Zain Abidein, came to visit, since Sheima was helping him with the organization of the conference. Shelma introduced him to me, and after he had spoken

332   *A Journey Through Ten Thousand Veils*

to me for several minutes and learned something about my journey, he asked me if I could please make a presentation at the conference.

I was inspired to speak about "The Beauty of Islam," not about architecture and art but about the beauty in the heart and soul of the people who love and surrender to the One Most Loving and Most Beautiful. Although I had nothing at all prepared, as was par for my course, the speech flowed like a river into its source. I was inspired, simply by looking into the beautiful faces of those who were listening and felt that I had always known them and that these were, as the dream had foretold, people of paradise I was destined to meet. That was the night that I met Sheikh Harun Rashid Faye al faqir and his circle of companions, the *fuqara* of Monck's Corner.

This was also the beginning of a long and deep connection that I was to have with Isra Islamic Research Association, a Sufi Collective dedicated to sharing in blessed assemblies like this one, celebrating the knowledge, love, birth, ascension, invocation and supplication of the Holy Prophet (saw) who was sent, as we have been led to experience, as Mercy, for all the worlds. I was blessed to speak and share God's grace at these gatherings, celebrating the mawlid or birth of the Prophet (saw) many times, and many deep bonds were thereby formed.

Having been introduced to Sheikh Harun at the Isra gathering, Issa and I went to visit him and his community in his mosque and center in Monk's Corner a little later. He made a prayer for us that touched us very deeply. I had the sense that he knew us and our spiritual potential in a profound way. He was extremely kind and loving to us and to everyone. With the community we sang beautiful songs of remembrance (dhikr), which strongly evoked the love and the presence of the Holy Prophet (saw). When our initial visit was complete, filled with love of Allah subhana wa ta'ala and His Prophet (saw), we set out to drive on the night journey back to Philadelphia and sang the dhikr the whole trip back.

A few days later I flew to India for the journey to places in peril in the presence of servants of the Light, described earlier. When Sheikh Aly said to me that the circle was complete and that I should prepare to rise, I sensed subtly and deeply the spiritual impact of our meeting with Sheikh Harun.

Shortly after emerging from the hospital the second time, walking, step by step, down the corridor with the knowledge that my life had been preserved with a purpose, I returned to South Carolina to speak at another conference and, more importantly, to continue to learn what that purpose was and how to fulfill it. The more time that we spent with Sheikh Harun and his community, the more deeply I sensed that he held in his hands — keys of divine knowledge that would open doors of spiritual awakening, enabling me to become a more activated, inspired servant of the Divine.

As we watched the Sheikh in action throughout the day and night, serving and caring for everyone, teaching from such a deep level divine knowledge in its essence as well as, its application, I was moved to go to the source of what was really moving him, what gave him such tireless energy to give all that he had for the sake of God. By what means were the secrets of the spiritual path placed in his hands? What deep source of generosity enabled him to give this knowledge so graciously to those who surrounded him? By what blessed decree had he thus become an agent and vehicle through which the Nur Muhammadiyyah was shining, transforming the lives it was blessing, including our own.

Unraveling the divine mystery, by turning to the source, I learned about the extraordinary house in Senegal, West Africa in which Sheikh Harun grew up, a house totally dedicated to the dissemination of divine knowledge, a house that became a center of light and enlightenment for the countless numbers of people that frequented it.

I deeply felt that the divine treasure, the legacy of the Holy Prophet (saw), had been passed through the generations, by means of an unbroken chain, to the people of this house whose blessed duty was to share it with the seekers of divine truth throughout the world.

I came to learn about how deeply inspired were each of the beings who were pillars of light in this dynamic divine work — the blessed mother of Sheikh Harun named Khadijatu Kubra (ra) who transmitted to countless beings the light of the Holy Qur'an, Sheikh Samba Gueye (ra), his grandfather who had made of his home a great center of learning and spiritual transformation, and Sheikh Moustafa Gueye Heydar (ra), Sheikh Harun's uncle, who would mobilize his journey and his mission in Senegal and around the world.

Whatever was to come to pass that would transform the lives of myself and so many others began in this humble, deeply dedicated house, which was a repository of blessings, a treasury of the secret knowledge of Allah, *subhana wa ta'ala.*

Sheikh Samba Gueye (ra), to whom this divine treasure had been passed down from one noble representative to the next through forty-four generations from the Holy Prophet (saw), knew what powerful medicine, what powerful tools had been placed in his hands. So, as he was guided, he made of his home a school of divine teachings that was filled with students, day and night. The students in this school of light were seated in concentric circles, each circle receiving a different level of knowledge and training.

The Sheikh's daughter, his first-born Khadijah (ra), and his son Sheikh Mustafa (ra) were, as God willed it, at the epicenter of this transmission and transformation.

Khadijatu Kubra (ra) set the highest standard for women on the path to God. She was fully immersed in the light of the Holy Qur'an and transmitted that powerful light and blessing to all who she met, all who were blessed to receive the wonderful divine teaching that passed through her. Her son, Sheikh Harun, among many others greatly blessed by knowing her, never ceases to bear witness to the immense impact his mother's prayers and teachings had upon his life and mission.

Her brother Sheikh Mustafa (ra) also had a very important role to play in the transmission of the light of Muhammad (saw) to the sincere hearts and souls, wherever they were, who were seeking Divine Truth.

Sheikh Mustafa (ra) was pious and inspired from birth. He was one designated to receive the bounties of his Lord and to transmit these bounties to the creations who were spiritually dwelling in dry, parched lands, awaiting the descent of the rain of grace. Born into such an illustrious and blessed family, he was destined by Allah *subhana wa ta'ala* to receive the wealth of blessing and manifest it throughout his life.

As a young man, when other young men were drinking, dancing, and searching for women, Sheikh Mustafa (ra) went into seclusion in search of divine illumination *(ilham)* and guidance *(hidaya)*. When he was seventeen years old and reading about the life of the Prophet (saw), he became overwhelmed with longing to see the Prophet (saw), so he wrote:

O Allah! Answerer of all our prayers! O Allah!
Grant us visitations from Al Mustafa (Prophet Muhammad)
that will give us honor both in the unseen and manifest in the
open for our eyes to see, O Allah! O Allah!
Visit us, O Mustafa, out of your generosity with the best of all
visits so that our hearts can be cured as well as our eyes!

O Allah!

At twenty-three, deep in seclusion in a village near the city of St. Luis, Senegal, he was visited by the Holy Prophet (saw) who placed in his hand the *wird* (a blessed series of prayers to be used every day in invocation) and a *tariqat* (school of Tasawwuf) which was to be called the *Mustafawiyya* or *Muhammadun Tariqah*.

Sheikh Mustafa (ra) was, as we were told, the youngest person ever to enter the *dairat'ul awliya* (the divine assembly of illuminated ones). The Sheikh (ra) lived a secluded lifestyle, very rarely going out because his inner life was so utterly complete, so full of the love of Allah *subhana wa ta'ala* and the light of His Messenger (saw).

Illuminated, intoxicated with the love of Allah *subhana wa ta'ala*, he did not go out to advertise what it is that he had to offer to the seekers. But sincere seekers, from the humblest to the leaders of lands, wherever they were, were magnetized by the light of the piety of his being and direct connection to the Divine. They came to see *him,* in his abode, to receive the great gifts that the One of Infinite Mercy had to give through him.

And I, along with the other sincere seekers, was guided to this house and this holy assembly to receive the bounteous gifts of Allah's grace and the blessings of Muhammad (saw) transmitted to me in this blessed stage of my journey through the Mustafawiyya Tariqat, a community of spiritual education with the blessed Light of Muhammad (saw) shining through.

The light of the most meritorious of humankind removed the
veil from my eyes, so they could see the essence of the Prophet,
during the state of witnessing in the unseen realm of the uni-
verse.

He unveiled for me, secrets of the unseen and presented himself to me without a blemish, erasing sins and sorrow in his honorable circle.

I was honored sitting therein as he chose me from amongst the many. He protected me from harm and taught me from his wisdoms.

Praising him causes me to drink from the cup of his openings. From his existence I was conferred lights, like continuous rain.

I attained that (spiritual) drinking point from those who were noble in their manners.

That is what is desired and sought by those who are most firmly rooted on the path.

The guidance of the Prophet leads my way, unveiling my Lord for me. He does away with my faults, a station of eternal adornment.

He unveiled for me the secret of (spiritual) arrival as well as the knowledge of the hearts and of existence.

That is the gift from His pre-existent excellence that comes with (divine) witnessing.
His book is from Ar-Rahim, the Compassionate, and he is the agent for those who want to visit the beautiful garden.

O Allah! Give me the book (of my deeds) upon the Day of Reckoning with the Prophets and the Companions and every great triumph.

That would be the best of endings, having reward and completion and the attainment of the shade of the Prophet's cloud, along with lasting goodness.

Grant us, by him, openings with salvation and piety and the achievement of brilliance, with Mustafa as the example for character.

Grant us, by him and by Your noble countenance, enlightenment with our every glance, and profound bliss.

He will be the benefit of protection for the souls in the eyes of Al-Quddus (the Holy), allowing them to gain victory and the privilege of drinking from the cups (of love) on the Day when all people will stand for reckoning.

Sheikh Mustafa Gueye Haydar (ra),
—Excerpts from *Bahr'ul-Muhit* (The Vast Ocean)

CHAPTER TWENTY-FIVE

THE WAY OF MUHAMMAD AS MANIFESTED IN THE LIFE AND TEACHING OF SHEIKH HARUN FAYE AL-FAQIR

With Him are the keys of the unseen; none knows them but He. He knows what is in the land and sea; not a leaf falls, but He knows it. Not a grain in the deep darkness of the earth, nor a thing green or dry, but it is recorded in a clear book.

—The Holy Qur'an 6:59

As for the muttaqun—those who are conscious of their Lord unseen, for them is forgiveness and a great reward. And whether you hide your word or publish it, He certainly has (full) knowledge, of the secrets of all hearts. Should He not know, He that created? And He is the One that understands the finest mysteries and is well-acquainted with them.

—The Holy Qur'an 67:12-14

O Seeker of Truth! How amazing and overwhelming it is to contemplate and begin to truly grasp that God, our Beloved Lord, knows everything we are doing. He knows everything that is happening everywhere.

He is with us every moment of the day and night. He walks with us everywhere we go in search of Him. He hears every prayer we utter in the innermost depths of our heart and soul. For it is He who inspired and brought that prayer to life within us, the Lord of boundless Compassion and Love, the Eternal Guide, the unfathomably boundless Source of Divine Knowledge, that *Treasure* that wills to be known.

From the moment I received the message as a child, *"Seek and the Truth shall make you free,"* as much as I could, I dedicated myself to seeking that Truth. And yet, how much more powerfully did that Truth seek me. When we take one step toward the Bountiful Source, we are told He takes, and has already taken, ten steps, a hundred steps, *a thousand steps* toward us — for how much infinitely greater are the Creator's steps than ours!

And that is why I say *not* that I decided to move wherever I liked on the face of the earth but, instead, only that I yearned for God and was moved, by His Power and Grace, towards the wondrous Goal. I took one step, as it were, off the edge of a cliff, and He enabled me to fly into the unknown realms.

I set out on a journey having no idea where I was going or what I was actually seeking. It is He who guided me where to go. The places I arrived were not determined by me but by One who knew me and the places I was destined to go far better than I knew myself or where the journey was leading me.

The Holy Qur'an tells us, *"Whithersoever you turn, there is the Face of God"* (2:115). From the time we took our first steps and learned to speak, He was there, but we did not know how to perceive and acknowledge His Presence. In one way or another, He kept calling, "Come closer, My dear servant. Draw near!"

I heard that *call*, night and day, and that is why I say I felt that, like a magnet, He was seeking and pulling me. He is seeking us! Calling us! If only we could open our eyes and see, open the ears of our heart and hear, then, gratefully, obey.

Through the veils I traveled, internally and externally, guided and propelled. What I found in the endless end was guiding me from the very beginning. But I did not know what it was, that magnet, that Light shining, through all the veils.

It is the light shining at the end of the tunnel and also at the beginning and, truly, all the way through. However dark that tunnel we are passing through may appear to us, the Light and Power of our Creator is shining *within* us, sustaining us, empowering and directing our blood to circulate perfectly, our heart to beat, our eyes to see. Why are we not aware of this? Why are we not truly grateful for the wondrous gifts that every moment we are being given?

There are countless miracles of His Grace taking place at this very moment, and no matter what we think that we are going through, we must not overlook these wondrous signs of His Presence and Power, which are keeping us alive, sustaining us in every way, and subtly revealing to us the ways to return to our Source.

The great journey is long, intensive, and challenging. Along the way, we may get distracted, get caught up in a detail, and forget the great ideals that motivated us to journey to our Lord. We may have a pain, a wound, a weakness, or illness and we become completely absorbed in and exclusively focused upon this dysfunction, this distress, this disease.

But as we focus only upon the dysfunction, the illness, this one area of blockage or distress, we are not conscious of all the billions of molecules and cells within us that are functioning perfectly, swimming along in perfect harmony — which by their very existence, as they flow in the divinely orchestrated dance, are proclaiming His Praise.

Although we may be sick in one part of our being, we are not aware of how well we truly are, not aware of that Power, that Love, that is directing the divine dance of the billions of cells and molecules within us, just as He is directing the dance of the planets and stars in the galaxies above. And He, the Best of Planners, will guide our steps, guide our thoughts and awareness if we allow Him to, just as He is flawlessly directing all of our molecules and cells. He will guide our spiritual evolution, bless and direct our journey to the degree that we place our life in His Trust. We realize what an amazing story it is — this journey of our life — only when we begin to see with certainty What is behind all the appearances, what Power is making everything move. This is what I have learned and am learning from the story of my life and journey.

It is not the story of *me*, the small leaf blown in the wind, that is important but what Wind blew this leaf, to what places, to what stations, it was blown and for what purpose it was blown from one place to the next. So many years of a life have passed by, and I am now assessing all this, contemplating the countless signs. I have hoped and prayed that the story would have a happy ending, both for me and for you, O seeker of Truth. And I believe, God willing, that this journey does lead to an abode of eternal joy and peace, if only we hear the words of Truth, follow the way ordained for us by His love and grace, and gratefully obey.

We have been given a heavenly invitation, and we have the choice to accept or reject it. What makes the ending happy is the acceptance of the Divine *gift*. What Allah *subhana wa ta'ala* inspired me to search for from the beginning, I saw manifesting before my eyes in the end.

From the beginning to the end, I saw manifesting in my heart and soul each step and station of the way.

The weathered traveler, having journeyed through so many deserts, up steep mountain slopes, across rivers and seas, and down into deep ravines, in search of the way that leads to God, came upon the next oasis, a place at once of peace and intensive training, of vital restoration.

And what was this inspiring, sustaining vision that I came to see — an exalted vision, manifesting in real life?

I had arrived in a station in which I could see the stained-glass win-

A Journey Through Ten Thousand Veils

dow of my life becoming more and more radiantly clear, and I could see that the light I had been arduously seeking was shining through my very being. I was able to see that, in this station, the understandings bestowed upon me along the way were integrated into the illuminated picture all as signs of the existence of the Eternal Guide, the One Most Loving and Kind.

Thus, it was in this, as in other oases of light and divinely inspired life, that the Most Merciful guided me — to a manifest vision of light and hope shining in the middle of a world shaken to its core by the forces of destruction which threaten to imperil its very existence.

Appearing in the midst of this world of confusion, this endless desert of the world disconnected from its Source, what kind of oasis is this? What is the nature of the water flowing from this wellspring, the restoration, inspiration, illumination, guidance, and peace that I found here? And what relevance or significance does this have to you, dear reader, who have traveled with me through all the pages, states and stations of the journey manifested in this book?

The water flowing in this oasis is Divine Love and Knowledge, from which all thirsty travelers are invited to drink. In a world shaken and shattered by war fueled by constant conflict between worldly powers with their unholy agendas and ideologies, it is an oasis filled with divine guidance, inspiration, and peace.

In the midst of the world bitterly scarred by the brutal wounds of racism and slavery, it is a flower garden filled with and made more beautiful by the different colors of the flowers growing together, a place in which all colors, all races, are united in one humanity as the Creator willed it to be.

In a world in which so many children are tragically "left behind" with no real education and training for their life's journey, it is a place where children are given real knowledge, love and deep training from the moment that they begin to see. And when each child begins to walk, he or she is walking on the path to God. When he or she truly begins to speak, it is with the words of God's remembrance. We pray that these children, brought up by the light of God on His path, may become ambassadors of peace and illumination, ambassadors without borders, and teachers of divine knowledge for the world so much in need of peace and light.

In the midst of a world in which women are often discounted, abused, and debased, it is a place in which women and men, as well as children, are appreciated for who they truly are and equally guided directly and profoundly on the path to liberation and fulfillment as the Creator, in His Mercy, has willed it.

When the elderly, ailing, and disabled are so often cast away and locked up in homes or simply abandoned in the streets, when the poor have no chance to better their condition, no advocacy at all, this is the gathering of beings specifically, intentionally caring for the needs of others, especially concerned with the needs of those who are helpless to care for themselves.

In the midst of a world filled with music, dance, and entertainment as well as drugs and alcohol specifically aimed to distract and seduce, I arrived in the presence of a circle of souls immersed day and night in *dhikr,* the profound remembrance and continual invocation of God.

In the midst of a world in which so many people passionately seek the freedom to do whatever they want, it is a community *(ummah)* intently pursuing the path toward the liberation that comes from doing what the Creator, Most Merciful and Wise, wants us to do.

What kind of *oasis* was this that appeared again in a new form as it had throughout the sacred journey? And what made it such a beautiful vision for the eyes of the soul to behold? It was a community based inherently upon the pattern of living established by the Messenger of Allah (saw), guided by the Grace and Wisdom of the Creator *subhana wa ta'ala.*

To understand *this pattern of living,* this deeply humane and compassionate mode of operation, to truly believe that it can and does exist and to be guided in the direction it is going, we need to know with ever deepening knowledge who the Prophet Muhammad, the Messenger of Allah (saw), truly was. Contemplating the profound meaning of the passage in the Qur'an in which Allah *subhana wa ta'ala* says to the Prophet (saw), *"We have sent you not except as a mercy for all the worlds"* (21:107), it is crucially important for us, the creations of the one God, to realize this: that Muhammad (saw), the last of the line of Prophets (as), was sent not to bring terror but to bring mercy to the worlds, to exalt and transform our lives and guide us to become the exalted creation that Our Lord, Most Merciful, created us to be.

For those who have been brought up to fear Islam and Muhammad as the enemy, the fear of what we were told Muhammad was will be re-placed by *knowledge* that he was created and sent, to all the worlds, as mercy, light, and healing for us all.

For those who have been brought up in a world of intense strug-gle, conflict and war tragically to become terrorists, even as children, how great would be the impact upon their lives, their destinies, and their practice of Islam, if they could learn and begin to experience the real meaning of these words: *Muhammad was not sent but as a mercy to all the worlds!*

What is needed for those growing up in Islam is the opposite of the training in terrorist camps. It is training in the curriculum of the compassion and love of Allah *subhana wa ta'ala* and all of His beautiful qualities including love, justice and wisdom. These are the qualities, the tools, most necessary for fighting the war against oppression and injus-tice as well as against terror and terrorism.

It is the *Islam* that is the manifestation of divine mercy, justice, knowledge and peace that these children and all of us need to learn about and be nurtured by. This grace is what will save and exalt all our lives, in this world and the next. The Prophet Muhammad (saw), in contrast to what we may have been led to believe, was the kindest, most charita-ble, most loving, and most just of human beings. He loved children and would shorten the prayer if even one child was crying, so caring was he for both the child and its mother. He cared so deeply for the poor that he fed everyone before himself and so often went to bed hungry. His love and care for all extended to animals and trees. He guided those who followed him to be kind to all living beings.

He was sent to this world specifically to right its wrongs — to free those bound by slavery and grant them equal rights and status with their former masters, to protect the rights of orphans, girls and women, the elderly, and the needy, and to create a community within the human family in which every member is called upon to care for every other.

Islam, from its inception, spread as a result of such qualities of the Prophet (saw), his great kindness and forgiveness, as well as his profound piety and inspired diplomacy, as the Holy Qur'an describes:

It was by the Mercy of Allah that you dealt gently with them. And had you been harsh or hard of heart, they would have scattered away from you. Pardon them and seek forgiveness for them. And consult with them on the conduct of affairs. And when you are resolved, then put your (whole) trust in Allah. Surely Allah loves those who put their trust in Him.

The Holy Qur'an 3:159

The divine beauty and grace manifesting through the Prophet (saw) were so overwhelming to the people around him that, just by being in his presence, they were utterly transformed. Khalid Ibn Walid (ra), one of the most skillful and dangerous enemies of the new Muslims, after a battle in which he bitterly attacked the Muslim army, entered the tent of the Prophet (saw) and was enabled by the grace of Allah *subhana wa ta'ala* to really see the Prophet (saw) for the first time.

Khalid (ra) was so overwhelmed by the light, the power, the beauty, kindness and grace pouring through the Holy Prophet (saw) that he immediately surrendered to that grace, embraced the reality of Islam and, from that moment on, became one of Islam's greatest and most courageous supporters.

This beauty and grace, power and light that manifested through the Prophet (saw) radically transforming the lives of the people who encountered him, is not something I and those around me learned about as we were growing up in America.

His divinely inspired being, which not only transformed the lives of those who lived with him but has continued to transform the lives of billions of people who have remembered him and invoked his presence ever since, is a divine mystery that has been very much hidden to many of us growing up in the non-Islamic world as well as many others who have grown up in the so-called Muslim world. And we have been led to believe things about him that are greatly contrary to the truth. And that is why the *discovery and experience* of the mercy he was sent to bring so much transforms the life and understanding of all those who are blessed to receive this.

The stories of the kindness, compassion, and love shown in the life of the Prophet (saw) as well as the great wisdom and diplomacy that he manifested and taught his Companions (ra) to manifest fill vast volumes.

But they are seldom read with deep, life-transforming sincerity and less often comprehended and implemented with wisdom. And that is why the light of true Islam is often obscured like a brilliant sun that is hidden behind dark clouds.

Many of the things being done in the *name* of Islam, like much of what have been done in the name of *religion* throughout the ages, present to those who have not penetrated the veils a perception of Islam and all religions that is absolutely contrary to the teachings sent by the Creator through the Prophets and Messengers (as) to humankind and revealing to us the way that the One Most Merciful wishes us to live and interact with other living beings.

To begin to clarify this deep misrepresentation, misinterpretation and misunderstanding, let us replace the word hate with *love* and experience the way that love illuminates the teachings and makes these teachings come to life. For the pure teachings coming from the Merciful Source to be truly comprehended and put into action is what is so greatly needed today to end the wars, heal the wounds, and guide the souls, wandering and lost in darkness to the clarity and light of the path taught by all the Prophets and Messengers (as) leading most directly to the Merciful Lord.

It was such a divinely inspired way of living that I discovered unfolding in the small town of Monck's Corner, South Carolina and in the holy land of Senegal, West Africa and Palestine, Sri Lanka, Kashmir, India, Bangladesh, Philadelphia, Canada, and other sacred assemblies I have been guided to around the world. After the Prophet Muhammad (saw), there will be no more Prophets (as). He was the last and the Seal of the Prophets (as).

But there are the *inheritors* — the custodians — of the wealth of knowledge he received from the Source of illumination and bequeathed to humankind. They are the real Sufis.

This distribution of wealth coming from the divine treasury is what drew my soul, at this stage of my journey, to unite with the *Tariqat Mustafawiyya*, which, as I perceived it, was a pure and beautiful manifestation of the *Way of Muhammad* (saw).

What does this mean? How does this work manifest? What do we see and how do we experience what is taking place? What I saw was that the teachings of the Holy Qur'an and *ahadith* that I had read and loved so much were manifesting in life. Beautiful passages that had so much inspired me were emerging from the page into life, like these:

> *And the believing men and the believing women, they are pro-*
> *tecting friends one of another; they enjoin the right and forbid*
> *the wrong, and they establish regular prayers and they pay the*
> *poordue, and they obey Allah and His Messenger. As for these,*
> *Allah will have mercy on them. Undoubtedly, Allah is Mighty,*
> *Wise.*
>
> The Holy Qur'an 9:71

> *And when they hear what has been revealed to the Messenger,*
> *you will see their eyes overflowing with tears because of their*
> *recognition of the truth. They say: "Our Lord, we believe, then,*
> *inscribe us among the witnesses (of truth)."*
>
> The Holy Qur'an 5:83

> *What actions are most excellent?*
> *To gladden the heart of a human being*
> *To feed the hungry,*
> *To help the afflicted,*
> *To lighten the sorrow of the sorrowful,*
> *To remove the wrongs of the injured.*
> *That person is the most beloved of God*
> *who does the most good to God's creatures.*
>
> Hadith of Prophet Muhammad (saw)

Such were the qualities and actions, the states of being, understanding, realization, and love that I saw manifesting in many different ways within the assembly of souls to which I had now been guided.

What I perceived on the outside was, as it always is, a mirror reflecting what was coalescing within me. I had thus arrived in the realm, or station, in which I saw the beautiful teachings of the Qur'an, the teachings sent to us by our Creator Most Loving, Most Kind, manifesting before and within me.

Every step I had taken in the journey led now to this unfolding state of awareness. In what place or station had Allah (swt) willed the traveler to arrive? It is a station in which, one by one, the words and teachings of the Holy Qur'an and other Scriptures became alive within my heart.

This teaching and transmission of the Way of Muhammad was being shared by Sheikh Harun both internally, specifically as he led me through a series of deeply guided retreats referred to as *khalwah,* and externally, in the sense that I was able to perceive these living truths in the actions and activities of the Sheikh and the circle of those that he was training.

Shortly after I met him, I saw the Sheikh in a dream. He was standing in the center of a brilliant swirling vortex of light. I was able to see, fading in and out of that vortex of light, the forms of his students — his companions, all the lives that he was inspiring and empowering.

Later I saw Sheikh Harun standing in a parking lot surrounded by the *fuqara,* his circle of students. He was wearing a white robe and a red kufi (prayer hat). In the dream he had been wearing a white robe and a red turban. From this moment on, I saw manifesting in life what I had seen in the epiphany of the dream.

I witnessed the symbol of the Sheikh, as had manifested through all my *Shuyukh,* as the catalyst, galvanizing the circle, by the power of Allah *subhana wa ta'ala* and the blessings of the Prophet (saw) manifesting through him, igniting the souls of all those surrounding him so that each one of his dedicated students was inspired and energized to make the real journey and, station by station, proceed to accomplish what he or she was created to do.

I could see that the Sheikh was not appearing as a figurehead, an idol to be worshipped by those following him, or a distant venerated figure that the disciples were lucky even, rarely, to see. He was manifesting as a light of guidance within them, an extremely vital element in their lives and spiritual journey, a powerful catalyst activating their transformation and elevation.

Such a noble, humble, and empowered teacher, one authorized by the Divine to teach the deepest truths, is not looking for disciples but for companions or, as Sheikh Bawa (ra) addressed us, "Children born with me, Precious jeweled lights of my eyes." He does not want to imprison his companions for life but to set everyone free. The disciples are not to remain disciples forever, but every capable person is trained to become a Transmitter of the blessings, Teacher or Friend, who will then continue to catalyze and transform others through the transmission of the knowledge, understanding, and blessing that he or she is blessed to receive and give.

The amazing tool that the Sheikh wields by the power of Allah *subhana wa ta'ala,* the instrument of transformation, is divine knowledge made manifest in action. The Sheikh teaches by example. The example that he himself embodies is one that devotedly follows the example set by the Messenger of Allah (saw).

To study with and be guided by such a person, who is the living heir of the transmission of all the Prophets (as), is to witness the teachings of the Holy Qur'an and all Divine Scriptures continuously manifesting in everything that is taking place in our lives.

Much of the Qur'an was revealed in the context of what exactly was taking place in the lives of the Prophet (saw) and his Companions (ra). From this we learn that the wisdom revealed to us by our Creator is not abstract but can and should be applied to all the dimensions of our life in this world.

This is the kind of profound practical teaching we gain as we travel inwardly and outwardly with such a Sheikh. Living and studying with such a teacher is a deep and dynamic way of coming to understand the real meaning of the Message of God and how it impacts upon human beings who are truly open and surrendered to it.

Shortly after I met Sheikh Harun, I was standing in line with him at Rite Aid. Behind us was a young woman in a wheelchair, disabled physically and mentally. His first impulse was to put her before us. Then he paid her bill. And then he put money in her hand. . Just as he gave her what she needed, I came to realize, so did he give me what I needed.

William Penn spoke in a beautiful statement about this inclination to goodness and the importance of utilizing every opportunity to express it when he said, *"If there is any kindness I can show, or any good thing I can do to any fellow being, let me do it now, and do not deter or neglect it, as I shall not pass this way again."* To be profoundly inclined to goodness, kindness and charity for the sake of God, Who is Most Loving and Kind, is the sunnah of the Prophet (saw), divine knowledge manifested continuously in action. It is the way that, in any situation, the Prophets (as) — those who are representatives of God on earth — would have acted. It is the way that most purely and directly manifests the Divine

Qualities. It is the way that the Creator, Most Merciful, wills and guides His servants to be.

Such a person, a true Sheikh who, following the example of the Prophets (as), is an agent for the manifestation of God's mercy on earth, will go out in search of those who are hungry and needy if they have not already lined up at his door, seeking food and help. He or she will spend sleepless nights praying and seeking divine guidance for everyone linked to him in any way, everyone he will ever know, and those that he does not know. He will be continuously engaged in serving others, taking care of their needs, never waiting to be himself served. This is the way a true Sheikh functions, and all those who follow him sincerely, all those who are being trained by him, become like this.

Wherever such a Sheikh is, that house, that mosque, that fellowship, that corner *(zawiyyah)* of the universe will become a refuge for all, a place of profound healing in the remembrance *(dhikr)* and supplication of Allah *subhana wa ta'ala,* open twenty-four hours every day.

In this contemporary world where mosques, churches, and synagogues are closed so much of the time, this example of a place of refuge, healing, solace, nourishment, and continuous guidance precisely follows the pattern of the mosque built by the Prophet (saw) and his Companions (ra) in Medina, which was a sanctuary, clinic, and place of continual teaching and illumination for the believers.

The Prophet Muhammad (saw), except when he retired to a cave for periods of profound isolation and prayer, was always in the presence of his Companions (ra), always teaching them, always sharing with them. The proof of this is in the vast number of ahadith (records of what he said and did) that were written down by those who lived with him day and night.

A true Sheikh, who profoundly adheres to the sunnah established by the Prophet (saw), will, following his example, live and interact in spiritual intimacy with his companions, deeply aware of what they are going through and how to help them progress on the journey.

The true Sheikh, one who is carrying an unbroken chain of transmission which he is blessed and empowered to give to the sincere disciple, perceives every disciple with x-ray vision. He sees what no one sees and feels what no one feels, and his love, which is divinely inspired, is thus powerfully transformative.

What may appear to others to be an abandoned lot filled with weeds and even piles of trash is, to him who sees what it can become, a fertile, bounteous garden filled with rare and beautiful flowers full of fragrance. He sees the potential in every seed lying dormant in the ground. And he has been entrusted with the life-giving water he pours upon the seeds so that, one by one, they push through the soil and, moment to moment, reveal the inherent beauty and fragrance each one possesses.

No ordinary love is this, but love which knows about us what we know not, loving and thus bringing to life ever-deeper dimensions of our being — our spiritual potential — of which we were not even aware. These are the seeds planted within us by our Creator when He created us.

CHAPTER TWENTY-SIX

GUIDANCE ON THE INNER JOURNEY AS
SACRED TEACHINGS COME TO LIFE

If Allah guides you to remember Him, it is a sign that He loves you.

— Imam Ali (ra)

Allah *subhana wa ta'ala* has placed within us secrets and mysteries that only a person of wisdom can see and make us know. These are the Divine Names that link us to our Lord and, when we know them, show us the way that He has decreed for us to return to Him as directly as possible. May every soul that is filled with longing realize its purpose is to be guided on a path that unlocks and activates these divine mysteries. Connected to the physical body but not limited by it is our spiritual being that only Allah *subhana wa ta'ala* and a person of God can see. And this is what the Sheikh enables us, ourselves, to see on the inner journey, as veil after veil is penetrated. As we are purified and illuminated, we draw closer to our Lord, less and less obscured by the veils of the world and all that it contains, closer to realizing and fulfilling the purpose for which God created us.

In one after another of the inner journeys we are blessed to make, the Sheikh is inspired to know what words of the Holy Qur'an we are ready to read, behold and, to some extent, understand. It is a feast that he is serving us in the depth of our solitude of divine knowledge that we assimilate and absorb.

No food that we have ever been given is like this food. This food is the light of Allah *subhana wa ta'ala,* and by eating it we become light. Every divine word, every teaching that we assimilate, illuminates our journey within.

Thus, on the inner journey, we come to realize that we, in our true nature, are composed of these beautiful words, the messages of our Lord, which are, one by one, being revealed to us and also, God willing, bringing us back to Him.

Such is the medicine given to us in perfect doses to heal and transform everything within us that has throughout our journey blocked our progress and caused us to be separated from the pure Love, the Majesty and Bounty of our Beloved Lord.

This is the divine therapy. The Sheikh is the vehicle, the agent for the grace of Allah *subhana wa ta'ala* and His Messenger (saw). So, he does not give, but the Most Merciful God in His infinite generosity and love gives, through the agency of the Sheikh's guidance, whatever are the secrets of the knowledge that we are blessed to receive at every stage of our journey.

No journey in the outer world can compare to the journey that leads us to our Lord within us. Everything that we have gone through is only a preparation for this ultimate journey.

After all of the conveyances, all the trains and planes, boats, buses, cars, and horse-drawn carts, I traveled on in search of the Creator and the path that leads to Him, at this stage of the journey in the process of Divinely inspired evolution, I was guided by the Sheikh to make the inner journey, being transported by Allah's Words, His Revelations coming to life within me.

The inner journey is a journey of doorways within doorways and openings within openings. To arrive at each new level of realization, we have to go through a doorway, a process of awakening and transformation. Just as we do in the outer journey, as we are traveling inward, we must deal with roadblocks, hardships and tests deeper and more intense than what we have experienced in our outer journeys. This is because we are now encountering the very essence of everything within us that we need to truly understand, overcome and transform.

But as we penetrate through each difficulty and go through the door, we are blessed to enter the next radiant space, the next dimension of the knowledge and love that brings us closer and closer to the Presence of our Lord.

We have to profoundly face our fears, pains and all other negative attributes and accept and understand them in order to access that grace that has the power to overcome them utterly.

In one of the retreats, I went into the inner space, seeking the grace, the peace and light of my Lord. But what I saw within my heart, filling it, was a mass of bristling, electrified fibers intertwined with each other, vibrating intensely, filling the wide-open space with intensity. I understood. This is what is blocking my heart. This is what is standing in my way.

This configuration that I watched, fiercely burning and bristling, was somehow the embodiment of all the anxiety, fear and pain I had been carrying along with me throughout my life.

It was in a sense so terrifying to behold that I wished to run out of the room, but I did not move from my spot, continuing to focus intensely upon the prayer. I sensed that Satan, the dark force, had his hand on that mass. The satanic force was controlling that energy, and I had to summon the inner strength, the power of unshakable faith to overcome that force and send it out of the room.

I beseeched the One of Infinite Mercy and Grace to come and take this heart out of my body, wash it, purify it, liberate it and then put it back again, purified and renewed. I prayed and prayed, supplicating profoundly. No one came. No resplendent vision appeared. No words. No message… But, at a certain moment, in the midst of the deep prayer, I realized — the space was entirely clear. That burning, bristling mass was completely gone. With what profound subtlety had the Most Subtle One (Al-Latif) cleansed and restored my heart to a state of deep peace.

The One of Infinite Mercy, Compassion, and Kindness is Formless. So, all that was obstructing and oppressing me was dispelled, outside of time, by One that I could not see.

Such is the miracle of the Kindness (Al-Karim) of our Creator. When we surrender to it, when we realize the depth of our powerlessness to make it through even the next step of our journey, His Power (Al-Qawiy) is the means by which we travel to Him.

When we are battling with the illusory force of our pain and fear, it is His Peace (As-Salam) flowing through our faithful heart that can easily dispel all this illusory pain and stress.

When our hearts or minds are closed, may we travel back to Him through His Attribute, the Opener (Al-Fattah). When we are broken and in need of restoration, may we travel by means of His Attribute, the Restorer (Al-Mu'id). When we seek protection and divine friendship — let us invoke Al-Wali, the Protecting Friend. When we are in darkness, may we return to our Beloved Lord through His Attribute, An-Nur, the Light. And whatever may be our difficulty or need, we may travel to Him through His Attribute, As-Samad, the Satisfier of all needs.

The beautiful 99 Names of Allah are secret ways and means by which we can return to our Lord, leading us to the One that is Unfathomable and Unnamable. The beautiful Names and the teachings that He has sent to us are the very means by which we can make the journey back to Him.

Did we think that, like the builders of the Tower of Babel, we could build a tower or create a means or method to reach Him? It is only by God's Grace and His Power and His Will that we can discover and follow the path that leads to Him. We have no ability on our own to make this journey. But only if we bow down and give all that we have to that Source of Infinite Bounty can that One of Infinite Love give to us all that He has for us.

I saw this in the depth of my solitude where I went to draw closer to the Lord. But I know that it is the truth at all times and in all situations. Allah *subhana wa ta'ala* created us to worship Him so that the infinite Treasure of His Existence could be known. At every moment that we accept what He is giving us, that gift is the power to dispel everything else. At every single moment of our life we can make this exchange. It is to bow down and give Him all that we have. In exchange for what we have given, and what we have given up, we receive what He has to give us. What a great exchange!

I also perceived in the inner journey, in the center of the courtyard of the space within, the fountain of *al kauthar*, abundant grace, ever overflowing with compassion. And I felt the wind of grace pass through my heart like a current, establishing a channel of peace flowing toward everyone I have ever known as well as to innumerable beings that I have never met.

I felt the love and forgiveness of God passing through my heart and moving in all directions. And, I very sincerely hope that it has come through the pages of this book to you!

This was the level of therapy that the Sheikh was teaching me as he guided me again and again to take refuge and do the necessary work in an extensive series of spiritual retreats. It was through this profound inner process of transformation, passing through doorway after doorway of purification and elevation, that I received the white, red, black and green mantles of the tariqah — becoming a Sheikha, one who has the blessing and duty to serve. I am deeply thankful for the wondrous gifts that I was blessed to receive in one after another of these inner journeys and sincerely request of the Giver of all Grace that I may be used as a servant to aid the purification, transformation, and elevation of other sincere seekers on the sacred journey.

In one of the many inner journeys, I was sitting in the deep solitude of my room, meditating upon the dimensions and aspects of Allah,
the Creator, the Fashioner, the One who brings forth all out of nothing,
infinitely Glorious and full of Grace is He. I sat in my room meditating
deeply upon the absolute power of the creativity of the Creator.

While contemplating this, the realization came to me that
everything surrounding me was man-made — the walls, the floor, the
windows. Here, within the sacred space of the sanctuary of my room, the
only thing that appeared to me to be made by the Creator — that which
was vitally alive, filled with the Divine secrets — was the human being,
the body and all that it contained. This was a form fashioned by the great
Creator in which He placed His treasures and His mysteries, such as His
Divine Attributes, the Asma'ul Husna, His Beautiful Names. Realizing
this — how filled with His grace was the creation that was my being — I
was carried into the dhikr, the state of remembrance.

Entering deep into the recitation and remembrance of the Sacred
Kalimah and the Names of Allah, *subhana wa ta'ala* I saw and felt them
spinning in all the cells and organs, in all the vital fluids circulating, in the
breath, in the heartbeat, in all the various systems which were enabling
this form to be sustained. This form, although vulnerable and impermanent, subject to disease and inevitably to death, was, in the moment, a
theater in which the divine mysteries were manifesting, a living temple
created by Allah *subhana wa ta'ala* as the place in which He should be
worshipped and known. And the center of this mysterious creation is the
heart. As the Holy Prophet (saw) told us, "*There is a piece of flesh in the
human body; if it is sound and well, then the entire body is sound and well
and this is the heart.*"

This is what the journey of transformation, the alchemical process, was leading to. The purified heart, that heart freed of negativity
and cleansed of the worship and praise of anything other than the One
Eternal Lord, was becoming a true sanctuary, the wide-open space, filled
only with His Love.

That Love, which I found at last most clearly manifested and which
was most certainly with me all along, is not specifically or uniquely for
me but for us all. If only we could turn, with open hearts, towards our
Creator, who is the unlimited Plenitude of Mercy and Love and receive
the sustenance and grace, guidance and knowledge that He, in His In-

finite Generosity, wills to bestow upon us. Whoever and wherever we are, whatever we have to undergo of trials in this earthly existence, may we be open to receive this gift of His Love. And may we travel by means of this, back to our Beloved Lord! As our eyes are opened, we can see these signs manifesting, both in everything that happens around us and in everything that happens within us. May we be the living witnesses who behold and acknowledge these signs!

Although this is an account of one person's travel, I truly believe that my story is linked with the spiritual journey of all beings. We all come from one Source, and to that Source do we return. As I write, I write for every journeyer, every seeker of Truth, just as every step of the way, I walked with everyone; all seekers were walking within me. When I set out on the path in quest of Truth, I had no idea at all where I was going, where the quest would lead me. Only Allah *subhana wa ta'ala* knew. Only He, the All-Seeing, All-Knowing, saw and knew where the traveler was, in what state and station, every moment of this journey.

Once we have set out consciously on His path, we come to see that it is He who is our constant Companion, Witness, Healer, Helper, and Friend. It is to Him Who has bestowed upon us all the infinite bounties and treasures discovered in the journey that we offer our deepest gratitude, submission, and praise. In this endless journey, leading us into the eternity of His Being, may we never cease to beseech our Beneficent Guide for the ever-unfolding gift of His Guidance, and, as we travel by Allah's Grace, toward the Divine Presence, toward the Exalted Goal, may we travel through the agency of His Blessed Attributes.

Allah's ninety-nine gracious qualities of the Asma' ulHusna are the windows through which we can see all of this world and the hereafter. Come, stand here and look with your divine knowledge through each of His Names and each of His Qualities. Once you have looked through these windows, then you will understand.

Do you see the complete and faultless treasure of Allah's absolute wealth which has been given to you? Do you see Allah's grace of Bismillahhir-Rahamanir-Rahim? This is the water which Allah made to be exalted in the world of pure souls, in alamul arwah and placed in the goblet of iman, within the faith of the kalimah. Take one drop of its benevolent grace and place it on your tongue of divine knowledge. Now taste it. How is it my children? Ahhhh! That one drop of the water of Bismillah-hir-Rahamanir-Rahim has seventy thousand exquisite tastes, doesn't it? How delicious it is! Can you compare its taste to any other you have known. Can you find a taste equal to it of any in the worlds? Do you feel any hunger now? No, you are filled with grace.

—Sheikh Bawa Muhaiyaddeen (ra),
A Mystical Journey

Allah unveils, unveiling with light. As You are the remover of coverings, remove my veil. Allah expands things, extending His benefits. As You are the Expander, expand my contentment. Allah heals imperceptibly, restoring to health. As You are the Healer, heal my debility. Allah gives prolifically, providing sustenance abundantly. As You give profusely, let my satisfaction overflow. Allah is acknowledged as the Sovereign, with open hands, to accept oaths. As You are the One Who accepts oaths of loyalty, let every atom of my being, be loyal to You.

—Sheikh Mustafa Gueye Haydar (ra),
The Remover of Coverings

CHAPTER TWENTY-SEVEN

TRANSMISSION OF GRACE THROUGH THE COALESCING NETWORK

The mystical journey ever continues to unfold as we gaze through the windows of Allah's Names and Qualities to behold His Will made manifest through whatever window He inspires us to gaze.

One evening in South Carolina I went with Sheikh Harun and a few companions into his office, as he guided us to do, to make special prayers requesting that this book may become a movie inspiring its viewers to make the journey to God. Sitting in the mystery-filled office with my dear spiritual sister Marjonah, we were united as always in the deep intention to behold the Plan of Allah *subhana wa ta'ala* manifesting within our lives and journeys and, in this case, to see how the journey of the book would unfold.

Sheikh Harun had already played a significant role in this book's development. When I met him and began to work intensively with him, as well as being guided by him through inner doorways, I had only written ten chapters of the book. He saw the potential of the book to serve a purpose, just as he saw the potential within me to serve. It was as though he put a key into the ignition of the vehicle of my heart and soul, igniting the deep intention to serve within me. Through that transformative process, the book — the story of my life and the lives of so many others in an ever-expanding network of light — organically unfolded.

Speaking of the light in the context of this book, it is important now to acknowledge my discovery of this book's publisher. In 2008, I was guided to the Book Expo in New York and at the Expo to an illuminated booth filled with Sufi teachings, with a beautiful glowing edition of the Holy Qur'an placed visibly on high.

Everything taking place in the expo seemed to disappear as I arrived in this abode of light and disappeared within it. There I met a wonderful Turkish man, Huseiyn Senturk, representing Tughra Press, also accurately referred to as the Light Publishing Company. As the light of Divine Guidance had ordained, thus the book was published by Tughra in 2009.

Now, twelve years later, the book, having made its way around the world, has sold out, and I am presently working on the revision, remembering what I forgot to mention earlier, while I continue to take notes as a deeply grateful witness beholding the miracles of the journey as they continue to unfold. The reason why the book must now be adapted and expanded is that, most certainly, the sacred journey has not ceased revealing, through every passageway and in every fertile garden along the way, the ripening fruits of knowledge and blessed spiritual experience coming forth from so many blessed seeds having been planted throughout the quest.

And like this was the night that I sat with companions in the Sheikh's office, supplicating the One of Infinite Grace, if He willed it, to make the book into a movie.

Our prayers and supplications are the offering that we lay down at the feet of Allah's Vast Unlimited Authority. But it is the way in which the prayers are answered, not what we think we are asking for that reveals to us His perfect Plan.

Having made the prayer, I set out onto another dark night journey into the revelation of the unknown, the wondrous manifestation of God's Will which we deeply intend that we are able to perceive and surrender to with unwavering gratitude and joy.

Driving with companions on the journey back to Philadelphia, we arrived home at about one thirty in the morning. I went to my room and was inspired to open the computer, which, as I perceive it now, became an instrument of the Divine Will. I was guided directly to the website of an Afghan Imam, Taha Hamid, host of a TV program called *Islam in the West*. Having been guided to him, not knowing what we were to share, I was inspired to send him some paragraphs from the book about my amazing and deeply awakening experiences traveling through the deserts of Afghanistan.

I sent these paragraphs to Imam Taha Hamid. I knew nothing about him, who he was or what he was engaged in doing, but I was simply, definitively, guided to him.

The next day, without delay, I received an incredibly warm and loving invitation from him. He said that he very much appreciated the message and passages that I sent in the email and that he would like me to come to address their community in Dallas, Texas in two weeks and that 400 to 500 members of the community would be gathered at their center to welcome me and hear my talk.

Of course, I could not refuse this amazingly energetic and caring invitation. He sent me tickets, took care of all expenses, ultimately sold about 50 books and also offered me an honorarium. As he had said would happen at the event, a large number of people were gathered together to graciously welcome whatever I was presenting.

It was especially interesting to note that many of the people assembled there had come from the places abroad I had been blessed to land in, such as Afghanistan, India, Bangladesh, Palestine, Kashmir, and different parts of Africa. Many of the assembled guests were young and had only seen their countries in perilous conditions, engulfed by hardship and war. They had not been able to see the radiant peace and light in their native lands that was their ancient heritage, which I had been blessed to see, experience, and imbibe.

So, it was my blessed duty to share with the assembly that night radiant glimpses of their sacred heritages which they themselves could be carrying within them as seeds of a legacy that could come to bloom within their beings. It was truly a blessing and a joy to meet and mingle and share with everyone, all as members of my eternal family.

This event was filmed, and the next day Imam Taha took me to his home to meet with his lovely family. We went into the backyard where he made another film in which he asked me to speak about my journey. I realized later that behind me in the film was a luminous river with geese floating by in a row. The river and the geese were also part of the sacred story.

On the last day, Imam Taha took me out to breakfast and told me that the next time I was in Southern California I should visit a special community he was connected to there. This, itself, was a very important gift that would open many marvelous doors in my ever-unfolding journey.

Why did Imam Taha do all this for a person that he did not know, just because he read some paragraphs in a book she wrote about the country of his origin? Why, based upon those few paragraphs, did he ask me to speak to a gathering of five hundred of his community members, men, women, and children? What inspired him, after so generously hosting me, to send me to the Afghan community in Southern California, through which so many more doors of the sacred journey would open? I believe it is that he was and is a devout activated servant and instrument of the Divine Will. And when I saw how the Divine Will then manifested so amazingly through the agency of this open heart, I came to realize that the movie we had prayed to be made seemed to be unfolding, from one scene to the next, in *real life*.

Let me now describe the scenes, as they continued to unfold. The next time I went to Southern California to attend a conference, I called Zia Noorzay to let him know that I would be in town and would be happy to attend a gathering at his home as Imam Taha had suggested. I was in LA to attend a conference I regularly participated in, the Conscious Life Expo. It is interesting to note in this context that *conscious life* is really what the ever-unfolding story is about.

I was picked up at the LA airport and taken to a gathering in the San Fernando Valley, where I had happened to grow up, by a dear friend from Hyderabad India, Dr Faizy, whom I had met in South Carolina. We arrived at the warm and comfortable home filled with people from various parts of the world but mostly Afghanistan.

As it was in Dallas, with deep meetings with people from so many countries I had visited, it was deeply meaningful for me, a girl born in Hollywood, to share with these gracious people born in Afghanistan and now living in Southern California my life-transforming experiences in the ancient land of their origin. Here we were meeting in the middle of the worlds. Where did we really come from and where were we really going?

I had left the consumer world I knew in America in search of my true origin and discovered in the deserts of their land of origin the call to prayer that transformed and illuminated my life. And they had come to live in the land where I was born, ultimately also to rediscover the mysteries of their spiritual destiny.

As we were sitting together in this warm and loving circle, sharing stories and understandings of our journeys, someone came in and sat down on the couch next to me. This was Massouda, the Afghan sister-in-law of the host. She told me later that she had been so tired that night that she hadn't felt she could make it but ultimately simply had to make it. We had to meet. And she became one of my closest friends and truly devoted helpers.

The next time I arrived in Southern California, Massouda picked me up at the airport, as she would do so often in the future. As soon as I got into the car, she told me that we were going directly to a *zawiyyah* (spiritual center) in Ervine, California where I would be interviewed on a radio program called Soul of Islam by its spiritually inspired hosts, Emil Ihsan Alexander Torabi from Afghanistan and Ahmad Sakamini from Syria.

As soon as we entered the room and Massouda introduced me to these gracious hosts, we sat down and began recording. I, of course, not knowing that this was to occur, had nothing prepared, and they knew very little about me from which to prepare questions for an interview. But this didn't matter. As the meeting of hearts and souls organically unfolded, with so much to share with each other and, ultimately, with so many others, it seemed clear that this joining together was arranged by the Hand of Divine Grace to fulfill a purpose beyond our comprehension.

What mattered was the meeting of our souls on that day and our uniting in the light of our longing to serve our Beloved Lord and fulfill the purpose for which He created us. With no planning but the power of the Plan motivating and carrying us along, we made a two-hour radio interview that day which went out to people in 126 countries. Through what then unfolded we learned and are ever continuing to learn the power of media inspired by God's Grace to transmit light, knowledge, understanding, peace, and love.

Having been brought together by the power of God's light and love, Ahmad, Ihsan, Massouda and I have continued to work together in a variety of ways. Through Massouda, I also came to connect deeply with Mariam, my beloved Qur'an teacher with whom Issa and I have classes every week on the telephone. This was another blessed gift from Allah *subhana wa ta'ala* that He bestowed upon us on the sacred journey leading to Him.

As the blessings continued to descend, Massouda, having visited Sophie with me in the marvelous and mystical home in which I had so many profound experiences, suggested that we have a spiritual gathering there. I asked Sophie if we could invite a group of people to spend the night in prayer there. She, as usual, said," Fine!" So, we invited a large international group of guests from different Sufi orders to spend the night at the home of Lennie and Sophie and celebrate all that had taken place there, praying for the best, most blessed journey for all who were inspired to unite on that night.

When we were getting ready to leave for Santa Barbara — as Ahmad, Ihsan, Massouda and I were sitting at Massouda's table, sharing yet another feast of love — Ahmad said that he would like to create a website for me and then continue to maintain it. He asked me what name the website should have. The name that came was *Unite in the Light*. Thus, as he promised, Ahmed made and continues, wherever he may be in the world, to maintain for us the website www.uniteinthelight.org.

Having established and then embodied in a light-form online our shared commitment to unity in the light, we drove to Sophie's museum of stained glass, all made by her and surrounded by illuminated gardens, to welcome our dear friends, Sufi mystics assembling from a variety of countries around the world.

On the day we arrived, we gathered with a small group of people including a lovely, kind, and gracious sister named Tasnim who is the niece of the head of the well-known Islamic website *Islamic City*. The afternoon was beautiful and the garden itself full of light. Here, in the garden of succulents planted by Lennie now in full bloom, Ahmad made a film of Tasnim interviewing me about the light and beauty of Islam as I have been experiencing it throughout my journey.

What is especially significant about this to me now is that, many years later, someone called me and shared with me that he happened to come across that video online. Watching it and then speaking with me, he said that his faith and spiritual practice were strengthened and re-generated after some kind of spiritual crisis he had been going through.

This, then, for me is the purpose of making and transmitting any manifestation of our faith, understanding and spiritual experience, intending that it may inspire another life to reconnect more deeply and effectively with the Divine Source. And this is another manifestation of the prayer that we made to make the book into a movie we then beheld unfolding in real life.

The next day, many more people came to join in our prayer assembly to be held that night in Sophie's house. We stayed up through the night, praying and singing God's praise. Wonderful food was served, and the greatest feast was the gathering of souls that assembled that night, both seen and unseen, from around the worlds.

Thus was this house of light filled with light once again, bringing to completion the many prayers that had been made within it throughout the years. How many Imams and Sheikhs had come to visit and pray there? These blessed visitors would then appear in photographs standing with Sophie at the front door of the house, regularly addressing Sophie as "Sufi." In respect to the fact that the door of this house was always open to receive people from all countries, religions and walks of life and that prayers were always welcome here, I pray that Lennie and Sophie are finding a warm and radiant welcome in the next world abode.

Soon after our last celebration of praise there, the house was sold, and Sophie moved into a place of independent living. On the night of our Sufi assembly gathered there, before she moved, I was very grateful that we were able to thank Allah *subhana wa ta'ala* for all the beautiful manifestations of His Grace He had bestowed upon us there, also praying that the abodes awaiting us in realms to come are yet infinitely more welcoming and radiantly clear.

Now, it has come to pass that, as Allah *subhana wa ta'ala* ordained, Sophie returned to Him on the blessed Day of Ashura, upon which, we are told, very holy occurrences happened to many of the Prophets (as). I pray that the goodness, kindness, and generosity that she has shown to so many others, she may find awaiting her in akhirah (the hereafter), insha'Allah.

Just as Lennie was taken care of by Sophie with such loving care during the completion of his life's journey, Sophie also received deep loving care during the completion of her life's journey from her loving children, Judi, Deena, Glenn and Brian. Judi has also been distributing the estate with the deep and consistent consciousness of love, justice and respect for all. Thus, even in this process that often divides families and tears them apart, does this family legacy of love and light continue to flow forth.

CHAPTER TWENTY-EIGHT

UNITING IN THE LIGHT

My very precious children I give you my love. My very precious children who are the life within my life, we have come to this world from our Father who is God. During the period when we existed as a soul composed of light, we knew our Father. When we were nothing other than light, that light perceived and bowed down in reverential obeisance. That light form still exists within us as a mysterious secret, a mysterious secret light body, an atom, a ray, the soul. It is the treasure of wisdom which can be seen in the state of God's love. The soul, this light form, is God's mystery, and its life is God's life. Its actions are God's actions, and its love is undiminishing, endless, and indivisible.

When we came to this world, we brought that form with us along with its actions, its behavior, its qualities, and its compassion. That is our mysterious secret. It is that love which makes us instinctively show compassion to others, makes us aware, and prompts us to soothe and comfort others. The quality of compassion is just one aspect of that light form. My precious children, we must realize that this compassionate love is a ray of God's infinite love, and we possess that quality of compassionate love, that resplendent light. The act of showing compassion towards others, that ray of light, the life which is the soul, that grace and wisdom are within us and the secret story of the kingdom of God is within us. We must understand this.

—Sheikh Bawa Muhaiyaddeen (ra),
The Book of God's Love

Shortly after the radio interview by Soul of Islam went out to people in 126 countries, two spiritual seekers — Shaykh Hamdi ben Aissa from Tunisia and his wife, Anse Shehnaz Karim from India — made a journey to the mazar of Sheikh Bawa Muhaiyaddeen (ra) in search of Divine aid and guidance.

They drove from their home and spiritual center in Ottawa, Canada to the mazar of Sheikh Bawa (ra) in Coatesville, Pennsylvania to beseech the living spirit of the Sheikh (ra) to send them a representative of his grace and, in reality, to send them the transmission of his teaching and his grace. They came to the mazar to make this prayer and then drove back to Ottawa without speaking to anyone but the living spirit of the Sheikh (ra).

A few nights later back home in Ottawa, in the middle of the night, they heard the interview we had made on Soul of Islam. Later, they told me that they listened to it again and again, weeping.

The next day, they called the number posted on the interview and invited me to co-present with them at a gathering to be held lakeside in Quebec. This would be the first of many beautiful, transformative, soul-inspiring gatherings we were blessed to share.

Let us thus behold again the potential capacity of inspired media to bring souls together so, with the Grace of God, we may unite in His Light. And what is the Power shining through, empowering all that we see manifesting? It is the Hand of God that moves all. This was what brought us to Ottawa, Canada, and everywhere else we have gone, inspired by Divine Guidance.

In contemplating the storyline of my journey, I must acknowledge again the power and influence of the Divine Will in guiding me to the most beautiful people, situations, and teachings. In observing the unfolding events throughout the journey, the influence of this Grace is so profoundly obvious, and I bear witness that, without this, I would not have a clue where I was to go to meet all of the truly extraordinary beings and situations I was blessed to meet.

Being moved by this Grace and nothing else, upon arriving at the airport in Canada we did not even know the address of the place we were going. This created a problem at the border! After waiting at the airport for some time, unable to move on, I realized that, although I had no address, I had the phone number of our hosts in my phone. I gave the phone to the border police. They called the number and discovered that our hosts were waiting for us right on the other side of the door. We passed right through the border to meet them, got into their car, and proceeded with the wondrous journey.

As we rode off into the lovely landscape and began to share experiences with our gracious hosts, it was truly amazing to discover how deeply we were already connected — how many mysteries of our lives and journeys were linked together, intimately intermingled, in the coalition of souls united by Divine Grace.

As we drove, they introduced us to their inspired mission and organization called Sanad Collective. In this context, I came to learn that Sanad refers to spiritual transmission through the ages and Collective refers to the process of unifying souls in receiving and then transmitting that transmission.

Sanad Collective, we came to immediately and deeply experience, was bringing people together from all over the world. Our loving hosts mentioned a recent Collective gathering in which 44 people had been brought together, 40 of them from 40 different countries, to seek and share knowledge of the path toward spiritual realization. What a victory it is for the realization of the Absolute Unity of all that exists, when more and more people coming from so many places unite in the Light and manifest that grace in dedicated service to the Source!

This very image, of people from so many different countries joining together in harmony, reminds us to be actively conscious that all lives are sacred and that we must love all lives as our own, no matter where they come from or where they may be going.

In light of this ultimate truth, let us be aware that any wall that we or anyone may try to build or maintain that seems to separate us from our brothers and sisters in the universal family is counterproductive and a hopeless illusion or delusion, defying the ultimate truth of Unity. And the remedy and cure for separation resulting from the construction of illusory walls and barriers is for us, with the Grace of God, to unite in the Light.

As Sheikh Bawa (ra) tells us so often and in so many ways, it is our faith in Allah (swt) and His Qualities in our hearts that bring us together in His Love, and thus does true Islam spread from heart to heart and land to land.

Throughout my journeys across the world, I have experienced more and more deeply and powerfully how this process works and how hearts and lives are transformed by the transmission of the Divine Qualities, inwardly and outwardly, heart to heart and soul to soul.

And this knowledge and inspired activity in which our faith in God spreads from heart to heart, making the light of True Islam (the light of Divine Peace) spread, was that which we witnessed activating the Sanad Collective, manifesting the teaching of Sheikh Bawa Muhaiyaddeen (ra) and all true Teachers whose aid our loving hosts had come to the mazar to seek. So, it was for this purpose of continuing to share the light of the teachings of true Islam that we were now being guided to Ottawa, Canada to pass through one single door at the border, to unite on the other side and then travel insha'Allah, more and more deeply, with our spiritual companions in Sanad Collective. This journey began with Shaykh Hamdi ben Aissa and Anse Shehnaz and went on and on as we came to embrace more and more lives as our own. This "collective" process of souls uniting in the Divine Presence did not begin for me here in Canada but is the ever-present truth revealed in every place and stage of my journey.

Now, in Canada, after traveling and immediately sharing so much with our seemingly ancient friends Shaykh Hamdi and Anse Shehnaz, we arrived at their beautiful light-filled home and met members of the community there. We then went to spend the night in the lovely home of Stephane and Asma, with whom we also felt eternally connected.

The next day, we set out on a journey into rural Quebec. After some hours of driving, we arrived at a lovely piece of land surrounding an ancient lodge. When we entered the lodge, our hosts, knowing about my business, which I refer to as *Treasures from the Silk Road,* invited me to set up shop there.

Since this ancient, wooden lodge was two stories high and very well built, I was able to hang tapestries and rugs from on high, lay out our bags and shawls below, and create a kind of mystical artistic museum where, in accordance with Silk Road tradition, we were able to do business as well as share knowledge, blessings and peace with the assembly gathered in this blessed oasis.

We were given a room in the ancient hall, and I was very happy to see Issa lying stretched out on his bed, completely relaxed and peaceful, as I had seen him from time to time in oases of blessing and peace throughout the years of our sacred journey together.

The following day, when the guests had come and the conference was to begin, I was amazed to behold that the event was not to be held in a conference hall but in an expansive, radiant field in front of the lodge and close to a beautiful lake on the property.

Gazing out at the assembled guests, I saw that it was the light and purity and sweetness and openness in the hearts and faces of those assembled that were at the center of the beautiful picture I was beholding.

They were the flowers blooming in the midst of this garden whose fragrance in heart and soul I inhaled and whose light I beheld as I spoke.

There is, for me, a lifetime experience relating to moments of sharing with assemblies like this. Even when I was a child, a teenager, and young woman acting in theatre, when I looked out and spoke to the audience, I felt we were sharing a kind of spiritual intimacy and that my performance was not a staged act but a deeper spiritual communication. This was a foretaste of experiences yet to come.

In later years, whenever I was asked to speak at spiritual gatherings such as this, I have beheld, as I did in the radiant field in rural Quebec, a kind of assembly of ageless beings gazing back at me with, it seemed, light pouring through their eyes. This, as they told me, is also what they saw pouring through my eyes, as the words flowing through me entered and touched their hearts and returned back to me in the form of joy, gratitude, and prayer — the celebration of the praise of our Beloved Lord.

This is an amazing experience, an ecstatic exchange, that I, along with so many others, have been blessed to share in spiritual gatherings around the world, focused upon love, remembrance and invocation of the Divine. Alhamdulillah! All Praise be to God!

Let us now contemplate what could be occurring in places and times like this. Could this not be an assembly in this world spiritually linked to our gathering in the world of souls *(alam'ul arwah)* where we all together proclaimed the sovereignty of our Lord?

Considering this powerful possibility, the gatherings of Sanad Collective that I was so blessed to attend were, I believe, inextricably linked to such gatherings I had been attending all around the world throughout my life. Thus was the collective all-inclusive — an assembly of souls united in the Light of Allah *subhana wa ta'ala* including all the Believers throughout eternity traveling to the Divine Source on the Straight Path that leads directly to the Source. This is really what I was experiencing as I addressed the souls assembled in the field of radiant light.

Issa and I then walked to the nearby luminous lake, and we, along with two celestial children, Shaykh Hamdi's nephew and niece, walked on a bridge right onto the lake. There too, standing on the lake of light, suspended from the earth, did we celebrate the praise of God as though suspended in an eternal realm of grace.

We then returned to land and went to join with Shaykh Hamdi who was leading dhikr with a group of children dancing in a circle of joyous praise. I joined in dancing joyously with them. Noticing this, Shaykh Hamdi said, "Sheikha Maryam seems to be our elder, but really she is the youngest one among us."

I learned several years later from Moaz, who was with us in that wonderful gathering and has been with this group of children as they were growing up, that these children have kept love for the songs and prayers they sang there, love for one another, and beautiful memories of these experiences alive in their hearts. What they learned there in that blessed, joyous sharing is still shining within them. And so are those who will become *Ambassadors of Peace* often instilled with the spirit of Divine Love from childhood.

Such was my first blissful experience with Sanad Collective lakeside in Quebec. It was seemingly my first trip to Ottawa. However, I felt I had always been there and would always be there, merged in the assembly of remembrance and prayer. And so it is with all the places of worship in which Allah *subhana wa ta'ala* has invited us into His Presence. *Alhamdulillahi Rabbil' alamin.*

While never really leaving, I did return to Sanad Collective to participate in sacred gatherings many more times. On the next trip, Shaykh Hamdi and I travelled to sacred assemblies held, amazingly, in universities in Ottawa and Montreal. Shaykh Hamdi had been cultivating the consciousness of many students in these universities, and, as I was addressing the students, I saw that awakened consciousness permeating the space. In this exalted context, I came to see what "higher education" really is about, and it filled my heart with joy to perceive the light activated in the hearts of university students receiving true teaching and training. Returning to the road, filled with light after such gatherings in town, we travelled from the cities back into the luminous landscapes of rural Quebec. Our next wondrous location was a great, glowing hall by a radiant lake in a place called Notre Dame du Laus.

The vast lodge and surrounding lakeside property had been built and developed by the owner of the property, who was himself a dedicated spiritual servant of the Most High, as were his family members. In the service of the Creator Most Merciful, they had been dedicated for many years to serving the poor, disenfranchised, and disabled members of our human community in this glowing lodge and on these beautiful healing grounds. And this, too, as we learned about it from his daughter, was for us a sign from God that made us appreciate more and more how this sacred space was blessed — as we had understood and experienced the blessings inherent in dedicated service to humanity.

For one week in August every year, we have been gathering in this glowing, consecrated hand-hewn lodge by the radiant lake and sharing more and more deeply such manifestations of the Divine Assembly here on earth. Many inspired beings, both seen and unseen, have come to join with us and inspire us with radiant gems of wisdom and powerfully practical understandings of eternal spiritual truths.

We spoke to our beautiful and deep companions collectively and individually, beholding with much gratitude and joy the process of awakening, healing, transformation, and elevation that it seemed many of our brothers and sisters, as well as ourselves, were passing through. Such was the living truth of the awakening consciousness shared by the Collective.

Some of the messages I found to be most useful and spiritually effective in activating the process of healing were, "Ours is not a Caravan of Despair," as Mevlana Rumi wrote so many centuries ago, and "Ours is a Caravan of Prayer!" (as I was inspired to add). And when we say these words, we say them in harmony with all travelers on the journey everywhere, certainly including all those caravan travelers seeking sanctuary and refuge everywhere, at every border, at every passageway, and in every state. May all travelers on the sacred journey, through whatever challenges they are facing, come to realize that they are being sustained by the embrace of Divine Grace. And may we, as servants of the Divine, honor each life as our own.

Along with this, I say to myself and others assembled at the retreats who are passing through emotional, mental, and spiritual challenges, "Be blessed, not stressed, distressed, or depressed." And, as we behold the ever-unfolding mysteries of the sacred journey, revealed to us in many profound ways, with every true step we take to the Source of Blessing, our illnesses, pressures and depressions can be healed and dispelled in our true acceptance and welcoming of the ease that comes with every difficulty.

At one of the last gatherings, Shaykh Hamdi, Anse Shehnaz, and I were very much blessed and graced to be joined by two more deep facilitators of spiritual healing who were also our ancient companions on the journey, Shaykh Adeyinka Muhammad Mendes and Emil Ihsan Torabi.

It was indeed through the facilitation of Ihsan and the Soul of Islam radio transmission that I had come to meet and unite with Sanad Collective, so it was deeply appropriate that he had come to pour the light of his soul, his intention, and teaching into the blessed assembly and to be himself restored and reactivated by this coalition of Grace.

Shaykh Mendes is also, I have discovered, the very embodiment of the ancient friend and companion on the eternal journey. The more that I share with him, the more we realize that we have always been together on this journey, travelling upon the sacred path with many of the same companions at different times and in different parts of the world and realms of knowledge and grace. And now our souls were united once again in dedicated service on the shores of this illuminated lake to celebrate and activate the consciousness of the Divine Assembly among sincere seekers gathered together here on earth.

In gatherings in the deeply spiritual pre-dawn hours and throughout the day, Shaykh Mendes, Ustad Ihsan, Shaykh Hamdi, Anse Shehnaz and I shared knowledge and love of the Divine with the seekers assembled. Thus did the seeds implanted in our collective garden of hearts continue to be nourished by the water of grace to occasionally, moment to moment, burst through the soil and fragrantly bloom.

As our deep spiritual adventure continued to unfold, Shaykh Hamdi requested that we all be silent during the hour preceding the Maghrib prayer. Day after day, we sat beholding the illuminated water and sky and beautiful trees blowing in the wind, making du'a for all in the celebration of praise. The silent meditation we experienced at that time, as we gazed at the illuminated water, was extremely beautiful and healing, inspiring of deep peace. When I returned home to Philadelphia, I dreamt for many nights that I was continuing to gaze at the illuminated waters in deep silence and prayer, and I pray that the awareness of that illuminated silence and peace may always remain shining in the depth of my consciousness, whatever else seems to be happening.

At these blessed retreats, later every night we sat together at a great bonfire where all those assembled were encouraged to express their prayers, intentions, challenges, and realizations. At the first great campfire we shared, Shaykh Hamdi told us all stories of how he met Anse

Shehnaz, very much touching our heart and soul. He told us about the way in which they came to enter the spiritual presence and teaching of Sheikh Bawa Muhaiyaddeen (ra) through the books of Michael Green and Coleman Barks, *The Illuminated Prayer* and *Illuminated Rumi*. He then shared how this deep connection was amplified by their journey to the mazar and the prayers they made there, which led directly to their meeting and deep connection with us.

As we all sat together on those beautiful nights surrounding the campfire, we developed a practice of casting our anxieties, conflicts, problems and fears into the fire, beholding them turn into light. Sharing this experience, as we shared so many meaningful experiences and feelings offered into the circle by the assembled guests, once again, the presence of the Sheikh Bawa (ra) and all Shuyukh were powerfully sensed in the circle assembled in the Presence of Allah *subhana wa ta'ala*. It is only by the All-Powerful Grace of Allah (swt) and His Messenger Muhammad (saw) that such a Collective could be formed and perpetually sustained, including all the Prophets (as), Angelic Beings, Awliya, and Believers united in Allah's Light. May we all always be united in this Divine Assembly and never depart.

What we learn from true Teachers, the living Truth of the Teaching that they are transmitting from the Source of Knowledge, cannot be learned by reading books. I've often mused over how Sheikh Bawa (ra) once told me, "you may have read many books, but you cannot cook a paper squash," or how he began with, "jeweled lights of my eyes, you who were born with me" almost every time he spoke to us. It would seem that the Sheikh is referring to a connection we have had in the Divine Presence before our birth in this world. And the blessed Teaching that we are receiving and, insha'Allah, transmitting is transcendent of any limited human social norms and is defined by the Divine.

> *Our study of religion has not served its ultimate purpose until we transcend that which we study, until our chains of transmission become ropes of redemption, until our performance of piety becomes rays of Reality, until our tomes of information become ladders of liberation for all beings.*
>
> —Shaykh Adeyinka Muhammad Mendes

CHAPTER TWENTY-NINE

THE UNENDING CIRCLE OF PRAISE

Our Prophet (saw) said: "People will not sit in remembrance without the angels surrounding them, mercy covering them, peace descending on them and Allah mentioning them among those who are with Him."

—Muslim

The Prophet (saw) said: "When you come upon the pastures of Paradise, be nourished by them." When asked what the pastures of Paradise were, he replied that they were circles in which Allah is remembered."

—Tirmidhi

Everyone has a path of light that can be traveled, circles, orbits and universes. The path is that of the divine pilgrimage of the soul. And when one is accompanied by Sages and Saints, the circles or spheres through which one travels, become illuminated and the journey takes on a whole different meaning. One shares their nectars of wisdom; drinks of sacred sustenance served in the abodes of the Exalted Ones.

—Sheikh Tamer Degheidy

Allah *subhana wa ta'ala* is the Source and Provider of every drop of the Provision by which He sustains us and every ray of the Light of Guidance by which He guides us on the path that leads us most directly back to Him. As He wills, He introduces us to His Friends and Representatives in the other worlds and to those who represent them in this world.

Although, even as a child, I dreamt about such beings and heard them calling me to the Spiritual Path, contemplating, now, the beautiful blessed beings I have been inspired to meet and make the sacred journey with, words cannot express the gratitude and joy I feel to be a participant in this blessed Assembly.

I have never sought after or chosen my Teachers. They are all gifts of God, sent by Allah *subhana wa ta'ala* to guide me and so many others back to Him. They are shining clear mirrors on the journey in which we can see ourselves with greater and greater clarity, as Allah *subhana wa ta'ala* wills.

Thus, as Allah, the One Most Merciful had willed, one day, some years into the unfoldment of the Canadian retreats, I was inspired to call Ihsan to check in and share blessings and peace. A few minutes after we talked, he called me back to say that he was driving with a Sheikh named Sheikh Tamer to a retreat in Pope Valley, Northern California. The Sheikh was requesting that I also come and present there. Sheikh Tamer sent me a ticket immediately, and, thus, I was able to join them and many other friends assembled there when the retreat began two days later. Alhamdulillah! How this happened so quickly and transcendently was a sign to me of the Higher Power at work.

The gathering was taking place on a lovely piece of land where a center had been built by followers of Sidi Sheikh Muhammad al Jamal (ra), a Sheikh from Jerusalem I had studied with on the Mount of Olives many years before. There was a very warm and comfortable *zawiyyah* (gathering place) for meetings, with an adjoining kitchen. The grounds also held a University for Healing and a gift shop. I went into the gift shop to take a look around and to meet the people there. I bought a few beautiful gifts, and, as I was leaving, one of the shop's caretakers gave me a gift. It was calligraphy of the Name Allah in Arabic, and it was exactly the same calligraphy given to me by Sidi Sheikh Muhammad (ra) approximately 40 years earlier. I was to focus upon it in my first *khalwah* (spiritual retreat) that he guided me to make one holy night on the Mount of Olives.

This too, I felt, was a sign from Allah *subhana wa ta'ala* indicating the completion of a circle — the mystery of the circle that would come to manifest as the journey continued to unfold, in so many realms and in so many ways.

As we all came together in a circle in the *zawiyyah,* I found that sitting in the presence of Sheikh Tamer was like sitting with an ancient companion in another realm. This was definitely not like meeting someone for the first time. We were not just meeting but were already, by the Blessing of Allah (swt) and the wealth of His Grace imparted to us by our blessed Teachers, united in His Light.

Sensing, when I looked at Sheikh Tamer, the proximity of ancient Friends of Allah *subhana wa ta'ala,* it was as though I was swimming in the ocean of remembrance, filled with the sense of nearness to Friends existing in other realms and was not really aware of what was actually taking place in this realm.

When I was asked to speak, a dream that I had came forth to share. In the dream, our souls were assembled, as usual, in a circle. We were all making du'as (supplications and prayers) to Allah *subhana wa ta'ala* with deep yearning and intention. We watched the prayers rising up and beheld in the sky above us a circular configuration of Angels. There, in the center of that Angelic Assembly, our prayers were being received and recorded.

Then they rose higher into the Divine Presence. From there came the descent of His Grace, and we were told God answered our prayers as He willed, not necessarily as we were expecting or requesting. The answers were much greater than the questions posed, and the sense of both the Angelic and Divine Presence was very powerful and inspiring in the dream. Sheikh Tamer said that the dream was a sign that I would see/be with the Holy Prophet (saw). Insha'Allah! Alhamdulillah! Allahu Akbar!

This dream was related and connected to other celestial dreams that I would have with Sheikh Tamer in them, in the years to come. For example, in one dream, Issa and I were sitting in a circle with Sheikh Tamer and companions on top of a tall mountain and he was looking directly at us and transmitting a wonderful message to us there. In another dream I was traveling with Sheikh Tamer, as though propelled by powerful light and grace through the realms. While we had to navigate the passage from one realm to the next, as we travelled through the realms we were transported solely by Allah's Grace and no effort of our own. This was a tremendously liberating and transcendently energizing experience.

It was through such dreams and spiritual experiences that I came to understand and appreciate his presence in my life and journey and the radiant mirror that he was holding up, reflecting to me the history of my journey and the spiritual development of my heart and soul.

In another dream, I saw Sheikh Tamer sitting in the corner of an illuminated room. He was formed of blue light, sitting upright and asking students who among them was ready to make the journey. I said with energy and certitude, "I am ready." I then realized that I was the only student in the room, and it was not me saying that I was ready to make the journey but the Lord saying this for me and through me. And I realized once again that it was always the Divine Will that was propelling me to make the spiritual journey leading back to Him.

Also, it is important to acknowledge that what I saw in that mirror was not myself alone but a blessed assembly of souls united in the Light of the Divine Presence, Beauty, and Majesty. I saw and felt this upon meeting Sheikh Tamer, and the vision and experience were enlivened and clarified as the journey continued to unfold.

The next time I met with Sheikh Tamer, in an assembly of souls brought together for spiritual advancement, was at the Moroccan Caravan Hotel in the blessed mystic center of Meknes, Morocco in January of 2017. The retreat was aptly called *"At the Heart of Spirituality is the Spirituality of Hearts."* As the plan for the gathering was unfolding, I felt the magnetic rays of Grace pulling me into its heart.

I was going to be travelling insha'Allah with a lovely sister and brother, Anjum and Muhammad Was'ia, who I had met at the Pope Valley Retreat. Muhammad worked for American Airlines and was able to give me a complimentary ticket, which was quite helpful at that time.

All the travel plans were put in place. Then suddenly, a few days before our flight, as Issa was dropping me off to teach my weekly class at prison, I found that I could not walk. I could not get up the steps to go into the prison, so I had to limp back to the car and go home. On the way, Issa got me a knee brace which helped me limp up the stairs to my bedroom and contemplate how the proposed journey could possibly unfold. I made it to the bed, stabilized there, and tried to imagine how I could possibly venture across the world, in a few days, in this condition. The answer as always was: "Surely, with the difficulty, comes the ease."

I called my dear friends with whom I had planned to make the journey to Morocco and relayed to them my condition. I proposed that I could speak with those assembled in the retreat in Meknes through Skype. They told me to wait for them to call back in five minutes. In five minutes, they called back to say they were sure that I must come on this holy journey. And since Muhammad worked for American Airlines, he would arrange for wheelchairs throughout and thus carry me across the world.

Abandoning self-direction as a matter of course, I who had walked across so many pathways, mountains and valleys, fields and streams and stood for so many hours on trains rolling through amazing landscapes, now had to be carried across the world, on the sacred journey. Sheikh Tamer later wrote to me about this transformative mode of travel, saying that at some points in our journey to God we must be broken. We have to completely surrender, having no ability to move on our own. Then miraculously by the Grace of Allah *subhana wa ta'ala* we arrive at the goal!

At this stage of the sacred journey, the destination was the holy city of Meknes. We had been picked up at the airport by a taxi driver who kept stopping in fields, trying to figure out where we were going. But ultimately, not knowing how we got there, we arrived!! Across the street from the hotel! A broken seeker, without a ticket, driven by someone who didn't seem to know the way arrived! Indeed, it is amazing how Allah *subhana wa ta'ala* conducts His business. As we arrived in that mystic realm, I very strongly felt the *himma* (spiritual yearning) and presence of Abdal-Hayy Moore (ra) and his companions, in their love for their beloved Shaykh Ibn Habib (ra) with whom they had so deeply communed in this holy place.

After the long trip, I was certainly in fragile condition, and it was difficult, even, with help, to cross the big street and busy thoroughfare. But then, as we entered the hotel, our place of arrival, what a wonder it was! It was the most beautiful, mystical gathering place, unlike any hotel I had ever seen or even imagined. With magnificent architectural patterns formed in tiles on the ceilings, walls and floors, white light was emanating and radiating throughout this amazing building!

Then, one by one, I met the people — the ancient ones and eternally young ones — who had assembled within this Hall of Light. And I understood why I truly had to get there! I came to see that this Hall of Light was, at the same time, a Cave of Refuge, a Cave of Deep Contemplation and Prayer, and the people assembled here, the companions and students of the Sheikh, were, through their *ibadat* (worship) in the deep realms of remembrance, manifesting the illuminated teachings that he was transmitting, as Allah *subhana wa ta'ala* had ordained.

What was being transmitted were teachings for this time — teachings of preparation for and transcendence of the time of destruction, which Sheikh Tamer explored intensively in his instructions to and training of Companions of the Cave. Sheikh Bawa Muhaiyaddeen (ra) also prepared us for this in many discourses, such as "A Contemporary

Sufi Speaks: The Signs of Destruction," in which, at the end of the book-
let, he teaches us how to escape from the destruction.

Through the teachings of the Holy Qur'an, the teachings of Allah
subhana wa ta'ala transmitted through His Prophets (as) and the illuminated sages who follow them and carry on the transmission of true
Guidance, we are led from the destruction of the temporal world, into
the Abode of Eternal Truth. This is what I found manifesting so clearly
and beautifully in the blessed circle surrounding Sheikh Tamer in Meknes, as I had been graced to discover in such Sufi circles around the
world where we are reminded that everything on earth will perish, *"But
will abide (forever) the Face of thy Lord, — full of Majesty, Bounty and
Honor"* (The Holy Qur'an 55:27).

The blessed gathering of Sufis I envisioned in ancient Fez was now
manifesting in the present time in the deeply mystical oasis of Meknes.
What a beautiful vision for the soul to behold and unite with. Also wondrous for me was the experience of addressing this blessed assembly of
those immersed in the remembrance of Allah *subhana wa ta'ala*, beholding tears flow from their eyes as the words flowed through my mouth, by
Allah's Mercy and Grace. Further revealing the specialness of this gathering was the fact that the receptionists, workers and administrators of
the hotel also often attended our talks. We celebrated unity in this way
as well.

At one moment in the midst of the unfolding mysteries we were
all sharing, I had a meeting with the Sheikh. I walked delicately across
the glowing hall to greet him as he sat on a regal couch. In this somehow deeply spiritual encounter, he told me that his journey and mine
were, in some sense, parallel or interconnected in that we had both been
guided by truly extraordinary Teachers to pass through extraordinary
stations on the journey. I certainly felt that as well and was celebrating
the sense that I was so deeply feeling, as I expressed earlier, that all the
True Teachers were uniting in this coalition of the Divine Light. *Alhamdulillahi Rabbil' alamin!* All Praise to the Lord of all the worlds!

What, inherently, I believe that we have shared is the deep blessing of a living teacher and living teaching, the reception of a true transmission of divinely inspired knowledge, wisdom, and grace. Such is the
awakening, transformative effect of gazing into a radiant clear mirror.
The light that we behold in such a mirror is what we need to receive, to

give, and to share. Underscoring the spiritual connection of the seeker and teacher, Sheikh Tamer writes:

> *The communication between the Master and the disciple takes place in the visible and invisible world, and the students feel the presence of their Master wherever they go in wakefulness and in sleep such that the Master becomes a window or a gate in which divine guidance and inspiration comes. The wise student understands it is not the brilliance or the ingenuity of the Master, but it is understood that he is the window through which Allah's grace shines.*

> *All of the answers are inside of you. The teacher is inside you with you. When you sit in his proximity, the crystals of his light permeate through your being. You will be sustained. Through his prayers and love. You will be nourished by his breath. He loves you and that is what will make you go forward. He inherited this love and this caring from the greatest soul that ever walked the earth, our respected, Rasul (saw). Through this transmission, Allah makes the Master a source of light and doorway of light and grace to bring healing to his beloved brothers and sisters who are ill.*

As Sheikh Tamer and all true Sheikhs often remind us, we cannot teach ourselves this knowledge or gain it simply by reading books! A living, divinely inspired transmission of the blessed Grace transmitted through one referred to by the Holy Prophet Muhammed (saw) as "an Inheritor" is needed to awaken us to the potential which we were created to fulfill.

My meetings with Sheikh Tamer thus inspired me to realize what was being transmitted to me through the ages, the deep blessings and peace of the Prophetic legacy transmitted through all true Shuyukh. Sheikh Tamer further teaches that, as the circle of time is completed in the last days, the Shuyukh who appear at this time will be carrying an illuminated assembly of teachings gathered as a living legacy from many previous sages and saints. They will be carrying a focal point of the light, reflecting all the journeys of those who traveled before, representing all paths walked and becoming true mirror images of the unifying light of the Seal of Prophethood, Muhammed (saw)!

Sheikh Tamer, carrying the permission and the light of multiple spiritual orders, made, as he said, the collective blessings into a potent spiritual drink that connected his guests to the lights of those great saints and teachers, removing from them the sense of selfishness that prevents one from beholding the Divine Light.

As all this was taking place and so many transformative blessings were descending upon us, the inner activity within my heart and soul was so dynamic, buoyant, and inspired here in blessed Meknes — I was not identifying with the physical realm.

So, I had forgotten that, at this point in my unfolding journey, it was actually very difficult for me even to walk. But now, as the blessed event was concluding, it was time to go home. Once again, not really being able to walk on my own, I was so grateful to be carried across the world and then delivered to my home.

Shortly thereafter, I got an MRI and found that I had two torn meniscus in my left knee. From a dear friend, Ron, who was, it turned out, a knee therapist, I learned of an excellent surgeon.

On the day of the operation, I entered the hospital and instantly felt that it was a sacred domain. When I was given the anesthetic and transported to another world, the building that I saw I was in was a vast illuminated shining white mosque, shining with a light very much like the light I had seen shining in the illuminated hotel in Meknes. In the course of the movement from one illuminated space to the other, I was transformed from being almost completely immobilized to being completely healed and restored. I bounced off the surgery table and was completely mobile. I needed no crutches, no medication. I was both broken and healed by God's Grace alone.

The next time I was blessed to meet with Sheikh Tamer was in Massouda's house in Southern California. It was a short but, as always, deep visit. After the gathering there, as I was flying home during the night, the Sheikh had a dream.

He told me the next day that he dreamt that he was travelling through sylvan forests and waterfalls en route to Bawa's mazar. What he described from the dream was exactly like the physical landscape leading to the mazar, a place he never visited in this physical realm. He said to me in the dream, "This is your beautiful land!" referring, I believe, to the realms of barakah of Bawa's grace. So, in this unique fashion, my spiritual connection with Sheikh Tamer connected him to Bawa's sacred soul, and thus I learned how Allah *subhana wa ta'ala* connects His people through each other to His people. As the deep mystery of this relationship has continued to unfold, it is clear that the Grace of Allah (swt), the living spirit of His Messenger (saw) and the illuminating presence of the Inheritors of the Prophetic Legacy, specifically Shaykh 'Abdul Qadir Gilani (ra), are what unites true Sheikhs such as those mentioned here in the Divine Light.

In the Hajj, the pilgrimage, in which we die before death in uniting with the Divine Will, all sincere seekers are travelling together in an unceasing circle of praise *(tawaf)*. And this, I keep coming to realize, in different realms and different ways, is what is mystically unfolding in the journey of my life, the course of which is certainly not determined by me but by the Lord of all, Most Merciful and Wise, the Best of Planners, from Whom we all came, to Whom we all belong, and to Whom we all return.

CHAPTER THIRTY

THE ALCHEMY OF JOURNEYING WITH THE SHEIKH

The Holy Qur'an and the ahadith of the Prophet (saw) are filled with blessed words to be uttered by those in the ummah of Muhammad (saw) in all ages to come. These are the holy words recited by the Sufis in their circles of dhikr. The Source of all the words uttered in dhikr (zikr) is thus the Holy Qur'an and the ahadith of the Prophet (saw). These are the words of supplication, repentance, praise of Allah (swt) and His Attributes and salutations to the Prophet (saw) that they have been inspired by the Creator to say.

True Sufism is not an innovation but the continuation of the living legacy of the Light of Prophetic knowledge, the Light of *Nur Muhammadiyyah* that the Prophets (as) were sent to this world to bring. After the Holy Prophet (saw), the Seal of the Prophets, left this world, what hope would there be for humanity if his light did not continue to shine, illuminating and guiding the sincere believers in the ages to come? The process of this transmission of the Light, like everything else in the Divine Plan, has been perfectly organized. The divine knowledge is an infinite treasure, passed from one hand to the next.

There are those who sing and dance, wearing colorful turbans and robes who may call themselves Sufis. The Sheikhs may truly believe that they are Sheikhs, representing different Sufi Orders. But only if the Sheikh or Sheikha is one who has received the transmission in the unbroken chain, can he or she completely illuminate the path for those who follow him or her. And only then, will the follower be able to pass through the stages of transformation in the alchemy of journeying with a true Sheikh or Sheikha.

This is the transformation of the self, heart, and soul that the word Sufism ultimately refers to. It is a journey that leads the seeker with clarity through all the stations of his/her self, heart and soul from earth, fire, water, and air to the heavens above, to the station of the Awliya (Friends of God), to Angelic realms, to the station of the Anbiya (Prophets and Messengers, upon whom be peace), to unite with the Divine Reality. Only the true Sheikh has the Divine tools, the secrets of the Divine words and teachings, which he gives, one by one, to the sincere seekers whose journey through all the veils is facilitated by these divine keys. About this journey and the alchemy which can take place only with a true Master, this subject is intimately related to the spiritual path. Sufism is not simply dancing and singing or bearing robes and titles or even representing the various Sufi orders. It is the passing on in the marathon journey to Allah the eternal torch, the light of *Nur Muhammadiyyah,* from one soul to the next, which makes it possible for every soul receiving that beacon of light to complete its journey across all realms to the Goal.

The *Alchemy of Journeying with the Sheikh — fana-fis-sheikh, fana fir-rasul, fanafillah* — is a subject of great significance and relevance to the path we seek to tread. Especially at a time such as this, when natural disasters, devastating illnesses, tragic political struggles, tragic conflicts and wars are sweeping across the earth, we need not to stand alone, not to travel alone, nor to be swept up in the current of fear that is seizing those who do not know how to comprehend the phenomena we may behold. But, in these times when the signs of Allah (swt) that we have been reading about and reciting are manifesting on the earth with great intensity, we need to be traveling, insha'Allah, with those who are the nearest of the near, the purest of the pure.

Each of us on our own may read about the Rasul (saw), contemplate his wondrous attributes and invoke his presence within us. And such thoughts are the best thoughts we could have. But, according to the school of *Tassawuf,* the means of access to the *Haqiqqat Muhammadiyah* is through the true Sheikh. The *wasila,* connection and arrival at the goal, is through the *silsila,* the chain of transmission. The true Sheikh is one whose hand is in the hand of one who gave *bayat* (pledged, devout commitment) to the Rasul (saw). And as Allah reveals in Surat'ul Fath of Holy Qur'an, *"Verily, those who give bayat to you, O Muhammad, they are giving bayat to Allah. The Hand of Allah is over their hands"* (48:10).

So, it is the bayat (mystic bond of commitment and surrender) under the "Hand" of Allah that is the activating principle of the eternal, mysterious alchemical formula referred to as *fana-fis-Sheikh, fana-fir-Rasul, fana fillah.* And this is the galvanizing principle of the journey on the Sufi Path. In the imagery of alchemy, the true Sheikh (or Sheikha) is pure gold. He is one who has completed the journey and become burned completely clean in the crucible of the Way so that no alloy is mixed with the gold. If the Sheikh has not completed the journey, he cannot lead the disciples to completion. But the completed Sheikh, *insan al-kamil,* one who has travelled the road completely and has become annihilated in *Haqqiqat Muhammadiyah,* the truth of Muhammad (saw), is the only one who knows *fana, baqa, and liqa.* He has absolutely covered the terrain. He knows all of the holes in the road, the detours, the dangers, the traps.

If, by the grace of Allah (swt) and by the power of His Decree, they have found such a Sheikh, even then, before the disciples can begin to travel with the Sheikh, an authentic channel of communication must be established between the Sheikh and the disciples. This clear channel of communication is established between them in the bayat (pledge of fidelity) and activated in the wird (the living transmission of the dhikr, or collection of prayers).

The bayat, not necessarily occurring physically but spiritually, is the eternal activating principle of the union between the disciple, the Sheikh, the Rasul (Messenger), and Allah (swt). And the wird (practice of invocation and prayer) is a channel of continual communication in prayer between the Sheikh and the disciple. (Although Sheikh Bawa Muhaiyadeen (ra) did not externally enact formal practices such as bayat and initiation with his students, he certainly activated such unifying bonds spiritually.)

Then, before setting out on the difficult journey, the disciples must grasp the significance of the journey and access within themselves the deep longing, the strength and determination to make the journey and to go through whatever they must go through to reach the Goal.

After the bayat (spiritual alliance) is established, the Sheikh puts the disciples in a stable place called initiation. While the disciples are in this place, the Sheikh prepares them. He (or she) tells them about the beauty of the journey and the beauty of arrival at the Goal, to motivate them and inspire in them the zeal to make the journey.

The Sheikh tells them about the difficulties, the hardships, the fear, and the struggles they will have to face. But he also makes them know that the difficulties will not last and that the journey will have a glorious end. This knowledge, this commitment, this longing and love, are transmitted from the Sheikh to the disciples during the period of initiation.

The Sheikh knows the time it will take, the changes of the climate along the way. He knows when to run and when to walk and when to sleep. The journey is long, and one must use the provisions carefully. The Sheikh knows exactly how the provisions must be used and guides his disciples with precise wisdom as to how much to eat at each moment so that the provisions will last. The Sheikh knows how to avoid every danger and pitfall that will arise on the difficult road.

As they travel, they see that this world is full of temptations and that any step, any glance, any word, any smell, any touch, any sound, any feeling will affect the journey in one way or another. The journey is so delicate and so difficult because at the end of the journey is a mantle of light and the greatest victory. And the Goal cannot be obtained with tricks.

The real, sincere students of a true Sheikh are, slowly and surely, struggling to cover the distances which separate them from the Goal. The beauty in the journey is that, as they overcome many obstacles, they begin to see a brighter picture of the future, a picture full of hope and encouragement.

One who completes the journey of illumination and transformation and unites with the Messenger of Allah (saw), receives from him the tools he needs to use to rescue humanity. Then, when he goes back to the people, he will be able to liberate them from the influence of the satanic force. He will be able to protect them from any harm and guide them to the Illuminator of the illuminated.

One cannot complete this great journey and reach, through all the temptations and tests, its glorious end and then come back again to liberate humanity, except by precisely following the guidance of one who has completed the journey.

And how can we determine if the Sheikh is true? Because, if we place our trust in one who has not completed the journey, we can never attain the Goal with the guidance of that person. We can go with the Sheikh only as far as the Sheikh has gone.

As we are searching for the true Sheikh, the Sheikh is also searching for us. As we are looking to see if he has the signs and the qualities of one who has completed the journey and can lead us directly to the Rasul (saw) and Allah *jellajellahu* (may his glory be glorified), the Sheikh is also looking at us, assessing our capacity to follow him and become those who will also complete the journey. It is the very discernment and sincerity within us that enables us to see that he is the pure and true Sheikh that he is searching for in us.

So, even at the outset, we need to develop within ourselves the capacity to see, the capacity to distinguish the true Sheikh, the complete Sheikh, from those who can give us only a part of the knowledge but not the total transmission.

So, we must know what are the signs we are looking for. If the Sheikh has been annihilated in the presence of the Prophet (saw), then we will see the qualities of the Prophet (saw), the attributes of Allah (swt) manifesting through him. We will see the beauty of the Prophet, the light of the Prophet (saw) shining through his face, his heart, his words, and his actions. This is a sign not that he is a great person but that he is annihilated in the state of the perfection of the Prophet, the state of *fanafillah* (complete surrender to God). Anyone can be called "Sheikh" by himself and others. But we must look to see. Are the signs of Allah (swt) upon him? Does he (or she) have the capacity, by the permission of Allah, to transform his disciples and bring them to completion? The true Sheikh does not imprison his or her disciples for life but brings them to completion and liberates them.

In this time of deep crisis, when the earth and its inhabitants, our brothers and sisters, all children of Adam (as), are being inundated, shaken, broken, and tried so deeply, how many conscious, completed, liberated beings are needed to be walking on the earth? The true Sheikhs know this, know that there is no time to lose, and that each disciple who has the capacity to be transformed must be moving, Godspeed, down the road. This is a reality that all the true Sheikhs know. And it is also a reality that the disciples, the sincere seekers, must know. Every one of us must take responsibility for the sacred opportunity we have to become true human beings. The first thing that is necessary is for every one of us to realize the preciousness of our existence, that we were not created just to do what we feel like doing but to fulfill a divine purpose.

Brothers and Sisters, we have a limited amount of time to fulfill this purpose and accomplish all that each of us is meant to do. So, may we be clearly guided and constantly active, realizing that, every second of our life, we are on the pilgrimage leading us to union with our Lord and the fulfillment of His will. May we realize that every moment is sacred. Every moment, we may draw nearer to our Lord. Any moment we may be called back to Him and asked what we have done here and what provision of conscious prayer and dedicated service we have sent ahead of us. So, may we use our time well! May we get into a plane that truly flies, take the wisdom and rise!

Beloved Companions on the Sacred Journey, as we are contemplating the deep significance and transformative power of studying and traveling on the spiritual journey with a True Sheikh, let us now reflect on understandings gained in this process by a sincere student of such a

406   A Journey Through Ten Thousand Veils

Sheikh. May we imbibe the blessed teachings of Sheikh Bawa Muhaiyadeen (ra) as they have been absorbed in the heart of his devoted student, Ahamad Muhaiyadeen:

> *"Pray in a Natural Way"*
>
> *Anyone seeking the liberation of the soul will at some time feel
> an inner urge to pray. Whether another person is actually pray-
> ing or not is occluded from our perception. It occurs in the inte-
> rior of the heart and cannot be seen by anyone's eyes.*
>
> *However, we can observe whether our own activities constitute
> authentic prayer. We must be honest with ourselves at all times.*
>
> *What I learned about this matter came from being in the pres-
> ence of Bawa Muhaiyaddeen with whom I lived and studied
> for over a decade. Simply being in his presence stimulated
> an awareness of the sacred and prayerfulness. Here are some
> points he taught me:*
>
> *An important aspect of a healthy inner life is living prayer. It
> honors the mystery that gives us all breath, heart beats, and
> each other. It reminds us that we depend upon a Power of Life
> that we did not create but creates us. The remembrance of the
> gift of each breath brings gratitude and peace. It opens the heart
> to living prayer.*
>
> *The evidence of real prayer is that it opens the heart to love,
> regardless of whether we pray quietly, out loud, within a tradi-
> tion, out of a tradition, facing the east, the west, up or down. If
> it's true prayer, it opens the heart to selfless pure powerful love.
> If it doesn't, it's not prayer.*
>
> *The evidence of prayer is loving kindness and compassion and
> the evidence of loving kindness and compassion is caring for
> other lives. The evidence of that caring, and that compassion
> is service. And the evidence, experientially, of service is a clear
> conscience. The evidence of a clear conscience is inner peace.*

Inner peace gives us the capacity to receive wisdom. Wisdom further reinforces our humility as we realize it is a gift, not something we can achieve through egocentric willful effort.

Gratitude follows, and with that gratitude, openness and illuminated love. Wisdom tells us that we are connected to the Source of life and that all other lives are also connected.

All lives, all objects, all things are relational and have a beginning and end. Source, the mysterious Power that sustains and gives life, does not depend on anything with a beginning and end. It is Sovereign, Absolute, and demonstrates generosity, grace, love, and being, Itself. It demonstrates these qualities through the human heart that is pure and awake.

A consequence of that realization is a deep tranquility of heart, a profound appreciation for the miracle of consciousness, knowing, and clarity of purpose. This brings love, beauty and harmony — coherence and profound meaning — into every moment of life. This is an aspect of plenitude and fulfillment.

This is everyone's birthright, regardless of historical circumstances, regardless of joy and sorrow. It must exist independently of attraction and repulsion. It must exist independently of identification with race, tribe, religion, gender, and class. It sets us on a journey. We travel in upward spirals. We move by inspiration.

In this journey we can become sanctuaries of peace. That's what the world needs more than anything: examples of what it is to be a peaceful secure human being. It means that, regardless of circumstances, what governments do, what the person sitting next to us does, what our spouse does, what our children do, what our parents did, and what our neighbor does, we know there is no excuse for not doing this. This is the work that we have to do and it's a personal secret work.

The world needs peacemakers in a state of peace.

Make no mistake, we are responsible for doing this work. If we don't do this work and we do everything else, we will not be saying "thank you" at the end of our lives and we won't be ready for the next part of the journey.

Do this work, begin this work now and you will not have fear. If that love is alive in a heart, it is like a magnet for grace. That heart is electrified and illuminated because that heart has the appropriate humility to serve. Politics informed by such qualities guide toward policies of compassion and justice exercised with the humility that affirms our capacity to work together.

Such policies alone bring peace and security to a family, to a community and to the world. We can't get angry. We can't give up. We can't answer real questions about complex issues with slogans. We have work to do. The opposite of fear is love. The politics of love affirms human unity. Yet, there is a deeper unity: God lives in us and we live in God.

There is an Ocean of love that is our birthright. It is more powerful than the energy in the atom which, when harnessed with weapons, can destroy the earth. That Ocean of love has put a great power in the core of each of our beings. We come from that Power and that Power has also given us the wisdom, and the abilities, to meet all challenges, even those that nuclear weapons pose. We do have the resources to find peace and security for all peoples.

We do have the audacity to assert that all people have a right to peace and security. We do have a duty to work to help all obtain this right.

May that Power make us sanctuaries of peace, inspired and guided by loving kindness and compassion. For a journey, a compass is needed. Prayer reveals the direction we must turn. These are but a few of the reasons we should pray.

—Ahamad Muhaiyaddeen (aka) Jonathan Granoff,
President of the Global Security Institute

CHAPTER THIRTY-ONE

THE CIRCLE IS COMPLETED AND THE SPIRAL ASCENDS

Praise be to Allah, the Lord of All the Worlds in every situation. Praise be to the One who has established the ascending levels as a protection for the worshipful servants, and the stations of nearness for those who come to know by experience
—Shaykh 'Abdal Qadir Gilani (ra)

You have completed the circle. You have come back to where you started, and the circle of your life is complete. Now you are ready to rise.
—Sheikh Aly N'Daw, Kathmandu Nepal, 2004

Within the power of the circle, which was formed for invocation and thanksgiving, I found that the sense of creative potential was unlimited. I knew, even then, that a circle had the power to accomplish what no individual could do, and that is why I felt empowered and inspired in the circle, turning to the Source in thanksgiving and in wonder, sensing the potential of all that was to unfold. These joyous, energized, and liberating experiences in camp were a foretaste of the joy of Sufi fellowship that would later bloom from the seed planted within the circle itself, the seed of the divine assembly, awakening within the soul... ancient memories.
—*Journey Through 10,000 Veils* (First Edition)

On this path, our progress cannot seem to be measured by a straight line, but rather, our movement seems to progress in something like a spiral configuration, in the sense that we go through a certain set of experiences and we think that we have studied and mastered them, but then we find that we are reliving the same experiences once again, the difference being that, now, we are seeing the experience from a different perspective. We have learned something in the process and now we are beholding it through the perception of the more evolved person we have become. Then we go through the same set of experiences again. We thought that we were done with those experiences, and we find that we have to go through them all over again. But now we have attained a still different perspective.

This is related to the structure of the DNA molecule, which is understood to be in the form of a spiral or double helix. Thus it is in the context of a spiral that we progress. Every set of lessons. could be duplicated almost 1000 times. We meet them step by step in our progress.

Each time we meet them again, we receive a promotion; we have moved up a step through the lessons learned. We were in one state when we learned them the first time. If we meet them a second time, it means that we have gained a promotion. Our countenance has changed. There is a brightness in our countenance, and in the way that we approach things. The fact that we encounter these repeatedly is proof that we are progressing. This continues to occur until we reach a certain stage and then we just go through the door :we have completed the process and, now, we are free.

A bird does not fly straight; It flies up step by step, layer by layer. In the same way, our wisdom, our qualities, and the explanation, the understanding that we attain also go up step by step. They fly up step by step. Then where it is not so easy to fly up, they might have to come down a little at one stage in order to fly up to the next one.

So this is the way we progress in our life, climbing up step by step. And this is the proof. We can see the proof within ourselves. Our eyesight seems to be keener. When we look, using glasses, binoculars, or a microscope and even further than that with a telescope, with the same set of eyes, we are able to see more. In the same way, as our wisdom grows, it seems to have increased in its perception, like eyes that can see further. It is like this that our understanding develops and there is a corresponding growth in beauty, a growth in peace. That state develops by itself, naturally, and as that state matures within us, we reach the state in which we become truly free. This is how the study proceeds, and this is what we have to achieve or attain.

—Sheikh Bawa Muhaiyaddeen (ra),
"The Spiraling Progression of Experience"

Dear Respected Reader, as we are coming to the completion of this book, this journal on the path of awakening, I would like to explore with you some of the many ways in which I perceive circles coming to completion in my life and journey, which then impel the traveler to rise to new realms or dimensions of consciousness and, thus, as the spiral ascends by the Grace of Allah *subhana wa ta'ala* — to rise up to new stations of spiritual realization. And, as I am contemplating, with you, this deep process of individual and potentially collective spiritual evolution, I ask you to take note of the details of your development and ascension through the realms so you too may better comprehend and appreciate your challenges and subsequent victorious transformations as we all proceed, insha'Allah, in accordance with the great blessings of Divine Guidance being bestowed upon us, to return to our Exalted Beloved Source in a blessed and exalted way.

As we complete our sharing here, I would like to express my appreciation for your presence in this journey and pray that you may be clearly inspired and guided through the stations of the spiritual quest to fulfill your true purpose and reach the Goal. Also, please know that I am not someone isolated in an ivory tower somewhere. I am here with you, ready to share. If you would like to communicate, please email Sheikha Maryam at eternalblessingsandpeace@gmail.com.

The image of a collective journey in the form of a spiral ascent came to me in a dream some time ago. In the dream, I was traveling with many companions on a miraculous journey from one illuminated oasis to the next, rising up, layer upon layer, in a spiral formation as we collectively ascended. Alhamdulillah! As we were travelling through different stations, one or another of the travelers would behold an intensely energized vision revealing to the journeyer his or her station of awakening in the process of the collective ascent. We were thus individually and collectively experiencing a series of awakenings on the journey to our Lord.

On the night of my birthday, December 26th, 2018, we had a gathering of blessed friends. We recited Surah Yasin together, and when du'as were being made afterward, a picture was taken of this beautiful assembly. In the photo, the stairs rising up from the first to the second floor were resplendent with light. It was an ascending stairway of light. So, the image of the collective spiral ascent and the illuminated stairway became for me signs of this time, revealing the possibility of collective spiritual evolution which, I believe, we are now invited to participate in. The spiral formation that I saw and experienced led me to Sheikh Bawa's deep and practical teaching on this subject.

Now, I would like to contemplate the completion of the circle by acknowledging — with profound gratitude, wonder and amazement — this, the fortieth year of my journey, physical and, then, spiritual, in the presence of our Beloved Sheikh, Bawa Muhaiyaddeen (ra). How many divine seeds have been planted in the garden of my heart and soul, life and journey, throughout these years, that I now behold bursting into bloom, generating seeds that, insha'Allah, can make other gardens also come to life.

As Bawa (ra) has instructed us, in his teaching about the spiral progression, we come back to the same experience again and again, each time realizing the experience with another level of understanding and realization. God willing, our process is dynamic, not static, and we are rising in the direction of spiritual evolution, rather than descending into a mire of unresolved karmic baggage and bondage.

Such positive growth and development require, as the Sheikh so often tells us — *faith, certitude,* and *determination.* If we are truly dedicated to progressing on the journey, following, without wavering, the guidance and example of the Sheikh (ra), we cannot, as he tells us, just stand around and chat. We must be profoundly focused upon realizing the Gifts of Divine Grace that we are so blessed to be receiving.

As we are rising in consciousness, so does our comprehension of the messages that are, by the Grace of Allah *subhana wa ta'ala,* being bestowed upon us by the Divine Teaching passing through the living transmission of the Sheikh. We may have heard the words repeated   so many times, and, suddenly, they come to life within us through the powerful grace activating our awakening consciousness. And like this, as we truly receive the living transmission of the Teaching, we can see the seeds burst through the soil into bloom. The multi-colored beauty of the garden can then be seen, as its fragrance fills the atmosphere of our consciousness. Such is the wondrous experience of the Teaching that we have been blessed to receive, throughout the years of our journey, coming to life, within us!

The Sheikh has also instructed us that, as the good plants of wisdom come forth, we must harvest our crop and winnow away the chaff, such as all the dimensions of worldly karma (repeated unconscious patterns of behavior) so when the Angel of Death comes and we return to our Lord we have only the pure crop, *amanah,* the heavenly harvest of the vast treasures that He has imparted to us, from the time He brought us into existence and throughout this journey, to return to Him. Let us consider here what Sheikh Bawa (ra) taught us about this:

> *Your Father, Allah, your Rahman, is watching you. He has entrusted you with His property, and you must return to Him all that He gave to you. Return the wealth and the truth that came from Him. Return His good qualities and return His duties and actions, His Wilayat.*
>
> *In the form of Nur Muhammad, God has given these to you as a trusted property, as the wealth of grace, the wealth of your soul, the wealth of truth, and the wealth of the divine knowledge of ilm. If you return this knowledge to Him in its original form without destroying it or spoiling it, He will give you His wealth, just as He gave it to me. You must know this. Do not waste that which was given to you.*
>
> —Sheikh Bawa Muhaiyaddeen (ra),
> *A Mystical Journey*

Bawa (ra) further explains:

> *Within your heart in a space no bigger than an atom, God has placed the 18,000 universes, good and evil, and the wisdom to differentiate between them. That is your farmland. If you plow that land deep with your wisdom and sow God's qualities and actions with the knowledge of the difference between good and evil, you will receive the wealth of your soul, the bountiful harvest of undiminishing grace.*
>
> — Sheikh Bawa Muhaiyaddeen (ra)
> *The Golden Words of a Sufi Sheikh*

Dear Readers, Beloved Companions on the Sacred Journey, the *amanah* referred to here is a profound trust and transmission bestowed upon us by our Creator, Most Merciful, imparted to us when we came into existence. Only He, the One of Infinite Grace, knows what He implanted within us. By His Grace alone can we return this trust to Him in its pure form. In the accomplishment of this profound task, we deeply seek His Aid. Every step we take in the sacred journey seeking to realize the nature of this *amanah* and return it back to our exalted Source is truly, solely a manifestation of His Grace. Let us contemplate this deeply.

I do not have words to express my gratitude for the fathomless bounty of Divine Grace transmitted through Sheikh Bawa (ra) while he was here in this world, and as he is now in akhirah, Alhamdulillah! May we be conscious recipients of the wondrous gifts of guidance transmitted to us from the realms of the Divine Presence, and may we cherish and protect these gifts and share them with generosity of heart and soul, acknowledging and celebrating the infinite Generosity with which they have been shared with us.

In the context of acknowledging a living legacy that continuously elevates my soul on the spiral journey upward, I must also witness that I am the deeply grateful bearer of so many prayers transmitted to me by Sheikh Harun Al Faqir through *khalwahs* (spiritual retreats) and other deep transmissions. Throughout the years of spiritual study and practice with him, the Divine Attributes and Teachings have been brought to life within me by the infinite Grace of Allah (swt). These are eternal treasures alive within my heart and soul, and I very much anticipate, with longing and love, the possibility of going deeper into these blessed realms, rising up into the Divine realms, carried by the light inherent in these beautiful blessed prayers, invocations and manifestations of the *amanah* entrusted to us by our Creator in His creation of us, the sacred treasures we must return to Him in pure form. And it is my sincere intention and longing to make these spiritual practices available to other sincere travelers. Every transmission is a manifestation of Nur Muhammadiyyah. And, may the Light that we have received be transmitted, as Allah (swt) wills, Light upon Light, through our hearts and souls and intentions and actions, to the open hearts of fellow seekers on the sacred journey.

In the contemplation of another circle being completed, I would next like to share with you, dear friends and companions on this journey, teachings and understandings I have received while working in prison, where I have taught Islamic Studies for many years. This part of my life brings to completion an experience I had while in college in Berkeley, as I was reading about the transformation of Sri Aurobindo, a great Indian teacher who was imprisoned for a year in jail for acts of civil disobedience. At first, separated from his community, their activities and life as he knew it, he became very depressed, disassociated from life. Anyone imprisoned, whatever form the imprisonment may take, knows how this can feel.

But then, as the story was told, Sri Aurobindo, Social Activist dedicated to liberating humanity from oppression, was himself liberated from the oppression of his mind and limited understanding by realizing that the Divine Presence was pervading his prison cell and filling his heart with inspiration and light, a realization which affected his life and mission ever after. We have also heard of the experiences of other people, such as Malcolm X, being awakened and transformed in prison.

This story greatly affected me in my late teens, communicating to me at that moment the understanding that we are all imprisoned in one way or another and that our liberation from any sense of imprisonment comes from realizing that our Creator, our Beloved Lord, is with us in every situation and that He Alone has the keys to unlock every door.

In light of the depth of my feeling about this in my youth, as the destinies of my life unfolded, I found myself sharing deep love and teaching with women in prison with whom I was able to share the significance of this story in many ways. In this way also, I witnessed the power of the circle being completed again.

During these years of visiting my friends and students — spiritual sisters — in prison, I have seen such beauty, sweetness, and goodness in them as well as openness and yearning for transformation. And, I found the hearts of the sisters are open to the realization of the power of God's love to transform their lives. My belief is that even their realization of the meaning of Surat'ul Fatihah can save and transform their lives and, insha'Allah, by keeping them on the Straight Path, prevent them from being engaged in activities that might bring them to prison again.

With this as the foundation upon which we stand together, we have met regularly and shared the Light and Compassion of Allah's Wisdom and Grace as well as studying the Arabic language, especially focusing upon the meanings of what we are saying in prayer. I feel that it is an honor and blessing to meet with them, and I deeply pray that the sharing of the teachings of Grace will free them from the oppression that tainted their past and guide them on the Straight Path ever more.

In recent years, Issa and I attended a very special event hosted by the people responsible for prisoner-volunteer relations. It was called a Banquet for the Volunteers.

Like all of the sacred assemblies that I have been so blessed to participate in, taking place around the world, this too, I felt, was another manifestation of the blessed assembly occurring, here, on earth. What was immediately visible was that all the people in the room — prison officials, employees, volunteers, and the prisoners who were serving us

— were emanating love and light. We were seated at a table with Chaplain Regatti, my kind guide into the prison every week, along with two friendly volunteers and another very friendly person who, it turned out, was now seemingly well adapted on the "outside" after having lived many years in prison.

Following our meal, my dear friend, Dr. Scott Barrett, Re-entry Affairs Coordinator, with whom I have been sharing the light all these years, began the program by thanking all the volunteers for their self-less service. He mentioned that they were different from the employees because they offered their services to the prison and the prisoners, without being paid. In response, one of the volunteers spontaneously stood up to say how much in goodness and joy we, volunteers, were paid, much more than money! And he noted how often we may have come to the prison exhausted but left rejuvenated, full of life! I completely agreed!

Then Dr. Scott introduced the guest speaker. The speaker, John Pace, was notably gracious and eloquent. The message he delivered was exceedingly moving. He had been sent to prison at the age of 17 and remained there until he was released in 2017. What happened to him over the course of his prison term was one of the most amazing stories of the transformation of the human condition that I have ever heard.

When he entered the prison system, committed at that time to a life sentence without parole, he was sent to a prison in a very isolated location where no volunteers could come. This was very difficult for him in the context of his life circumstance. But, after some time, he was moved to Graterford Prison, a much more reachable location. There he met and began working intensively with many volunteers.

It was, as he explained, his extensive involvement with volunteers in the prison system that totally transformed his life. First, there was an in-depth literacy program by which he and so many others became literate. Then he described more advanced, high-level college programs, such as a very popular extended course in creative writing.

Not only did he receive a very good and extremely helpful education during his years in prison, but he became a highly trained and effective facilitator of this educational system that was now activated in the prisons. As he spoke to us, the clarity of his thinking and communication skills and the inspiration activated in his heart, as a result of his unique educational development and life experience, were truly apparent in his face and in his message.

It is also important to note that after 37 years he was finally released from prison, and thus were we so blessed by his inspiring presence at the banquet. I am sharing these stories with you, dear readers, because many of you reading this may never have been inside a prison. What we are shown on TV and in the movies is often so frightening and traumatizing that we could never know about the beautiful, truly inspiring stories of the transformation of lives that I and others have been witnessing — from the most desperate conditions to liberation from negative patterns, to the real possibility of peace, joy and fulfillment through transformative education and true service to humanity. The message I received through the transformative power in John Pace's life is a message for humanity particularly when so many of our brothers and sisters in the human family are facing many profound challenges and trials by which they may feel imprisoned. And, if John Pace could make it through all that he had to go through to become such a beautiful example of what a human being can be, so can we all, by Allah's permission and with His Grace, complete our mission in this world, leaving a truly beneficial legacy of service, light and love — seeds of light — to be planted in gardens of grace yet to bloom and bear blessed fruit.

Being trained by blessed teachers in the curriculum of *loving all lives as your own,* the story of each person I meet on the sacred journey becomes inscribed in the text of my memoir, and thus does the all-inclusive circle of God's Grace embrace us wherever He guides us to go.

Contemplating the circle in the sphere of education and service, I would next like to share with you, dear reader, the unfolding blessings of

Issa's education and, in this light, the potential of us all to become Ambassadors of Peace. Intending to walk in the footsteps of our Prophets (as), Messengers (as) and all the Friends of Allah *subhana wa ta'ala,* both he and I have been pursuing an international peace curriculum learned in many ways during our travels around the world.

Issa and I began traveling together when he was eight months old. Later, we went on long train trips to Canada, on which we read amazing books about the spiritual journey. When he was four-and-a-half, we went with Ahamad Kabeer to see his family in Southern India and our Kashmir family to the north of India and to share the light with them all. There followed many trips to Africa in which we were both engaged in countless hours of *dhikr* (remembrance of Allah), Quranic studies, and teaching with Sheikhs as well as many mystical journeys. All of these journeys were, in some sense, formative of a broad and universal consciousness guiding us along the path of the *Ambassadors of Peace.*

From a very young age, Issa was moved by an instinct towards compassionate awareness. When he was in Waldorf kindergarten, his teacher told me that she often saw him lifting up stones to liberate entrapped insects. On our African journeys, I often found him helping the disabled and the needy.

Guided by Sheikh Dieye to a village mostly composed of children needing clothing and blankets, we then went back to his Quaker School in Media, PA where we spoke about the needs of these village children. We were immediately flooded with abundant supplies provided by the generous Friends, which we then sent to the children in that village, continuing to affirm our commitment to serving the human family.

In high school, Issa was accepted into an excellent charter school, Friere Charter, which itself was dedicated to peace, where he was engaged in so many different kinds of charitable educational endeavors that were inspired and supported by the school. In the end, he made valedictorian and received the school's annual honorarium, which paid for half his undergrad education — so many blessings rewarding the blessings!

All of these, as well as many other pieces in a circular peace-puzzle, ultimately led him to get his first master's degree in International Peace and Conflict Resolution, a program which trained us both in very deep practical and spiritual studies, such as Restorative Justice, Conflict Resolution and Trauma Healing. It also took him on very meaningful journeys to countries such as Ireland, Costa Rica, and Germany which are actively engaged in these processes of peacemaking and social transformation.

In contemplating and appreciating this global practice of bringing peace to areas and people who have suffered so much from conflicts, let's remember and invoke the passage of Scripture, *"Blessed are the Peacemakers, for they will be called Children of God"* (Matthew: 5-9). And as we walk in the footsteps of Peacemakers, or Ambassadors of Peace, may we realize that to overcome and resolve conflict and make peace in the world, we must first resolve the conflict and make peace within ourselves. This, indeed, is a practice in which we, both mother and son, must be continuously engaged.

Deeply affected by this training, Issa then received a master's degree in Comparative Religion and was guided into CPE Spiritual Care, or the Pastoral Care programs, in which he has been working as chaplain in several hospitals including UPenn, Einstein and Lankenau, to aid and support people in transition, and their families, as the patient is in the process of passing from this world. The duty of a chaplain is to heal, sustain, guide, reconcile, holistically nurture the person — their body, their mind, and their soul.

While I was concluding this chapter, Issa applied to a Doctorate in Ministry program that will complete his chaplaincy education. He was accepted the next day. And one year later, when the blessed program was complete, he received his Doctorate in Ministry (Chaplaincy). As he prepared to make his final presentation in a virtual assembly of teachers and students, he was inspired to share with the blessed assembly many pictures from a book of dreams, visions and teachings that I had made 50 years earlier traveling throughout India and neighboring lands. These visions transmitted so inspired the assembly celebrating the completion of the doctorate program in the New Seminary that they collectively expressed that the book should be published, that they each wanted a copy, that I should be given an honorary Degree : A Doctorate in the Spiritual Journey. And thus did they tune in to the depth and signinificance of my journey. That Issa's reception of his Doctorate should be honored and celebrated by pictures of dreams and visions that I painted and wrote about on my solitary journey so many years ago was certainly another sign of the sacred circle being completed, Alhamdulillah!

That same week that he was accepted into the Doctorate program at New Seminary, Issa was hired to teach remotely for his beloved high school, Tech Friere, and in his second year of teaching there, he is being trained, in person, to teach Special Needs children, through which he is developing many deep, compassionate skills. As I have listened to him engaged in both learning and teaching, the word most often repeated by both teachers and students in this program is "appreciate." Mutual appreciation seems to be flowing through the educational process as he is experiencing it, and this, even more than any academic discipline, could be a life-saving teaching for both students and teachers. As all the various degrees are bestowed upon him and he is being trained to serve in many ways, I pray deeply that the degree of his spiritual awareness and awakening, manifested through loving service, may bring him and me into greater and greater realization and nearness to the Source of Eternal Knowledge.

From freeing insects in childhood, to seeking conflict resolution and healing for countries and people in need of peace, to aiding people in transition from this life and their families, to teaching in the high school that he so loved to attend, thus does the circle of compassion and care continue to comfort, aid, and sustain one life after another, insha'Allah. And, as we aid others to make the journey beyond this life, may we be preparing to make that journey ourselves. Everything that we may have experienced or learned up until now is being put to the test.

Now, Dear Reader, I would like to share contemplation of another circle completed and its spiral of ascent. And this was the homecoming of Issa's father, Seyed Ahamad Kabeer. After our beloved Sheikh Bawa (ra) left this world, Kabeer and I had different missions to accomplish. I, in making 17 trips to Senegal, where much knowledge and blessing were received — while he made many trips to Canada, serving Bawa's community there, as in Philadelphia, in so many ways.

After several years of travel, I came home to really land again at the Fellowship, rediscovering ever more deeply the sanctuary of peace that I find every day in the mosque, particularly at the time of dhikr (4:30-6:00 every blessed morning). Returning to this base, I am able to reach out, making many more connections with other spiritual travelers around the world. Ahamad Kabeer had been living in a small room at the Fellowship and was almost completely immobilized after some stays in the hospital and rehab. He was not really feeling too well.

One afternoon after we went to visit him, he was very excited, putting on his belt, asking us with a certain passion to take him home! We said that, of course, we would, and Issa got him in the wheelchair and brought him home. As he made it up the few stairs and into our back glass room, he seemed immensely relieved, so happy to have made it back. He remained there in that state of deep relief for about an hour.

Then we brought him to a room where he could rest in the middle of the house. It was a special room with large windows overlooking the garden and beautiful tapestries on the walls, the first ones we had made in Kashmir thirty-five years ago. When a group of friends who were healers came over to visit in this room one day and commented upon its special energy and beauty, I said that I had received the understanding that this was to be a healing room. And, as it turned out, it was to be Ahamad Kabeer's healing room.

Ahamad Kabeer was extremely happy and peaceful in his room, but we could not just keep him there as though we had absconded with him. So, we took him back to the Fellowship. A few days later, however, when we visited him again, once again he pleaded with us to take him home, and, knowing that this was truly what he wanted, we could not refuse.

This is, so simply, how he moved back into our house. In a worldly sense, he and I were divorced. Yet this was not a matter of worldly marriage but of deep commitment to serve the Divine. The happiness and peace that Ahamad Kabeer found in the house made me so happy and peaceful. Whenever I came into the room to serve him, he was making du'a, or prayers, and when I entered, he told the One that he was addressing that I had come. He was exceedingly grateful for everything given to him and addressed me as "Mawlana Maryam" or "Bawa Maryam." Whatever struggles we may have had, from time to time in the past, they were gone now, any manifestation of darkness now dispelled by Divine Light. And this was the realm in which he was to abide as he prepared to make his journey back to the One of Infinite Mercy and Grace.

Ahamad Kabeer lived in our house again for almost four years. While he was almost immobile when he moved in, with the loving service of his therapists Greg Hussein and Ron, he soon became almost completely mobile. He was very happy to see everyone living in the house and those visiting; this was his family. As he had been serving the Fellowship Community in various countries, now, it seemed, he was being served — on platters of Light — Blessings of God.

Such was the luminous, joyous, and prayer-filled realm in which he abided as he prepared to return to Allah *subhana wa ta'ala*, insha'Allah, pleased and well-pleasing.

During these final years, Kabeer suffered almost no health problems, simply blocked tear ducts in his eyes for which he received minor surgery. The trips to the hospital were a little challenging, but we made it through. And, every time, he was so very happy to be home again. Then during the final few weeks, we noticed that his mouth was open in a circular formation and he was not really breathing. We called an ambulance and were in the emergency room in a few minutes.

Kabeer was diagnosed with pneumonia and admitted to the hospital. This was the beginning of two relatively chaotic hospital stays, stressful, with invasive treatments and conflicting medical assessments. From the first visit, he was suddenly sent home. Then, a day or so later, when a nurse came to visit, he was immediately sent back to the hospital, where he did not want to go.

Shortly after we arrived there the second time, a doctor appeared. We were not introduced. He seemed to me like a mystical presence. He asked me if I thought Kabeer wanted to be in the hospital or would rather be at home. I said that I was sure that he would rather be at home. The doctor, who mysteriously appeared and then mysteriously disappeared, agreed.

In the next day or two, while at the hospital, we became connected to the hospice-palliative care network, composed of a variety of caretakers who, when Kabeer returned home, would be coming every day to visit him. Linked with this heart centered compassionate team, we went home. When Kabeer arrived in his room and laid down on the bed, he kept pointing his finger at Bawa's picture in a kind of deeply peaceful ecstasy. Alhamdulillah! The little struggle was over, and he was home again, to rest.

The last week of his visit here on earth was deeply peaceful, with caretakers attending and many members of the Fellowship praying with him and sitting in vigil throughout the house. Since the trip to the hospital, he had not really been breathing properly. Then, simply, as Allah *subhana wa ta'ala* ordained, he took his last breath. *Inna lillahi wa inna ilayhi raji'un* (To Allah do we belong, and to Him do we return). Members of the Fellowship family sat throughout the house, and the Holy Qur'an was played throughout the night.

When we visited the Funeral Home the next day, and the Islamic ritual of washing the body was complete, I went in to give Kabeer (ra) salaams, my last greetings of peace in this station of this sacred life. When I looked at him with the final gaze, I bear witness that it was as though I was gazing through the Divine veil. I have never beheld, in this world, such a beautiful face. I have been told such is the beauty of the face of the believer after receiving one's final ablution. May his journey and the journey of all sincere travelers be blessed forever with the light of eternal *ibadat* (worship, service, and love of Allah *subhana wa ta'ala*).

Forty days after the burial, we recited Surah Yasin in the masjid for Seyed Ahamad Kabeer (ra), and a week later we gathered in the Fellowship Meeting Room, welcoming everyone to share their memories. The fact that people were so deeply impacted by his prayers and presence was, I believe, not personal but simply because of the barakah manifesting through him as an instrument of the Divine Will through the blessed transmission of the Sheikh (ra).

In response to many sincere condolences offered, I do not have words to adequately express how much we have been benefited and gained from his presence here and the blessed way in which he departed, returning to Allah *subhana wa ta'ala*. And we pray for him an exalted ascension from this world to the realms of Allah's Presence and Eternal Grace. Ameen!

> *Inna lillahi wa inna ilayhi raji'un (To Allah we do belong and to Allah we do return).*
>
> The Holy Qur'an 2:156

In honoring the life of Kabeer (ra) and all other sincere servants of Allah subhana wa ta'ala in their time of passage and return, let us consider the message transmitted by Imam Ghazali (ra) as he was passing from this world:

> *Imam Al Ghazzali woke up one early morning and as usual offered his prayers. He then enquired what day it was and his younger brother, Ahmad Ghazzali, replied, "Monday." He asked him to bring his white shroud, kissed it, stretched himself*

full length and saying "Lord, I obey willingly," breathed his last.
Underneath his head rest they found the following verses; com-
posed by him, probably, during the night:
"Say to my friends, when they look upon me, dead,
Weeping for me and mourning me in sorrow,
'Do not believe that this corpse you see is myself,
In the name of Allah, I tell you, it is not I.
I am a spirit, and this is nothing but flesh,
It was my abode and my garment for a time.
I am a treasure, by a talisman kept hid,
Fashioned of dust, which served me as a shrine,
I am a pearl, which has left its shell deserted,
I am a bird, and this body was my cage,
Whence I have now flown forth and it is left as a token.
Praise to Allah, who hath now set me free,
And prepared for me my place in the highest of the Heavens.

Until today I was dead, though alive in your midst.
Now I live in truth, with the grave-clothes discarded.
Today I hold converse with the Saints above,
With no veil between, I see Allah face to face.
I look upon "Lauh-il-Mahfuz" (The Guarded Tablet)
and therein I read,
Whatever was and is, and all that is to be.

Be not frightened when death draweth nigh,
It is but the departure for this blessed home,
Think of the mercy and love of your Lord,
Give thanks for His Grace and come without fear."

May we all come to realize the light and peace of our Loving
Creator during our lives in this world and throughout the journey
beyond.

Blessed is the man who always kept the life after death in his
view, who remembered the Day of Judgement through all his
deeds, who led a contented life and who was happy with the lot

that Allah had destined for him.

– Imam Ali (ra)

Oh brother! Bear in mind the fact that at the time of your birth everybody was rejoicing while you were crying. Live such a life that when you die everybody weeps on your departure from this worldly life while you are smiling. If you always wholeheartedly think of your Creator with devotion and with enthusiastic zeal, then as a matter of fact, when you are on the point of leaving this world, you will remember your Lord and your heart will be illumined with the light of Almighty Allah.

—attributed to Shaykh 'Abdal Qadr Gilani (ra)

Die before you die., for the act of shedding off a lowly quality is a small death, every sacrifice for the sake of others is another small death whereby the individual gains new spiritual value; thus, in a series of deaths, the soul rises to immortality or to a level of spiritualization that it has never dreamed of.

— Annemarie Schimmel

I have seen many die, surrounded by loved ones, and their last words were 'I love you.' There were some who could no longer speak yet with their eyes and soft smile left behind that same healing message. I have been in rooms where those who were dying made it feel like sacred ground.

— Stephen Levine,
A Year to Live: How to Live This Year as If It Were Your Last

"Pray as if it's your last, for it very well may be." - this was what Imam Sohaib Sultan would always say out loud before he would lead us in Jummah prayer. Every single week, for as long as I can remember, he reminded us about death. Here was a man who was preparing for death long before death came knocking on his door. So when it finally came, he welcomed it

with grace. Here was a man whose remembrance of death led him to have presence in every moment. Just one encounter with Imam Sohaib was enough to change your life forever. One of the things he mentioned is that every person we come across offers an opportunity to practice pastoral care; each person we speak to is a full human being who just had a full day and has a day coming up that they might be worried about. It's remarkable how he approached every person he met with such sincere care, compassion, and concern. In the death-averse culture that we live in, it might seem like constant awareness of death would make us somber, but it only made Imam Sohaib live his life more joyously in the service of others, love that much deeper, and spread beauty and light everywhere he went. There was always a warm smile on his face and he had this sense of urgency to do good til his very last breath. Of course, the thought of separation from his loved ones and leaving the work that gave him deep purpose and meaning saddened him, but one thing that consciousness of death does for the theologically grounded is give perspective. His conviction in the everlasting abode and the mercy of God, his hope for eternal reunion with all of his loved ones, all brought him to a state of beautiful contentment with God's decree.

—Sabrina Mirza

I am going to Allah! I am going to Allah! I am going to Allah!
—Imam Sohaib Sultan, as he was transitioning

CHAPTER THIRTY-TWO

THROUGH DOORWAYS OF LIFE AND DEATH, FOR ALL HUMANITY: A CALL TO PRAYER, A CALL TO AWAKENING

O You Who spreads forth the banquet of Your gifts and opens wide the doors of relief and blessing; Spread over us Your abundant goodness, and Your provision. Enable us to recognize what is right, and what is the truth. Adorn us and beautify us with sincerity and truthfulness. Protect us from the evil of anything in creation, and when the moment comes to depart this Earth, conclude our lives here in the most beautiful way, with your gentleness and while we are in a state of well-being, oh Lord!
—Supplication after praying Salat'ad Duha

Dear Readers, Beloved Companions on the Sacred Journey, as Allah, Most Merciful, has decreed, may we discover and fulfill the true purpose of our existence in the time allotted. Let us now contemplate the station in which we have individually and collectively arrived. What are we perceiving within and without? As we are less able go outside our homes during the global pandemic, what are we discovering — what lessons are we learning, as we go more and more deeply within? Let us take notes – day by day, moment by moment, step by step, station by station, in this process of facing the challenges, hearing the call, and, God willing, awakening. In this mysterious epoch of our collective journey when many of us cannot go out to work, we are learning, day by day, how much we can discover about ourselves as we do the needed inner work. What, within ourselves, have we not had time to address, comprehend, pray for healing of, and hopefully transform? Let us explore these inner worlds, cleanse and organize the inner realms, work on discovering and healing the unhealed traumas, and bringing the Divine Qualities, such as Peace, Wisdom, Justice, Love and Light to life within. As much as we are able, with the Grace of Allah *subhana wa ta'ala* to bring the plenitude of the Divine Attributes and Teachings to life within ourselves, it is that much healing power we will have, as He wills, to share with our brothers and sisters on the sacred journey. And, as much Light and Healing Grace may be awakened and liberated within us, may that Light shine through us to illuminate others.

At this time, it is important to appreciate that while we as global travelers are for the most part not able to go beyond our homes, it is amazing and awe-inspiring how many connections are being established and deepened at this time with fellow seekers across the world. Thus, it has been normal for me to receive many calls a day from spiritual seekers in Canada, Botswana, Pakistan, India, Spain, Ecuador, South Africa, England, Scotland, Australia and many other countries who have simply seen a video that we made and been guided towards us, light upon light. Then, the process of healing unfolds — heart-to-heart and soul-to-soul, as the Healer decrees and ordains. And, as is clearly revealed, it is through focusing upon and imbibing the blessings that are being bestowed that we are being liberated from being stressed, distressed, or depressed.

This process is very deep at this time, when so many members of our human family are being challenged so profoundly, physically, mentally, emotionally, psychologically, economically and spiritually. It is certainly a time when unhealed traumas on all levels are coming to the surface and requesting, intensely, to be addressed, and, hopefully, *insha'Allah*, to be he healed. And such is the focus and substance of many healing sessions that I am sharing with others, day and night, as with myself.

And, as we have been experiencing so often and so deeply in our prayers and in our lives the message, "Surely with the difficulty comes the ease," as expressed in Surat'ul Inshirah, this divine message is especially relevant now, to lead us from the difficulty to the ease. As often throughout our journey we may have read and recited these words and been guided by them to the light which shines not only at the end of the tunnel but right in the middle of it, this is fundamental, powerful, transformative guidance now when so many challenges are facing our brothers and sisters, aunts and uncles, grandparents and grandchildren.

Yet, in the midst of this collective trial, let us behold how much compassion, kindness and care within many members of the human family have deepened and increased. This is one vital step in our collective awakening: gratitude. In the midst of the deep struggles, the crises facing our fellow beings across the earth, let us appreciate and celebrate the loving dedicated service and care, manifesting in so many hearts and souls, prayers and actions. And let us invoke the mercy of our Lord, Most Merciful, to enable us to become instruments through which His Mercy, Compassion, and Transformative Love may flow.

As we learn how many families are facing the death or suffering of a loved one, or we ourselves are facing illness or death, may we deeply contemplate the teaching we have just read of Imam al Ghazali and the teachings of other great sages regarding the potential liberation of our passage through the doorways of difficulty and death into the Eternal Presence of our Beloved Lord.

I would like to share with you, dear friends on the journey, who are hopefully being awakened by seeing your souls and profound inner intentions reflected in the mirror of the journey transmitted in this book, some of the dreams that I have been having during this time of spiritual seclusion, hoping that these reflections may encourage you to be more and more conscious of the messages that are coming to you, while encouraging myself to be more and more conscious of the messages that I am receiving.

In the first of a series of dreams, I was sitting at an extended table upon which our goods were laid out as they had been throughout our shows for the past 35 years of our business, Kashmir Dream, Treasures from the Silk Road. An ancient blessed being, frail and subtle, seemingly not composed of earthly substance, approached from the distance and came to the table to bless it, to bless us and all our endeavors. A few nights later, I saw in a dream that I was sitting next to the table again laid out with our goods. Laid out also on the *maidah* (outspread table) was a feast of provision. Let us here reflect upon the ayat of the Holy Qur'an:

> *Issa son of Maryam said: "O Allah, our Lord! Send us from heaven a table spread (with provision) that there may be for us – for the first and the last of us – a festival and a sign from You; and provide us sustenance, for You are the Best of sustainers.*
> The Holy Qur'an 5:114

Then in the dream I received a message, saying, "The business is thriving!" Still in the dream, I remembered how we had packed up all of our goods from the Philadelphia Flower Show in mid-March 2020 and from that time on business was over. We could not go out again. I asked, "What business?" I was told, "The business of praying ever more deeply and sharing all the blessings received with the seekers who come to you in search of Allah's Grace. By this message, I am continuously reminded what I am to be doing here on earth at such a time.

Another dream also came in which our house became a vast healing space. One by one as people arrived, I gazed into their eyes, praying for each one to realize and fulfill the purpose for which he or she was created, for the circle of their life to be completed. Each one began to turn, slowly, then whirl as dervishes do, in smaller and greater circles, according to their needs, processing, and inspiration, in a state of ecstatic praise. My hands were raised in supplication, and at a certain point I realized that coins were falling abundantly into my uplifted hands, symbolic, I felt, of Divine Provision for all.

A few nights later, I was in the process of reciting Surah Yasin many times for the provision and protection of humanity and also Su-rat'ul-Waqiah, when I went to sleep and dreamed. This time, I was in our home, but the house was expanded, and radiant light poured through many vast windows. There was a knock at the door. One by one, the most beautiful beings entered. Their faces shined beautifully, and they wore splendid robes. They seemed to be visitors from another realm who had come to bless us, bless our home, and bless humanity. They came in smiling deeply and sat down, filling the house.

I served them all food from an expansive tray. I knew that I could never have prepared such food as was needed to feed this vast assembly, and that it was the provision of Allah (swt) for all. Once the blessed guests had eaten, they raised their hands and sang together — in celestial harmony — salawaats upon the Prophet (saw). The house seemed filled with heavenly light. Awakening from the dream, I realized that this house – dedicated to being a sanctuary of peace that had been filled with so many spiritual travelers from around the world who arrived for nourishment: dhikr, remembrance and the celebration of praise — was now, when people could not even come into the house, filled with beings from other realms assembled here for dhikr — the celebration of praise of Allah *subhana wa ta'ala* and salawaats upon the Holy Prophet (saw). The dream showed me that in a time of seclusion and "social distancing" beautiful and powerful meetings can take place in the spiritual realms of our heart and soul, and the light generated within such assemblies can then be shared with our companions in this world, even virtually, on the telephone, or through our prayers.

When the dream was over, the salawaats did not cease. We must realize that the depth and sincerity of our prayers and salawaats flowing within us are sustaining our spiritual well-being. Like the blood that sustains our physical existence, our ever-flowing dhikr, prayers, and salawaats sustain and guide us on the journey back to our Beloved Lord.

A few days after this dream, the members of our household gathered in our prayer room for a salawaat night. As we were celebrating the Presence of Allah *subhana wa ta'ala* and His Messenger (saw), I was gazing at the large photograph of the Ka'aba on the mantle. It seemed radiant and activated. As much as we have been told that the Ka'aba is now vacated, with very few people able to gather there, the Ka'aba that I beheld in front of me was surrounded by a vast, luminous congregation, beings circling powerfully around it, light upon light. As this vision manifested before me, questions arose within. What is the Ka'aba? Where is this central place around which we turn in *tawaf*? And how can we make the Holy Pilgrimage at a time like this when we cannot physically travel across the world?

Gazing at the resplendent Ka'aba now shining within me, I prayed, asking how to make the journey there at this time in our collective history. I was guided directly to a book by Sheikh Bawa Muhaiyaddeen (ra), *Hajj, the Inner Pilgrimage*. Its many deep teachings reveal how we can make this blessed journey to our Exalted Source, whether or not we can travel to the physical manifestation of the Ka'aba.

Although I have been aware of Sheikh Bawa's (ra) profound teachings about this for many years, I feel they are powerfully coming to life within me now in this time of great challenges and transformation for the human family. While we cannot travel to the Ka'aba physically, at this time, the Sheikh (ra) is guiding us on the journey internally to the Divine Heart within us, to make the appropriate sacrifice – to give our life and being to Allah *subhana wa ta'ala* as He gives His Life and Being to us, infinitely transforming our existence, insha'Allah. Then, if and when we are blessed to make the physical pilgrimage, may we make this hajj with ever-deepening love for and awareness of the Divine Call and the Divine Presence around which we turn. As the Sheikh (ra) says about the inner dimensions of the hajj:

> *What is Hajj? It is to destroy separation and dispel ignorance, to bring about peace, tranquility, serenity, unity, love, and harmony, and to know that God is love. Without deviating from*

virtue, truth, and the state of bliss, to know, with certainty that God is one, and that there is one family, to become one with Allahu, and to establish that state. It is to proceed in unity as one family, one people, with one God and one prayer, to dedicate oneself to Him. To surrender to Him, to make the world within die, giving life (hayat) to His Grace, His Wealth, and His treasure is Hajj.

Unity is hajj, love is hajj, the qualities and actions of Allah are hajj. His wisdom is hajj. Establishing patience (sabur), contentment (shakur), and trust in Allah (tawakkul) and unshakable faith (iman) is hajj. To bring about peace and wisdom is hajj. To see the divine world (akhirah) within yourself, and to realize the qualities of Allah is hajj. Unity and love are hajj.

Allah will answer any heart that is filled with this love and unity. Anyone whose heart attains such a state is accepted by Allah. The resonance comes from His Grace and Resplendence, saying, "I accept you." This world then becomes the Divine World for people in this state. The wealth of the Divine World is given to them in completeness, while they are in this world. When that state comes, this is hajj. You and I must reflect upon this.

My love you, my grandchildren. Each one of you must think about this state. No matter what race, religion, or caste you are, you must have this peace, this unity, compassion, love, tranquility, and all the qualities of Allah. You must embrace each other in this state, heart to heart, and gaze at each other's face, speaking His names and His words, and acting according to His actions, His ninety-nine Attributes (wilayat), His compassion and love.

You must join together and do this, no matter to what group you may belong. Acquire this state of peace, tranquility, unity, justice, compassion, patience, and tolerance. Acquire the loving qualities of Allah, live in unity, have love for Allah, join your hearts to Him, and unite with Him. If you exist in this state, He will make this world into the Divine Kingdom (akhirah).

You will dwell in the freedom and happiness of heaven. This is the absolute truth. These are the teachings given to the Prophets. You must think about this. You must have this certitude of iman. With wisdom and love, you must praise Allah and show compassion to everyone, Then the world will be made into heaven for you. In your life, you will have peace, tranquility, light, and beauty. Allah will protect you. Understand this, Amin, Amin, Allah is sufficient unto us all.

All of everything experiences life and death. In life and in death, the way to fulfill the hajj is to make the world die within oneself and to turn one's life into everlasting Life while still living in this world. This hajj is to make this world (dunya) die in the world (dunya) and for life to become eternal (for hayat to become Hayat). To fulfill this Hajj is to cut the connections of one's life, the connections to the base desires (nafs), it is to cut the four hundred trillion varieties of 'illusory' qualities and to establish with clarity that there is no Lord other than Allahu.

You must understand what divine knowledge (ilm) is. Allah is One Who has so much wealth. His treasures will never diminish by one atom. He holds the wealth of all three worlds in His hands.

He holds the wealth of all three worlds in HIs hands.

What will those that have received this wealth every lack? It is certain that the wealth of the three worlds; the beginning (awwal), this world (dunya), and the divine kingdom (akhirah) are in His Hands. Whatever wealth you are to receive in this world is in His hands. Whatever wealth you are to receive in the realm of the soul is in His hands. The wealth of the divine kingdom is in His hands. When one receives the wealth of the three worlds (mubarakat), he will receive completeness. If a human being understands the five furud and fulfills the fifth fard of hajj, then what will he have? Nothing will be lacking. He will be fulfilled. But as long as one does not fulfill this hajj, there will always be deficiencies in one's life and in one's prayer...

Millions upon millions of people attempt to complete the hajj... If one truly fulfills this state, the sound of Allah will resonate within. On that day, he will receive the wealth of Allah, the grace of divine knowledge (ilm) the mercy of His grace, the grace of His qualities, the grace of certainty, the grace of love, the grace of wisdom, and all His undiminishing grace and mercy. On that day, one transforms his life into heaven, into Allah's kingdom. After completing the hajj by dying within Allah, one's life will be in heaven and not in hell. Even though one still has the body, life will be heaven. Even though one lives a life in this world, it will be a life filled with Allah.

When one looks, it will be with Allah's resplendent gaze. When one listens, it will be with the ear that hears Allah. When one smells, he will smell the fragrance of Allah, when one speaks it will be the speech of Allah. When one tastes, it will be the taste of Allah. One's actions of giving and receiving will be the action of giving and receiving Allah's wealth. When one walks, one will be walking on Allah's path, focusing on Allah. One's heart will be Allah's heart, the throne of a true believer (arsh'ul muminin), the heart of light. All one's qualities will be the qualities of Allah. Such is the state established by those who have fulfilled the fifth fard (obligatory duty) of hajj.

—Sheikh Bawa Muhaiyaddeen (ra),
Hajj, the Inner Pilgrimage.

Dear Friends, fellow travelers on the Sacred journey, let us contemplate the significance and relevance of these messages to our life and journey. At this time, when we cannot make the physical hajj, let us explore the possibility of making the Inner Pilgrimage as suggested here. The more deeply and completely we can surrender our existence back to the Source which brought us into existence, the more completely can our existence become solely a manifestation of His Grace, insha'Allah. The phrase: "Die before death' is completed by "that you may live forever."

What will live forever is not our temporal being but the Divine Being within us.

Let us consider these words a call to awakening, a transmission of light from the One Who is Infinite Light, an invitation to return the blessed *amanah* to the Source of all being that entrusted it to us and an invitation to receive, for all our ailments and illnesses – the cure. When we bow down in prayer, we give to Allah *subhana wa ta'ala* what we have to give Him — ourselves, and all that we have within us. We surrender. And He gives us what He has for us of His infinite Grace. What a great exchange!

As we continue the journey back to our Source in the midst of the trials and tests that we may be encountering, may we realize that with every illness, Allah (swt), the One of Infinite Mercy, has sent down the cure. Let us address the challenges facing us all while seeking the Divine cures made manifest in His Exalted Qualities. In the context of the trials of racism, religious conflict and other forms of aggression and strife experienced collectively and individually throughout the ages, let us truly seek the realization of Divine Unity to heal a deeply distorted consciousness. May our fears and anxieties be dispelled by the power of tawakkul (trust in Allah) and iman (unshakable faith) made manifest in Al Yaqin, His Certainty. May our sense of poverty and need be dispelled by the reception of the wealth of Divine Provision. May conflict and aggression, within and around us, be dispelled by the invocation and living reality of Divine Peace circulating within and around us, insha'Allah. May our fear of death be cured by our experience and realization of the Eternal Life, *al-Hayy al-Qayyum*, within us.

During this period of seclusion, of inner rather than outer travel, may we beseech our Lord, Most Merciful, Most Kind and Most Powerful, to awaken our hearts and souls to the presence of His Secrets that He has implanted within us — as He wills us to realize them. If, by His Grace, Allahu subhana wa ta'ala blesses us to unite with all the Believers in the tawaf encircling the Ka'aba, the Divine Essence, and enables us to return to Him in purity the treasures of His Grace that He has Most Mercifully entrusted to us, thus will the Ultimate Circle be completed as the Spiral ascends.

CHAPTER THIRTY-THREE

LAILAT'UL ISRA WAL MI''RAJ —

THE EXALTED NIGHT JOURNEY OF THE HOLY
PROPHET (SAW) AND ITS SIGNIFICANCE FOR
HUMANITY

Glory to Allah Who did take His servant for a Journey by night from the Sacred Mosque to the furthest Mosque, whose surroundings We did bless, in order that We might show him some of Our Signs. For surely He Alone is the All Hearing, All-Seeing
—The Holy Qur'an 17:1

Praise be to Allah Who has chosen His praiseworthy servant Muhammad for the Message, distinguished him with the sudden rapture on the Buraq, and caused him to ascend on the ladders of perfection to the high heavens to show him of the greatest signs of his Lord. He raised him until he reached to the Lote-tree of the Farthest Boundary where ends the science of every Messenger-Prophet and every Angel brought near, where lies the Garden of Retreat, to the point where he heard the sound of the pens that write what has befallen and what is to befall.
—Sayyid Muhammad ibn Alawi al Maliki

Dear Companions on the Sacred Journey, we thank Allah (swt) profoundly for the Infinite Blessings of His Mercy and His Grace, descending upon us and guiding us, step-by-step, through this amazing journey, Alhamdulillah! As I have been sharing with you, since the beginning of this mystery-filled journal, I am truly not the creator of this story or the determiner of the unfolding journey. Step-by-step, we are being guided from one dimension to the next of the spiritual journey back to our Exalted Source. Having been immersed in the ocean of salawaats, in the celebration of the Divine Assembly, in the vision of the illuminated ascending stairway and the transmission of the inner Hajj, as the book was being finalized, I came to realize that I would be completing this book on the night of the celebration of Lailat'ul Isra w'al Mi'raj, the unfathomably exalted journey of our Beloved Prophet (saw), then I realized that I must add a chapter dedicated to this blessed subject and I was, again, overwhelmed with profound awe, in beholding the Divine Plan.

For, there are so many points of deep significance brought into focus by the completion of this work in conjunction with the supremely exalted event: the Night Journey and Ascension of our Beloved Prophet Muhammad (saw). And it is truly by deeply contemplating what we are able to comprehend of his journey, that, with Allah's Grace, we may be able to experience and understand the significance of our life journey on the path leading us to our Lord. Where has my life's journey been leading me from country to country, realm to realm, teaching to teaching, Sign to Sign of Divine Grace, if not to such a completion?

To comprehend, in the context of all that we have shared and may share in the future, in coming to understand the tremendous importance and relevance to us, of the Ascension of the Prophet (saw), let us begin by contemplating the multidimensional usage in our personal and collective awareness of the "spiritual journey" itself. Let me begin by considering how many times I have used the word "journey" in this memoir and how much I consider my life (our life) to be a journey, from one station, one state of realization, one test and transformation, one blessed realm to the next. I feel deeply connected to the word journey, and the multi-dimensional experience of the journey, along with the ever-unfolding realization of the relevance in every rigorous passage that we make of the Quranic teaching that we so often return to, "Surely with difficulty comes ease." Thus do we ever more deeply come to realize that our journey is, God willing — a guided passage through doorways, or veils, leading us, inshaAllah, to our ultimate Goal.

In order to contemplate the possibilities of our ever-unfolding journey, let us consider the potentially immensely powerful impact of the journey of the Holy Prophet (saw) upon ours. It is the Blessing and Grace of the exalted journey of our Beloved Prophet (saw) on Lailat'ul Isra w'al Mi'raj , and all throughout his life, that enables us to make the divinely inspired journey, following in the footsteps of our Exalted Guide (saw). In this context, as we contemplate the Ascension of the Holy Prophet (saw) it is very important for us to deeply, heartfully contemplate how profoundly the Holy Prophet (saw) suffered during the Year of Sadness preceding his Ascension, with the loss of his beloved wife and blessed companion, Khadijah (ra), and his beloved Uncle and protector, Abu Talib (as). May we contemplate these profound losses that he endured in the context of all that the Blessed Rasul (saw) was called upon to endure both before and after the Year of Sadness, such as the death of his father, Abdullah (as) before he was born, the death of this mother (ra), when he was quite young, separation from Halimah (ra) his wet nurse, the death of His grandfather, Abdul Muttalib (as) the extreme trials he and his Companions faced while enduring extreme tribulations such as the years of the ban in Mecca, extreme persecution that he endured at the hands of even members of his family and tribe and then the most difficult day of his life, as he expressed it, in which he was intensely assaulted by people of Ta'if. It is deeply important for us, who yearn to walk in his exalted footsteps, to deeply contemplate that, through all these profound challenges, he was the manifestation of Divine Light and Mercy for all the worlds, and that his journey and the extreme trials he faced in Ta'if, as well as in Mecca, and elsewhere, led him, through these profound challenges, to the boundless exaltation that he experienced on the Blessed Night Journey and ever after. His example, through profound difficulties and challenges, and then exalted Ascension into the Divine Presence, is the deepest invitation to us, dear companions on the journey, to, God willing, follow his greatly inspiring example, as we face every hardship and challenge, and, step-by-step, station-by-station, penetrate the veils in our journey back to our Beloved Lord.

I am therefore deeply grateful, dear Reader, that this book could be brought to completion at such a blessed time, and I pray that this may be a sign that our journey is being guided by the light of his journey and by the One Who guided him on his blessed journey through the realms.

May our journey come to completion through the blessings bestowed and the prayers that he made for his ummah on his journey into the Presence of the Divine, and may the illuminated power of the Night Journey of our Beloved Rasul (saw), as the rain of Grace, pour down upon our prayers: the celestial gift that we were given upon that blessed night, inspiring, guiding and illuminating our worship of and our meeting with our Beloved Lord (swt).

> *Let us always remember, as we pray - that " It was during this great night, that the transmission of the practice of our daily prayer, whose cycle began with the Prophet Adam (as) and was brought to completion with the Holy Prophet (saw) was given as a gift to all of humanity. When performed properly and with total awareness, this prayer becomes the vehicle that we travel in, to ascend through the seven heavens to the presence of Allah (swt). It has been said that prayer cannot be valid without the presence of the heart. The Holy Prophet Muhammad (saw)*

said *"The prayer is the ascension of the believer". This is our own, personal 'Vehicle of Light', which has the power to enlighten us, open our heart and the subtle centers of the heart, and bring us nearer to our Lord. Then we will realize the true meaning of the verse: "Prostrate yourself and draw near." (The Clot 96:19).*

Murshid Ali El-Senossi

May we deeply come to realize that our daily prayers are not simply a ritual practice, but actually a means, as divinely ordained, of drawing near to our Beloved Lord, and may we behold in the wondrous significance of the Night Journey, coming to life within our prayers: the mystery of the Ascension of the Prophetic Spirit and, as the light is rising, experience the descending Grace made manifest in the Divine Gift to us of our daily prayer, Alhamdulillah! Then, as deeper and deeper as we go in our prostration, surrender, and submission, may the ascending light of the celebration of praise guide us to ascend and unite with the One to Whom all Praise is due.

Let us now contemplate the deep messages about the Night Journey as transmitted through blessed ahadith. It is important to note here that there is a great wealth of amazing information describing the Night Journey of the Prophet (saw) throughout verified ahadith, but we have selected a few to focus upon, through which a sense of the powerful light and momentum of the blessed journey may be awakened in our consciousness and inner vision, inshaAllah!

When the Prophet (saw) was sleeping in the house of Umm Hani (ra) in Makkah he said, 'the roof of my house was opened and the Angel Jibril [as] descended' (Bukhari). Scholars reconciling between various narrations, say the Prophet (saw) was then taken to the Hijr, the semi-circular wall of the Ka'bah, where the Prophet (saw) said that Jibril (as), 'opened my chest, and washed it with Zamzam water. Then he brought a golden tray full of wisdom and faith, and having poured its contents into my chest, he closed it'. [Bukhari]

The Prophet (saw) continued, 'I was then brought a white beast which is called al-Buraq [from the Arabic word barq, meaning lightning], bigger than a donkey and smaller than a mule. Its stride was as long as the eye could reach'. [Muslim]...

At several points along the journey, Jibril (as) stopped Buraq and told the Prophet (saw), 'Dismount and pray'. The first stop was at 'the place of emigration' i.e. Madinah - and soon after this night the Prophet (saw) would meet the Ansar and migrate to Madinah. The second stop was at Mount Sinai, where Allah (swt) revealed the Torah to Musa (as). The third stop was at Bethlehem, where 'Isa (as) was born.

The fourth stop was the grave of Musa (as), 'I happened to pass by Musa [as] on the night of my Night journey by the red sand-hill whilst he was standing praying in his grave' (Muslim).

Safra Faruqi,

"Al-Isra' wal-Mi'raj: The Story of the Miraculous Night Journey"

The exalted journey of the beloved Prophet Muhammad (saw) proceeded until he reached Jerusalem, al-Quds, the Holy.

[The Prophet (saw)] continued traveling until he reached the city of the hallowed house, and he entered it by its southern gate. He dismounted the Buraq and tied it at the gate of the mosque, using the ring by which the Prophets tied it before him. The Prophet (saw) entered the mosque from a gate through which the sun and the moon could be seen when they set. He prayed two rakaats and did not tarry long before a large throng of peo-ple had gathered. The Prophet (saw) recognized all the Prophets (as) there, some standing in prayer, some bowing, some pros-trating. We have also been told in other ahadith that a great number of angels descended from the heavens above to join in this celestial prayer assembly. Then a caller called out for the prayer, and the final call to prayer was made. They rose and stood in lines, waiting for the one who would lead them. Jibril

*(as) took the hand of the Prophet (saw) and brought him for-
ward. And the Prophet (saw) led (the exalted congregation) in
two cycles of prayer.*

Sayyid Muhammad ibn Alawi al-Maliki,
The Prophet's Night Journey and Heavenly Ascent

Alhamdulillah Rabbil'alamin! Alhamdulillah! How graced we are to
behold this blessed congregation, manifesting on earth as in heaven!
And then to discover how deeply we may be connected to it, as we
realize that we, too, Insha'Allah, are praying in the presence of all the
Prophets and Messengers (as), all the Angels and all the believers. Is
this not the Divine Assembly that unites us all, as I have been writing
about in previous chapters that, I felt, was manifesting in so many wondrous experiences that I have been blessed to participate in, in prayer
assemblies around the world? And it is this that I feel is coming into
completion now in the inner worlds as we celebrate the exalted gathering of worshippers which took place in the Hallowed House on the
sacred ground of Haram Ash-Sharif but, truly, unites all worshippers
together forever, as our blessed Prophet (saw) eternally leads us in
prayer. (Beloved Friends, Companions on the journey, as we envision
the assembly of all the Prophets, and Messengers (as) of God, praying
together in one exalted assembly on the hallowed grounds of Al Quds,
the Holy, may we pray that all of us, servants of the One God, may
follow the example of the exalted assembly of Prophets (as) and unite
in prayer and submission to the One Most Merciful in these sacred
precincts and thus end forever the unholy wars that have prevailed for
so long covering up the light of all the Prophets and Messengers (as)
praying together in this blessed realm.)

Also, may I share with you, dear fellow travelers, the realization
arising within me now, approximately 40 years later, of the powerful
blessing that guided me to pray in this wondrous Masjid, shortly after
I embraced Islam. One day, after having embraced Islam in El Khalil,
I was impelled to go to pray in the Mosque of the Dome of the Rock,
by a force beyond my comprehension or personal motivation. By that
inspired force, or momentum, was I sent to the Haram Ash-Sharif, the
grounds surrounding the Masjid, and was passing through the gate onto
the blessed grounds, when I was stopped by some guards, there, who
said that I could not enter. They said that only Muslims could enter these

grounds. I said, "I am a Muslim." They asked me to recite passages from the Qur'an, which I did. Then they said that they would have to take me to the Chief of Police within this sacred vicinity, which they did. As we entered the police station, the police chief jumped out of his chair, and said to them, "That is Maryam. You must take her into the Mosque to pray." And that is what they did without delay.

Upon entering the blessed Masjid, I found that no one else seemed to be there. (It was not a time for the formal prayer.) I was alone in that vast illuminated space and went up to the prayer mat in front, where the imam stands to pray, and prayed there, possibly in or near the place, where our beloved Prophet (saw) stood as he led the exalted congregation on the Night Journey. What a great wonder!

So, this is where the One Most Merciful, Loving and Wise, the Best of Planners, inspired me to pray, along with all the souls gathered in the Divine Assembly in this blessed Masjid Al Aqsa, shortly after I had embraced Islam in a zawiyyah/cave a few minutes away from the blessed mazar of our father Ibrahim (as). Now, forty years later, I am realizing the journey that, step-by-step, I have been guided to make, and asking you, too, dear companions on the journey, to remember and thank the most Generous Giver, for the gifts that you have been receiving, and the steps that you have been guided to make on the sacred journey leading back to our Exalted Source.

In contemplation of the greatly meaningful and blessed circle in my spiritual journey back to the blessed day forty years ago when I was invited into Masjid al-Aqsa to pray in that illuminated blessed space, brought to completion in the celebration of the Exalted Mystery of Lailat'ul Isra w'al Mi'raj, so many years later. what can be said — but the proclamation of "Alhamdulillah!" uttered in a state of profound awe, gratitude, and joy. The blessed seeds planted in the garden of the heart, so many years ago, seem to be blooming in the form of spiritual awakening to this great mystery — now.

Further, to come to experience more of the mysteries that are moving us deeply along the path, let us continue to contemplate the wondrous events that unfolded on the miraculous Night Journey of the Holy Prophet (saw). And may we be guided through the transmission of such transcendent events, through His Grace, into the Presence of our Beloved Lord (swt) and the blessed ones that He has sent to guide us, and to pray with us.

Of the continuation of the mysterious signs manifesting in the Night Journey, scholars relating details found in the ahadith write:

> *After the Prophet (saw) finished praying with the Prophets (as), he was asked by Jibril (as) to choose between a cup of wine and a cup of milk. He chose the cup of milk, and Angel Jibril (as) told him that he had chosen al-Fitrah (innate nature), for his ummah, which is inclined to choose that which is natural, unchanged, pure, beautiful, and leads to growth.*
>
> Amany Shalaby,
> "Reflections On the Isra' and Mi'raj"

The next step in the journey took the beloved Prophet (saw) to the sacred site now found within the Dome of the Rock mosque.

> *Allah ascended the Prophet (saw) from the Dome of the Rock through the skies, where he not only saw many miraculous sights and numerous angels, he also met the past Prophets (as). Along the way, he (saw) was greeted with excitement and delight, as his arrival had been much-anticipated.*
>
> *It is hard to imagine how he (saw) must have felt upon meeting his brothers (as), all of whom had gone through trials and difficulties, as they met him with the warmth and love his own tribe had isolated him from. He was greeted with the words, 'Welcome O pious Prophet and pious brother!' (Bukhari). (Adam (as) and Ibrahim (as), however, welcomed him as 'pious son').*
>
> *The Messenger of Allah (saw) said: " Then we ascended to the first heaven [the first layer of the sky and end of the known universe]. Jibril [as] then asked the gate of heaven to be opened (by knocking on one of its doors). [Bukhari]*
>
> *And It was said, "Who are you?" He said, "Jibril [as]".*
>
> *It was said, "And who is with you?" He said, "Muhammad [saw]".*

(In other narrations it mentioned the angelic gatekeepers rejoiced at the arrival of the beloved Prophet (saw) and proclaimed, 'Welcome unto him! What an amazing arrival has come!' [Muslim] and 'He is most welcome, and amongst family!' [Bukhari]).

In other narrations we gain more details of the meeting of the Prophet (saw) and the Prophet Adam (as):
'There we saw Adam (as) sitting with a large group of people on his right and a large group on his left. When he looked towards his right, he smiled and when he looked toward his left, he wept. Then he said, "Welcome O pious Prophet and pious son!" (or in another narration, "Welcome you are amongst family, O my son! What an amazing son you are!" [Bukhari]).

The Second to Sixth Sky

Then the Prophet (saw) continued to ascend the layers of sky with Jibril (as). Again, permission was sought to enter, and the angelic guards were delighted and welcomed the Messenger of Allah (saw).

At the second sky, he met the maternal cousins, the Prophets Isa (as) and Yahya (as).

At the third sky, the Prophet (saw) met the Prophet Yusuf (as) whom he described as having 'been given half of (the world's) beauty' [Muslim]. The Messenger of Allah (saw) had himself been blessed with all beauty, ma sha' Allah!

At the fourth sky, the Prophet (saw) met the Prophet Idris (as) whose soul was taken there, and he is praised in the Qur'an: 'We raised him to a lofty position'. [The Holy Qur'an, 19:57] At the fifth sky, he met the Prophet Harun (as); and in the sixth sky, he met Prophet Harun's younger brother, the Prophet Musa (as)...

At each one of these levels, these Prophets (as) welcomed the Prophet (saw) and supplicated good for him saying, 'Welcome O pious Prophet and pious brother!"[Bukhari]

The Seventh Sky

At the seventh sky, the Prophet (saw) met his... ancestor, the Prophet Ibrahim (as) who was reclining his back against al-Bait al-Ma'mur...

Bait al-Ma'mur literally means 'the much-visited House'. It is the heavenly Ka'bah directly above the one on earth.

In another narration, Ibrahim (as) conveyed his salaams to the ummah of the Prophet (saw) and shared the knowledge that Paradise has pure soil and delicious water, and that its seeds are (saying), SubhanAllah (Glory be to Allah), Alhamdulillah (All praise belongs to Allah), La ilaaha ill-Allah (There is no god but Allah), and Allahu Akbar (Allah is the Greatest)'. [Tirmidhi]

Yasrab Shah,
"Al-Isra' wal-Mi'raj: The Story of the Ascension to the Skies"

Then the Prophet (saw) was raised to the Lote Tree of the Farthest Limit, Sidrat'ul Muntaha, as described in the Holy Qur'an:

Near the Lote-tree beyond which none may pass:
Near it is the Garden of Abode.
Behold, the Lote-tree was shrouded (in mystery unspeakable!)
(His) sight never swerved, nor did it go wrong!
For truly did he see, of the Signs of his Lord, the Greatest!
The Holy Qur'an 53:14-18

But here at the Lote Tree of the Farthest Limit, the point in creation beyond which none may pass, the journey of the Prophet (saw) did not end!

> *At Sidrat al-Muntaha, Jibril asks Mohammed to proceed alone. No one from among all of Allah's creation has ever gone beyond Sidrat al-Muntaha for beyond it lies the throne of Allah the Almighty. Prophet Muhammad proceeds alone and reaches the climax of his journey. He stands in the presence of Allah the Almighty at a distance of "two bow-lengths away or even closer."*

Dar Al-Itfa Al-Missriyyah,
"The Miracle of the Night Journey and Heavenly Ascension of
Prophet Muhammad"

> *In one of the oldest commentaries, based on the sayings of the Prophet, it is said: "The Lote Tree is rooted in the Throne, and it marks the end of the knowledge of every knower, be he Archangel or Prophet-Messenger. All beyond it is a hidden mystery, unknown to any save God Alone." At this summit of the universe Gabriel appeared to him in all his arch angelic splendor, even as he was first created.' Then, in the words of the Revelation (it is said)l: When there enshrouded the Lote Tree that which enshroudeth, the eye wavered not nor did it transgress. Verily he beheld, of all the signs of his Lord, the greatest.' According to the commentary, the Divine Light descended upon the Lote Tree and enshrouded it and all else beside, and the eye of the Prophet beheld it without wavering and without turning aside from it." Such an answer to the supplication implicit in his words: "I take refuge in the Light of Thy Countenance."*
> *The Prophet (saw) was taken up to a point where he heard the scratching of pens (writing the Divine Decree).*

Martin Lings

"Muhammad, His Life Based on the Earliest Sources"

Then, the Prophet (saw) saw his Lord, the Most Glorious, the Exalted, and he fell prostrate.

> *At the end of this phase of the journey, the Prophet (saw) was brought into the Divine Presence, the ultimate source of strength and relief. It is impossible to imagine the beauty of this scene, or how loved, honoured and humbled the Prophet (saw) must have been.*

> *"Then Allah revealed to His servant [saw] what He revealed."* *(Qur'an, 53:10).*

> *As the Prophet (saw) mentioned, 'Then Allah revealed to me what he revealed and then He made obligatory for me fifty prayers every day and night'. [Muslim]*
>
> Yasrab Shah,
> "Al-Isra' wal-Mi'raj: The Story of the Ascension to the Skies"

Through the suggestion of the Prophet Musa (as) who he met when he descended, the Prophet Muhammad (saw) was inspired to go back to Allah (swt) to ease the pathway for his ummah from fifty daily prayers to a smaller number. Ultimately Allah (swt), the One Most Merciful, while keeping open the doorways for sunnah and nafl prayers, brought the number of obligatory prayers to five times a day, each one carrying the weight of ten, so the command could be, through Divine Mercy, fulfilled. It was thus that Allah (swt) gave this ummah the gift of salat, a daily source of strength and inspiration to Muslims because it gives us the opportunity to communicate with Allah (swt) and draw closer to Him, every day, all throughout the day and night. It is truly the believer's ascension!

May we receive the deep blessings of the Divine Gift and through the sincerity of our response be guided day and night on the blessed path leading us directly to our Beloved Source.

Finally, the Prophet (saw) was taken back to the Blessed Masjid Al-Aqsa and returned to Makkah on the Buraq. Thus was the circle completed and filled with the Light of Divine Guidance for all seekers of Allah's Grace in ages to come.

Dear Friends, Beloved Companions on the Journey in search of the Truth that will set us free, the Truth that will guide us to the Source of Truth — everything in the finite world comes to an end. The pages of this book and its cover are made of paper that is perishable. But the Truth within it that comes from the Source and leads back to the Source is eternally alive. Let us remember that everything perishes but the Face of our Lord, full of Majesty, Bounty and Honor (The Holy Qur'an 55:27), and that Allah (swt) leads to His Light whom He wills (The Holy Qur'an 24:35). May we beseech the One Who has power over all things to enable us to fulfill the purpose for which He created us: for ibadat: to love, serve and worship the Divine Being Who brought us into existence with a Divine purpose. May the Light of Divine Revelation, pouring through the Book of Allah (swt) guide and illuminate our journey through this temporary world into His Eternal Abode, as He, Most Merciful, wills. Abundant Blessings and Peace be upon the Holy Prophet (saw) (and his family and companions) who was sent as Mercy from the One Most Merciful to lead us all in prayer, guiding and illuminating the way that may guide us in the Ascent to unite in the Light of our Beloved Lord.

> *Allah is the Light of the heavens and the earth.*
> *The example of His light is like a niche with in which is a lamp,*
> *The lamp is within glass, the glass as if it were a pearly [white] star,*
> *Lit from [the oil of] a blessed olive tree,*
> *Neither of the east nor of the west,*
> *Whose oil would almost glow even if untouched by fire.*
> *Light upon light.*
> *Allah guides to His light whom He wills.*
> *And Allah presents examples for the people,*
> *and Allah is Knowing of all things.*
> 　　　　　　　　　　　　　　　　—The Holy Qur'an 24:35

> *O You Who is closer to me than myself, place light in my heart, light in my grave, light in my body, light in my blood, light in my bones, light in my nerves, light in every hair of mine, light upon my skin, light between these two hands of mine and in front of me, light behind me, light on my right side, light on my left side, light above me, light underneath me. Make me light.*

Grant me light. O My Dear Lord. closer to me than myself, increase the light You have granted me. Make me light upon light.
—Du'a of Light,
from the Hadith of the Prophet Muhammad (saw)

Dear Lord, let not our hearts stray, now that you have guided us, but grant us mercy from Your Own Presence, for You are the Giver of bounties without measure.
—The Holy Qur'an 3:8

Salatus-Samawiyyah Allahumma salli 'ala Sayyidina Muhammadins-sabiqil-lawami'i anwarauhu mil'as samawaati sallallahu aleyhi wasahbihi 'adadarimali wa 'adadanujumis-sama

O Allah, Send Blessings upon our Master Muhammad, the one who precedes all others, the one whose brilliant lights radiate and fill the heavens. May Allah bless him and his family and his companions in the amount of every grain of sand and every star in the sky.

CHAPTER THIRTY-FOUR

THE ENDLESS END: ETERNAL PRAYER

Bismillahirrahmanirrahim
In the Name of Allah, the Merciful, the Compassionate

Our Dear Lord, In You we trust, to You we turn, and to You is the final return.

—The Holy Qur'an 60:4

Dear Lord, O You Who are closer to me than my own self and Who see perfectly the secrets of my heart. When You show me something of truth, allow me to firmly put down roots in it, so I can never be shaken from it or lose hold. When You show me that goodness is found in a particular matter, grant me determination in that matter, so that I never let go of such opportunities and gifts You send to me. Guide me to good actions that You have made by Your Grace worthy of Your Love and Acceptance; and guide me to prayers that, by Your Promise, will guarantee me Your Pardon and Mercy.
***

This prayer, Du'a al Kunuuz, was sent to respond to all human needs and provide protection out of every dead-end. It addresses the crisis of resolve faced by humanity. It was one of the favorite prayers (du'as) of the Holy Prophet (saw).

The Prophet (saw) taught this prayer to his Companion, the noble Shaddad ibn Aus, telling him: "If people all race to store up gold and silver as an insurance against hard times ahead, my advice to you is to do the following: Amass these words of prayer which are all that will be able to protect you in times of your spiritual need."

—Du'a al Kunuuz (Prayer of Treasures),
translated and with commentary
by Shaykh Hamdi Ben Aissa and Anse Shehnaz Karim

Your extinction to self-will (irada) through the action of Allah is indicated by your never formulating any personal goal, your lack of self-interest, and the fact that you no longer feel any want or craving; for, besides the will of Allah, you wish for nothing else. Instead, the action of Allah is at work in you, so while you are experiencing Allah's will and action, your limbs become relaxed, your mind becomes calm, and your feelings surrendered, your face begins to glow, and your inner being thrives. In contact with their Creator, you feel no need of things.

The hand of Power will move you as it wills, and the tongue of unity will summon you. The Lord of all religions will teach you and clothe you in beams of His own light and special raiment and install you among those possessed of ancient knowledge.
—Shaykh 'Abdal Qadir Gilani (ra),
Revelations of the Unseen: Futuh al-Ghaib

Lord, make me an instrument of Your peace. Where there is hatred, let me sow love; where there is injury, pardon; where there is doubt, faith; where there is despair, hope; where there is darkness, light; where there is sadness, joy.
O, Divine Master,
grant that I may not so much seek to be consoled as to console;
to be understood as to understand;
to be loved as to love;
For it is in giving that we receive;
it is in pardoning that we are pardoned;
it is in dying that we are born again to eternal life.
—St. Francis of Assisi

O You who are closer to me than myself, I beg of You Your love and the love of those who love You and I ask of You that I may perform such deeds which will bring me Your love.
—Tirmidhi

Praise be to the One Who freely bestows upon all people benevolence, even before their worldly existence.
Praise be to the One Who undertakes to sustain them, whether

they act toward divine will with compliance or resistance.
Praise be to the One, Who extends support to everything living,
through the prior existence of Divine Giving.
Praise be to the One, Who safeguards the being of all creation
with Self-Sustaining Effusion.
Praise be to the One, Who appears in the world through traces
of wisdom's subtleties, Who manifests in the heavens by evidence of powers' potency.
I witness that there is no God but Allah, the Singular One, Who
shares in no partnership. These words of witness come from a
person who has handed over all his concerns and cares to Allah's decision, who has peacefully submitted to the current of
Allah's decreeing and executing. I witness that Muhammad
(saw) is Allah's worshipful servant and messenger.

My brothers and sisters you were made to experience Allah's
Love. You have been granted the rare gift of nearness to Allah's
Being. Allah has offered you a taste of the blessed nectar sipped
by the people of divine intimacy. Allah's continual intimate connection to you has been safeguarded from any chance of opposition or termination.
Allah has made you the followers of those people who are chosen
to bear divine messages. Their hearts break with longing when
they realize that their vision cannot perceive Allah — then their
broken hearts are strengthened through insight until Allah becomes actual in their lives, bestowing upon them lights. Allah
has opened for them, the gardens of divine nearness, stirred up
from this garden fragrance of His in-dwelling Presence, wafted
its inspirations over their hearts, and showed them the depths
of His prior concern for their well-being. In this way, can Allah reveal the subtle artful actions through which their lives are
sustained and thus they desist from resistance and obstinance
of will.

In this way they have fully submitted themselves to Divine
care and completely entrusted it to oversee all their concerns,
for they know that nobody reaches the goal of satisfying Al-

lah except through being completely satisfied with Allah. They acknowledge that nobody arrives at the purest sincerity except by the fullest inner submission that the Divine dictates and decrees. Thus their disposition is never sullied by the dark gloom of distraction as one among them said poetically: "Fluctuations in time never beguiled them in vain. In the most intense trial they keep hold of the rein."

The Divine decree flows over them, and they act appropriately. They react with respect for its might and allow themselves to be led by its powerful current.

— Ibn Ata' Illah Al-Iskandari,
The Book of Illumination

Allahumma salli 'ala sayyidina Muhammadin al-faatihi lima ughliqa. Wal khaatimi lima sabaqa. Naasiril Haqqa bil Haqq. Wal haadi 'ila siratiqal mustaqeem. Wa 'ala aalihi Haqqa qadrihi wa miqdaarihil 'adheem.
O Allah! Send blessings on our master Muhammad (saw), who opened what was closed. Who sealed what had gone before. The helper of Truth by the Truth. The guide to Your straight path. And on his (saw) family, may these blessings be equal to his immense position and grandeur.

—Salat'ul Fatih

Subhana rabbika rabbil 'izzati amma yasifun. Wa salamun alal mursalin. Walhamdulillahi Rabbil 'alamin.

Glory to thy Lord of Honor and Power. He is free from what they ascribe to Him. Peace be upon the Messengers. Praise be to Allah, the Lord and Cherisher of the Worlds.

—The Holy Qur'an 37:180-182

Subhanallahi w'alhamdulillahi wa la'illaha ill'Allah w'Allahu Akbar wa la hawla wa la quetta illa billah.

Glory be to Allah and all Praise be to Allah and there is no

God other than Allah and Allah is the Greatest and there is no power or strength except in Allah.

Allahumma Antas-salaam wa minkas-Salaam wa ilaika yar-jius-salaam. Fa hayyina ya Rabbana bis-salaam wadkhilna dara-s salaam bis-salaam. Tabarrakta Rabbana wa ta'alait ya dhal jallali wa ikram.

Exalted are You, O Lord of Majesty and Honor. O Allah, You are the Peace and from You comes the Peace and to You returns the Peace. Greet us, our Lord, with the Peace and enter us into the House of Peace with Peace. Blessed art Thou our Lord, O Possessor of Majesty and Generosity.